CONSUMPTION IN THE AGE OF AFFLUENCE

Dieting and overeating go hand-in-hand; food scares and the incidence of coronary heart disease have made a healthier diet the explicit goal of government policy; and the range of foods and the ways of eating seem intimately connected to our lifestyles. This is the age of biotechnology, huge supermarkets, all-year-round exotic fruits and vegetables, fast food and ethnic restaurants, and the microwave. Here, the authors argue that in order to comprehend these extensive, dramatic and crucially important developments in the world of food, a new interdisciplinary approach is necessary. *Consumption in the Age of Affluence* successfully addresses food consumption in this way. The volume:

- argues for the importance of socioeconomic and cultural factors over diet, in influencing the production, marketing and consumption of different groups of foods;
- places food systems theory on sound analytical foundations;
- draws critically upon food systems literature;
- includes case studies from the sugar, dairy and meat systems;
- employs novel statistical techniques to identify and explain distinct patterns of food consumption.

The book is a valuable and path-breaking addition to the revitalized discipline of food studies and points the way forward for the continuing study of food consumption. As such, it will be invaluable to students, researchers and policy-makers engaged in the world of food.

Ben Fine is Professor of Economics and Director of the Centre for Economic Policy for Southern Africa at the School of Oriental and African Studies, University of London. His previous work includes *The World of Consumption* with Ellen Leopold and was published by Routledge in 1993.

Michael Heasman is Senior Research Fellow at the Centre for Food Policy, Thames Valley University, London. He has researched widely on different aspects of the food economy.

Judith Wright is a Research Officer at the Social Statistics Research Unit, City University. She has undertaken research using a variety of large social survey datasets.

CONSUMPTION IN THE AGE OF AFFLUENCE

OF AFFLUENCE

The World of Food

Ben Fine, Michael Heasman and Judith Wright

London and New York

First published 1996
by Routledge
11 New Fetter Lane, London EC4P 4EE

Simultaneously published in the USA and Canada
by Routledge
29 West 35th Street, New York, NY 10001

Typeset in Garamond by LaserScript, Mitcham, Surrey
Printed and bound in Great Britain by
Mackays of Chatham PLC, Chatham, Kent

British Library Cataloguing in Publication Data
A catalogue record for this book is available from the British Library

Library of Congress Cataloging in Publication Data
A catalogue record for this book has been requested

ISBN 0–415–13155–3
ISBN 0–415–13579–6 (pbk)

CONTENTS

Part V Whither food studies?

FIGURE AND TABLES

FIGURE

ABBREVIATIONS

A	appropriationism
ABF	Associated British Foods
ACP	African, Caribbean and Pacific
ADI	acceptable daily intake
AID	almost ideal demand
CAP	Common Agricultural Policy
CATFI	Common Approach to Financial Information
CSA	Commonwealth Sugar Agreement
DTF	Dairy Trade Federation
EC	European Community
EEC	European Economic Community
ESRC	Economic and Social Research Council
EU	European Union
FES	Family Expenditure Survey
GATT	General Agreement on Tariffs and Trade
GHS	General Household Survey
GIS	geographical information systems
HFCS	high fructose corn syrup
IMF	International Monetary Fund
MAFF	Ministry of Agriculture Fisheries and Food
MMB	Milk Marketing Board
MMC	Monopolies and Mergers Commission
MMS	milk marketing scheme
MRM	mechanically recoverable meat
NFS	National Food Survey
NPQ	negotiated price quota
NRS	National Readership Survey
OAQ	overall agreement quota
OECD	Organization for Economic Co-operation and Development
PP	producer-processor
PR	producer-retailer

RHM	Rank Hovis MacDougal
S	substitutionism
SCF	Scientific Committee for Food
SCP	structure–conduct–performance
SOP	system of provision
TLS	Tate & Lyle Sugars
WSE	white sugar equivalent

Part I

FROM FOOD STUDIES TO FOOD SYSTEMS

1

INTRODUCTION AND OVERVIEW

BACKGROUND

In deference to the commitment of the United Kingdom's Economic and Social Research Council (ESRC) to wider dissemination and popularization of results, 'What We Eat and Why' was ultimately settled as the shortened title for our research project which had previously been paraded under the guise of 'Food Consumption: Social Norms and Systems of Provision'. The project was one of the first eight to be funded under the ESRC's programme, 'The Nation's Diet'.[1] The programme was intended to explore the topic by research drawn from across the social sciences in the hope of providing interdisciplinary explanations for food choice. Not far in the background were two motivating themes: first, that eating habits were changing rapidly and, second, that healthy eating campaigns, attached to dietary guidelines, were at best meeting with limited success. Could social scientists complement the progress made by dietitians in order that healthier diets could not only be identified and publicized but also adopted by consumers?

The intention of the ESRC's continuing programme, then, has been to develop a rigorous and interdisciplinary social science of food consumption, together with the drawing out of policy implications, where possible. This book, and its forthcoming companion volume, contains the results of our endeavour to meet these objectives and, whatever their merits in content, arguably represent a landmark in the development of food studies as a discipline within the social sciences.

The case for such a bold claim can in part be justified by the content of Chapter 2. There we review the existing discipline of food studies, even if partially and cursorily with much greater attention to methodology and analytical principles than to detail. The chapter is organized around a number of themes. First, the discipline of food studies is highly fragmented, with little or no genuine integration between its separate components drawn from the various social sciences (which are our main concern) and nutritional sciences (which are not).

3

Second, the isolated contributions from the separate disciplines tend to fall into two types. From economics, psychology, geography and nutritional sciences, for example, diet is understood as the consequence of regular, determined individual behaviour and outcomes but from which there can be deviations. Each discipline identifies these determinate patterns in very different ways according to its own preoccupations (as due to prices, incomes and tastes for economics, and dietary requirements for nutritional science). By contrast, social theory, as represented by sociology and anthropology, tends to focus upon specific social determinants such as stratification or ritual, with a corresponding degree of indeterminacy depending upon how these social processes materialize in practice. This, however, has generally resulted in a fragmented approach to food studies within these disciplines, one intensified by the predilection to exploit food to illustrate previously derived social theories (stratification, inequality, patriarchy, etc.) – rather than to develop food-specific theory and insights.

The third theme taken up in Chapter 2 is that food studies as a whole and in its constituent parts has been shaken out of its fragmented complacency by a series of empirical developments, ranging from disarray in international food markets to growing incidence of nutritional disorders arising out of affluence and overeating. Food studies has been unable to address these adequately, and the lack of interdisciplinary integration has been sorely felt as a deficiency – particularly in identifying practical and effective policies.

As a final theme, apart from providing an overview of the 'old' food studies even as it is currently experiencing dramatic changes and challenges under the weight of its inherited inadequacies, Chapter 2 provides pointers to the analytical directions and themes to be pursued in this and the subsequent volume.

Our project was the only one in the first set of the ESRC's programme to be attached to an economics department although, as will be abundantly clear, it broke completely with mainstream economics in its approach and motivation. Far from taking prices and incomes, together with the optimizing, constrained and rational individual as the determinants of food choice, emphasis has been placed within a fully interdisciplinary framework upon the social processes generating both uniformity and difference in the patterns of food consumption. Indeed, the project's origins resided less in economics, or a break with it, than in the continuation of research, previously funded by the Leverhulme Trust. Accordingly, the content of this research is worth outlining briefly, even if the contribution of this research to food studies is not immediately apparent.

The research concerned the relationship between female labour market participation and household ownership of consumer durables. There is a presumption that households with working wives (and/or children) would have a greater incentive to possess consumer durables because of their greater worth as labour-saving devices – this over and above any effect arising from

4

the availability of higher levels of income. This simple hypothesis, however, prompted a number of much more complex areas of investigation.

The first was to employ an entirely novel way of *identifying* patterns of consumption empirically (in the context of ownership of consumer durables). Essentially, this is based on the idea that society orders or ranks durables according to their popularity in ownership. This reflects, from the potential adoption of a common culture through to the imperatives of mass production, the outcome of a range of socioeconomic processes. In addition, it also proves possible to investigate the extent to which separate socioeconomic strata of the population either conform more or less to the overall population norms or rankings or whether they exhibit a sharply distinct 'norm' of their own.

Although these methods are elaborated in detail in the body of the text, where they are applied to foods rather than durables, it is crucial to recognize that the derived norms, whether for the population as a whole or for subgroups, are concerned with the *ranking* by frequency of ownership or purchase, not with overall *levels* of ownership. Thus, rich households almost inevitably own *more* durables (although not always purchasing more foods) than the poor households, but the *norms* for the two groups could still be the same. In this case, the implication is that the purchase behaviour, or order of acquiring durables, is the same and the poor aspire to, but do not generally achieve, the same patterns of consumption as the rich. Of course, it is equally plausible that the poor not only consume *less* but also *differently*, acquiring or ranking durables in a distinct sequence. In terms of food, then, do different types of households have the same patterns of consumption even if at different levels (because of income or household numbers), or do they simply consume differently altogether both quantitatively *and* qualitatively?

In principle, then, it proves possible to estimate consumption norms and their variation across the population, according to socioeconomic factors such as the presence of a working housewife and/or children, as well as income, class, age, etc. A separate task is to explain why these norms should prevail, with empirical associations between socioeconomic variables and consumption patterns at best being suggestive of causal links. This was broached through a critical review of theories of consumption across the social sciences, thereby constructing an alternative approach based on what is termed *systems of provision*.

The results of this research are fully reported in Fine and Leopold (1993). It is found that theories of consumption are usually concerned with 'horizontal' factors, those that are presumed to apply equally across society as a whole or a broad range of consumer goods. One example among many is provided by emulation and differentiation of status through consumption, with its corollary of the trickle-down of tastes and consumption habits. Such horizontal theories, as in this case, also tend to project existing theories, constructed for other purposes or in other contexts, on to consumption and to be derived from within an academic discipline. The result has often been neither to address consumption specifically (it is simply a reflection of class, or diffusion, or some other analytical category that could equally be applied to other areas of study), nor to open up the potential for an interdisciplinary study of consumption other than as the stacking of otherwise unconnected theories. A further feature of the literature is that specific moments in the more or less direct determinants of consumption, such as production, retailing, culture, etc., have also been examined horizontally as if they were appropriately understood as general, undifferentiated categories. We would argue, however, that it is inappropriate to construct a general theory of the impact of production, retailing or advertising, etc., upon consumption. Rather the influence of each depends upon what is being produced, sold or advertised and how these separate activities are specifically attached to others along the system of provision of specific consumption goods.

In contrast, the systems-of-provision approach argues that consumption must be investigated within a 'vertical' framework in which each commodity or group of commodities is differentiated from others. Consumption of a specific commodity is linked to a chain of activities, originating in production, which are structured and reproduced in a way that is both integral and distinct from that of other commodities even if the separate components are shared in common. Analytical reliance upon systems of provision resolves the problems previously identified – creating an interdisciplinary approach, appropriate and targeted for consumption, and distinguishing the different impact of socioeconomic factors according to their specific role from one area of consumption to another.

Before pursuing these lines of argument further, connecting them to their development in this volume, it is helpful to consider the results of the research on female labour market participation, reported in Fine (1992), even if focusing upon their methodological significance. This work was concerned with a historical explanation for the changing patterns of women's paid employment and, in particular, why labour market participation rates of married women, especially those with children, had increased over the post-war period in the United Kingdom (and in many other developed countries). This is treated not so much as a matter of detailed estimation of elasticities – how much more female employment for an increase in women's wages – as one of causal factors and historical timing.

Traditional explanations in one way or another, most notably in the new household economics associated with Gary Becker,[2] have relied upon the increasing productivity of the commercial relative to the household sector, so that comparative advantage has shifted in favour of women taking paid work to finance household goods rather than providing these or their equivalent directly through domestic labour. This, of course, all depends upon assumptions concerning presumed skews in preferences and abilities by sex, and the net effect of rising real wages (and the potential negative effect on women's employment from higher male earnings), but also upon decisions over fertility and family size. Each of these assumptions can be rationalized through further reasoning – the choice of fewer, 'higher quality' children in the new household economics, for example, to save a housewife's time for waged work without skimping on the level of enjoyment as parent.

The argument in Fine (1992) is of a different type. It seeks a much stronger, systemic connection between the rise of mass production and consumption, the demographic transition to a family system of households with fewer children, and the shifting patterns of women's employment. The logical connection between these is established, although their historical chronology is troublesome with an apparent sequence of lags between them; why did fertility falls and greater female labour market participation not occur earlier?

The details of the answer need not detain us, other than two important methodological points. First, the presumed shift of comparative advantage in favour of the commercial sector and against the household is not only uneven across products, it may even be reversed. Increases in productivity in the commercial sector have the effect of both undermining domestic production *and* of enhancing its viability through, for example, the provision of consumer durables and other household goods that are used in the home at the expense of bought-out commodities. Sewing machines, textiles, cooking ingredients and equipment illustrate the point as do, of more recent vintage, a range of equipment providing for home self-entertainment.

One way of accommodating such observations is to appeal to net outcomes and greater levels of detail in disaggregating to specific goods and services. Our approach is different in, first, regarding the separation between the commercial sector and the household as a social structure that is reproduced in a much wider context than is encompassed by the economics of shifting comparative advantage. Moreover, while non-economic factors can be understood as simply impeding or even accelerating the outcomes attached to comparative advantage (with custom or culture, for example, competing with or complementing what are perceived to be purely economic factors), we reject such simplistic dichotomies. Second, then, we perceive the economic pressures upon the structural division between commerce and the household as contradictory, underlying forces whose outcome is complex and uncertain – neither generalizable nor reducible to a simple balancing act in allocating activities across the structural divide between the household and the commercial economy. In other words, we emphasize the tensions inherent within and between socioeconomic forces and how these reproduce social structures.

While apparently unduly abstract and removed from the issue of the

7

determinants of food choice, the relevance of this discussion for our continuing work on food is twofold. First, it is directly of significance for analysing the relationship between the household and the commercial provision of food. Second, it is indirectly of importance because of its methodological implications for examining the reproduction of socio-economic structures other than those at the boundaries between commerce and the household – within commerce itself in terms of the vertical integration of economic activity, for example. How are we to understand, for example, the relationship between production of (manufactured) foods and their retailing as well as the separate activities attached to production itself? How is the relationship between agriculture, as a source of inputs, and food manufacturing to be addressed and, by the same token, agri-culture's own increasing dependence upon manufactured inputs, such as fertilizers and insecticides and, most recently, new varieties of seeds resulting from the leap forward in biotechnology?

This, and related issues, make up the subject matter of Part II of this volume. It furthers the work of Fine and Leopold (1993), where the virtues of analysing the determinants of food consumption in terms of systems of provision have already been established. Food is attached to a distinct series of systems of provision like other commodities – and we only refer to the food system when referring to all food systems taken together. However, food systems are further marked by the extent of their 'organic' content. With origins in agriculture and an ultimate destination in human ingestion, food is inescapably dependent upon biological processes at the extremes of its provision and, consequently, throughout the chain of activities attached to consumption. Moreover, the imperatives of food systems' profitability have subjected the food system to economic forces that continuously shift its relationship to the organic – through the industrialization of processes and products (as in the 'technological treadmill' in agriculture, and the use of additives in food manufacturing). The shifting balance and content of the organic in the food system are intimately related but not identical to the restructuring of the chain of activities along the food system.

OVERVIEW

These insights around the nature of food systems are explored in Part II. It argues for a number of propositions that build upon and reconstruct existing food systems theory. First, emphasis is placed upon differentiation between foods. There is not a single food system, either across all foods or even globally for a single food, with differentiation between one country and another even if it serves a common world market to a greater or lesser extent. Each food system is potentially structured differently and has a distinct chronology. This contrasts with the presumption that there has been a global, Fordist food system over the post-war period that has

8

suffered crisis and fragmentation from the 1970s onwards. It follows that uniformity in the food system has been exaggerated for the earlier period and, ironically, differentiation and fluidity have been unduly emphasized currently.

Second, as in the previous methodological discussion, irrespective of the balance of shifts along the food system (between agriculture and industry, industry and retailing, commercial and household provision) and their separate connection to the organic content of the food system, the restructuring of the food system should be examined in terms of contradictory forces acting upon the division between its various components. This contrasts with much of the literature which presumes that the industrialization of food is at the expense of agriculture and the household, with a correspondingly simple shift in structural boundaries in favour of commercial provision.

The second chapter in Part II, Chapter 4, develops food system theory further by defending the system-of-provision approach, whether for foods or other commodities, against a range of criticisms which essentially boil down to a reassertion of the primacy of horizontal analyses because consumers and consumption forge connections across commodity systems. Specifically, then, what defines the boundaries around a group of commodities to form a distinct system of provision as opposed to a more or less loose connection between different systems of provision? *Reductio ad absurdum* would lead either to an analytical proliferation of food systems to reflect minor differences between one food or even food brand and another or to an all-encompassing single food system to incorporate each and every connection in production, retailing or the culture of consumption. It is argued that this conundrum cannot be resolved abstractly. For the integration across the structures that define distinct food systems are the contingent outcome of underlying socioeconomic forces. It is a matter of identifying empirically how integrated are the various components of the food system across commodity groups and assessing how they are being reproduced or transformed in the social structures to which they are attached.

Thus, connections across distinctly defined food systems do not contradict their separate existence, and establishing the difference between a single food system and two that are closely integrated cannot and need not be an exact science. However, so extensive and potentially pervasive are the connections between food systems at the level of consumption (as commodities are consumed together or culturally identified with one another, especially with the support of advertising or projected lifestyles) that we reject this as the basis for assigning commodities to a single system of provision even though, from the horizontal perspective rooted in the culture of the consumer, this forms the grounds on which to reject the system-of-provision approach altogether.

9

Part III is concerned with a number of applications of food system theory. Chapter 5 provides a detailed study of the UK sugar system – how it has shifted over time and how it is distinctive relative to other sugar producers. The restructuring of the sugar system is shown to reflect its organic properties (whether in terms of crop source – cane or beet – industrial uses, or potential substitutes whether artificial or not). Although sugar is affected by other sweeteners, we do not consider that the two products are sufficiently integrated with one another to constitute a single system of provision. Thus, by use of the UK sugar system, we have been able to show how food systems are differentiated from one another, by product, structure and history and from one country to another. Chapter 6 considers artificial sweeteners, making the case that they should be considered as belonging to a separate system of provision than sugar, even though both serve the market for sweetness.

Part III closes with a critical examination of the application of standard neoclassical demand theory to the determination of diet, specifically assessing the evolution of its use empirically with UK National Food Survey (NFS) data over the past fifty years. Such theory and its statistical counterpart are far removed from food system theory. The assumption of fixed preferences and the reduction of all other changes to shifts in the prices and incomes faced by consumers are an obstacle to understanding why we eat what we eat. Indeed, the empirical results have persistently and increasingly undermined the assumption on which they are calculated – since the unexplained residual, normally assigned to exogenous shifts in preferences, has become of growing numerical importance.

While Part IV draws more constructively upon National Food Survey data, the NFS does not escape criticism. We employ the techniques for consumer durables mentioned earlier to calculate norms for food purchases, although the translation of the method from the one application to the other is not without problems. This need not detain us here, and the approach is covered at length in Chapter 8, devoted to the methods, with further coverage in following chapters. In Chapter 9, however, we do highlight a major difference with the analysis conducted by the NFS. For the latter depends implicitly upon the calculations of consumption norms by the average quantities consumed across the population as a whole or for selected subgroups. Our concern is to tackle first whether a food is liable to be purchased at all or not. The analogy with smoking might be helpful (although our favoured food example is provided by sausages). Quite clearly, average levels of consumption across the population are misleading according to the proportions of smokers and non-smokers (and even finer divisions might be important between heavy or habitual and light or occasional smokers). The more (less) smokers there are, the less (more) acute is the incidence of heavy smoking. Similarly, if presumably of less stark significance, the calculation of average levels of consumption may conceal the presence of heavy concentrations of consumption of certain foods within particular subgroups of the population (and, correspondingly, there is the possibility of abnormally low levels of consumption). This issue is examined for a variety of foods for which there have been changing patterns of consumption over the past decade, with special attention paid to the impact of low levels of income and the presence of children or not.

Chapter 10 calculates food norms for a variety of meat products. Perhaps the most important result is that whether in the influence of socioeconomic variables such as age or class or in the interpretations attached to particular meat products (as healthy or convenient, for example), there are not consistent variations. For example, the young have a particularly pronounced bias, conforming to the trend over the period from 1979 to 1989, against many meat products. This can be interpreted as supporting an ideology of health or vegetarianism. But for some products, attached to convenience and innovation for example, the young are particularly favourably inclined. This leads us to the conclusion, contrary to much of the literature across the social sciences, that meat is a heterogeneous category and should be analysed as such. It is inappropriate to view meat as a natural symbol (since it is a variety of symbols), to focus upon meat and two veg as a 'proper meal' without specifying the, possibly shifting, nature of the meat concerned, nor to derive Engel curves for meat as a whole since these conflate aggregates of divergent patterns, etc.

A different factor in the meat norms concerns the greater overall purchases of meat products by those of lower income or class status, a reversal by 1989 of the previous association of meat purchases with higher status. This suggests that meat consumption, and possibly food more generally, has become a form of gratification for those who have more limited alternative outlets, whether these be through other forms of food provision, such as eating out, or through other aspects of personal or social life (holidaying, prestige car or house ownership, etc.). Paradoxically, in order to link these features of meat consumption to the food system, we emphasize the presence of a single meat system, rather than a series of individual meat systems for chicken, beef, etc., even though we have insisted upon the heterogeneity of meat products in consumption. This is because of the interdependence between the provision of different meat products along their systems of provision, although the nature of that interdependence has shifted over time with the character of the meat system itself.

Food and class is the subject of Chapter 11. Food norms are calculated by class for a variety of foods and these are shown to differ by class for some but not for all foods. It is argued that the influence of class upon food cannot be simply read off as a form of distinction pitched and determined exclusively at the level of consumption. Rather the class content of diet

11

varies across foods and needs to be situated within the functioning of the various food systems as a whole.

Chapter 12 examines the dairy system. Food norms for dairy products reveal a number of patterns, but the most consistent are those associated with levels of food expenditure. Not surprisingly, the absolute frequency of purchase of any product tends to increase with food expenditure – more money is being spent, presumably across more items as well as more of the same items – although inferior foods might be expected to fall in frequency of purchase. This monotonicity of absolute frequency of purchase with overall food expenditure is particularly striking in the case of dairy products. However, while those who spend more might be reasonably expected to purchase more (and more of all) foods, there is no reason to believe that they should change their ranking of the foods. But, for dairy products, there is a peculiar pattern for some of the foods. Those who spend more rank 'healthy' products, such as skimmed milks, less highly and an 'unhealthy product' such as cream more highly. This seems likely to reflect common innovative behaviour across *both* healthy and unhealthy foods, and the 'lite'/heavy syndrome in which consumption of something healthy justifies the consumption of something unhealthy. Our analysis, however, moves beyond such explanations to show how the dairy system has functioned to sustain the consumption of what are deemed to be unhealthy products despite the widening range and consumption of healthy dairy products. There is a parallel with the persistence of sugar in the nation's diet, as examined in Chapters 5 and 6.

Part V contains a single chapter. It is devoted to summing up the implications of our contribution, with particular emphasis on the directions that might be usefully taken by future research. To some extent, it also anticipates the content of the future companion volume.

NOTES

1   The programme began with its first wave of eight projects in 1992, followed by a second wave of a further eight projects in 1994. The programme is co-ordinated by Anne Murcott, currently at South Bank University. It was due to last for six years. Our research has been funded by the ESRC through grant L209252016. We thank MAFF and the ESRC Data Archive for making data and documentation available on the National Food Survey, and for helpful suggestions and responses to enquiries.
2   See Becker (1981) and Fine (1992) for one of many critiques. See also the debate between Fine (1995e) and Kotz (1994), (1995).

2

FOOD STUDIES: AN INITIAL ASSESSMENT

INTRODUCTION

The determinants and significance of food consumption have attracted increasing attention over the recent period. It has led to the introduction of food studies into more general courses of study where it was previously absent. And it has induced those already embroiled with the problems of food to venture towards broader approaches than are defined by their narrower specialisms. What has brought about this enhanced pre-occupation with food, and why has it led to the breaching of inter-disciplinary boundaries?

The most obvious answer to the first question is to be found in the extensive changes that have occurred within the world of food. Over the past two decades, food prices on international markets have continued to decline relative to those of manufacturing, but they have exhibited increasing volatility. At the same time, there is perceived to be a world food problem in which a significant proportion of the world's population suffers from endemic hunger and is liable to famine. This is not due to global shortages in the supply of food, even on a per capita basis, but concerns unequal access to food.[1]

However depressing, this situation is far from new even if its more dramatic manifestations are more familiar as a result of the activities both of relief agencies and the mass media. Consequently, the impetus to food studies has derived less from the problems of hunger and poverty in the developing world and more from those of affluence in the developed world. This is most notable in the shifting concerns over healthy eating. Less than a century ago, even in what is now the developed world, little was known of vitamins and proteins. Much more was known of hunger and poverty. Policy in the intervening period has predominantly been concerned with ensuring that the majority of the population gets enough to eat and in the right proportions – what ensures a balanced and adequate diet has been the name of the game.

13

More recently though, within the developed world, failure to attain sufficient to eat has shifted well away from being a common problem to being one of what might be termed deviancy – something that has to be explained as out of rather than as the ordinary. It has had its counterpart in an entirely different but no less familiar problem, that of overeating in general and of particular food ingredients, so that the question of balance within diet has also remained a considerable cause for concern.

An important reason then for the greater exposure of the various analytical elements that make up food studies is that they have been required to address new problems of increasing importance – the so-called diseases of affluence. In addition, the conventional wisdoms attached to food studies, designed however adequately to deal with the older problems of under- or malnutrition, have proved sorely inadequate to the new tasks with which they have been confronted. The search for more broadly based solutions has prompted interdisciplinary overtures across the various aspects of food studies as well as promoting the discipline where it has previously been weak, as in the sociology of food.[2]

So, food studies has been given a shaking out of the old and has moved on to new preoccupations. But much more than this has been involved. For the changes in diet and dietary concerns are transparently linked to a range of other significant changes in the provision and consumption of food. And these changes have challenged the legitimacy of interdisciplinary boundaries and the assumptions under which they have been employed. Food studies needs to address: changing technology in the household (microwaves, freezers, convenience foods), lifestyles and culture, the rise of fast foods, the erosion of traditional meal patterns, changing preferences over foods, technological advances in food preservation, processing and packaging, the use of biotechnology to raise yields and all-year availability, etc. Further, the need to address these issues has sucked in other considerations, some of them more prominent recently, even if they are not specific to food. Thus, feminism has concentrated attention on food as an aspect of intra-household gender relations; increasing interest in the culture of the commonplace has brought food forward from the back burner; and food has been studied as one aspect in the role of the state and international relations.

In short, food studies is in disarray. It has been hit by a set of material developments that it is far from capable of addressing, not least because it has always been a disparate collection of fragments. Indeed, those following a course in food studies might well have felt themselves to be back at school, benefiting from a general education in which food happens to appear on the timetable for each period. This fragmentation of food studies has been cruelly exposed by recent events and should lead us to question whether the old studies was even adequate for the old problems that it sought to address. In a sense, this is one of the purposes of this chapter.

14

What follows is a very cursory and uneven, some might say crude, review of the 'old' food studies – although this form of the discipline still remains very much alive and predominant. Hopefully, the lines of argument that we develop will encourage others to provide more nuanced critiques of the existing body of orthodox knowledge and teaching that currently prevails. For a second purpose of this chapter is to show how the old approaches are incapable of satisfactorily addressing the new problems that have arisen to confront food studies.

The first sections begin with the approaches that, from different perspectives, have explained diet in a deterministic way. Diet has been construed as a norm from which there are deviations. Thus, paradoxically, diet is understood by what it is not (a deviation from a standard), with otherwise excluded factors, particularly human agency, used to examine these deviations. Within this broad category of approaches falls economics, nutrition, (agricultural) geography, nutrition and much of psychology. The later sections are concerned with the contributions of social theory, especially sociology and anthropology. It is found that they have considerable difficulty in integrating their insights together let alone with those from the other disciplines.

THE ECONOMICS OF FOOD[3]

We begin with economics because it illustrates in simpler form, in some respects, what is characteristic of the approach found in other disciplines. In food studies, economics is often presented in terms of the supply of, and demand for, food with corresponding supply and demand curves giving rise to equilibrium outputs and prices at their intersection. More sophisticated analyses set about deriving the supply and demand curves from what is termed first principles. The demand curves come from the aggregated behaviour of consumers, each of which is presumed to be 'rational'. By this is meant that each consumer determines demand for food as part of a more general set of purchases (and decisions to save and supply labour to earn interest and wage labour income, respectively). Utility, representing a given and fixed set of preferences, is maximized subject to prevailing prices and available income. The supply curve derives from the aggregated behaviour of firms. Entrepreneurs decide how much to produce by maximizing profits, subject to given prices for inputs and outputs and given technologies from which to choose production methods.

The notion of equilibrium is a central organizing concept for understanding what happens or might happen. Taxes or other forms of state intervention, for example, shift the supply and demand curves to generate a new equilibrium. Market imperfections, whether due to monopoly or externalities (as in environmental considerations), also shift the equilibrium from its optimum. Even where equilibrium does exist, it may prove unstable – as in the famous cobweb in which supply and demand (and prices) explosively alternate between being too high and too low.[4] Frequently, however, the underlying role of equilibrium (and its associated assumptions) slips into the background, and the focus is placed upon supply (the farmer) or demand (the consumer) alone.

For the latter, what we eat is empirically estimated by assuming that variations in demand over time (or across households of a similar type at the same time) are explained by variations in income and prices.[5] The models concerned have performed far from perfectly, but any residual variations in demand are generally understood as due to other omitted factors, not least shifts in underlying preferences. In the 1980s, such residuals grew in importance, so that price and income effects seem to have been of limited use in explaining food choices. In principle, each consumer could have different preferences. But, for the purposes of estimating demand curves, it is usually assumed that the economy incorporates a single representative consumer or, if using disaggregated household data, that households of the same type have the same food preferences.

On this basis, it is possible to derive a standard pattern of consumption for each of a number of different household types depending upon prevailing income and prices. Although such sophisticated procedures are not employed in practice, this opens up the possibility of discovering when households are unlikely to attain an adequate diet if prices are too high or incomes too low. Policy can be used to support the poor directly through income support or indirectly through price subsidies (the latter generally thought to be a less efficient form of policy in that it targets all consumers, not just the poor, and it also distorts the system of relative prices).

What if diet is either inadequate or unhealthy even where the level of income is not a constraint on meeting a healthy diet and acceptable standard of living? Either the economist assumes that the consumer is poorly informed, and this justifies healthy-eating campaigns so that given preferences *and* dietary norms can be truly satisfied,[6] or, by the same means, an attempt must be made to shift preferences towards healthy diets. In this case, as for price and/or income subsidies, the sovereignty of the market and even of the consumer is overruled in pursuit of the greater good. This creates a tension between whether the consumer or the government knows best.

As a simple application of demand analysis, economists and other social scientists have seized upon Engel's Law, the notion that the proportion of income spent on food declines as income increases (and it is also generally reckoned that the proportion of food expenditure shifts away from staples and towards meats). Note that, as a *law*, this is merely an empirical regularity which may or may not be valid over time and in a cross-section across a population at a given time. As such, it also is a law that does not *explain* anything. Rather, to the extent that it is well defined and valid, it

16

poses a problem rather than offering a solution.[7] Engel's Law, however, is important in setting the scene for the economic analysis of the supply side. For, quite apart from a declining share of expenditure on the demand side, farmers are seen as squeezed on the supply side by a secular increase in productivity at a greater rate than for other sectors of the economy and especially industry. This gives rise to the 'farm problem' in which agriculture must adjust to falling prices, fewer producers and low and unstable incomes to the extent that adjustment is slow and imperfect.[8]

The farm problem is essentially perceived to be a feature of advanced capitalism. At earlier stages of development, the agricultural sector is more likely to be poorly treated by government policy, with taxation used to obtain a food surplus to support urbanization and industrialization. But this gives way to the goal of food security or national self-sufficiency and, ultimately, heavy subsidies to the agricultural sector to handle the farm problem. Such reversals of policy are evident within countries but have now been elevated to the international arena as in the European Union's (EU) Common Agricultural Policy, (CAP). So great have agricultural subsidies become that they have been included in the Uruguay Round of GATT (General Agreement on Tariffs and Trade) which has incorporated agriculture as a target for reduced protection for the first time.[9]

The scale of the problem is significant in a number of ways. First, subsidies to (and protection of) agriculture have been growing, reaching $25 billion in the United States and the EU respectively in 1986, and over $160 billion in OECD (Organization for Economic Co-operation and Development) countries, estimated at $13,000 per full-time farmer equivalent. Second, such direct costs are complemented by indirect costs as consumers face higher prices, thereby reducing their potential welfare. Third, even though nominally designed to support low-income farmers, larger farmers have benefited disproportionately, especially if support is linked to output. Fourth, the administration (including monitoring of corrupt practices) and political lobbying around agricultural support is costly. Finally, the dynamic of agricultural protection at the international level generates its own competitive momentum. As support is raised for one set of farmers, so it is nullified by a matching response elsewhere, and so on. Thus, it is estimated that 40% of US support simply neutralizes the negative impact generated by the support of other countries.[10]

In this light, Tyers and Anderson (1992, p. 75) point to three key characteristics of world food markets:[11] developed countries support agriculture in contrast to developing countries which pursue policies of cheap food and taxation of the agricultural sector; as development proceeds within a country, agricultural support tends to displace economic bias against farming; and all countries have been insulated from world food prices whose downward trend has entailed a rising gap between domestic and international prices. Given the costs of the policies involved, Tyers and

Anderson set themselves the task of explaining why they should have been adopted.

Their answer is based on use of the new (international) political economy. Essentially, this extends the workings of the market to the political arena. Interest groups, such as industrialists and farmers, gain or lose to a greater or lesser extent from different policies; and the costs of realizing a preferred policy depend upon how fragmented and difficult to organize are those who would benefit from collective action. Tyers and Anderson argue that agricultural policy is endogenous, shifting over time with economic development. Initially, farmers are numerous and fragmented, whereas industrialists suffer disproportionately from high prices for foods (and raw materials) since they are a major part of their costs in the form of wages. As development proceeds, farmers constitute a smaller, concerted interest group with much to gain from agricultural support which, in turn, is of considerably lesser significance to industrialists in terms of their proportion of costs.

Thus, at a world level, it is as if (groups of) countries are playing a game in which the attempt to gain by each worsens the outcome for all. The analogy with the cold-war nuclear arms race is appropriate for this inspired the new international political economy. While everyone would be better off without nuclear weaponry, given its costs let alone the danger of use despite mutual deterrent, each player-nation is better off with arms irrespective of what the others do.[12] Such arguments carry over to agricultural protection, although the analysis is refined by the inclusion of the process of domestic policy-making as costs and benefits shift between different domestic interest groups. There is also a greater heterogeneity of international players – the 'war' between the EU, the United States and others incorporates developing countries and the Cairns Group (that is the relatively unprotected producers who seek free trade to promote exports in which they have a comparative advantage).

The discussion has wandered far from the initial concern with simple supply and demand curves and has been extended to include a political economy of policy-making. But the increasing sophistication of the analysis, especially when applied empirically through complex models, should not blind us to continuing weaknesses. First, the theory is heavily deterministic, with patterns of agricultural development laid out in advance, or extrapolated from the past, and policy outcomes are equally mechanically linked to evolving economic interest groups.

Second, setting aside food for the moment, the economic theory of international trade that has been employed to justify trade liberalization for industry and, increasingly, internationally traded services, has long been fundamentally flawed both empirically and theoretically. It has failed to explain the origins of comparative advantage or different rates of increase in productivity between countries. In other words, technological change has been taken as exogenous, and there is no place for increasing or dynamic returns to scale in production. Given the limited analytical distinction that is made by orthodox economics between agriculture and industry, it is hardly surprising that the benefits of negotiated free trade, or reduced protection, should emerge for agriculture as they have for other sectors, such as industry and, increasingly, internationally traded services. If agriculture were to be considered as an infant industry, in the context of imperfect competition, as a dynamic source of surplus for domestic industrialization, etc, it would render traditional analysis redundant. The point, then, is not so much to dispute the costs of agricultural support, but to question the theoretical basis on which they are explained and criticized.

Nor is traditional trade theory able to explain for manufacturing why countries should both export and import the same goods since it relies upon a logic of each country specializing in goods for which it has a comparative advantage.[13] While agricultural trade is less perverse in this respect, although countries do import and export some of the same foods, this does not justify the use of an economic theory for agriculture which is demonstrably unsuccessful in explaining industrial trade, especially when the same sorts of assumptions are made for both – technology given at any moment, no economies of scale, limited market imperfections, etc.

Third, the theory of the state and of policy-making is extremely simplistic. Economic interest groups are identified with corresponding policies and the means to achieve them. In other words, politics is simply a particular form of economics by other means. More general issues of political power and the formation of political parties, institutions and alliances are necessarily overlooked.

Fourth, the same applies to the exercise of power at the international level where, for example, the difference between developed and developing countries is primarily seen as one of differences in stages of development. The benefits of free trade, equitably distributed, are intended to support development. But, as is all too apparent, trade policy, whether protection or liberalization, has long served the interests of the developed countries and has reflected the exercise of economic and political power over the developing world.[14]

Fifth, the relationship between agriculture and industry is far more complex than one of a shifting balance of favour towards the farmer. During development, surplus is transferred from the agricultural sector to promote industrialization, but it involves a range of other changes – such as land reform and proletarianization – which are varied in their content and outcome.

Sixth, this complexity is overlooked by the highly aggregated understanding of the farm and food problem. Often the analysis is explicitly restricted to a few staple crops, such as grains and sugar. But there are differences between and within these, and there can be no presumption of a common theory to cover them all.

Seventh, the food issue has primarily been reduced to agriculture alone. The intervening roles, prior to consumption, played by traders, processors and retailers are primarily passive. These can be important, shift over time and have different impact from one country to another.

Finally, it is worth speculating on how treatment of food is distinguished from other products. Essentially, there are three simple factors alone – the declining income elasticity of demand (Engel's Law), the high rate of productivity increase over time, and the corresponding political economy of interest groups. It is remarkable how little should be employed to explain so much!

In short, the economics of food as theory has shifted very little in response to recent empirical developments, although it has shown considerable sophistication in explaining what has happened on the basis of limited analytical raw materials. Consequently, a more deeply rooted political economy of food has to be sought elsewhere. This is taken up in the next chapter but it is distinguished from the orthodoxy in its starting point by the following:

1 taking the imperative to increase output and productivity as a crucial driving force rather than as an exogenous trend;
2 focusing upon the exercise of economic and political power at national and international levels rather than seeing these as the response to problems or interests as they emerge;
3 incorporating the role of all economic activity around food rather than examining agriculture alone.

NUTRITIONAL APPROACHES TO FOOD

Nutritional studies are a mirror image to the demand analysis of orthodox economics. While the latter is relatively unconcerned with the physical properties of food and is only concerned with the utility that they generate, the former is centrally preoccupied with the physical properties of food itself and, in the first instance, the physical properties of human beings as feeding animals. The starting point is to identify an appropriate (minimum) diet on the basis of the balance and levels of nutrients. This serves as a standard to be attained by each consumer. Where this is not achieved, an explanation is sought and, where possible, remedying policy undertaken. Experiments are even undertaken to examine whether humans, like other animals, instinctively or unconsciously seek out foods that contain essential nutrients, otherwise missing from their diets, as a result of physiological stimuli.

In this way, a balanced diet is taken as a norm, and actual diet is explained by divergence from that norm whether due to physical, psychological or social factors. For the latter for example, there might be insufficient income or inadequate knowledge of a healthy diet or information concerning foods. There is a paradox here. For, while nutritional studies is heavily based upon the idea of humans as animals with a well-defined and even instinctive predilection for a healthy diet, deviance from such a diet is to be corrected by appealing to the conscious capacity to make and change choices. Essentially, there is a presumption of obstacles to the adoption of an appropriate diet (just as economists see market imperfections as an obstacle to economic efficiency).

The problems with this approach are highlighted by, but do not originate with, the incidence of modern dietary disease. For, while incomes were low, the gap between actual and recommended food intake could be readily explained by factors beyond the control of the individual consumer. It could be more reasonably presumed that a deficient diet was the consequence of lack of capacity or deviancy in habit or knowledge which could, hopefully, readily be corrected. Once, however, the majority are both able to meet dietary requirements and failing to do so, it is apparent that dietary norms defined by nutritional standards only play a limited role at most in determining what is actually eaten. What we *do* eat is not appropriately understood by reference to what we *ought* to eat. There is a role for nutritional standards and advice in explaining diet, but it is only a small part of a complex system of what constitutes food knowledge and the translation of that knowledge into food choice.[15] Certainly, consumers do not in general make a detour via what they ought to eat in deciding what they will eat (as if we were all self-disciplining naughty children exhorting ourselves to eat our spinach).[16] Nor is there any reason for food studies to take this route. It can only exaggerate and simplify the role played by nutritional knowledge in the choice of foods.

THE GEOGRAPHY OF FOOD

Traditional approaches to the geography of food have taken their lead from economics. In principle, the analyses of supply and demand should be the same across the two disciplines, and they often are – especially where the two disciplines overlap within agricultural economics. But, geography is more concerned with the differences engendered by location and space. Consequently, differences in the production and consumption of food by country are examined for empirical regularities. This is so, for example, in the series of contributions by Grigg (1993a–c and 1994). He observes how food consumption changes with income and prices and adds the environment (weather, fertility, etc.), culture, trade and government policy as other factors that broadly explain variations across country and over time.

This is limited in that, while it provides a range of empirical regularities, it offers little or no explanation for them. Olives are produced and disproportionately consumed in a Mediterranean climate; ruminants are prevalent where pasture is exclusively available rather than arable land, etc.

Further, in seeking empirical generalizations, the presence of difference tends to be overlooked. In addition, what is essentially an ahistorical set of correlations between food-related variables takes no account of differences in products, how they are produced, and how productivity differences have been generated over time.

This treatment of food clearly has its intellectual roots in physical geography even though it is concerned with humans rather than rocks. For the land has a particular physical relationship to the production of food, and humans are presumed to have stylized patterns of consumption, reflecting incomes (Engel's Law is prominent) and a sociocultural land-scape. In the mid-1980s, unlike economics, a reaction against this form of analysis gathered strength within geography, partly reflecting more general developments within the discipline towards a more firmly grounded theoretical basis within social theory. Bowler and Ilbery (1987) complained that the traditional field of agricultural geography had been obsessed with the production function in agriculture (how much output from given inputs). They emphasized the need to examine food systems up- and downstream from agriculture and to promote political economy to explore issues such as uneven development, the persistence of the household farm, restructuring in and around rural areas, and the sources and role of state policy. Atkins (1988) pursued their critique further, seeking to forge a link between the geography of food supply and that of consumption.[17]

This has led geographers to construct theory without suffering the deadweight imposed by orthodox economic analysis. Thus, Bowler (1992b) is concerned with the industrialization of agriculture and the third agri-cultural revolution, terms that do not fit comfortably within supply and demand curves. This leads to a focus upon systemic economic processes such as intensification (growing share of non-farm inputs), concentration (at enterprise and regional levels and in food-related industries), and specialization. Rather than take technological change as exogenous, it is intimately linked to government policy, both as cause and effect:

> The process of intensification has been described as 'treadmill' for those working in agriculture . . . costs of production tend to rise at a faster rate than the prices obtained for farm produce, thereby creating a cost–price squeeze; innovative farmers gain a short-term financial advantage by reducing their production costs or increasing the output for each hectare of land using new farm technology; as output increases and product prices fall, other farmers are forced to apply the new farming methods in order to survive; further downward pressure is exerted on agricultural prices thus causing the cycle to be repeated. But when governments intervene to support farm prices and incomes, they also tend to reward the process of intensification. (p. 14)[18]

It is insights of this sort that inform our own work.

THE PSYCHOLOGY OF FOOD

The psychology, economics and geography of food appear to be miles apart but they have one crucial characteristic in common – they seek regular relationships between food as a physical and as a social object (and nutritional science minimizes the latter component and may even see it as a source of deviancy from beneficial instinctive feeding). In many ways, the economics of food demand can be seen as a limited model for the psychology of food. For economics, the individual consumer has a limited personality defined by given preferences, and limited motivation and behaviour, given by utility maximization. Psychology considers the relationship between the consumer and the consumed more broadly, albeit upon an individualized basis.

A starting point, for example, can be made with the well-known Fishbein–Ajzen model adopted from marketing in which (food) choice is heavily associated with attitudes and beliefs.[19] This is already problematical in that individuals may have a structure of beliefs that are mutually inconsistent. Positive choice also depends upon whether conditions are favourable or facilitating, and this extends beyond prices and incomes to forms of approval, habit formation and the pleasurable and sensory attributes of foods.[20]

This all begs the question of where attitudes, habits, food properties, etc., come from in the first place. In defining a relationship between human motivation and behaviour and the properties of food, the psychological model tends to be drawn by analogy with a rat in experimental conditions. But we are not rats nor rat-like and, although we both learn and need to meet physiological requirements to survive, these do not determine our food choices. As Shepherd and Farleigh (1989, p. 49) observe, there is only the weakest of links between sensory responses and food intake because of the weight of influence of other factors involved in food choice.[21]

None the less, the psychology of food continues the attempt to extract that part of consumer behaviour which is rat-like or, more exactly, human-like if humans were not bound by social relations. By analogy, the scientist might study a bee's power to fly without regard to its social role in the community of bees, and this can be a meaningful exercise for certain purposes (in understanding aerodynamics). Yet, it cannot tell us anything about why the bee flies where it does. Similarly, humans eat to live but they do not live to eat, except very rarely in extreme cases of the gourmand or gourmet! Consequently, the psychology of food choice has to be integrated with, and set against, its social determinants.

We cannot, then, explain eating patterns by human nature whether this be physiological or psychological. Even though humans are omnivores, this does not necessarily induce obesity, as some have argued, as a consequence of abundance and an intrinsic appetite for variety and security against future food shortages (Rolls and Hetherington 1989). Nor do we simply learn about, and hence accept or reject, foods through Pavlovian conditioning, sensory factors (smell, taste and appearance), but through any number of cultural factors. As Rozin (1989, p. 220) concludes, like many other psychologists who recognize the explanatory limitations of their discipline, there is a long list of mechanisms that lead to acquired likes and dislikes: 'It is difficult to assign particular foods to particular mechanisms partly because many substances are consumed for multiple reasons.'

In this respect, psychology has some parallels with geography. The latter searches for irreducible generalizations from the physical environment whereas the former seeks them within human nature. This is so, for example, in the omnivore's paradox (Fischler 1980, 1988 and 1989) – we are able to eat many things but this creates uncertainty and tension around new foods as greater availability has to be set against risks of poisoning. Some would extrapolate this dilemma to contemporary capitalism – from an idealized primitive society (presumably it would have to be Robinson Crusoe's island with nobody to tell us what is safe to eat). The grounds for doing so are the consumers' limited knowledge of foods that have their origins in distant factories and fields. While these are important features of the modern food system, their impact in determining what we eat and how we receive it psychologically is only obscured by attaching them to an intrinsic and immanent omnivore's paradox.[22]

SOCIAL THEORY AND FOOD

Unlike the approaches previously considered, the sociology, anthropology and history of food create a much greater space for human and social agency and contingent outcomes.[23] Not surprisingly, anthropology has long been concerned with food given the extent of its importance in the societies that it studies. Particular attention has been paid to the symbolic aspects of food, how its meanings have been socially constructed, and how this has related to food habits, taboos, kinship, nutritional wisdom and health beliefs and practices. Over the past decade, however, particularly as anthropological insights have been applied to advanced capitalism, material factors have become more prominent in the anthropology of food.[24]

To use a favoured example to illustrate this, why do we not eat pets? The earlier structural approaches, especially associated with Levi-Strauss and dealing with the symbolic aspects of food, would have answered in terms of pets not being 'good to think about' as food since they have been assigned human attributes in a variety of ways. Consequently, eating pets is symbolically paramount to violating the taboo against cannibalism. An alternative 'materialist' anthropology, however, reasonably observes the wide variety across societies and cultures in what are designated as pets and, correspondingly if not exhaustively, what is not eaten. But what determines what animals should become pets? This is not arbitrary. Rather, it is accepted that pets are not good to think about as food, but the structuralist causation is reversed. Animals become pets because they are not eaten, not vice versa, and this is the ideological source of their lack of palatability.

By material here is meant much more than the comparative advantage associated with orthodox economics – that cats and dogs do not make good cattle from a commercial point of view. More broadly, apart from productive potential, the choice of foods ultimately reflects material conflicts for power between different interest groups. Thus Ross (1980a), in rejecting cultural explanations for patterns of meat consumption (is pig more palatable than beef), seeks to show how in the United States the interests of large-scale beef interests prevailed over those attached to pork. Only then could it come to symbolize American eating habits, most notably in the form of the beefburger (which, ironically reflecting its origins in the victory of beef over pork, is often termed a hamburger).

What is remarkable about the anthropology of food is that there is such a sharp contrast between the two schools of thought. While our own sympathy lies with the materialist school, that the structure of symbolic representation of food is heavily determined by economic factors, it is equally necessary to recognize that material factors interact with one another and with the cultural and symbolic content of food in different and complex ways which can themselves have material effects. Thus, the current form and extent of concern around healthy eating, and what (symbolically or otherwise) constitutes a healthy diet, is in part a consequence of the ways in which the food system has developed materially, with productivity and profitability pursued at the expense of consumers' well-being. But, equally, the food system has also moulded to, even if it has itself moulded, the demands for a healthier diet.[25]

Sociology has taken a much later interest in food than anthropology and has tended to traverse the relationship between the material and the symbolic content of food in the opposite direction. For sociology has used its central and longstanding preoccupation with social relations, structures and processes and has applied them to food. Issues covered include (class) stratification, rural restructuring, ethnicity, gender, inequality and welfare, and how these are reflected in food consumption. Food is used as a means of illustrating an underlying theory – the proper meal with meat and two veg and husband at the table as an index of intra-household power in the preparation and consumption of food, or the distinctions in diet between households of different social class, for example.

The rise of the sociology of food, however, has been accompanied by a greater interest in the sociology of culture and of consumption more generally. Consequently, sociology has increasingly been concerned with the symbolic meaning of food, especially in the wake of post-modernism, just as anthropology was at an earlier stage. The result has been to create an extremely fragmented set of contributions and themes, more around traditional sociological concerns, with food as a handy illustrative vehicle, than in the formulation of a coherent understanding of food itself. This is amply reflected in the survey of Mennell *et al.* (1992, p. 118):

> The discipline of sociology is like a cake: it can be cut up in many different ways. Food and eating have not until very recently generally merited a 'sociology of' to themselves. Even now, the sociology of food and eating is hardly a very unified sub-discipline – if, indeed, it ought to become one.

CONCLUDING REMARKS

As previously observed, food studies has always been a disparate discipline or collection of disciplines. This proved more or less acceptable while each fragment could remain exclusively preoccupied with its own concerns in isolation from the concerns of the others. Developments over the past decade in the production of food, the composition of diet, the politics and content of policy-making, etc., have sorely revealed the inadequacies of food studies. This holds not only for the analytical and policy challenges that are currently posed but it also reflects back upon the conventional wisdoms that were previously prevalent.

Many of these points can be illustrated by *The Food Consumer*, a volume edited by C. Ritson, L. Gofton and J. McKenzie in 1986. The preface observes, 'that there was no volume which provided an integrated approach to the study of food consumption in the industrial world' (p. ix). The book seeks to rectify this by providing coverage for the specialists in fields other than their own. Essentially, this is then attempted by a sequence of separate contributions addressing different topics or disciplines.[26] An integrated approach is offered by McKenzie (1986) but it simply pieces together selectively a number of the separate influences concerned without their interacting satisfactorily.

Hopefully, Ritson *et al.* (1986) will increasingly prove a redundant product of its time, demonstrating both the then fragmentation of food studies and the inadequacy of the intrinsic content of each fragment. The remainder of this volume is concerned to promote and to apply a more adequate analytical basis for food studies, one that is both interdisciplinary and appropriate from the outset.

NOTES

1 For discussion of the world 'food problem', see Grigg (1993d), Dyson (1994a and b) and Smil (1994). Debate over famine over the past decade has been dominated by Sen's (1981) entitlement approach. See Fine (1995c) for an assessment from a food studies perspective.

2 Thus, Sobal *et al.* (1993) provide advice on how to design courses in three different areas – the sociology of food and nutrition, food and society, and nutritional sociology.

3 For an overview of theories of food, generally with a different coverage than that presented here, see Fine and Leopold (1993).

4 For an exposition, see Tarrant (1992, p. 245) for example.

5 This approach is thoroughly assessed in Chapter 7.

6 Some economists doubt whether false information will necessarily persist, as good information will chase out the bad just as good quality displaces bad quality. See discussion in the second volume, but also Fine and Leopold (1993) and Fine and Wright (1991).

7 The analytical status of Engel's Law is discussed in greater detail in the second volume.

8 See Gardner (1992) for a review in the US context.

9 For this account and what follows, see Rayner *et al.* (1993).

10 It has also been suggested that one cost of agricultural protection has been to hold up the completion of the Uruguay Round.

11 See also Anderson and Tyers (1991) and Anderson (1994).

12 This is a classic example of the prisoners' dilemma, termed the isolation paradox by Sen (1967) when there are more than two players. He also discusses the assurance game, in which each player is willing to hold to a mutually beneficial strategy as long all others are. The difference in this context depends upon whether protection by an individual country is better for it or not, given that other countries are not protecting. For the prisoners' dilemma, each country has an incentive to breach GATT whereas this is not so for the assurance game once the treaty has been negotiated and implemented.

13 For an exposition of the empirical anomalies surrounding orthodox international trade theory, see Henderson (1989). For an alternative to the orthodoxy, see Krugman and Smith (eds) (1994).

14 For a stunning account of this in the context of an advanced industrial sector, see Hills (1994), who shows how the United States has sought to reverse its position on free international access to domestic markets (to protect its own) now that it has established a dominant position in the domestic markets of others.

15 See the second volume and Fine and Leopold (1993) and Fine and Wright (1991).

16 The prominence of spinach as healthy originated with a mistakenly placed decimal point in nutrient analysis. Its subsequent rise owes much to that of Popeye – revealing how food knowledge moves in mysterious ways.

17 It is ironic that Grigg (1994) sees himself as responding to this call by replicating for consumption the old geography of production.

18 Note that support also tends to sustain inefficient producers and excess supply even if the advantage accrues disproportionately to lowest cost, large-scale producers.

19 See Shepherd (1989a).

20 As argued in Fine and Leopold (1993), especially when psychology is used in marketing, there is an indeterminately large number of food attributes, forms of consumer gratification and relationships between the two.

21 See also James *et al.* (1980, p. 3): 'In man, control of food intake is complex, and the primitive hypothalamic reflexes are so buried under so many layers of conditioning, cognitive and social factors that they are barely discernible.'

22 The omnivore's paradox is taken up in greater detail in the second volume.

23 We do not cover the economic and social history of food. It is extremely diverse and perhaps offers more insights than other disciplines because of its goal of explaining major changes over time. Accordingly, it is significant how little attention is paid to history in other branches of food studies.

24 See Murcott (1989) and Messer (1984) for overviews of the anthropology of food.

25 This is discussed at length in the second volume.

26 The same is true of the NCC (1992) which provides a more recent overview of the contribution of various disciplines to the issue of food choice.

Part II

SPECIFYING FOOD SYSTEMS

3

FOOD SYSTEM THEORY[1]

INTRODUCTION

Increasingly, the idea that what we eat depends upon the functioning of the food system, or a number of food systems, has gained in strength in both popular and analytical discourse. Central is the notion that the passage of a food from farm to mouth comprises a sequence of distinct activities that are, none the less, structurally bound into a unified whole that is integrated with other economic activity, such as transport, shopping and domestic labour. Equally important is the recognition that such food systems are intimately connected to international and political influences. In this context, even the neoclassical orthodoxy implicitly acknowledges that food is structurally distinct from other products by locating it within an international political economy in which bargaining 'games' are conducted at different levels, such as domestic, international and, potentially, regional.[2] This chapter argues for the necessity of employing the concept of a food system. But it is concerned to review some existing notions critically and to bring out crucial differences from our own perspectives.

In particular, we need to take some view about the structures and processes along the food system, how they interact with one another, and what is distinctive about food as opposed to other systems. These are abstract theoretical issues. They are complemented by what are occasioally more concrete concerns such as the role of global factors and the role of the state. Each of these is discussed in turn, although the emphasis is primarily upon the more abstract set of issues since, as will become apparent, we are not convinced that much progress can be made at a general level in determining the relationship between food and the role of the state and of global factors.

WHAT IS A FOOD SYSTEM?

Perhaps the commonest form in which the idea of a food system is used is as a descriptive or narrative framework. Economic and social histories or

31

contemporary accounts of particular commodities focus upon the distinct stages of agricultural production, industrial processing, marketing and consumption. Often within an informal framework of supply and demand, the fortunes or the misfortunes of price, quantity and quality are documented as technology, state support, global developments, changing tastes and other factors are perceived to create particular systems and levels of provision.

Over the past two decades, however, rooted if not originating within political economy, much more sophisticated theoretical analyses, with a richer causal content, have been brought to bear upon the understanding of what comprises food systems and how they evolve in practice.[3] Essentially, as Goodman and Watts (1994) have perceptively observed, much of this analysis of the global agro-food system is wedded to the notion that agriculture has been increasingly industrialized and, in particular, has experienced developments that parallel industrial capital and close the gap with it. This implies that an image of industrial capital is projected upon agriculture. Specifically, the latter is perceived to have experienced a Fordism of mass production and consumption. This has required homogeneous commodities that are durable and, consequently, open to trade and postponed consumption without running the risk of perishing. Production methods and consumption patterns have been internationalized (the world steer in production, McDonalds in consumption), and the financing and marketing of agriculture have also been heavily monopolized and internationally integrated. Further, Fordist agriculture has suffered a crisis from the mid-1970s onwards, matching the collapse of the post-war boom and the declining hegemony of the US economy in international competitiveness. The past twenty years have witnessed a continuing industrialized development of agriculture but one that has more closely followed the diversity associated with post-Fordist patterns of production and consumption, geared towards flexibility in production methods and market tastes.

Methodologically, three particular issues have been addressed, however explicitly. The first concerns the rationale for the *structures* that comprise the food system. Moving beyond a descriptive narrative requires an explanation for the existence of the separate elements along the food chain and what activities belong within each of these. Most prominent here has been investigation of the relationship between agriculture (or farming) and industry (agro-industrial complex furnishing inputs and processing outputs). However, attention has also been devoted to wholesaling and retailing as the corporations involved are acknowledged to have become increasingly monopolized and powerful in dominating conditions of supply and demand – that is, attention has also focused upon the *other* elements along the food system apart from agriculture and industry. Further, it is often observed how important access to finance is in determining the position of agricultural producers. In addition, the dependence of the food

32

system upon consumption has led to a focus upon the household, not simply as a source of demand, but as a site of consumption, and even (domestic) production, structurally differentiated within the food system. This is especially so in considering the role of women's (paid and unpaid) work, changing domestic technology in advanced countries (microwaves and convenience foods), and consumption habits (shifting and flexible mealtimes). Thus, to view the food system as a sequence of economic activities undertaken within a definite structure is to open the question of what the dividing lines are between those structures, and how they are reproduced, shifted or transformed over time – a matter to be taken up shortly. In some respects, in the specific context of food, this is to raise more general issues within social theory. On what basis do we distinguish one activity from another in denoting them as (social or economic) structures? And what is the position and status of such structures in theoretical analysis as a whole?

Apart from interrogating the structure of the food system itself, other structural considerations have been raised of a less abstract character. In particular, emphasis has been placed upon corporate structure and the industrial structure arising out of vertical and horizontal integration, the structure of world trade, and the institutional structure within which the food system operates, particularly the role of state institutions and their (shifting) relationships to the private sector. This reinforces the need to place the structures of the food system within an appropriate analytical framework rather than taking them as self-evident on a more or less casual empirical basis.

The second methodological input of the new food systems literature has been to stress the presence of inherent *tendencies* linked to the imperatives of capitalist accumulation and profitability. These have been most prominent in the discussion of technology and farm size (both for acreage and labour force), particularly in the idea that farming has been increasingly squeezed by industrialization of its activities, forcing it onto a technological treadmill, comprising artificial fertilizer, hybrid seed, protective chemicals, mechanization and, most recently, biotechnology.

Third, there has been a methodological appeal to historical *contingency*, although this functions in two distinct ways. One is to recognize that the structures and tendencies interact differently across the various food systems, thereby differentiating these from one another. The other is to allow for the intervention and resolution of conflict between competing interest groups, whether this be through the market or the state, or in the domestic or the international arena.

The preceding paragraphs represent a simple attempt to distil three separate but common methodological elements from a range of literature. Inevitably, it does rough justice to those other factors that are only sporadically present, which range from broad analytical stances derived from grand theory – such as appeals to long waves, or the Fordism of regulation theory – to the more mundane dependence upon Engel's Law. Also some violence to the literature is perpetrated by artificially divorcing structural, tendential and contingent components from one another since each conditions the content of the others. None the less, the implicit framework developed around these three methodological elements exhibits considerable strengths because of its generality and yet its sensitivity to particular foods and their histories.

It does, however, have the potential for certain weaknesses as a general methodology for examining the food system. Since the latter is most readily understood as a sequentially ordered set of structures, it is these that most readily appropriate analytical priority. Subsequently, the analytical role of *tendencies*, even if abstractly understood initially, is translated into that of empirical *trends*, which are considered to be constrained by the structures within which they operate. Ultimately, the tendencies and structures prove incompatible and the food system is necessarily restructured if only to be subject to renewed, possibly different, tendential strains. It is predominantly, if not exclusively, during a period of restructuring that conflict resolution and historical contingency are seen as most pertinent for, then, they are liable to influence the character of the transformed food system that is to be put in place.

The political economy of food can then be thought of as being based upon a more or less conscious dialectic of structure, tendency and contingency. Out of this, how well-defined are the structures comprising a food system? What is meant by a structure in this context? Often it is empirically unambiguous – as between one activity and another (agriculture and industry, for example), or one institution and another (the 'family' farm as opposed to the capitalist enterprise). On the other hand, such structural distinctions are far from analytically innocent and take on deeper meanings and a causal content in assuming, often implicitly, a correspondence with the categories of economic and social theory; the division between activities and between institutions has affinities with class relations or other stratifications (peasants and capitalist, producers and consumers, etc.). There is, moreover, an inherent danger of deriving a spurious causal content out of such tentative structuralism. For empirically identified divisions are construed as deeper analytical structures which are, in turn, employed to explain the empirical evidence from which they have been derived. Thus, if a division is identified between backward agriculture and advanced industry, it inevitably leads to a corresponding theory of the one blocking the penetration and advance of the other, or of one ultimately converging upon the other.

In short, the analytical basis for structures cannot be satisfactorily rationalized in isolation from other theoretical considerations. The role of the state, most prominent in the political economy of food, illustrates this

34

most readily – as it comprises both structures and is itself the *product* of the forces that act upon it. This raises a second methodological issue of whether the order of analytical priority between structures and tendencies is generally acceptable. It is arguable that tendencies do not simply develop within and against the structures of the food system but also serve to (re)produce them. Does the industrialization of agriculture, its penetration by specifically capitalist methods of production, work upon the structural separation between the two sectors of agriculture and industry or is it the source of that separation or the means by which it is sustained?[4] In terms of classic Marxist theory, for example, economic development is perceived in terms of the dialectic between the relations of production (crudely, structures) and the forces of production (crudely, tendencies). Whether in this analytical context or others, it is essential to bear in mind, then, that the relationship between tendencies and structures in terms of causal priority is open to question – although, as observed, there is most often a simple treatment of structure as prior to tendencies which are themselves treated as trends operating within structures. Empirical developments are more easily and immediately accommodated within such a framework but only at the expense of explanatory content. This is to be found, for example, in the explanation of agricultural over- or underproduction in terms of the structured levels of support to producers being set at too high or low a level, respectively.

The third methodological issue is whether analysis of food provision as a system is unique to food and, if not, what distinguishes the food system or food systems from other systems of provision – from the energy, housing, transport, clothing and education systems. Are they simply systems that are analytically indistinguishable from one another even though they are concerned with different products? Indeed, as Fine and Leopold (1993) have argued at length in examining consumption in general, the economy should be understood in terms of a series of such systems of provision. These are distinguishable from each other in that the ways in which production, distribution, marketing, consumption, etc. are integrated differ from one commodity (group) to another; and the signifi-cance of each of these factors is dependent upon its relationship to the system of provision as a whole. Yet, while this does suggest that each system of provision, including the food system, is potentially different from other systems of provision, it does not specify what is liable to make the food system specifically different from other commodity systems.

There have been two very common answers to this question which are intimately related to the issue of structure along the food system. The first concerns the relationship between the food system and consumption; food is consumed in a particular way which means that its 'organic' properties are of crucial importance.[5] By 'organic' is meant the physical properties of food and how they are created by, and relate to, the socioeconomic conditions within which they function. Thus, food has specific use values – around nutritional content, perishability, etc. – which are important and distinctive but these must not be taken as isolated determinants. Despite the goals of nutritionists and dietitians, what is consumed is not determined by the organic content of food, but the latter does set food apart from other items of consumption which are primarily, if not exclusively, inorganic in content. And the relationship between food and consumption is mediated by the structural separation between the commercial world and the household, given the latter's responsibility for the acquisition and preparation of food.

The second unique aspect of the food system is often perceived to be its dependence upon agriculture. Whether agriculture is organized capitalistically or not, its use of land as a major factor of production and the role of climate and soil fertility, etc., are taken as important influences upon the internal organization and development of the sector and upon its integration with the remainder of the food system. Essentially, however, there is a strict analogue with the relationship between the household and the food system, only around production rather than consumption. Agriculture has an organic relationship to production which is associated with its structural separation from the capitalist production of food (using agricultural commodities as raw materials).

Combining these two insights together suggests that the defining characteristic of the food, as opposed to other, systems of provision is the crucial significance of organic factors at both of the extreme ends of the system of provision. For any process of production or consumption, there will be what might be simply summarized as a ratio of organic and inorganic content.[6] Some have a high ratio at the outset as in those dependent on agriculture or land. But this ratio might decline along the system of provision – as for textiles or minerals, for example. Clothing is an apt example here, since its dependence upon agriculture might persist through to the final product, as in a cotton or woollen garment, and clothing performs many of the roles of food in terms of its symbolic and other functions as an item of consumption. But it is consumed on, not within the body, and its organic properties as such are liable to be negligible at this stage.

On the other hand, there are items of consumption whose organic ratio is negligible initially, within production, but whose organic properties are crucial to consumption. The example of medicines immediately springs to mind. In short, what distinguishes the food system is its high organic ratio at both extremes of the system of provision (SOP for short). This is so whatever the organic ratio at intermediate stages – due to the use of chemical food additives, for example, and whether organic materials can be treated, in production, distribution and sale, as though they were inorganic. The use of the three Ps in food production – preparation, preservation and packaging – reflects the integral nature of food systems, in seeking both to accommodate and to minimize the impact of the organic content of the food system. Thus, sugar is grown as an agricultural product in the form of beet or cane, but its properties allow it to be treated almost as an inorganic raw material prior to consumption where its nutritional and other organic properties become increasingly important again. On the other hand, for dairy products, the intermediate properties of the raw materials derived from milk depend upon how it is processed – as in the distinction between liquid milk and cream as opposed to butter, cheese and dried milk.

Consider what we have termed the 'organic' content of the food systems further. First, as suggested, all systems of provision, for food or otherwise, are differentiated from one another, with each constituting a vertical structure and chain of activities. But food systems, in addition, are distinguished by a particular feature. As Beardsworth and Keil (1993) have recently argued, food has a physiological character since it is eaten and, consequently, is broken down into nutrients that are used by the body.[7] We would extend this understanding of the organic content of food as having an influence along the whole SOP, either indirectly because of the ultimate purpose to which the activity leads or directly because of the organic nature of the chain of food provision itself.

Some have criticized this sort of argument for embodying a degree of natural determinism, and this is a potential danger. Unfortunately, Beardsworth and Keil (1993) skate on thin ice by viewing the distinctiveness of food in terms of its necessity and indispensability (as opposed to clothing, housing, warmth?), although this is qualified by the observation that food cannot be reduced to physiological determinants as a 'fuel for the body's metabolic process and physical activities' (p. 11). Our stance is different in simply acknowledging the necessity of physiological or biological content of food systems, whether this entails that they are positively embraced or functional as in agriculture (or fermentation, for example) or subject to control and avoidance as in preservation from spoilage. This is not to suggest that other SOPs are without an influential organic content or that the latter is an unmediated, asocial and ahistorical determinant. Rather, food systems incorporate an organic content both systematically and pervasively (in the same way, by analogy, that an energy system must incorporate the generation, distribution and use of power). In other words, food systems do have general material properties in process and in the created use values for consumption (irrespective of how these are socially constructed) which are themselves open to restructuring and transformation.[8]

Thus, even though the specificity of the food system is identified with its particular balance of organic and inorganic content along the system of provision, this does not imply an analysis based on biological and/or natural determinism. Even if the pattern of the organic ratio does distinguish the food from other systems, it does not follow that it is determined by its organic characteristics at the expense of other social and economic factors – just as it would be equally incorrect to suggest that non-food

37

systems are determined by their inorganic content as such. None the less, such naturally based theories of the food system do exist and persist – most notably in the idea that agriculture is inherently unstable because of its dependence upon the weather, etc. In this respect, our position is distinctive in recognizing the organic but without ascribing to it a prior (and fixed) causal role, whether this be in terms of the physiological or biological determinants or, as in the work of Goodman and Redclift to be discussed shortly, a more abstract dialectic between the social (represented by capital) and the biological or natural.

Second, the argument made here, concerning the specificity of the food system, has referred to the structural position of agriculture and the household within the food system in order to bring out the degree of organic dependence at the two extremes of the food system. But those structurally located extremes serve purely in an expositional or descriptive role; there can be no presumption, to return to an earlier theme, of the priority of such factors in a causal analysis – that such structures are as or more important than others or that they are more significant than tendencies within the food system.

Finally, it is worth observing that the dependence of food provision upon a tenacious organic ratio has encouraged commentators to focus upon the idea of a food system – acutely in the context of food scares – however that might be understood. For the concern with the organic content of food in consumption necessarily leads to attention to the origins of the food in a way that is not true of inorganic products. The mineral origin of a car is of less interest than its design, performance and appearance. Yet the production of food crops, and their processing, are less amenable to neglect in considering their ultimate use. In order to comprehend the organic quality of food (whether we consider it to be served well or badly), we have to trace it through to its origins. We have much less interest in the origins of products that are primarily inorganic. There are exceptions that prove the rule, for there can be the wish to trace the combination of organic and inorganic influences through each system of provision, whether food or not.

The most obvious example is in studying environmental impacts of consumption for which the origins of energy or metal are important. But then the desire to examine the SOPs is motivated by a general concern that potentially applies to all products – whereas there is a necessary concern with the organic content of food (even if the extent and form is socially constructed).[9] Note also that the dependence of diet upon food systems may lead, contra green consumerism and healthy and safe eating concerns, to a desire for detachment from knowledge of food's origins. We do not want to know how cruelly animals (or workers) have been treated in providing our meal – it would ruin our enjoyment and even our appetite! This is an important point since it demonstrates that cultural attitudes to, or ideologies of, foods cannot be derived simply from the material conditions under which they are provided. For the same material conditions can yield the potential for opposing attitudes.

DOMESTIC LABOUR

In the previous section, food is distinguished by its uniquely organic profile over its SOP. In doing this, the issue was raised of the implications for the structural and tendential characteristics of the food system, in particular in light of the positions occupied by the household and agriculture. This matter has been extensively explored within the literature at both extremes, particularly under the more general problem of the process or tendency towards commoditization. For agriculture, the relationship between agriculture and the food system has concerned the impact of capitalism upon rural society. For the household, the matter arises in the context of the domestic labour debate, and how food production is potentially shifted from the home by mass production of the items of (working-class) consumption. We begin here with the household and how, in part, it relates to the food system. This is because it will help to illustrate an analytical principle of importance (how to understand shifting comparative advantage) and because the weight of the existing literature is primarily concerned with the agricultural–industrial divide, with production rather than with consumption. Indeed, consumption has only recently entered the food system literature to any extent, often with a dramatic impact, exaggerating its causal significance on the basis of limited and cursory analysis. This is because of the notion that varied and shifting tastes can have a major influence upon production rather than consumption being seen as a passive response to the latter's dictates.

Before returning to this point and focusing upon the division of production between the household and the commercial sector, it is worthwhile to begin by recalling the domestic labour debate, which has been assessed in great detail in Fine (1992). Essentially, leaving aside the issue of whether domestic labour produces 'value' or not (which it does not), a wide variety of analyses have been concerned with how the developing productivity of capitalism undermines the viability and desirability of domestic (household) production. In other words, the tendency for capitalist productivity to increase leads to the displacement of domestic production. In the most extreme analyses, within the new neoclassical household economics associated with Becker (1981), there is a smooth and harmonious reallocation of resources from the household to the formal economy in line with shifting comparative advantage.[10] Other analyses, which often counterpose themselves to such orthodoxy because of appeal to a wider range of factors and an alternative economic theory, are, none the less, organized around such shifting comparative advantage. It is recognized that the household is something more than a unit of production and consumption, not reducible to a pseudo-marketplace, that it is governed by inner conflicts, and that its relations to the external world are both social and also not reducible to a pseudo-market exchange. Yet, for all of these genuine insights, they merely serve to modify and obstruct what is an inevitable invasion of domestic production by commercial products.

Significantly, each of these analyses depends upon a structural separation between the household and the (capitalist) economy, and the tendency for the latter to increase productivity is treated as a trend with the empirical outcome of diminished domestic production. While the structure around the family is economically eroded, this does not lead to its destruction because the nuclear family is taken as a systemic component of capitalism – although there are plenty of analyses, from a variety of points of view, that suggest that destruction of the family is intimately related to these economic pressures, through women's two roles (of wife/mother and wage labourer) and greater economic independence.

There are a number of serious deficiencies with this sort of approach. First, little or no account is taken of a crucial countertendency to the erosion of domestic labour – the mass production, at ever cheaper prices, of the items that serve as the raw materials and machinery of domestic production. This is not only a logical implication of increasing productivity under capitalism but one of considerable empirical importance, both historically and in the contemporary world. The mass production of food ingredients and cooking equipment, of textiles, cottons and sewing machines enhances the viability of domestic production. Similarly, most notably in microwaves and videos, the home production of cooking and leisure has been promoted and integrated in particular ways with mass production of convenience foods, leisure products and consumer durables. Indeed, it is frequently observed that the rise of television heavily impaired the commercial position of the cinema.[11] Convenience foods, for consumption within the home, also have a complex relation to the commercialization of food consumption through eating out – since both can depend upon the same raw materials, pre-prepared foods, and the same technology, the microwave.

The simplest way to deal with this tendency to promote domestic production is to accept that it has been overlooked but that, on average and historically, it continues to be outweighed by the tendency for capitalist productivity to outstrip domestic productivity. There may be exceptions, from time to time, to the average, and it might even be argued that these are more liable to be present for food than for other commodities given the concern with certainty or confidence in organic content. Manufacturing processes and manufactured ingredients might be treated with mistrust.

While an advance on the previous neglect, this resolution of the issue is deficient because of its reduction of tendencies and countertendencies to

40

simple empirical trends. First, the interplay between the two tendencies associated with commoditization is an underlying factor in determining the structural boundaries between the household and the formal economy, and it needs to be situated within broader economic and social changes. Second, for this and other reasons, the household cannot be taken as an ahistorical category which is well defined and subject to tendencies/trends irrespective of the society within which it is situated. The family system is very different according to the stage of development of capitalism.[12]

Essentially two simple points are being made here, and they are of general applicability, not just to domestic labour and capital. The process of commoditization is associated with two underlying tendencies whose interaction is complex. One, associated with the superiority of capitalist methods of production, tends to undermine non-capitalist production because of superior productivity. But there is a simultaneous strengthening of non-capitalist production. Second, precisely because non-capitalist production, even if integrated with capital (in reproducing labour power), is a form of production, the resolution of these conflicting tendencies cannot be determined abstractly. It depends upon the historical, social and contingent content of the non-capitalist production itself.

The discussion has wandered to some extent away from the immediate issue of food into the more general problem of the relationship between capital and domestic labour. This, however, remains highly relevant to food because of the central role that its consumption plays in the reproduction of the labourer – even if this declines in proportion with rising living standards. None the less, there is a complex relationship between factors such as family formation, domestic and waged labour, the development of capitalist production and products (e.g. eating out as opposed to, or even promoted by, the microwave, changing meal patterns and content as women take waged work, etc.). The argument here is that these are not best understood as the trend to commoditization eroding the structures of domestic provision other than by way of exception. Rather, commoditization involves tendency and countertendency whose complex interaction in specific historical and social circumstances gives rise to particular outcomes, including differences in family systems themselves even if they appear to belong to a single 'nuclear' genus.

AGRICULTURE

As previously observed, the relationship between the capitalist (food) system and the (consuming and producing) household has its counterpart in the relationship between capitalism and agriculture. Although reliance upon the idea of food systems suggests that they need to be analysed in their entirety, the focus of the rest of this chapter will be primarily upon the division between agriculture and industry. Much of the literature's concern with agriculture takes as its starting point the persistence of pre-capitalist production or less than fully or relatively backwardly developed capitalism within agriculture. Accordingly, agriculture (especially a peasantry, however categorized) is structurally separated from (more developed) capitalism whose tendency to greater productivity is a force upon the former.

It is not the intention to rehearse fully the debates that this has generated. But it is worthwhile outlining its main parameters. To caricature, at one extreme, associated with the Chayanovian model of the peasantry, the latter is endowed with a dynamic and vitality that enables it to resist successfully the disintegrating impact of *commoditization*, defined as the displacement of production for use by production for the market, and the increasing reliance upon the market for inputs. At the other extreme is the view that disintegration does occur even if subject to obstacles. The way in which this has been examined has been increasingly sophisticated. The process of dissolution has been linked to differentiation of the peasantry, drawing upon Lenin's two routes to capitalist agriculture,[13] and the rejection of deceptively appealing analyses based on notions of the peasant mode of production.

Ultimately, although there are differences within the latter position over the point at which commoditization of agriculture has occurred given the coexistence of non-commodity production (for subsistence, say), it views capital as a disintegrating force. The strongest expression of this is to be found in Bernstein's (1979) notion of the simple reproduction 'squeeze'.[14] Essentially, this involves the drawing of producers into commodity relations and their being progressively undermined by the superior productivity of large-scale capital (and subject to external surplus appropriation). However, this implies that the role that capital plays in potentially *enhancing* non-capitalist production is primarily set aside or, at best, is perceived as a contingent obstacle. Yet, integration with capitalism provides the availability of cheaper inputs and alternative opportunities with which to earn income – whether through access to markets, including those seeking labour power.[15] That these are overlooked is not surprising given the notion of 'squeeze', since the presumption is that competition operates on output prices (as one side of the scissors) and on input costs as well (the other side). But capital cannot reasonably be argued to be both increasing and decreasing the prices of its commodities. This is subject to qualification where agriculture's non-produced inputs are concerned, such as credit and land. These, however, concern conditions of access to means of production (and surplus appropriation), a matter to be taken up later.

Thus, for this approach, the countertendencies to commoditization tend to be neglected or categorized as historically contingent obstacles to (further) capitalist penetration.[16] Not surprisingly, the school opposed to the commoditization approach (arising more out of the Chayanov tradition) places much greater emphasis upon these countertendencies. First, their antagonists are perceived as the victims (or perpetrators) of a series of -isms – teleologism, dualism and essentialism. Their own emphases are upon the rejection of agricultural producers as backward or anomalous, and greater recognition of the internal organization and adaptability of producers, their strategies for survival and resistance to disintegration, and the variety of forms and means of incorporation into the external economic and social environment.

Significantly, the distance between the two positions has narrowed. Each has examined the internal dynamic of agricultural production and its variety of forms of existence; each has emphasized the impact of the external environment (in which state policy has assumed prominence); each has argued that agriculture may be characterized by production units governed by an internal logic other than the imperative of profitability; and each has recognized the persistence of a structural separation of agriculture from and, possibly, within capitalism. As the two schools approach one another in analytical content, the difference is more one of relative emphasis upon survival versus penetration or how the transformation of agriculture is to be understood. The movement onto a common analytical terrain reflects the recognition that agriculture, whether capitalist or non-capitalist, does survive and prosper in ways that distinguish it from capitalist production in general – not only in pre-capitalist forms but even in the family farms of advanced US capitalism.

What both sides share in common is the idea of a shifting comparative advantage associated with rising capitalist productivity, although the commoditization school is inclined to place greater emphasis upon it. Consequently, it pushes towards the view of agriculture as backward and subject to erosion but for the presence of historically contingent obstacles whereas these impediments are seen as more permanent, varied and shifting in the Chayanovian model. Interestingly, van der Ploeg (1990, p. 273) considers that there is 'an astonishing convergence between commoditization theory and neoclassical development economics'. While false in specification of analytical perspective, the germ of truth is to be found in the core emphasis upon the role of shifting comparative advantage. However, exactly the same accusation can be made in the opposite direction, against the Chayanovians – only the conclusion is that shifting comparative advantage transforms and restructures without any overall imperative necessarily to disintegrate non-capitalist agriculture.[17]

The reason for this affinity between the two schools is their common adoption of a structural differentiation between agriculture and capital and their interpretation of the tendencies associated with commoditization as trends that do or do not breach that structure. For the Chayanov-type school which, of necessity, has a greater interest in the countertendencies, commoditization inevitably becomes constrained within persisting structures. For example, Long and van der Ploeg (1988, p. 37), in response to

Vandergeest (1988), do recognize the relationship between structures and tendencies:

> Agricultural development is many-sided, complex and often contradictory in nature. It involves different sets of social forces originating from international, national, regional and local arenas. The interplay of these various forces generates specific forms, directions and rhythms of agricultural change.

But their subsequent exposition is exactly the reverse, concerned with 'agrarian structure' as the starting point for identifying underlying forces: 'Some concept of "agrarian structure" is necessary in order to identify and classify the types of agricultural development patterns, the forms of interaction between different sectors (agrarian and non-agrarian), as well as the specific driving forces.'[18]

In conclusion, it is suggested here that the tendencies and counter-tendencies associated with commoditization have to be understood as underlying forces whose interaction gives rise to more complex outcomes including the reproduction and transformation of agrarian structures within the food system. These observations are, however, extremely abstract, and they must remain so because the analysis has been restricted to general considerations of the interaction between capitalist commodity production and *any* form of commodity-producing agriculture. To proceed further, it is essential both to specify the internal organization of agriculture (what are its class relations of production, its conditions of access to land, etc.) and its socially and historically contingent relationships within the capitalist society of which it is a part.[19] Even where the agricultural sector is specified to be capitalist, the interaction with industry is historically contingent according to the form taken by landed property – as will be shown in the next section.

FOOD AND LANDED PROPERTY

While the organic content of food is important to the household because it is a site of consumption, it is important to agriculture because it is a site of production. Traditionally, this has been recognized in the political economy of food through various theories of rent and associated forms of tenure. At one extreme are those theories, perceived to originate with Ricardo, that take rent to arise out of the different natural fertilities of the soil. More sophisticated and wide-ranging theories include the conditions under which producers gain access to the land and, hence, construct a theory of landed property and its relation to capital which goes beyond the properties of the land itself. In terms of the distinction between agriculture and industry, it is not the dependence of the one on land as such which sets it apart (nearly all production depends upon some access to more or less favourable space), but the peculiar conditions governing access to the land for the purposes of production. These are distinct from the purchase of produced commodities as the typical form of inputs, and the payment of rent is the economic form in which the role of landed property is represented as a revenue. Within Marx's theory, landed property as a potential barrier to capitalist accumulation concerns the conditions under which capital gains access to the land (for which payment of rent, however determined, is only one, if often a principal, component). While extremely controversial in the variety of ways in which it is interpreted, Marx's rent theory can in part be seen to depend upon the ability of landlords to appropriate a share of the surplus profits that arise for individual capitals as they are accumulated upon the land – rather than this surplus profit becoming both generalized across the agricultural sector and redistributed to all capitals as part of the general rate of profit.[20]

Three further points need to be made here. First, Marx's preferred focus for this effect of generating surplus profit is through increasing size of capital which, if applied to the land, is susceptible to its associated additional surplus being appropriated by the landlord, thereby discouraging such intensive cultivation. Accordingly, Marx derives the result that the organic composition of capital (the rate of change of capital intensity) is potentially lower in agriculture than in industry more generally to the extent that extensive cultivation is induced in place of intensive cultivation, with absolute rent correspondingly raising the price of agricultural products at most to the level of their values.[21]

Second, however, the extent of this effect (both on prices and on the industrialization of agriculture) is historically contingent upon the form taken by landed property (the arrangements under which either landowners, farmers or others are able to accrue the benefits derived from intensive cultivation). Thus, the theory of rent is not based upon the unique properties of the land, nor upon the particularly strong dependence of agriculture upon land (for all production has some spatial requirements), but upon the particular way in which landed property intervenes into the accumulation process (an intervention that may be acute or not, and may apply to other activities such as mining and construction).[22]

Third, and closely related to the last point, the accumulation process as a pursuit of surplus profitability is not confined to competitive access to largest size of capital, important though this may be, but is governed by many factors including natural fertility, the law (terms of leases), the potential to lower wages or increase working hours, access to credit and markets, and not least, shifts in the vertical (dis)integration of production. Thus, the frequently observed dependence of farmers upon credit potentially represents the transformation of rent into the form of interest; their receipt of state support signifies rent in the form of a subsidy[23] (especially to large-scale producers who benefit disproportionately from policies designed to secure survival of the small-scale); and dependence upon the

45

'technological treadmill' of seed, mechanical and other chemical inputs, represents a system of landed property in which rent potentially accrues to industrial capital despite its separation from ownership of the land.

While mindful of not imposing theoretical propositions upon actual outcomes, generalized across a range of products, an ideal-type illustration of our arguments might prove helpful. In our perspective, accumulation of capital upon the land tends to yield surplus profitability. In other sectors, this is eroded by an inflow of capital, reducing prices and restoring a normal rate of profit. This is potentially obstructed in agriculture, as in other heavily land-intensive production, by the intervention of landed property and the appropriation of the surplus profitability as rent, the form it assumes when accruing to the landlord (although this relationship is both complemented and obscured by the continuing, if shifting, differentials in surplus that are attached to lands and their environment).

Should prices be allowed to fall more or less in line with productivity increase, implying a limited intervention by landed property, then there are liable to be dramatic consequences for those producers not matching the standards in rising productivity, with their suffering loss of income and even bankruptcy, as production is concentrated on fewer, larger, capital-intensive farms. Should such norms be contingent upon access to finance, then this may prove a proxy for landed property, appropriating rent in the form of interest, sustaining prices even if possibly moderating the pace of concentration of farming – although it appears as if debt-dependency is the source of (individual) bankruptcy. On the other hand, if prices are sustained through a cartel on behalf of producers – whether through a state or other form of marketing scheme – then surplus profitability arising from productivity increase is retained by producers. But, depending upon the price – or state-sponsored income support if this is used as an alternative – there is the prospect both of surplus production as price–cost margins widen and/or increasing direct and indirect costs of moderating the pace of change across the farming sector.

Clearly, this theoretical account provides some immediate insights into the functioning and ultimate crises of many of the agricultural support schemes that have been characteristic of post-war food production.[24] Traditional explanations tend to focus upon the static inefficiencies of price or income fixing, setting them against, or within the context of, the political and economic interests of the various strata within farming. Where our analysis differs is in emphasizing the dynamic and systemic aspects of the problem arising out of productivity increase, surplus appropriation and the form in which landed property intervenes at one or other point along the food system. One implication is that policy interventions in the form of getting the prices or subsidies right are misconceived since they fail to recognize unevenness of the accumulation process. Further, the intended balance between efficiency and equity (i.e. support to poorer farmers) is open to being usurped by the differentiated impact created by links with the food system. Put simply, support to the agricultural sector is liable to be poorly targeted in terms of its overall level and in its direct (which farmers?) and indirect (will it accrue to farmers?) effects.

In short, the organic dependence of agriculture upon landed production entails its integration into particular forms of landed property. These give rise to the appropriation of rents which influence the scale and intensity of accumulation. And the conditions of access to landed property cannot be reduced to ownership and tenancy, but need to be situated in relationship to the functioning of the food system as a whole, since vertical integration (with traders, financiers, suppliers or the state) may embody a *displaced* form of the rent relation.[25] Consequently, the accumulation of capital along the food system gives rise to particular tendencies in relation to the forms of landed property that it confronts. What distinguishes food in this context from other commodities, even those with a higher dependence upon land (such as minerals), is the persistence of the organic component along the food system. This process is examined in the following section by a careful assessment of the work of Goodman and Redclift, for they focus on the food system in terms of vertical integration and disintegration, the dependence of food upon nature, and the tendencies of capitalist accumulation.

AGRICULTURE AND INDUSTRY

For Goodman and Redclift,[26] leading theorists within food systems literature, there is a structural separation between agriculture and industry as a result of the former's dependence upon nature over which capitalist production can only exercise limited control (Goodman *et al.* 1987, p. 1):[27] 'The key to understanding the uniqueness of agriculture . . . lies neither in its social structure nor in its factor endowment. Rather agriculture confronts capitalism with a *natural production process.*'

Now, as is apparent from the earlier discussion, the idea that agriculture is distinct from industry because it offers particularly strong resistance to capitalist development is far from novel. Mann and Dickinson (1978, p. 467) observe that 'Capitalist development appears to stop, as it were, at the farm gate'. They reasonably reject two common explanations, one depending upon a subjective preference for rural survival achieved through self-exploitation, the other relying upon agriculture naturally providing less fertile ground for large-scale capitalist methods. Instead, they offer an explanation based upon the inevitable separation between production and labour time, suggesting that this gives rise to lower and more uncertain profitability. Consequently, 'the capitalisation of agriculture progresses most rapidly in those spheres where production time can be successfully reduced' (to duration of labour time, p. 473). But, as Perelman (1979) notes, such sectoral disadvantages in the ability to generate surplus value within agriculture will be compensated for by appropriate transformations of rewards through relatively higher prices of production.[28]

Goodman and Redclift, develop a more sophisticated view of the way in which nature proves an impediment to the penetration of capitalist development into agriculture – although it is important to recognize that they reject the notion that there exists 'a pre-ordained or "natural" division of labour between "agriculture" and "industry"', (Goodman *et al.* (1987, p. 153). Nevertheless, they do take as key the biological or natural production processes. Initially, their work concerned the insensitivity of much Marxist analysis to the tenacity of peasantry, family farms and petty commodity production in surviving against the pressures towards proletarianization. They observe that agriculture is less susceptible to capitalist development for a variety of reasons, such as patterns of specialization, diffusion of standard technology, its spatial dispersion, and the natural rhythms associated with climate, growth and crop rotation (Goodman and Redclift 1981, p. 11). This analysis was more concerned with the transformation in rural class structure than with agrarian political economy and the associated confrontation between agriculture and industry as distinct spheres of production.[29] Goodman and Redclift's later work is more centrally concerned with transformations in the production process in which the division between agriculture and industry is crucial, and in which the survival of the family farm within advanced capitalism is to be explained.

These issues are addressed by developing two concepts – appropriationism and substitutionism.[30] The first refers to the encroachment by capitalist products and processes within agriculture itself. Examples are provided by mechanization, fertilizers, etc. Industrial capital is increasingly the source of inputs and these are increasingly tied to more factory-like methods of production. On the other hand, substitutionism is the displacement of products and the production process from agriculture into industry, most marked in food processing and the substitution of inorganic for organic products (Goodman *et al.* 1987, p. 6):[31] 'Although there are areas of overlap . . . appropriationist capitals are associated primarily with the rural production process and the primary transformation of crops, whereas substitutionist capitals are involved in later, downstream, stages of food manufacture.'

Quite clearly, appropriationism, A, and substitutionism, S, are concerned with vertical (dis)integration along the food system – what gets done where and with what, and the extent to which the where and what depend upon agriculture. A and S are associated with vertical disintegration at the expense of agriculture since it is peculiarly dependent upon natural processes. Before considering this proposition, it is first worth examining the issues associated with vertical integration in a context divorced from agriculture. In Marx's theory, for example, a distinction is to be drawn between the social division of labour and the division of labour in manufacture.[32] The former refers to the sectoral boundaries between products that are bridged by the market process. The latter is what occurs within the workplace in the absence of market intervention. Examples are provided, respectively, by car manufacture based on bought-in components as opposed to a single factory in which raw materials go in at one end and vehicles emerge at the other.

Marx argues that capitalist production is subject to two opposing tendencies: it might lead to the fragmentation into separate trades of what were formerly combined production processes, or it might lead to the unification of previously separate trades into a single trade to the exclusion of the market. It is not possible to determine abstractly whether such vertical integration or disintegration will predominate. While this will depend upon the nature of the production processes, it will not be determined by them since it will also depend upon historically contingent competitive pressures across industries. Suffice it to observe, however, that a shifting social division of labour and division of labour in manufacture is a systematic consequence of capitalist production. It is certainly not specific to the relations between agriculture and industry.

Now, for Goodman and Redclift, the preceding analysis would appear to be the appropriate starting point for specifying the distinct pattern and evolution of the division of labour within agriculture and between it and industry. Essentially, they place heavy emphasis upon the role of natural or biological processes and argue that these constrain the development of the capitalist division of labour. For them, the organic content of agricultural production can only be picked off by industrial capital in a piecemeal fashion, by discrete elements (Goodman *et al.* 1987, p. 2–3).

In debate, Goodman and Redclift (1994) deny that the obstructed processes of A and S imply an increasing encroachment of industrial capital into agriculture, although this was our earlier interpretation of the idea that the biological content of agriculture is displaced. Rather, they posit a fundamental dialectic between nature and capital which does not coincide with the division between agriculture and industry. There is no reason, then, why A and S (or shifting division of labour) should thereby be in a direction favouring industry over agriculture. Indeed, for particular crops, especially those most perishable, industrial processing may be compelled to be sited within the farm gate, and there is not even necessarily a shift of the inorganic over the organic. For the enhanced availability of the inorganic (as artificial fertilizers or food additives, for example) may promote as well as undermine the use of organic, agriculturally produced inputs. A further reason that the processes of A and S are indeterminate in fashioning the division between agriculture and industry is the scope of the rent relation. How far it is vertically displaced along the food system, and who are the beneficiaries of the surplus profits generated by intensive exploitation of the land, are intimately related to the division between agriculture and industry, irrespective of the shifting organic content of food production. Which specific activities take place within agriculture as opposed to industry will reflect competitive relations over who appropriates surplus profits as accumulation proceeds and how they do it. Either 'side' might seek to appropriate production processes from, or impose them upon, the other to gain competitive advantage (just as firms or industries engage in vertical integration or disintegration in pursuit of profitability).

Although they may deny it, that Goodman and Redclift's analysis is based upon a skewed pattern of vertical (dis)integration along the food system (between agriculture and industry) is confirmed by their treatment of biotechnology. For they see this as potentially enabling a radical restructuring of the food system because of the greater scope that it provides for both A and S. Indeed, biotechnology is perceived as substantially weakening, if not totally undermining, the impediments to the capitalist penetration of agriculture, for it raises the possibility of two extreme trajectories and conflicts between them. This is because of the greater potential to manipulate the biological production process on the farm through genetic engineering, and the greater potential to use products in the form of broken-down raw material ingredients in food processing.[33]

One extreme is factory production of food on a non-organic basis (perfect S) but the other is to enhance the farm production of basic foodstuffs, perfecting A. Thus, biotechnology appears to raise the prospect of a fundamental conflict or a process of convergence between A and S. In short, it apparently frees the food system from earlier constraints on vertical (dis)integration. And, in doing so, a methodological reversal is in prospect in the causal priority between tendencies and structures, with the first now predominating over the latter, even if subject to contingency. Where previously tendencies were primarily perceived as trends operating within and against a given structure, they have now become the abstract determinants of structure itself. Occasionally, prior to biotechnology, the contradictions between A and S are observed, as in the ability of each to strengthen the role of the agriculture through the other. Industrial inputs, S, enhance the industrialization of the farming process; industrialized farming, A, cheapens and encourages the production of the organic inputs that can be combined with the inorganic in processing.

But the presumed priority of structure over tendencies (interpreted as trends) in the pre-biotechnology period leads to a definite emphasis on A and S as promoting vertical (dis)integration only partially, discontinuously and through fragmentation of discrete products and processes, a consequence of capital's inability to confront each food system as an integrated whole (Goodman *et al.* 1987, p. 6). Despite, or even because of, reference to the technological treadmill, the integral nature of the system of provision is placed in the background relative to sharply drawn divisions between agriculture and industry, with attention to conflicts between A and S confined to minor or major skirmishes. In particular, Goodman and Redclift's stance leads them in part to set aside the organic nature of food once it departs the farm and enters the stranglehold of industrial capital. Subject to perishability, cropped agricultural commodities become like other raw materials (Goodman *et al.* 1987, p. 2). This reflects too heavy a dependence upon biological determinism (in constructing a theory of A and S) and, yet, a neglect of its importance through the food system as a whole.[34] For the organic properties of food remain crucial from farm to mouth since they affect processing, packaging, distribution and marketing, and are prominent once more in consumption.[35]

In short, Goodman and Redclift treat tendencies as trends, these giving rise to definite outcomes within structural constraints.[36] This precludes the recognition of tendencies as underlying forces in contradiction with one another (especially where one is a countertendency to another) whose resolution gives rise to more complex outcomes. The alternative analysis offered here is distinguished from Goodman and Redclift's in the following ways. First, the distinction between agriculture and industry is tempered, not defined, by organic properties and is based upon the historically contingent forms taken by the system of landed property in its relationship to the food system. Second, the latter is subject to underlying tendencies that reproduce and transform the structural divisions along the food system. Third, such differences in methodology leave open empirical developments that are arbitrarily prejudiced against by the particular form taken by Goodman and Redclift's understanding of A and S – that these are liable to operate at the 'expense' of agriculture as the primary domicile of the organic, at least until the arrival of biotechnology.

Despite these reservations over Goodman and Redclift's contribution, it has allowed them to characterize much of the new work in the political economy of food with considerable critical acumen. Goodman and Watts (1994) point to a dual distortion in the literature. The first is in the categories used to examine post-war *industrial* development. Following the collapse of the post-war boom, which had been explained by the success of Fordism, a binary opposition has been constructed between Fordism and post-Fordism, the latter based on small-scale, flexible special-ization in production to serve niche and fragmented markets. With this, there are a number of problems, not least the construction of two ideal types of industrial organization into which a much more complex and varied range of empirical possibilities do not adequately fit. Thus, the approach has been faced with accommodating an increasingly varied range of empirical and historical developments within a constraining analytical framework. In other words, even when stretched analytically, chrono-logically and empirically, the categories of Fordism and post-Fordism are incapable of adequately encompassing either the post-war boom or subse-quent developments. This is all the more serious to the extent that the theoretical and empirical evidence for a category of post-Fordism is itself highly questionable.[37]

The second distortion, significant even if the Fordism/post-Fordism divide were both analytically and empirically acceptable, arises out of what Goodman and Watts term 'mimesis', the notion of a parallelism between industrial and agricultural developments – that agriculture is examined as if it too had to take the Fordist/post-Fordist itinerary. The two distortions have been combined to yield further putative analytical consequences. The US Fordist model of agricultural production has been exported to other countries some of which have been able to attain and surpass US levels of productivity. While the US model has gained hegemony, particularly at the expense of tropical products, for example, this hegemony has been undermined by the success of emulating countries. Increasing competition at a global level has led farmers to seek supportive national policies but, increasingly, the food system is being driven by multinational corporations which seek to displace the regulation of food systems to international state institutions. This is seen as reflecting a more general erosion of the national form of the state although, paradoxically, the nation-state is itself required to implement the very policies of trade liberalization that are pursued by international organizations such as GATT, the International Monetary Fund (IMF) and the World Bank.

This is all well represented in McMichael's (1994a, pp. 280–1) overview of the core of post-war food systems. He divides the post-war period into two eras, the national and post-national and, following Friedmann's identification of food complexes, he ingeniously juxtaposes the periodization with the separate food complexes. The wheat complex is attached to national regulation (in which the United States prospered through exporting surpluses), the durable food complex (sugar and oils) is attached to agro-industrialization (and transition between the two eras?), and the livestock complex to globalization. Where, however, does this leave other foods that do not belong to these complexes and where does it leave the latter themselves at the times outside their designated correspondence with the national and the global eras?

A further consequential feature of the Fordism/post-Fordism understanding of the agro-food systems is that it provides, especially if the categories are themselves used flexibly, an extremely broad and eclectic framework within which to accommodate empirical developments. Production trends can be examined to see whether they are Fordist, post-Fordist or both,[38] and policy can be scrutinized to see whether it supports national or global interests. There are also other theoretical fragments available which can be freely drawn upon, ranging from French regulation theory to ideological and cultural explanations for the shifting and refining of food tastes, whether for exotic fruits or environmentally friendly organic products. As Goodman and Watts (1994, p. 37) conclude:

The effort to build a theory of agrarian restructuring on foundation stones provided by the macro and meso-level categories of regulation theory, Fordism/post-Fordism and flexible specialization is at best problematic, and often deeply flawed. This edifice, we suggest, is weakened, and ultimately condemned, by two fundamental fault-lines: the weaknesses of the theoretical and empirical categories of Fordism/post-Fordism which a panoply of critiques have exposed, and the associated failure within the agrarian restructuring literature to interrogate the applicability of these concepts to the political economy of agriculture and rural space. In our view, this failure derives from the unexamined assumption that the sectoral dynamics of socioeconomic, cultural and spatial changes in agro-food systems are the mirror-image of industrial restructuring.

Essentially, the food systems literature has analytically faltered, even if prospering in weight of contributions, by seeking to impose models of industrial development upon agriculture. While this attempt has been undermined by evident empirical and theoretical weaknesses when Fordism was the only model available, the addition of the post-Fordist model and other variants has only served to conceal rather than to resolve the underlying problems of mimesis.

The strength in the critique of Goodman and Watts lies in its insistence upon the specificity of agriculture (and food systems which they dub 'filières' in line with the notion of Fordist food complexes that belong to the approach that they criticize), and the heterogeneity of these food systems both historically and presently. The source of this critical strength, however, appears to derive from what we have previously identified as an analytical weakness. For the notion of food systems as embodying the discontinuous and uneven processes of appropriationism and substitutionism of nature by capital (industrialization of agriculture) serves the purpose of exposing the limitations of mimesis even if itself open to question.

Consequently, in a separate paper,[39] Goodman and Wilkinson (1994) even replicate much of the analysis of Fordism and post-Fordism that has been previously criticized by Goodman and Watts. They maintain a distinctive position, however, by privileging the historically earlier, natural forms taken by food products. Unlike other industrial products which can discard their organic origins, 'In the food industry, by contrast, quality is judged essentially in terms of the closeness of industrial products to the original pre-industrial product' (p. 14). This is used to explain why food systems are distinct and heterogeneous – because of what is termed 'the polyvalent responses to changing economic, technological, social, and cultural tendencies' (p. 16). However, the notion that foods are especially inhibited by their traditional origins, even if these could be recognized and defined, is entirely spurious and arbitrary, reflecting an exaggeration and analytical elevation of green consumerism.[40] It is only necessary to point out how many foods have little or no connection to natural or historical roots (as in many snack foods) and how little interested consumers might be in these in any case. In short, Goodman and Wilkinson correctly identify the heterogeneity of food systems and the significance of their organic content but incorrectly explain the one by the other. Equally, it is erroneous to generalize over the role of the (nation-)state and the international nature of food systems whether such generalizations are derived from industrial mimesis or otherwise.

CONCLUDING REMARKS

In previous sections, attention has been directed at the agricultural/industrial divide in order to bring out certain analytical imperatives. Necessarily, the discussion has been both abstract (potentially testing the patience of those sensitive to the historically variable forms that these divisions take) and negligent of the other elements along the food systems – in processing, retailing, etc. Yet, such interrogation of theoretical foundations is essential and currently apposite. For the explosion of academic interest in food has built upon what was already a wealth of theoretical and empirical research, much of it generated to explain the conditions both before and after the collapse of commodity markets in the mid-1970s. Inevitably, simpler, general models concerning the various components of the food system, and how they are integrated, have been challenged by the emergence and observation of empirical anomalies and countertrends. Most notable has been the apparent decline, in theory and practice, of the globalization of food systems,[41] as attention has focused upon national differences and the rapid growth of new crops such as fresh, 'exotic' fruit and vegetables to serve affluent markets that have exhausted the scope for the mundane and homogeneous, mass products whether cereals, other staples or the traditional meats. This seems to provide the analytical recipe for a diet of eclecticism – a different food system for each product, country and circumstance.

At the level of consumption, researchers have been inspired by such a wide range of factors, ranging from the components of personal identity to those of the foods themselves, that the possibility of a coherent, integral account to create a field of food studies is in doubt even before it has had a chance to emerge. As it were, the consumption of each item of food is subject to determination like any other item of consumption, with no greater connection with other items of food.[42]

We hope that it has been shown here that a more satisfactory way forward is to distinguish between items of consumption according to their SOPs. Analyses need to pay careful attention to the relationship between the (re)structuring of the systems of provision, the role of (and distinctions between) tendencies and trends, and the scope for historical contingency. Further, the distinguishing aspect of SOPs is their exceptional dependence upon the combination of organic and inorganic factors through their systems of provision. Nor is there any reason for there to be a single food system or for different food systems to be replicas of one another. This is a consequence of the different ways in which underlying economic tendencies lead to the (re)structuring of food systems as well as of the different outcomes within those structures. This is further pursued analytically in the next chapter.

NOTES

1 This chapter draws upon Fine (1994a). See also the debate between Fine (1994b) and Goodman and Redclift (1994), Friedmann (1994a), Murdoch (1994) and Watts (1994).

2 See Avery (1991) and Hirschoff and Kotler (1989), for example, and discussion in previous chapter.

3 For some representative literature, see Arce and Marsden (1993), Bonnano et al. (1994), Busch et al. (1989), Buttel and Goodman (1989), Freidland (1984), Friedland et al. (1992), Friedmann (1982, 1987, 1990, 1993 and 1994b), Friedmann and McMichael (1989), Goodman and Redclift (1989), Kenney et al. (1989), Kim and Curry (1993), Lowe et al. (1990), Lyson and Geisler (1992), McMichael (1992, 1993a and b, 1994a and b), McMichael and Myhre (1991), Marsden et al. (1986), Marsden et al. (1990), Marsden et al. (1992), Marsden and Little (1990), Munton (1992), Raynolds et al. (1993), Reinhardt and Barlett (1989), Symes (1992). Marsden and Munton (1991), however, refer to the limited research in this area! Le Heron (1993) is a recent example of the culmination of the path taken by food systems – bringing together a host of analytical themes. More recently, as will be discussed, the literature has veered analytically towards post-Fordist themes without always abandoning Fordist models. Goodman and Watts (1994) provide a critical assessment.

4 In a representative review of, and contribution to, the food system literature, Munton (1992, p. 32) inadvertently stumbles upon the issue of the ambiguity of the relationship between structures and tendencies by referring to 'broad structural tendencies'! See also Le Heron (1993, p. 39), for example, who sees agricultural overproduction as a structural tendency.

5 Thus, Winson (1992) sees food's uniqueness as the intimate commodity because it is ingested. He also sees its production as distinct or atypical because of the limited penetration of capitalism and capitalist methods.

6 The term 'organic ratio' is used extremely loosely to incorporate a range of factors, of which the composition of the product is but the most obvious one. It also depends upon the degree of natural processes, for example, whether bodily or otherwise. Medicines, an example taken up later, may be inorganic but be taken bodily. Garnishes on dishes may be organic but might not be intended for actual consumption.

7 Even if 'nutrients' are not always healthy.

8 The word 'organic' was attractive for three reasons: because of the distinction between organic and inorganic chemistry, its affinity with the nature of content in general, and the analogy with Marx's notion of organic composition of capital with its division between dead and living labour. A defence of appealing to the

organic content of food in the abstract can be made by analogy to the discussion of the labour process in general that is made in Chapter 7 of Volume I of *Capital* by Marx (one of the most difficult against whom to bring the charge of biological determinism).

9 Thus, interest in the food system can be motivated by considerations of ecology and sustainability, as in Dahlberg (1993). The same applies to problems of hunger and malnutrition; see Hirschoff and Kotler (1989), for example.

10 This is complemented by much ingenuity concerning price and income effects, women going out to work, and the consumption of fewer, higher quality children, as the real wage rises along with productivity.

11 This example illustrates the importance of taking account of the role of public provision in mediating the relationship between commercial and domestic provision. There are also historically contingent, but systematic, opportunities for enhanced domestic production arising out of the development of the capitalist economy; taking in and providing for boarders is a significant factor during rapid periods of urbanization/proletarianization. See Fine (1992).

12 This is argued for at length in Fine (1992).

13 An implication of the argument here is that the two 'paths' to capitalist agriculture, loosely labelled large-scale and parcelization, should be seen as tendencies whose complex interaction gives rise to historically contingent outcomes – rather than as two alternative empirical outcomes or trends as is the almost universal interpretation. This cannot be taken up here but, for an exception, see the account of Iran in Afarinkia (1989). On the other hand, see Morris (1979) for an account of the development of capitalist agriculture in South Africa for which the process is transparently the working out of the two paths in conjunction with one another (as is inevitably the case for the co-existence of small- and large-scale production).

14 See also Bernstein (1982).

15 Hence the frequently observed phenomenon in which wage-labour by one household member provides a source of income which, paradoxically, supports the continuing viability of non-capitalist household production.

16 Note, however, that Gibbon and Neocosmos (1985) correctly argue that simple commodity production is a logical outcome within, and therefore not alien to, capitalism and even that capital opens up and closes opportunities for small-scale enterprises according to its rhythm of social productivity. But, from this stance, the most developed recognition of the opportunities for smaller-scale agriculture created by capitalism is to be found in the work of Friedmann, especially Friedmann (1978) and (1987). See also Reinhardt and Barlett (1989).

17 For an overview of the orthodox literature on why the family farm has persisted in the United States (and related issues), implicitly revealing its affinity with non-orthodox explanations within a framework of supply and demand, see Gardner (1992).

18 They continue, 'Agrarian structure includes not only the set of technical, natural resource and production factors involved in a particular farming system but also the legal and political institutions supporting the system, the rural–urban relationships, marketing structures, and the wider economic parameters.' In other words – everything! This is indicative, together with the ambiguity over the relative priority of structures and tendencies, of a failure to address the associated problems of causal structure.

19 This duality in defining agriculture involves the rejection of notions of the production unit in terms of peasant mode of production, household production, simple commodity production, or family farm, etc., since these are hetero-geneous according to their own internal organization and their external

interactions. This observation has a close correspondence with the previously developed argument that structures (such as the division between agriculture and industry) have to be theoretically located relative to the tendencies with which they are reproduced and/or transformed.

20 This is a desperate summary of what is an extremely complex and long argument to be found laid out in detail in Fine (1979). See also the debate between Ball (1980) and Fine (1980).

21 This result, usually seen as quantitatively arbitrary in Marx's theory of rent, is demonstrated algebraically in Fine (1979). See also Fine (1989).

22 For a detailed case study, see Fine (1990). See also Fine (1994c).

23 As all commentators observe, the role of the state in mediating the relationship between capital and agriculture is pervasive although, not surprisingly, it tends to be situated within the analytical framework adopted (does it or does it not support reproduction or disintegration?). It should, however, be seen as an arena of conflict, expressing a form within which the resolution of contradictory tendencies are expressed.

24 Others have readily identified the processes discussed here, Bowler (1992b, p. 14), Tarrant (1992, pp. 245–8) and Watkins (1991, p. 46) for example. But the relationship to the theory of agricultural rent has tended to be overlooked.

25 See, for example, Bhaduri (1977), but also Fine (1994c) where it is shown how common it is in the early stages of mining for the rent relation to be displaced through forward integration (looking at British coal, South African diamonds and US oil).

26 Here, the most important of their works is Goodman *et al.* (1987). Their earlier work, Goodman and Redclift (1981), was more concerned with the class implications of the relationship between agriculture and industry in the context of transition. Later work, especially Goodman and Redclift (1991b), has focused on environmental implications of food systems. See also Goodman and Redclift (1989) and Goodman (1992).

27 See also pp. 153–4: 'The central problem . . . is the industrial erosion of the rural, with the key variable being nature and the degree to which biological production systems are reproduced in the industrial context.'

28 Mann and Dickinson's position leads them to the perverse conclusion that agriculture is distinct because it produces both perishable and durable goods. Note, however, the dependence upon these organic/inorganic characteristics of food products.

29 For the distinction between agrarian political economy and rural restructuring, see Marsden *et al.* (1990). Interest in food systems was in part stimulated by the recognition, in studying rural restructuring, that it depended upon factors lying outside the immediate rural environment.

30 See especially Goodman *et al.* (1987), but also Goodman and Redclift (1991a) and Buttel and Goodman (1989). There are precedents for these notions in the broader context of externalization (out of the rural environment). See especially Long *et al.* (1986, p. 51), and also Pelto and Pelto (1985) for analysis in terms of 'delocalization'.

31 At times there is confusion over the difference between appropriationism and substitutionism, since the distinction might be taken to refer, respectively, to the mechanization of *processes* (away from, rather than within, the farm) as opposed to the displacement of (farm) *products* in industry. This seems to be the only interpretation of Busch (1990, p. 4) if appropriationism and substitutionism are to be distinct: 'Appropriation refers to restructuring that removes from the farm certain processes that once took place there . . . while substitution refers to wholly industrial processes that replace those on the farm.' At

times, Goodman and Redclift's intention, however (as understood by Bowler 1992b, p. 26), seems to be that appropriationism refers to what takes place on the farm, substitutionism off the farm, each involving products and processes – although they appeal to analytical rather than to spatially determined distinctions (Goodman *et al.* 1987, p. 2). Kim and Curry (1993, p. 61) refer to 'the substitution of industrial inputs and processes for natural ones and the appropriation of "traditional" or "pre-capitalist" modes of activity by industrial capital'. Friedmann (1994b, p. 264) sees capital as appropriating production from farmers and substituting for their products while, in the same volume, McMichael (1994a, p. 281) considers, 'appropriationist tendencies, such as the application of new energy and capital inputs in industrial agriculture', and 'substitutionist tendencies, such as the replacement of tropical crops by scientifically extracted components of temperate crops'. See the debate with Goodman and Redclift (1994) for some clarification.

32 See especially Marx's *Capital*, Volume I, Chapters XIV and XV.

33 See Goodman *et al.* (1987, pp. 140–4) and also Goodman and Wilkinson (1990) and Busch *et al.* (1989). See also Ruivenkamp (1987). For a discussion of biotechnology in the context of political economy, see especially Kloppenburg (1988) for whom

> The social history of plant breeding in the twentieth century is essentially a chronicle of the efforts of private industry to circumvent these twin obstacles (of farmers' seed supply from own crop or from the state). These efforts have involved the elaboration of two distinct but intersecting solutions to the constraints facing seed companies . . . the use of science to make the seed more amenable to commodification . . . A second solution is the extension of property rights . . . to continuously redefine the social division of labour in plant improvement, with public breeders becoming increasingly limited to activities complementary to rather than competitive with those of private capital (p. xiii).

Note that the latter process has led to increasing collaboration, and concern over the relations, between universities and private industry. See Busch and Lacy (1986). Note also that, for Kloppenburg, biotechnology has come to dominate agricultural production: 'The seed, as embodied information, becomes the nexus of control over the determination and shape of the entire crop production process' (p. 201). In one extreme form, this parallels Goodman and Redclift's view that biotechnology breaks down the (biological) barriers between agriculture and industry.

34 See Murdoch (1994) who argues that Goodman and Redclift veer between biological and social determinism according to whether they are addressing the agriculture/industry divide or the rest of the food system, respectively.

35 Some mention is made of the significance of the organic nature of food in its consumption in Goodman and Redclift (1991a).

36 This is especially transparent in the earlier work on the transition to capitalist agriculture, where the Marxist classics are interpreted (as by many before and since) as offering empirical predictions about paths rather than these representing simultaneous and contradictory tendencies. See Goodman and Redclift (1981) but also Buttel and Goodman (1989). The most controversial area, however, in which the distinction between trend and tendency is crucial within Marxist theory concerns the law of the tendency of the rate of profit to fall. See Fine and Harris (1979) and, for a more informal treatment, Fine (1989). In their first volume on *Marxism and the Agrarian Question*, Hussain and Tribe (1980a)

discuss the issue of tendency and countertendency as underlying determinants and even acknowledge the analytical analogy with the law of the tendency of the rate of profit to fall and its countertendencies. Yet they wrongly see both as involving a *hierarchy* of determinants with dominance between them rather than as their being of equal causal status. Nor do they take up the issue in the context of Lenin's theory of two paths in their second volume (1980b). But, for a dramatic illustration of the contradictory interaction of underlying forces in the context of food and personality, consider the medical condition of bulimia (alternating gorging and vomiting) which can scarcely be understood as a diet made up of the net effect of equal and opposite trends! See discussion in second volume.

37 Apart from citations in Goodman and Watts, see especially Curry (1993).

38 As in the study of the US chicken industry in Kim and Curry (1993) and the US dairy industry in Lyson and Geisler (1992).

39 This paper appears to be available only in mimeo and is referred to as such in Goodman and Watts (1994). The mimeo itself is indicated as forthcoming in P. McMichael (ed.) *Food Systems and Agrarian Change in the Late Twentieth Century*. This, in turn, seems to have been the working title for McMichael (1994), a conference volume, in which the Goodman and Wilkinson (1994) piece does not appear, possibly marking an intellectual breach as reflected in the Goodman and Watts (1994) critique.

40 Interestingly, Goodman and Wilkinson appeal to this natural basis through reference to the omnivore's paradox which is itself indefensible as a continuing explanatory factor in modern food systems; see the second volume for further discussion.

41 See Moran (1992) and Marsden (1992) for a broader discussion.

42 This has been termed the 'diet paradox' – that diet is both perceived to be integral and, yet, is shown not to be – and is the subject of a chapter in the second volume.

4

DIFFERENTIATING FOOD SYSTEMS

INTRODUCTION

The previous chapter has been primarily concerned with building upon existing food systems literature and upon the work of those who, at least implicitly, appear to accept the SOP approach even if with food as a special case. The argument emphasized the role of tendencies in (re)structuring the food system and the distinctiveness of its dependence upon the organic content of food provision. The present chapter is first concerned with defending the food system approach against criticisms that the SOP approach is an invalid method for examining consumption in general. This, second, leads to the more constructive task of defining what constitutes the boundaries of one SOP as opposed to another. The results of the theoretical arguments presented will be deployed in later chapters when addressing the meat, dairy and sugar systems.

The SOP approach to (food) consumption provides a counterweight to recent studies of consumption. These have emerged within, and have often been inspired by, the intellectual milieu provided by post-modernist perspectives. Post-modernism has proved a fertile terrain on which to displace previous materialist preoccupations, rooted in production and determinism, and also to embrace the discourses of individual and social (de)construction. It is not that questions of power and work and of economic and social forces have evaporated altogether, but they seem to belong to some other world that provides the raw materials for the meaning rather than for the substance of our lives. For this reason, consumption has increasingly been situated within what we term 'horizontal analyses' – those that range, in principle, across consumption as a whole and which address the immediacy of consumption itself. It is perhaps best exemplified by the analytical demise of the passivity that is assumed to be attached to Fordist mass consumption, and the birth of the nuanced tastes and niche markets generated and served by post-Fordist flexible specialization.

Such developments are directly challenged in this book, both theoretically and through the specific application of an alternative approach to various food systems. The first section defends the theory of consumption based on *SOPs*. This analytical stance is fuelled by the idea that consumption is made up of vertically organized chains of activities and meanings, from production through to consumption, that are integral and, as structured systems, are differentiated from one another. Abstract argument is employed to show how the approach is able, indeed is required, to address pervasive (horizontal) aspects of consumption which appear to contradict a vertically organized analysis based on systems of provision. Specifically, two issues are broached: consumption (as in tourism, for example) or its determinants or features (the role of gender, for example) that straddles apparently otherwise unconnected commodity systems, and consumption that bridges commodity and non-commodity consumption and activity (as in DIY or the more general use of leisure time). It is argued that the SOP approach is essential for understanding such consumption, even if the latter cannot be reduced to discrete acts of consumption from a simple aggregation of isolated and distinct SOPs.

This defence, against what is otherwise a reassertion of the primacy (or equality of status) of a horizontal approach, has a more constructive aspect. For it is the basis on which the issue of how SOPs are vertically delineated can be broached. It is concluded that this should not be done through connections forged at the level of consumption (a sort of bread-and-butter and tea-and-jam approach) but, rather, through the integral connections established across earlier stages within accordingly defined SOPs. The theoretical conclusion drawn is that the formation of distinct systems of provision is contingent upon the way in which underlying economic and social processes (re)structure the food systems (and consumption more generally). These can be identified empirically but they cannot be predetermined theoretically.

These propositions are illustrated through their application to food systems. For the meat system, for example, in Chapter 10, it is first argued that the literature, in what are generally horizontal approaches to meat consumption, has suffered from treating meat as a homogeneous category whereas we would emphasize the heterogeneity of meat – not only in terms of a variety of products but in the direct determinants of its choice for consumption. This is confirmed by reference to the literature but also through detailed quantitative analysis of the socioeconomic patterns of meat consumption across households, through use of data drawn from the UK NFS. Paradoxically, we argue that this neglected heterogeneity in meat consumption is itself the consequence of the evolution of a *single* meat system, whose scope encompasses the variety of meat products, with the patterns of integral connection across the SOP having shifted vertically, and currently concentrated in activities such as feed grain provision, food manufacturing and retailing.

TOWARDS A METHODOLOGY FOR STUDYING CONSUMPTION

Elsewhere,[1] we have argued at length that the determinants of consumption need to be assessed in terms of SOPs. Each consumption good is attached to a vertically organized chain of activity, from the various stages of production through to distribution and retailing and to the processes and cultures of consumption themselves. Our emphasis is placed upon how such SOPs, whether, in popular parlance, the housing, food or energy systems, for example, form structurally integral entities which are distinct from one another.

This insistence upon vertically structured analysis in this form entails a sequence of corollaries. First, horizontal theories of consumption are rejected as they are not structured by, nor satisfactorily understood by, appeal to society-wide influences such as status, identity, symbol, utility, gender, power, etc. The significance of each of these for consumption differs according to the SOP to which it is attached and its place within it. Second, such horizontal analysis has been intellectually paramount because it is the natural consequence of the way in which such causal factors arise out of the social science disciplines to which they are attached. Each discipline tends to promote the application of its own theories and concepts to consumption in a general form, even if illustrated by case studies, without regard to other (horizontal) elements that make up SOPs and which fall within the domain of other disciplines. Third, this has led to a failure to develop a satisfactorily integrated and interdisciplinary theory of consumption applicable across consumption goods, not least because this is a futile goal. Rather, an interdisciplinary approach to consumption must necessarily address specific consumption goods, in correspondence to their SOPs, in order to meet the distinct ways in which causal factors are integrated in practice. Fourth, as already implied, it follows that there can be no general theory of the specific horizontal factors as applied to consumption whether for advertising, gender, class or whatever. For the particular role of each of these will be differentiated according to the specific SOP with which it is associated.

IN FAVOUR OF SYSTEMS OF PROVISION

The SOP approach to consumption has previously been outlined in Chapter 1 and developed in detail in Fine and Leopold (1993). Its most contentious aspect concerns its insistence upon vertically organized analysis at the expense of consideration of society-wide horizontal factors. This has undoubtedly been at the root of many, apparently powerful, criticisms. While these have frequently been made verbally from a variety of perspectives, we will focus on the contributions of Glennie and Thrift[2] since they are made in the context of a debate with our approach and have the virtue of laying out the issues with considerable clarity and supporting references.[3]

The first issue concerns the legitimacy of splicing through horizontal factors to form vertically integrated SOPs. Surely, Glennie and Thrift (1992) suggest, this 'will tend to neglect interactions between such systems (which are not just additive)' (p. 603), 'because these interactions themselves produce new effects which cannot be traced back to any single system' (p. 604). Later, Glennie and Thrift accept that 'certain systems of provision are vertical' but that most experience 'leakiness' which has both material and symbolic dimensions . . . that are not reducible to these systems of provision'. Such leakiness is then specified in terms of corporate conglomeration diversifying across commodities, advertising that specifically forges links across commodities, and the capacity of consumers to create such connections themselves (with or without the help of advertisers) in, for example, the construction of their sexuality or through counterculture or, presumably, other genres. The very notion of lifestyle, of the consumer, necessarily straddles a range of commodities which cannot reasonably be presumed to belong to a single SOP.

To a large extent, these criticisms appear to arise from an occasional, possibly understandable, misinterpretation. For they depend, correctly, upon rejecting a view of the economy (or even society) as a set of rigidly structured, non-overlapping, vertically organized SOPs. Our approach does not deny that horizontal factors apply across different SOPs and mutually condition one another; that racism, gender, advertising, etc., are, indeed, fluid across the world of commodities and are, in part, constructed out of their associated multiplicity of roles. Not surprisingly, this is why horizontal theories of consumption are so appealing. They seem to have immediate application to the nature and significance of different moments of consumption.

Unfortunately, however, such horizontal features are boundless in their potential variety, with some of them assuming prominence and others being neglected whether in the academic world of intellectual endeavour, in the practical world of making a possible sale (with the sexism of male orientation, if not targeting, in both, for example), or in the minds and acts of consumers. Essentially, to point to the horizontal factors, and their interactions, even if designating some areas as more important than others, is merely to recognize that consumption involves a relationship with (socially constructed) use values and, once the focus is upon consumption of commodities, that they have their origins in exchange value (and the market system, however this might be conceived).[4] The problem is how to go beyond these generalities and create a causal theory rather than a descriptive account of consumption, even if the latter is organized within some analytical framework prioritizing one or more horizontal factors.

Paradoxically, our approach is implicitly accepted by the very terms in which Glennie and Thrift seek to reject it. For, in appealing to *interactions* and *leakages between* SOPs, they have acknowledged the latter's existence as (logically) prior. Leakages and interactions between entities presume their prior presence. It follows that there seems to be a choice between two structuralisms – one vertically and the other horizontally organized, with more complex outcomes and nuances understood in terms of interactions and leakages. The attempt to retain both structuralisms simultaneously necessarily leads to the collapse of each in to what might be termed a *lattice* approach which is liable to degenerate in terms of causal content – consumption becomes a mish-mash of horizontal and vertical factors.

A number of very important questions flow from this discussion. One concerns the nature and status of the structuralism involved in constructing a theory of consumption based on vertically differentiated SOPs. This is particularly so in the context of the current intellectual preoccupation with consumption (and post-modernism) which has been associated not only with horizontal analysis but also with a committed rejection of the rigid and mechanical determinism imputed to any form of structuralism. However, while our approach can be employed and (falsely) interpreted as a variety of structuralism, this is not its necessary nor its intended content. In this respect, it is based upon a relatively weak proposition – that *consumption* must be understood in terms of differentiated SOPs. This methodological stance cannot be projected uncritically onto other areas of study. It is specific to consumption, although we have argued that the impact upon horizontal factors, and the relationships between them, are differentiated from one commodity to the next. Thus, our approach does not imply that it is 'possible to understand a modern economy by simply accumulating studies of individual industries' (1992, p. 604), but that this is the way to understand modern consumption – if industry is understood as a proxy for SOP. By the same token, we do not accept that it is appropriate to take an 'overall view of consumers' grasp and action' as an object of study other than 'as a series of accounts of production-consumption chains' *and* their interactions (even if Glennie and Thrift seem to think that the necessity for this particular overall view is self-evident).[5] Consumption and its deter-minants are so complex and heterogeneous that they cannot be taken together collectively as an appropriate object of study.[6] For, otherwise, consumption is a category that is simply chaotic, like the category of the consumer, since each potentially includes everything and everybody, respectively.[7]

In short, Glennie and Thrift appear in part to reject our approach because of a more general rejection of the validity of what they perceive to be a pure commitment to vertical analysis (which, for our purposes, is specific to consumption). How appropriate is vertical, as opposed to horizontal, analysis for other areas is an open question.[8] However, the earlier proposition that horizontal and vertical structuralisms are incompatible without analytical degeneration should not, once again, be conflated with a stronger proposition of the general incompatibility of vertical and horizontal analysis. Thus, for those committed to patriarchy theory, and the idea that gender divisions are the fundamental causal determinants, differentiated SOPs for consumption can be seen as the form in which male/female conflicts are, in part, resolved and reproduced. This is not our own view,[9] but a commitment to abstract categories such as gender or race is not incompatible with our approach to consumption. Otherwise, the very division of the capitalist economy into spheres of production and exchange for differentiated commodities would itself preclude the analytical legitimacy of abstract categories such as capital, labour and class.

None the less, the relationship between vertical and horizontal analysis has to be treated with care for we would propose an alternative approach to what has been the analytically prominent position within the food studies literature. This takes the vertically integrated food systems and their associated structures as the analytical and causal starting point. Thus, there is a division between agriculture and industry (the latter usually standing as a more general proxy for commerce external to agriculture) and between industry and the household (usually serving as a more general symbol for the non-commercial world). These are acted upon by economic and social relations and their associated forces – the imperatives of profitability, state and global power, etc. These factors are confined within the given structures of specific food systems, although these are often seen as going through a Fordist history, and press against them until their limits are reached. The food system is then restructured, most dramatically through crisis.[10]

Our own approach is to turn this analytical framework upside-down (or is it inside-out?). We take the vertically differentiated SOPs as the starting point for examining consumption but perceive them as the products of other underlying factors. Specifically, the class relations of production, the imperatives of capitalist profitability, the exercise of state power, etc. are the means through which SOPs are both (re)produced and transformed. By way of clarification, consider the *processes* of vertical integration and disintegration in the sense of the connections between up- and downstream activity and how they create the *structures* associated with the division of labour within firms or between them through the market. Competition creates pressures for vertical (dis)integration irrespective of the existing corporate structure across sectors of the economy but acts upon and transforms that structure.

Thus, while accepting an appropriate role for horizontal factors, we do not consider this to be incompatible with our approach to consumption even if we do not allow such factors direct leverage across a range of consumption goods. However, having identified consumption by means of

65

SOPs, what about that consumption that lies outside their scope? This is raised implicitly in a footnote by Glennie and Thrift (1992, p. 605):

> Finally, and more speculatively, it is increasingly necessary to consider 'what is a commodity?' In contemporary Western societies, resources are increasingly devoted to 'quasi-products' which are to do with how products are *used*, not with the production–consumption of the items themselves. . . . Examples of the 'quasi-products' might include participation in historical re-enactment societies or in events such as road races or mountain bike competitions.

This issue, and it is frequently raised in a number of different ways, requires further theoretical clarification and precision, both in general and specifically in relationship to consumption. The analysis here, and much of it elsewhere, has so far been concerned exclusively with consumption arising out of commodity production.[11] This is not, of course, to suggest that consumption is limited to the objects produced commercially nor that non-commercial activity is excluded. Rather the world of consumption in contemporary capitalism is primarily defined by the world of commodities; and the latter's world must be addressed before other forms of consumption can be properly understood.

This reflects a more general methodological point: capital, as the main source of commodity production, does define ideal or, more exactly, pure forms of economic and social categories. Take the example of work: productive labour, however understood (as that labour creating surplus value in Marx's terms), is an ideal category which does not exhaust all forms of work. Such pure, simple categories, once developed analytically, simultaneously define their own opposites or negation – by what is excluded from their scope. To point to categories defined in this negative way, or through their mirror image, is clearly not to deny their existence, nor their significance. Thus, wage labour has its counterpart in non-wage labour (and productive labour has its counterpart in unproductive labour, whether this, in not providing a surplus, is wage labour or not).[12] Indeed, it surely makes sense not only first to define and understand consumption based on commodity production (or, by analogy, first address wage labour), but also to see this as a precondition for understanding its opposite, non-commodity consumption (or non-wage labour). This follows, not as an abstract principle, but because of the logical and empirical weight of the prior categories.[13] Non-commodity consumption is defined by its not being commodity production, at least in a capitalist society, even if this does not totally determine its nature.

A further point is that the division between such core categories and their negations does not prevent an analysis of their interaction. Thus, the division between consumption derived directly from SOPs, and consumption less commercially determined can be articulated with one another (indeed, must be so as final consumption lies outside the immediate commercial sphere) to yield different and more complex outcomes. Again, by the same analogy, the presence of a category of self-employment can hardly be allowed to undermine an analysis based on a pure form of wage labourer and capitalist in confrontation with one another. These can be used, once previously developed, to define the self-employed as simultaneously capitalist and worker and, hence, neither.[14]

It follows that the core concepts are not negated by the more complex forms that they can assume. In particular, the notion of SOPs is not invalidated by complex forms of consumption, going beyond purchase of commodities alone and in which a commercial and non-commercial content are articulated. Further, given the emphasis that we would place on the importance of public, potentially non-commercial, forms of provision within and across SOPs – as in transport, housing and energy, etc. – it is imperative that SOPs be defined to incorporate the 'quasi-products' to which Glennie and Thrift refer but without accepting the analytical nihilism that this seems to involve for them. For them also, possibly unintended, there is an implication that such articulations between SOPs are only or primarily to be found at the consumption end of the activities involved – as if only consumers and consumption are caught between the world of commerce and its negation. SOPs are integrated at levels other than consumption alone, as is especially but not exclusively signified by the pervasiveness of the state in contemporary capitalism, and its interventions along most, if not all, the components constituting SOPs.

The above observations about what might be thought of as the domain of a central category, such as the commodity or capital, are general. They concern the corresponding domain defined by the negation of the central category and the relationship between the domains. In the case of consumption, this dialectic is particularly rich for a variety of general and specific reasons. First, the act of consumption is withdrawal of the commodity from the immediate economic domain[15] and, consequently, it is potentially incorporated into a range of uses and activities that are, in principle, infinitely variable across individual consumers and acts of consumption. It is precisely such variability at the level of consumption itself that encourages the adoption of horizontal theories of consumption in seeking regularities across the separate moments of consumption. And there certainly are general limits to, and uniformities within, consumption as in the need to guarantee social reproduction, create and maintain social distinctions, etc.

Further, the breadth of use and using associated with consumption is enriched, doubled or more, by the genres of counterculture. The commodity can even be sold as its own negation. This can be in two ways. One is the paradoxical rejection of the significance of exchange value in the world of the commodity even as it is obtained through purchase – as in conspicuous consumption where freedom from the constraints of money is demonstrated by its profligate application to what are, otherwise, 'worthless' objects; or, alternatively, commodities are promoted because they are traditional or authentic, created according to an old recipe, home-made, etc., in order to suggest that they are free of the taint of commerce even though, perversely, they once again are obtained through purchase. There is, then, a potential tension between being tied to the world of commodity production, through the money that it demands as an entry fee or the commercially determined nature of the products that are its inhabitants, and the desire to exhibit freedom from those ties, whether as an index of status, authenticity, morality or political outlook.

The second form in which the (genre of the) commodity is (symbolically) negated is through the rejection of its (pre-established) usefulness. This has been most apparent, for example, in punk culture, even if the negation can itself be commercially reincorporated. Dependence upon negation of the use value of the commodity through consumption has its most recent expression in the brand of 'Death' cigarettes which employs as a selling point what has normally been fiercely resisted, or concealed – that of ill-health as one of the 'use values' of smoking.[16]

In addition, the ideological rejection of the world of commodities in consumption may not be merely gestural since it need not always depend upon commodity consumption itself. There can indeed be home-cooking or DIY. None the less, these remain highly dependent upon commercial provision of ingredients, equipment, etc. The same is true of counter-consumption that is not substitutable for by commercial products – family heirlooms and antiques which are not (commercially) reproducible (except as 'reproductions'). However, once again, it would be mistaken to see these as items of consumption that are exclusively constructed and defined by their difference from the world of commodities (because they are defined by their commercial non-reproducibility whether through age, origin or obsolescence of product or process, or uniqueness through attachment to personal experience).

The purpose of the preceding discussion is to suggest that the presence of consumption which does not belong directly to SOPs does not in itself negate the latter as the basis on which to construct a theory of consumption. Interestingly, one of the studies to which Glennie and Thrift appeal is Charsley's (1992) book on the wedding cake. Quite apart from the fact that this can be interpreted as a narrowly defined SOP, within that of increasingly commercialized baking more generally, Charsley himself refers to the notion of 'marooning' as a causal factor. This term is borrowed from Cannadine's (1983) study of the growing idiosyncrasy of the existence, practices and customs associated with the British royalty. Certain consumption practices become marooned with the development of contemporary capitalism. This term is particularly apt because it suggests how the isolation is defined by the normality from which it is separated. Further, even if it is common practice for orthodox economics to present capitalism as the generalization of a Robinson Crusoe society (in the absence of Man Friday), it is entirely inappropriate to take consumption marooned from SOPs either as an analytical starting point or as undermining one based on SOPs. Desert islands in the world of consumption, and they may be many with complex interactions among themselves, can only be discovered and analytically colonized through a long passage originating in the world of commodities, from which they take their point of departure.

DEFINING THE BOUNDARIES OF SYSTEMS OF PROVISION

So far, the whole discussion has been defensive in tone and purpose in meeting criticisms of the SOPs approach. But it has provided sound foundations for a more positive and constructive response to what has been perceived as a destructive criticism but which is, in reality, a means of pushing forward and clarifying the approach. The issue is what determines the boundaries of one SOP as opposed to another. Although we have always stressed that SOPs are attached to commodities or groups of commodities, the criticism can arise in two forms of *reductio ad absurdum*. Either there are finer and finer differences between each sort of commodity (by brand, for example, or the different sorts of milk) so that the number of SOPs grows with the level of detail considered; or the leakages and interactions across commodity systems are so pervasive that they can only be accommodated by constituting the world of commodities as a single SOP encompassing them all.

Both of these criticisms tend to have the same root in common: they recognize the fragmentation between (the use values of) commodities with the first *reductio* proliferating and the second collapsing the SOPs, respectively. This is nothing more than the reproduction in another form of the case for a horizontal theory of consumption. It does, however, often degenerate into a focus upon consumption at its most immediate moment and/or reduced to the level of the individual consumer. Thus, Jackson (1993), to whom Glennie and Thrift refer, seeks to

> treat consumption as a process by which artefacts are not simply bought and 'consumed', but given meaning through their active incorporation in people's lives . . . how many different 'readings' is it capable of in the hands of different audiences or for the same listener in different times and places? Rather than limiting the discussion to the point of purchase, I will focus on many acts of appropriation and transformation that may be performed on any single artefact (pp. 208–9).

69

Here, apart from only tracing consumption back as far as purchase, the individual consumer is endowed with enormous potential. Thus, in noting different responses to the photograph of a nude, pregnant Demi Moore in *Vanity Fair* and the deliberately shocking Benetton advertisements, he finds it necessary to consider 'what the viewer [by implication, more generally, the consumer] brings to the photograph [the commodity]'.

In this way, consumers are allowed to enter, as they can in reality, their own individual world of consumption. But this is, of course, a fetishism – a real appearance which conceals and sets aside the mechanisms by which that reality has been created socially. Significantly, Jackson's case is argued in general terms but made by reference to specific SOPs, although these remain unexamined, namely that of women's magazines and mass-marketed fashion clothing. These have to be unravelled in order to understand who advertises or presents images, how and why (even if consumer interpretation retains a socially determined degree of lassitude).

Glennie and Thrift also close their contribution by citing the work of Cowan (1992), picking out short quotes to support the case for extensive horizontal content in consumption relations (something that we do not deny); the existence of 'consumption junctions', 'the infinitely expandable universe' of social groups, and the idea that 'any human being can enter the consumption junction under a number of different guises, depending on what is being consumed'. This leads them to conclude (1992, p. 606):[17] 'Empirical studies using such a concept would need to focus *both* on production-consumption chains *and* on networks among consumers; how these appear to consumers; and which elements are more important, more determinant, of choices in particular circumstances.'

This is to resort to what has previously been termed a lattice approach to consumption and aptly illustrates the more or less casual empiricism to be employed; apart from SOPs, theory is to be displaced by judicious selection of the appropriate choices actually made by equally contingent consumer groupings. Significantly, Cowan's own study does not rely upon this method, and her ideas have been torn out of context. For she is specifically, if unconsciously, concerned with the SOPs associated with stoves, and the networks to which she refers are those that are *vertically* organized – how the stoves are designed, manufactured, assembled, distributed and served by changing fuels and uses.[18]

However much these comments successfully criticize alternatives from the perspective of SOPs, they still leave unaddressed directly how this approach itself demarcates between such systems. Part of the answer is to recognize that there is no general abstract resolution of this problem. For, as has been previously argued, SOPs are structurally differentiated vertically on the basis of underlying relations that reproduce and transform these structures. Consequently, the latter are socially and historically contingent according to the linkages that are established between commodity groups.

This is readily illustrated by reference to industrial structure for which the competitive processes of horizontal and vertical (dis)integration in pursuit of profitability give rise to a definite corporate structure and divisions between sectors of the economy (however well these do or do not correspond to broad or fine systems of industrial classification for statistical purposes). Not surprisingly, economics takes for granted the division of the economy into well-defined and distinct sectors.[19]

Industrial, and the corresponding, but not identical, corporate structure is one form in which SOPs are *institutionalized*. This must, of course, be extended to include the other economic activities sustaining provision: distribution, technology, design, retailing, etc. And the structuring of SOPs can also be found reflected in other institutions, notably in the state and its formation of policy, together with quangos and other organizations within civil society. But economic and social structure cannot be legitimately reduced to institutionalization for there is also the structure of (global and power) relations to consider such as those of trade, investment and finance.

In short, as has been insisted upon from the outset in our work in defining SOPs, they depend upon the formation of an integral structure between the economic and social activities that provide for consumption (without, thereby, isolating such structures from others). These structures must themselves be rooted in the systematic forces and relations that create them even if the outcome is socially and historically contingent. Consequently, as a crucial corollary, it is necessary to reject the definition of SOPs by appeal to integral linkages forged exclusively or primarily at the level of consumption itself. For, as already seen, this potentially leads to the two extremes either of a proliferation of SOPs according to the more or less casual connections that are made by consumers across a range of products, activities or motives, or of a collapse into a single all-encompassing SOP. Essentially, these two opposites correspond to the identification of structure through categoricism – on the one hand, any empirically identifiable relationship is perceived to constitute a structure; on the other, everything is connected to everything else so that there is only one structure, the totality.

Thus, it is hardly surprising that the same stance that insists upon horizontal analyses, whether in synthesis with SOPs or not and especially if pitched at the level of consumption itself, should also have difficulty in identifying the structural differentiation between SOPs. For a commodity can be appropriated in isolation from all others as well as in conjunction, potentially with any other or all others – as, for example, in the formation and expression of identity or in the contribution to well-being (or utility, as economists would have it).[20] None the less, SOPs can be drawn across separate commodities that have integral relations at the level of con-sumption but only if these are also reproduced at other points in the chains between production and consumption, possibly brought about following links first established at the level of consumption. Thus, tourism does bring

71

together a variety of activities which (and the term is highly appropriate) when packaged gives rise to the SOP of a particular form of holiday.[21]

By the same token, and possibly more significant from an analytical point of view in moving away from consumption understood at an immediate level, a SOP may integrate activities or products even though they are far removed from one another in consumption. This is especially so where bi- or joint products are involved – as in petrochemicals, for example, although it must again be emphasized that such linkages, whether in production or elsewhere, do not in themselves necessarily lead to integral social and economic structures.

These have to be identified and justified both in content and type. There is no single model for the formation of SOPs for they are not only differentiated from one another, they are also different according to the way in which they are structured and the structures reproduced. More concretely, and by way of illustration, this has led us in our own work to distinguish between the men's and women's clothing systems, to suggest a dairy system that combines both liquid and processed products, a sugar system that incorporates cane and beet but which excludes artificial sweeteners even though all serve the consumer market for 'sweetness', and a meat system that incorporates a variety of products even though these are of mixed significance at the level of consumption.[22] These results are not the consequence of either the technical properties associated with the groups of commodities concerned, nor do they follow from the contingent connections established at the level of consumption alone. Rather, the SOPs are formed, and identified, through the processes that create and reproduce them.

NOTES

1 See Fine and Leopold (1993), Fine (1993a and b, and 1995b), Heasman (1993 and 1994) and Heasman and Schmitt (1994).

2 In the debate between Glennie and Thrift (1992 and 1993), with Fine (1993a).

3 Because debate with Glennie and Thrift is not our primary purpose, we do not provide a comprehensive response. Some points not covered fully and in detail include the extent to which the supporting case studies that they cite are open to our own, alternative interpretation of inadequately addressing consumption because of their undue confinement to horizontal analysis, as in Beck (1991), Giddens (1991 and 1992), Hooks (1992), Urry (1993b), and many of the studies in Brewer and Porter (1993); some even reflect our approach directly, if implicitly, as in Belk (1992b), Charsley (1992), Cook (1994), Sahlins (1988), Cronon (1990), Scranton (1983 and 1989), Urry (1993a), Wernick (1991) and Willis (1991). However, most of the latter studies waver between specific commodities and horizontal analysis. Giddens' (1991) discussion of anorexia, for example, fails to recognize that it is a condition that depends on both the compulsion to diet *and* to eat, with the absence in his consideration of the commercial pressures underlying the latter (even though commodification in general as an influence on self-identity is discussed elsewhere by him). For a critique of the sociology of anorexia from this perspective, see Fine (1995a). We

also suggest, contra Glennie and Thrift, that most studies are both horizontal and confined within disciplines without this being a necessary logical connection, and we dispute empirically that our insistence upon a vertically integrated approach 'is pushing at an open door in the study of consumption' (Glennie and Thrift 1993, p. 603).

4 Thus, in neoclassical economics, the generality and variety of use values are expressed through the goal of the consumer in maximizing utility; the presence of the market figures through the constraints imposed by prices and incomes.

5 It is a fetish of neoclassical economics that the consumer (represented by the theorist) takes such an overall view. We doubt whether this is so in practice, let alone that this is the way to embark upon a study of consumption even if it were true!

6 This is suggested in a novel way in Fine (1995d) where consumption is interpreted as adults at play.

7 Of course, this does not prevent these undifferentiated categories from being commonly used – but usually with an implicit, ill-defined, unrepresentative (e.g. males) and/or shifting meaning.

8 Current work on segmented labour markets, however, suggests that the radical approach – which sees them as the simultaneous outcome of interaction between horizontal forces, such as trade unionism, patriarchy, industrial structure, etc. – is misplaced. Rather, different labour markets are structured independently of one another even if subject to many of the same factors. See Fine (1987).

9 See Fine (1992) for the view that patriarchy is appropriate as a simple investigative category but not as an underlying causal category.

10 See Chapter 3.

11 The emphasis on private and/or commercially originating consumption erroneously neglects the direct and indirect impact of public provision and, where it does not, often treats the latter as if it were an alternative to private provision rather than generating consumption on an entirely separate logic.

12 In strictly Marxist terms, the distinction between productive and unproductive labour only applies to wage labour. But in non-Marxist terms, and in some versions of Marxist theory, productive labour is defined as being directly attached to any economic activity that attracts a profit.

13 The logical and causal hierarchies of concepts in this context do not have to be identical. Thus, for example, Marx begins *Capital* with the simplest form of economic activity associated with the commodity, but this is not, as such, the most important causal category which is given by capital itself.

14 Hence, the existence of self-employment undermines neither the category of wage worker nor of capitalist – even if the strictest neoclassical orthodoxy in economics does eliminate such distinctions by treating all individuals as owning a balance of material and human capital.

15 Although neoclassical economics recognizes this by partitioning time into mutually exclusive work and leisure, it treats the latter as if it is governed by the wage foregone for the former.

16 It is interesting to recall a spoof advertisement for a beer in which the slogan used was that it gets you drunk. Although the distinctions between presenting the commodity as something that it is not, as the opposite of what it is, and concealing what it is are conceptually distinct, they are often mixed together in practice. Of course, this leaves open what is the actual content of the commodity for the consumer, whatever its material and cultural determinants.

17 Note how the consumption networks are counterposed with SOPs (*production–consumption* chains) as if the latter could not be networked at points other than consumption.

18 Indeed, this is a particularly important illustrative case study of the role of technology and design in the restructuring of a SOP.
19 For a critique of the tendency of industrial economics to focus upon horizontal at the expense of vertical integration, see Fine (1994d). A particularly striking force behind the restructuring of the divisions between sectors has been the impact of new technology where, for information technology for example, telecommunications and data processing have been integrated.
20 Neoclassical economics formally recognizes the possibility of distinct SOPs, forged at the level of consumption, through restrictions on individual utility functions as in the property of additive separability. It can also do so at other points, such as production, through assuming the absence of joint production possibilities, as is usual, so that separate SOPs are defined by the sector of the economy to which they are attached.
21 Thus, we would argue that tourism as a whole does not constitute a SOP but it does range across a number of SOPs such as travel, entertainment, catering, etc., and, at times, does integrate these to form particular tourist systems. The initial part of Urry's (1993a) account can be interpreted in this way before it becomes unduly preoccupied with how the tourist receives tourism.
22 See later chapters and Fine and Leopold (1993), Heasman (1993 and 1994) and Heasman and Schmitt (1994). The EU and the US sugar systems are also distinct with greater reliance in the latter on high-fructose corn syrup (effectively excluded in the EC, within which the UK sugar system is unique in its dependence upon imported cane).

Part III

THEORETICAL AND EMPIRICAL APPLICATIONS

5

THE UK SUGAR SYSTEM

INTRODUCTION

The two previous chapters have laid out in considerable detail the theoretical themes underpinning a SOPs approach for the study of particular food systems. This approach has been discussed in the context of the body of food systems literatures, a tradition now termed as the 'new political economy of agriculture', and acknowledges the insights gained and intellectual debt to this wide-ranging research. The purpose of this chapter is to expose these theoretical writings to empirical test using an investigation of the persistence of sugar in the British food supply from 1900 to the present day.

The first part of the chapter discusses how the study of UK sugar supply using the SOP approach suggests anomalies within, and differences from, the methodologies promulgated by the food systems literature, in particular in the work of Goodman *et al.* and Friedmann. Our distinctive approach comes to light through the detailed study of the historical supply and consumption of sugar in the United Kingdom, treated as a sequence of separate SOPs. The stance taken here, therefore, will be complex since it attempts to pick a path between various contributions to the food systems literature which, by themselves, are often too general and piecemeal. They need to rely on considerable and arbitrary time-lags in attempting to explain the persistence of sugar in the UK diet.

In this sense, the analysis of sugar presented here makes its contribution to the political economy of agriculture by way of contrast, first in the method employed and then, by reference to a detailed empirical account of sugar supply. In doing so, it draws upon appropriate elements from the political economy of agriculture literature, modifies them and places them in a slightly different framework, namely analysing sugar in terms of SOPs. Reviewing sugar in terms of SOPs serves to distinguish sugar from other foodstuffs. Emphasis is placed on 'persistence' because sugar's survival and prosperity as the principal ingredient for 'sweetness' in the diet cannot simply be taken for granted.[1] From this perspective it is then argued that the United Kingdom has experienced three historically distinct, but consecutive, sugar SOPs: pre-1914; from 1914 to 1973; and from 1973 to the present day.

The three SOPs for sugar neatly illustrate the dialectic, suggested by McMichael and Buttel (1990), between agriculture as a politically mediated, historically defined sector and the industrializing role of modern food complexes. Included in the latter process in recent years has been the shaping of consumption patterns that, in part, has sought to turn foods into desirable and undesirable nutrients, with sugar falling into the negative category. This consumer trend is perhaps not surprising in the light of what Goodman *et al.* (1987) describe as product 'fractioning'. For the food industry has sought to extend its range and the concept of products even to the point of redefining conventional notions of what constitutes food. Yet still important to the modern food system is the taste of sweetness largely created by the widespread availability and use of sugar. However, in order to maintain its position as the United Kingdom's principal sweetening ingredient (more than 80% of Britain's market for sweetness is supplied from sucrose), the past decade has seen the sugar industry forced to defend itself against its product being labelled as less than desirable.

While these are important factors, changes in food supply involving sugar make more sense in the context of the persistence of sugar in the United Kingdom as the result of the functioning of three unique SOPs. These have extended the use and secured the supply of sugar in the United Kingdom, enabling supplies entering the UK food system to be sustained at around 2.3 million tonnes, an increase of around 1 million tonnes from the turn of the century (a per capita supply of around 38 kg in 1900 compared to 40 kg today!). In this light, the use of sugar in some manufacturing systems can be regarded, for example in the case of confectionery, as the consolidation of a long-term historical trend, rather than sugar suddenly turning up in these products. In addition, the industry's restructuring, as in the stock-market takeover bids of the 1980s, is regarded as the outcome of political processes and conflict resolutions in the operation of the market for the supply of sugar from cane or beet.

At a theoretical level (as elaborated in previous chapters), these events are captured by looking at the tendential strains within each sugar system as it produces and reproduces particular structures dependent on historically specific circumstances. Together with these underlying forces there is the organic role of sugar in food systems. For example, in the first two SOPs for sugar, it was sold for its energy value (calories); in today's sugar system this organic property of sugar is played down to the extent that it is advertised for how little energy a teaspoon provides. More specifically, each sugar SOP is distinguished by a number of features that can be broadly organized around five key, but interlocking, points: (1) the sources of sugar; (2) geographical location and political significance of elements in the sugar chain of activities; (3) the industrial processing of sugar and its use in manufacture; (4) food use and patterns of consumption; and (5) forms of state intervention. Each of these points is briefly elaborated below.

1 *Sources of sugar* The most important distinguishing feature of each SOP has been its principal source of sucrose and the capitals relating to them. Over the past ninety years the dominant agricultural source of supply for UK sugar has swung from temperate European sugar beet, to tropical sugar cane (for final processing in a temperate climate), and back to European beet. The relative dominance and the associated competing interests between the refiners and their respective sources of raw sugar for the final refined product have significantly shaped each SOP in terms of market structure, competing capitals and profitability, the role of the state and government policy and the change from one SOP to the next.

2 *Geographical location and political significance* While cane refining in the United Kingdom has become more industrially concentrated, especially in the second SOP, the geographical location of the agricultural crop and production of raw cane sugar has varied considerably. Cane production for use in the UK market has been derived from dozens of countries – from Cuba, through South Africa to the Pacific. The reasons for this and a discussion of the sugar industries in these countries is beyond the scope of this chapter. However, the political importance of colonial and imperial links between Britain and sugar producers is self-evident from the brief discussion provided later. Similarly, sugar beet production has its own, but very different, geographical history and development. Beet production in the United Kingdom, for example, is confined to specific areas of the country and closely related to the political influence and interests of the farmers in those parts. Within the European Community (EC) Sugar Regime, the geographical and political importance of sugar beet changed so dramatically as to contribute to a fundamental restructuring of sugar's second SOP.

3 *Industrial processing and use in manufacturing* The structures and patterns of capital accumulation within each SOP have had distinct influences on the nature and type of industrial refining. For example, refining operations for beet and cane have expanded in particular ways, been restrained or contracted or even gone out of business depending on their relative strengths and weaknesses within each SOP. This process has seen the evolution of cane refining and beet-processing monopolies which between them now supply more than 90% of UK sugar.

Sugar's use as an ingredient in manufacturing[2] is covered in detail in later sections, especially the importance of its organic properties throughout the food systems in which it is used. Three points, however, can be emphasized. First, there is the role that sugar has played in creating sweetness in food systems and disseminating this taste widely throughout food supply. Second, although its industrial use has today become concentrated in just three food categories – soft drinks, chocolate confectionery and sugar confectionery (50% of industrial sales) – it has been used and continues to be used in a diverse range of other food products and drinks. Decline of sugar use in one area, for example sugar in tea, often sees the sugar reincorporated in other areas, such as sugar in soft drinks and so on. Third, in many foods, its use has changed very little over time. The role of sugar as an industrial input was further strengthened during the second SOP when a number of trends within food systems – for example, Friedmann and McMichael's (1989) 'durable foods complex' – became important, but manifested themselves in ways specific to sugar's SOP.

4 *Food use and patterns of consumption* Mintz (1985) details how sugar became a staple food of the new industrial proletariat and argues that, by 1900, sugar in the form of processed sucrose had become an essential ingredient in the British industrial diet. However, this conceals who was eating sugar and in what forms. The most striking change has been in class consciousness in relation to sugar. Before the Second World War, consumption of packet sugar was greatest among high-income groups in comparison to lower-income groups, although average per capita consumption across all groups was fairly uniform. In the 1980s this position had reversed and the NFS, (MAFF 1991) shows the sharpest decline and smallest consumption of packet sugar for high-income groups. The most marked difference, in terms of sugar consumption, in the 1930s was the large amounts of sugar consumed in processed foods by richer people in contrast to those in low-income groups. During the 1980s, the removal of sugar from some products became part of the 'healthy eating' trend, and 'sugar-free' versions of products have often been targeted and priced for higher income consumers.

The long-term trend over the century has been for the use of sugar to move away from the packet to being used as an industrial input so that today more than 70% of sugar is sold direct to the food industry as an ingredient. Thus, it should be noted that the expansion of the sugar supply has gone hand in hand with its use in food manufacture and many food industries have grown and expanded using sugar as a principal ingredient. Part of this trend has been the swap of food 'manufacture' in the home to the industrial site and, in many instances, sugar has successfully moved its food use from the home to the commercially processed and packaged product.

5 *Forms of state intervention* In each SOP for sugar, the role of the state has been a significant factor in structuring markets and legitimizing the operations of cane and beet refining. In this sense, the state is not to be regarded as neutral, but as an institution that defends and manages

interests, particularly those of dominant classes. In other words, the role of the state in sugar's SOPs has not always been as an autonomous body but as working in partnership with competing class interests set around the supply of sugar.

The state can also serve to legitimize class interests. In the example of food, the state, through issuing public information, public relations activities and ministerial pronouncements as well as its policy-making apparatus, helps to justify and maintain the United Kingdom's existing food system by influencing and constraining the content of the 'food agenda'. The 'crises' of the mid- to late 1980s in the UK food system, for example, over food safety, represent a breakdown in this public information role. Pressure groups and different food industry interests aim to influence the legitimizing role of government and their own particular concerns.

To accommodate and elaborate on these points this chapter is divided into two parts. The first part focuses on theoretical and methodological issues in relation to what is understood as a food system and develops two major theoretical themes within a SOPs framework. Key features of food systems are identified and, where the literature uses sugar and sweeteners as examples, these are considered in more detail. It is suggested that too crude an application of food systems theory, for example Goodman *et al.* (1987), to the sugar systems leaves it unable to identify and explain the historical rhythms that it has experienced.

The second part of the chapter examines sugar's three SOPs. It is important to point out at this stage that the sugar system is not regarded as one system that has gone through three periods, but that there are three separate sugar systems historically delineated. Each structural period is examined in detail, and each can only be logically understood as distinct historical regimes based on the resolution of conflict between sugar-cane and sugar-beet interests.

More specifically, the first UK sugar system considered originated before the First World War. By the turn of the century, the United Kingdom was one of the world's most important sugar markets. Operating within a free-trade policy, supplies of sugar were predominantly from the European sugar industry based on sugar beet. The UK sugar industry, which refined raw cane sugar supplied from tropical countries, experienced increasing concentration and economies of scale in the face of European competition. At this time, no sugar was grown in British soil.

The second sugar system prevailed from the First World War to Britain's entry into the European Economic Community (EEC) in 1973. During this period, sugar cane interests were dominant, but the underlying, contra-dictory tendencies, described by Friedmann and McMichael (1989) as the 'culmination of colonialism' and the accedence of 'nation-state agriculture', are a key feature. A number of major changes took place in the development and characteristics of the system in the context of an expanding market for refined sugar. These include the increasing concentration of the sugar-refining industry with one company, Tate & Lyle, becoming dominant. Government became more interventionist, not simply to iron out market imperfections, but to regulate and influence the rate of expansion. Powerful and new market interests came into play, namely the creation of a home-grown supply of sugar from sugar beet and the associated industrial and agricultural interests involved. The end use of sugar in the food system was also undergoing change. There were shifts in consumption patterns with the increasing use of sugar as an industrial input in processed foods. By the end of this period the profitability and expansion of sugar used in the food system was firmly organized around a tripartite structure of the state, cane-refining interests (represented by Tate & Lyle) and beet interests (organized around the British Sugar Corporation).

The third UK sugar system runs from 1973 to the present day. It is evident that many of the key features identified by the food systems literature are in place: the growing concentration of the relevant food industries, including cane and beet monopolies. The final use of sugar develops more and more as an industrial input and is closely allied to just three main food sectors, namely sugar confectionery, soft drinks and chocolate confectionery. The state continues to play an important role in the structuring of the SOP, in particular with the EC Sugar Regime. This institutionalizes massive overproduction of sugar in Europe while demand falls. In Britain, a steadily falling market for sugar and the controls imposed by the EC Sugar Regime witness major structural changes in the refining industry. In addition, substitutes develop for sweeteners, both industrially and organically based. At the consumption end, sugar becomes the focus of new non-agricultural interests as healthy eating policies redefine the nation's diet and break food down into its constituent parts. In this new healthy diet, many nutrition experts suggest that carbohydrate from sugar should play only a minor role. The introduction of new sweeteners, especially aspartame which was given government approval for use in foodstuffs in 1983, further heightens class distinctions in the consumption of sweet foods giving impetus to the widespread introduction and development of sweet (but sugar-free) 'lite' foods and drinks (Heasman 1990a).

SUGAR AS A SOP

Sugar's organic properties

Goodman and Redclift (1991a, p. 90) argue that as a result of the biologically determined rigidity in demand and supply structures, the food industry has developed around specific agricultural products to form specialized food chains linking farm and table. Subsequently, from this foundation, the food industry could turn its attention to effecting qualitative changes in the organic composition of food and the general perception of what constitutes food (Goodman *et al.* 1987, p. 60). This last point, about the organic composition of food, is especially important in understanding sugar's persistence in the British food system.

Goodman and colleagues develop their 'natural' theme in the context of discussing the actual structures and patterns of accumulation within agrifood systems. The implications of this were discussed earlier, in particular the point that while the organic distinguishes food from other systems, it does not follow that it is determined by its organic characteristics at the expense of other social and economic factors. Goodman and colleagues stress the significance of biological factors at the extreme ends of the SOP in agriculture and the household. However, through the empirical investigation of sugar's SOP, it emerges that the organic is critical throughout the whole system and determines organic features both upstream and downstream, a factor to which they devote less attention.

The widespread use of sugar in industrial and household food supply is relatively new. Until the mid-1800s sugar was still a luxury item for the better-off, though becoming more widely used throughout society. Only by the beginning of the twentieth century had it become an 'essential' item in the British working-class diet (Mintz 1985). Sugar, therefore, needs to be regarded as a truly modern food and as a product of industrial society. In accomplishing this, the consumer has become divorced from the connection with sugar as derived from an agricultural crop and, therefore, the organic appears to evaporate from this end of the food chain, much like cotton or wool in clothes. However, the organic properties of sugar do remain important since it is still, literally, consumed.

Sugar in Britain is sourced from two very different crops – sugar cane (containing between 10–20% sucrose) and sugar beet (containing around 16% sucrose). Sugar cane is a tropical crop while beet is a temperate crop; sugar beet is grown as a rotation crop while cane is usually grown as a monoculture, plantation crop. Each has its own types of cultivation practices, inputs, handling, transport, processing, distribution, use of land and so on. However, the agricultural crop as such is irrelevant to most people's understanding of sugar since it is the refined product – sucrose, virtually 100% pure – that people regard as sugar. Cane refining (in refineries) and beet processing (in factories) acts as an equalizing process to produce white sugar. It is virtually impossible to tell from which of the two crops the sugar has been derived. From very early on, therefore, the agricultural product and its organic constraints, while apparently propping up the whole system, are dependent upon an industrial process that is needed to extract and crystallize the sugar from the plant source to make it available for consumption. The natural agricultural crop, without this industrial step, is of no use to the individual, the household nor the food industry.

The successful development of the refining industry has driven the intensification and extensification of agricultural production. In world terms, for example, the production of refined sugar has grown from around 50 million tonnes to more than 100 million tonnes since the Second World War, and nearly every country that can produce sugar (about 120) now does so (Abbott 1990).

The sugar-refining industry, providing this pure organic product, presents the food industrialist with an all-year-round input that has overcome the time-bound and sequential constraints of agriculture (subject to the refining industry organizing its supplies efficiently). Sugar also presents the food manufacturer with a range of organic properties as well as its sweetness. These unique technical and functional properties have been exploited to produce an extensive and diverse number of food and drink products, and whole industries have developed around sugar as a major input.

A primary purpose for using sucrose in food products is as a sweetener. The sense of sweetness is the subjective evaluation of the interaction of sugars, total acidity, pH level and the other constituents of a food (Wursch and Daget 1987; Frijters 1987). In general, as the concentration of sucrose is increased, so is the sense of sweetness, up to a limit. At higher concentrations, an unpleasantness develops (Moskowitz 1971). Relative sweetness, that is the comparison of sweetness between sweeteners, is also dependent upon temperature, concentration and acidity (Nicol 1982).

Another vital use of sucrose is to control water activity and humidity in food products. This is of considerable importance to many types of food products which are exposed to fluctuating humidity conditions when in storage or marketing channels – hence, the organic role of sugar in assisting the shelf life of many modern food products.

These points, if a little obvious when stated, have proved important for the successful industrialization of the food system. Sugar is able partly to resolve the problem that food is characterized by its frequency of consumption, while agricultural production is seasonal and dependent on sequential events (such as planting, growing, harvesting). Sugar aids the frequency and levels of its own consumption by its palatability and its making other foods more acceptable, for example in bitter beverages like tea, coffee and cocoa. While, in its earlier history, sugar can be regarded as an important source of food energy (calories), at times more recently it has helped food processors to overcome the human limits of consumption in the sense that there is usually room for a sweet. Sugar has also proved adaptable and versatile to changes in other food systems. It is no coincidence, therefore, that sugar has been used to develop products consumed outside 'main' meals – sweet courses, snack foods, treats – foods that are eaten with minimal or no preparation, consumed on the move or at times outside main meals (for example, mid-morning breaks, afternoon tea, supper). The importance of the organic properties of sugar can be summarized in four distinct but interrelated areas:

1 The time-bound and sequential constraints of agricultural production to the food system as a whole have been largely overcome by the need for the crop to undergo an industrial refining process controlled by external capital. Consequently, refined white sugar has presented the food industry with a mass-produced, standardized, predictable but versatile industrial input with a range of technical and functional properties. The consumer has been presented with a cheap source of food energy and an all-year-round food additive important for making foods and drinks more palatable or acceptable and for preserving some foodstuffs that would otherwise perish.

2 Many of today's modern, taken-for-granted foods and drinks have been 'invented' around sugar as a major ingredient. In this respect a number of food industries, such as confectionery, cakes and biscuits, have developed using sugar as an industrial input. In addition, these and other industries have persisted not only around more traditional sugar-based products, but have found new applications using sugar through product differentiation or new product categories. Sugar, in other words, has successfully functioned and performed within the underlying tendencies towards mass-produced, mass-consumed industrial products described by Goodman *et al.* (1987) and not least in producing 'durable' and 'hardy' products (Friedmann and McMichael 1989). Empirical evidence for these processes for sugar in the United Kingdom is described in more detail in the sections on sugar's SOPs.

3 The major organic property of sugar – sweetness – has been successfully and fully disseminated throughout the British food system as a whole. From sugar and sweetness being a relative scarcity 150 years ago, it is now universal and 'added' or 'hidden' throughout the modern food system.

4 Sugar's organic properties in consumption have been responsible for a countertrend in recent years. Although sugar has proved remarkably versatile and has been incorporated and reincorporated into the diet, more and more people are seeing its organic qualities (such as its calorific value) as something undesirable in the diet, in particular among higher-income groups. This attitude has been reinforced by scientific, medical and nutritional advice based on increasing knowledge about food and diet. However, as the popularity of foods and drinks using low-calorie sweeteners testify, sweetness itself persists.

In short, the organic role of sugar is important throughout its SOPs and, though not stated at every occasion, this is an underlying theme in this paper. Nor are these organic properties piecemeal and fragmented. The particular connections between sugar as an agricultural product and its ultimate consumption in one food or another often depend upon the integral combination of a variety of sugar's organic properties as they are employed along the food chain – whether as preservative, bulk additive, sweetener, flavour enhancer, etc.

SUGAR AND THE POLITICAL ECONOMY OF FOOD

As observed in previous chapters, the 'political economy of food' approach has centred upon a 'restructuring thesis', pointing to the decline of Fordist industrial and agricultural hegemony. Kenney *et al.* (1989), for example, examine this in the context of the crisis in US agriculture. They outline a general framework for understanding recent transformations in US agriculture based on the following points: (1) the motion of the non-agricultural economy largely determines the shape and structure of agriculture; (2) the current crises in agriculture parallel the current crisis of American capitalism; and (3) linkages forged between non-agricultural industries and agriculture have resulted in a present-day political economy in which the two have become entirely intertwined and inseparable. Within this framework they argue that the Fordist logic of accumulation has been played out within a distinct segment of American agriculture – the corn–soya–meat and wheat complex of the Midwest – and describe how this process has led to the present crisis in agriculture.

For sugar, there are two critical differences between the restructuring thesis and the SOP method to be adopted here. First, the work on the decline in US hegemony, especially its crisis orientation, is simply not relevant in the context of the historical examination of sugar in the United Kingdom. Put abruptly, it is empirically invalid. Second, those concerned with economic restructuring have been led outwards, that is to follow the horizontal disintegration and recombination of the spatial structure of society induced by the changing geography of capital accumulation. Our approach continues to emphasize the vertical integration that ties socio-economic activities together to form the sugar system.

However, research on food systems in the 'political economy of agriculture' tradition has continuing relevance for sugar's SOP, especially the work of Friedmann (1982 and 1993), Friedmann and McMichael (1989) and Goodman often in conjunction with his colleagues. There are two important differences between Friedman and Goodman, but each provides essential elements for a conceptualization of the sugar system. The first difference is Goodman's emphasis on the organic/biological characteristics of the food system which Friedmann hardly mentions. Second, Friedmann employs an abstract logic in which structures, such as the 'international food order' and 'food regimes', are produced and reproduced by underlying forces or tendencies. Goodman, by contrast, tends to discuss the role

of government in creating structures within which tendencies (often interpreted as trends) are constrained (Goodman and Redclift 1991a, p. 114, for
example). In the sugar systems, the organic, as discussed earlier, is a key
feature and will be incorporated here in the specification of the SOPs but,
paradoxically, more by following the method of Friedmann. Thus, both
authors address the character and features of the modern agri-food system.
Where the analyses are particularly relevant to an understanding of the
sugar systems, they will be elaborated but within an analytical framework
which differs from both.[3]

An important aspect of the work of Goodman *et al.* (1987) is the
increasing marginalization of agriculture as it becomes appropriated as part
of an industrial sector, with consumption of agricultural produce shifting
from final use to industrial input. Here, two points of departure are in order.
While arguing that the organic is a distinguishing feature of food systems
compared to other systems, too much emphasis can be placed on the food
system as being biologically determined. Consequently, a more appropriate
starting point for distinguishing agriculture and industry, as opposed to
Goodman *et al.*'s reliance on nature, is the role of landed property (and rent
as its economic form as a revenue) although this does incorporate, but is
not exclusively determined by, organic factors. Nor can the rent relation be
simply seen as payment for land use – since, with state quotas and other
forms of intervention over who produces and how, there can be a
displacement of control of landed property along the food system and its
structures.

Second, as sugar becomes more integrated into industrial food supply,
the agricultural source becomes marginalized in the sense that it is but one
link among many in the food chain. However, at the same time, as a
countertendency, agriculture becomes more important as a source of
essential raw materials to an expanding industrial food supply. Simply
because the net outcome of these two tendencies has been a reduction in
the proportion of value-added by agriculture, it cannot be presumed that
the tensions between them are analytically redundant – particularly in the
context of defining the structural divides along the food system, not least
between agriculture and industry.

Where Goodman's work is particularly important for sugar is in the
argument that agro-industrial development has taken place through the
dual processes of 'appropriationism' and 'substitutionism'. A particular
concern is the emerging biotechnology industries and how developments
in this area threaten to transform and 'refashion' our whole understanding
of nature and agriculture.[4] Much of the work on food systems addresses the
problem of how technology and science have transformed and are transforming commodity chains. Especially important is the idea of the technological treadmill, with farmers in particular locked into production
methods comprising, for example, artificial fertilizer, hybrid seed,

87

protective chemicals and mechanization. Biotechnology threatens to transform the treadmill. In short, now that the genetic code can be manipulated,
biotechnology has the ability to refashion nature according to the logic of
the marketplace. Biotechnologies have suddenly opened up new alternatives and paths of development for all the major actors in the food
system: farmers and input suppliers, primary processors, final food manufacturers and consumers (Goodman and Redclift 1991a).

Like other crops sugar has been subject to the technological treadmill,
and to the effects of appropriationism. For sugar beet in the United
Kingdom, for example, the mid-1940s to the 1960s saw the completion of
machine harvesting; precision drilling was introduced in the 1950s, herbicides from the 1960s, and monogerm seeds from the mid-1960s (Harris
1985). The location of sugar-beet growing has, in part, been dependent on
the location of the beet-processing factories and is characteristically a
product of large farms. In the 1960s more than half the crop was grown on
holdings in excess of 300 acres. The trend since the 1940s has been for
more concentration of production; average acreage per farm used for sugar
beet approximately doubled from under 10 to over 20 acres between 1950
and 1970, while the number of farmers who cultivated sugar beet dropped
by around 40% Holderness (1985).

Although not always made explicit by Goodman and others in discussion of substitutionism, two distinct routes for it are identified: either
through organic or through inorganic substitution for agricultural crops.
Both of these are important in an examination of sugar production in a
global context. Most worrying for the future of sugar has been the impact
of biotechnology in the production of the (organic) sugar replacement high
fructose corn syrup (HFCS). Goodman and his colleagues use the example
of HFCS (known as isoglucose in the EC) to illustrate the impact of
biotechnology on the restructuring of food systems. HFCS is derived from
glucose syrups by an enzymatic process (the former prepared by the
hydrolysis of starch, in the main corn/maize – known as the wet-milling
process). From the 1970s, from the sugar industry's point of view, HFCS has
had a devastating impact on the market for sucrose in the United States. It
accounted for 44% of the total US sweeteners market in 1988. Thus, HFCS
stands as an example of substitutionism and the way in which biotechnologies can drastically restructure commodity chains.

Looking at this example in more detail, however, it is not simply biotechnology alone, important as it is, that has to been seen as the driving force
of restructuring. There is no doubt that HFCS has dramatically changed the
composition of the US total sweeteners market. From a peak of more than 11
million tons in 1977, sugar use declined to 7.9 million tons in 1986, while HFCS
production rose from 1 million tons, dry base, to 5.5 million tons.

However, this substitution of sugar has been based on a number of factors.
HFCS is commercially available only in liquid form, comparable to liquid

invert sugar. This has made it especially attractive when used in liquid manufacturing systems such as soft drinks. It is primarily because this product category is so dominant in the United States, in terms of its purchase of sweeteners, that the displacement of sugar by HFCS has been so impressive. One reason for this switch, therefore, is the organic/technical properties of HFCS which has made its use more efficient than sugar (and vice versa in other food applications). In addition, the economics of HFCS production has been particularly favourable in the United States, with low corn prices and the byproducts of maize helping to keep the price down (Smith 1978). Further, the success of HFCS consumption has been dependent on state policies. The major feature of US sweetener policy has been the level of protection that it has offered not only to sugar producers but also to producers of HFCS. The subsidy equivalent afforded sugar producers and HFCS producers is estimated to be in the order of $1 billion each year between 1982 and 1988 and the costs to the consumer over the same period in the order of $2.5 billion (Borrell and Duncan 1990). As Mahler (1986) ironically points out, the US sugar industry found unlikely allies in the lobbyists for the manufacturers of HFCS. They also argued for high sugar support prices – but, not for the love of the sugar industry as such, but as a way to compete effectively against it within domestic markets!

Borrell and Duncan also point out how policy decisions influence the markets for sugar and HFCS in Japan. The very high consumer price for sugar in Japan not only reduces sugar demand directly, but also allows HFCS to be priced below sugar. Consumption of HFCS is subject to a small tax, but maize, its major raw material, can be imported duty-free, unlike raw sugar. The unequal treatment of sugar and HFCS has encouraged the production and use of the syrup in place of sugar. Within Japan, sugar policy is estimated to have given HFCS producers an effective subsidy of over $700 million in the three years up to 1987. Over the same period, sugar millers, processors and growers together also received an estimated subsidy of about $2,000 million.

Goodman *et al.* (1987) are correct, therefore, to show how bio-technology has helped to develop an effective competitor for sugar, but in a favourable (subsidizing) policy environment. HFCS continues to impede the growth of the world sugar market. At first, HFCS expanded mainly in the American and Japanese markets. More recently, consumption has spread to many other countries that are traditional sugar producers and exporters such as Brazil, India, Argentina, Taiwan, the Philippines and Thailand. In 1977 HFCS consumption was 1.45% of world sugar con-sumption; by 1980 it had increased to 2.97% and in 1988 reached 6.77% (Landell Mills 1989). However, world consumption of sugar continues to grow at a rate of 2% per annum. In Europe, the production and use of HFCS have been blocked by sugar interests when HFCS was incorporated into the EC Sugar Regime in 1977 under conditions making it too costly for their widespread industrial use. It is also important to note how, in some countries such as Brazil, sucrose has become a key player in reverse substitutionism where it is used as the raw material to produce ethanol, a substitute for automobile fuel.

An example of inorganic substitutionism, at the consumption end of sugar's SOPs, is in the area of low-calorie artificial sweeteners. Saccharin has been available for many years, being in commercial production from the early 1900s, and today is extremely cheap in comparison to sugar. However, its particular set of organic properties, especially the bitter aftertaste, have made it a poor substitute. Its industrial use has been restricted to products that use sugar, but where sugar content can be reduced slightly (thus saving on an expensive ingredient) with saccharin making up the sweetness, in fruit squashes for example.

Aspartame, on the other hand, has a far superior taste profile which is closer to mimicking sugar, but it is more expensive relative to saccharin. Thus, the combination of the organic property of sweetness with less calories and an acceptable taste profile, together with the high EC price for sugar, have contributed to the rapid introduction and diffusion of aspartame in food products and the retail market on the back of the up-market healthy eating and lifestyle revolution in 1980s Britain. This substitutionism, however, has probably only impeded the use of sugar, while simultaneously expanding the market for sweetness (Heasman 1990). In some products, the introduction of the diet version has also helped to revive sales of the full sugar product, in brands of fruit-flavoured soft drinks for example (Heasman 1988).

There are many other substitutes for sugar available on the market but these, like the sugar alcohols for example, have made little impact on the main UK sugar (sucrose) market. Substitutes like the sugar alcohols are more expensive than sucrose and have been restricted to specialist dietetic foods (an exception, possibly even an illustration, being 'sugar-free' chewing gums). Other manufacturers have, in the past, been reluctant to use them in more mass-produced products because of undesirable organic properties.

Thus, biotechnologies may have immense potential to restructure and change food systems fundamentally, as persuasively argued by Goodman *et al.* However, sugar's SOPs suggest that substitutionism needs to be modified in the context of other factors, not least the organic relationship between specific foods, the role of different ingredients in food manufacturing systems, trends in food consumption habits and state policies directed towards different commodities.

THE ROLE OF THE STATE IN ORGANIZING, STRUCTURING AND RESTRUCTURING FOOD CHAINS

For sugar's SOPs in the United Kingdom, described in the second part of this chapter, it is argued there have been three distinct structural periods –

pre-First World War, from 1914 to 1973 and from 1973 to the present day. In each case it will be shown that there is a stable set of complementary state policies, with impacts upon prices, specific patterns of specialization (cane refining and beet processing) and resulting patterns of consumption and trade. These structural features of particular food orders were first identified by Friedmann (1982) in her analysis of the 'international food order' built around the dominance of the world grain trade by the United States, with food aid at its axis. While there are obvious differences between wheat and sugar, and the types of dependency resulting from their cultivation and trade, it is interesting to note similar forces at work in their respective SOPs.

In a later work, the role of the state in shaping food systems is described in a more generalized way (Friedmann and McMichael 1989). They argue that the process has gone through two distinct periods, which they designate as the first and second food regimes. Although they do not explicitly date these, the first food regime is centred on the period 1870 to 1914 and ends with the Second World War. The Second Food Regime dates from 1945. Of particular relevance for sugar is the shift in regimes which they describe in terms of the culmination of colonialism giving way to the rise of the nation-state.

Generally, state intervention in sugar's SOPs has taken two forms. First, in terms of agricultural policy, there is the set of measures taken by the governments of nation-states to influence, directly or indirectly, agricultural factor and product markets, including state-to-state negotiations. Second, the state has intervened through negotiations with the sugar-refining and processing industry. However, far from these features in the United Kingdom being crisis-driven as suggested by much of the food systems literature, they have been resolution-driven, in the sense of abstract tendencies being played out through relatively harmonious structural change. The restructuring that has taken place has occurred around dominant and conflicting interests, in most instances to accommodate contingent factors. This has been most notable in the conflict between cane and beet interests. Friedmann and McMichael (1989) would presumably describe this shift between the two as synonymous with regime shift. But, significantly, the chronology that they employ for food regimes is inappropriate for the sugar systems in the United Kingdom.

First, they describe how in the late nineteenth and early twentieth century the supply of tropical products from colonial countries was expanded by metropolitan economies. For sugar in Britain, this did not happen. Under a free-trade policy, Europe became the dominant supplier of sugar to the United Kingdom (from temperate beet). From the outbreak of the First World War tropical cane interests became the dominant force in the UK market, resisting the tendency, described by Friedmann and McMichael, for (developed) nation-state agriculture to substitute for tropical products. At the start of their second food regime (the 1950s and 1960s), they describe the decline in markets for tropical exports, notably sugar and vegetable oils, through import substitution by advanced capitalist countries. It is precisely during this time that the United Kingdom strengthened its links with empire sugar and secured the supply of tropical cane through the Commonwealth Sugar Agreement.

However, as Friedmann and McMichael rightly point out, tendencies do not operate in isolation and there are often contradictory tendencies at work. While strictly regulated, the home-grown beet industry did gain in importance. With the full force of European beet interests allied to those of the UK beet industry, the conflict between the 'culmination of colonialism' and the 'nation-state' finally came to a head in the 1970s when, although delayed on Friedmann and McMichael's time-scale, domestic beet triumphed, if only partially, over tropical cane.

If, then, the analysis of Friedmann and McMichael were to be applied to the UK sugar system, it would require a considerable dependence upon lags and contradictions to explain the industry's history. A more palatable explanation is to set aside their analysis as too general – drawn from particular crops, albeit important ones, and particular aspects of imperialism, whose more concrete consequences cannot be simply read off from abstract propositions concerning world orders and food regimes.

While the presence of inherent tendencies are stressed here, these need to be understood as abstract and contradictory and not immediately realized empirically as trends or structures. In this way, therefore, the deductivist schemas, against which McMichael and Buttel (1990) rightly warn, can be avoided. Consequently, a more nuanced understanding of the UK sugar system can be proposed, as described in the following sections.

Also of potential importance for understanding the UK sugar systems is Friedmann and McMichael's concept of 'food complexes' created, they consider, during the second food regime. They argue that during this period, restructuring occurred mainly through two large complexes: the intensive-meat complex and the durable-foods complex. The intensive-meat complex drew upon the integration between separated and specialized animal and grain producers, dramatically supplemented by the vast expansion in soya bean production. The durable-foods complex, on the other hand, changed food from a local, perishable set of ingredients to a widely marketed and manufactured set of products with a long and hardy life, for example frozen and packaged goods.

While both of these complexes are important, the durable-foods complex will be discussed because of its implication for sweetness in food systems. After meat, the most important inputs to manufactured foods as a whole, Friedmann and McMichael argue, are sweeteners and fats. The durable-foods complex is created by the shift from farm produce to manufactured foods during the 1950s and 1960s, mirroring the larger trend to mass consumption and mass production of standardized products. Writing about the United States and advanced capitalist countries, Friedmann and McMichael (1989) argue as follows:

> This involved a double shift: first, the share of the total consumption shifted away from table sugar and cooking oils (both involving only processing that yields a final consumer product), to industrial sweeteners and fats as ingredients in manufactured complex foods; and second, domestic inputs substituted for imported ones, especially if we consider advanced capitalist countries as a unity (consistent with the increasing integration of their food sectors for sourcing and marketing manufactured foods). (1989, p. 109)

Sugar's organic qualities and its use in inventing or, as Goodman would describe it, altering the organic composition of foods, made it a natural ingredient for the durable-foods complex. However, it needs to be noted that long before the durable-foods complex was in full swing in the 1960s, nearly half of all sugar supply was already used as an industrial input in manufactured foods in the 1930s. With the exception of soft drinks, the major, mass-produced traditional products using sugar as an ingredient were already in place. During the second food regime, sugar continued to be used in what had long been its traditional industrial role, even as its food applications expanded to a numerous but diverse range of other food categories including mass-produced soft drinks.

In short, as in the previous discussion of production, the role of sugar does not fit neatly into the chronology of consumption associated with the pre-sumed creation of durable foods in the second food regime. This is not to suggest that the drive to mass production/consumption is a myth, nor that sugar, fats and meat only played a limited role in such development. But such abstract generalities preclude more complex understandings other than by way of appeal to exceptions or contingent factors. For sugar, though critically important in its organic role of rendering industrial food sweet, was in many respects an ageing product (or eternally youthful!) originating in an earlier food supply, and was not automatically appropriate for new food regimes. As well as sweetness, its other organic properties did enable it to occupy prominence as an ingredient in the era of mass consumption. But this was only so in the context of continuing countertendencies in ingredients, products, processes and changing food habits dependent upon durable goods, like refrigerators and freezers, in both stores and households and the more recent trends to fresh and healthy foods.

The food systems literature sheds light on the development and charac-teristics of the modern agri-food system. Taken together, however, they only allow a fragmented understanding of historical changes in sugar supply and its role in the nation's diet. But, with the two major themes in place, that is, the organic properties of sugar and its dependence on three distinct SOPs, a more detailed, historical account can be given of how sugar has persisted in the UK diet and how its integral unity within food systems has set it apart from other foodstuffs.

THE FIRST SOP: SUGAR BEFORE THE FIRST WORLD WAR

At the turn of the twentieth century Britain was one of the world's most important markets for sugar (at this time the United States was also a large importer of sugar), and around 1.5 million tonnes entered the UK food system. As well as domestic consumption through the sugar bowl, sugar was increasingly being used as an ingredient in foodstuffs like jams, biscuits and confectionery. At this time, Britain grew no sugar of its own and increasingly relied on supplies from Central Europe, produced from sugar beets rather than colonial sugar cane.

It is not the intention here to document the economic and social origins of the sugar trade and its links with the notorious triangular trade – depending on the flow of goods to West Africa, slaves to the Caribbean and a cargo of rum, molasses and sugar back to the United Kingdom.[5] However, these early sources of supply, developed in the seventeenth and eighteenth centuries by rich states to produce raw materials and luxuries for their home markets in return for outlets for capital and manufactures, was to continue to play an important role in the structuring of the sugar system in the 1900s. Indeed nearly all the characteristics associated with the recent globalization of agriculture – vertically integrated markets, extensive foreign investment, a problematic impact on development and distribution in peripheral areas – have been part of the world sugar trade for centuries. Caribbean sugar played a central role in the world political–economic system of the seventeenth and eighteenth centuries, and Britain was at its core (Mahler 1986).

From the point of view of the modern supply of sugar, an important change took place in the nineteenth century, fundamentally and per-manently changing the nature of the world market – the development of sugar beet (a temperate crop) in competition with sugar cane (a tropical crop). The sugar-beet industry was developed in Europe in the 1800s and, by 1880, had displaced cane as the principal source of sugar in Europe.[6] By 1913 continental beet accounted for nearly 80% of UK supplies (Monopolies and Mergers Commission 1981). The British market was a major target for exporters with around one-quarter of world exports and three-quarters of European exports going to the United Kingdom. Of the sugar exports from Europe to Britain, 75% came from Germany and Austria-Hungary (Albert and Graves 1988).

Before the First World War, Britain was the world's only major free market; duties on sugar imports were abolished in 1874. This, together with

Table 5.1 Comparison of UK sugar consumption with other countries in 1900

Country	Consumpion (lb per head of pop.)	Consumption (tons)
UK	83.65 (37.94 kg)	1,536,882
Germany	29.97 (13.59 kg)	752,974
Holland	26.57 (12.05 kg)	61,430
Belgium	19.74 (8.95 kg)	59,000
France	25.81 (11.71 kg)	448,134
Austria-Hungary	16.17 (7.33 kg)	327,866
USA	65.20 (29.96 kg)	2,219,847
Dominion of Canada	57.24 (25.96 kg)	136,009
Australian Commonwealth	107.09 (48.58 kg)	180,013

Source: Accounts and Papers 1907 *(334) lxxxi 893*, London: HMSO

the continued development of the beet industry in Europe, saw the British consumer becoming one of the chief beneficiaries (see Table 5.1).

Ironically, sugar produced from European beet was still a relative luxury in the producer countries while its price continued to fall in the consumer countries. The retail price of sugar in Britain in 1905 was (the equivalent of) two pence per lb, while in France and Germany the comparable prices were 44% and 19% higher, respectively (Tracy 1989). In terms of UK supplies available, in 1880 these stood at around 29 kg per person per year; in 1900, 36 kg per person per year – equivalent to about 1,500,000 tonnes of sugar entering the British food system.

Between 1850 and 1914, along with Hamburg, London was also one of the major trading centres of the sugar world, and the United Kingdom an important refiner. The crux of the sugar business is the production and sale of refined sugars. Historically, tropical colonies produced raw sugars from cane, which were then shipped and refined in the United Kingdom by British companies, for example into the pure, white granulated form that we would recognize today, but also into other products such as syrups, icing sugars and so on. These refined sugars were then sold on (traditionally through sugar brokers and merchants) for home consumption or re-exported to third countries – the latter being an important market for British refiners.

Technology has brought increasing capacity and economies of scale in the refining of raw materials to the final products. In the terminology of Goodman *et al.* (1987), sugar has been an industrial input from the very outset, that is grown and cultivated as a raw material (cane and beet) for refiners to turn into a number of final products in a variety of formats through an industrial process. In this sense sugar cane is not a natural crop of the Caribbean (it arrived for the first time in 1493 on Columbus's second voyage), nor is sugar beet naturally found in Europe, but was cultivated and developed from the start as an input that needed a factory process to produce its final product (sucrose). In terms of power and control, the success of metropolitan centres, such as the United Kingdom, had been to maintain inputs of raw materials from a variety of tropical sources, but especially colonies, while protecting the home industry (cane refining in the case of the United Kingdom) from the vagaries of the world market through protective duties and tariffs.

The last decades of the nineteenth century saw the closure of many refiners. In 1864, for example, there were 72 UK refineries processing 500,000 tonnes of sugar. By 1913, there were only 13 refineries processing more than 1 million tonnes of sugar (Chalmin 1990).[7] The refining industry was centred around three main locations: London, Liverpool and the Clyde. Of lesser importance were Bristol and Plymouth. The surviving refiners often developed specialist products to help them compete: for example, brewing sugars, or Abram Lyle & Sons' 'Golden Syrup', or the sugar cubes of Henry Tate & Sons.

It is against this background that the crisis of war gave the opportunity for British refiners to rally to the national cause as a solution to their industry's own crisis, in shifting to cane supplies. The result was that the structural arrangements for the supply of sugar were radically altered in favour of cane-refining interests which, in one way or another, were to remain dominant for the next six decades.

THE SECOND SOP: THE DOMINANCE OF SUGAR CANE, 1914–1973

Sugar during the inter-war period

The structure of the British sugar system changed in many important and substantive ways with the outbreak of the First World War. Sugar was the first foodstuff to receive direct government intervention. On 20 August 1914, a Sugar Commission was appointed with power to purchase, sell and regulate sugar supplies on behalf of the government. With the loss of European sugar supplies, the United Kingdom was forced to rely upon supplies from tropical sources (mainly Java, Mauritius and the Caribbean, chiefly Cuba). This meant that European refined beet sugar lost its dominant place in the UK market, and raw cane sugar, refined in Britain, took over the dominant position in the trade for the first time in recent history (Hammond 1962). State intervention in the market also meant that, for the first time, British refiners were able to work with a guaranteed margin without any risk in the fluctuation of prices – their main concern being to increase their productive capacity (processing raw sugars to refined sugars). As Chalmin (1990, p. 125) notes:

The First World War therefore marks the 'take-off' of British refining. After periods of uncertainty when the British market was the theatre of the fiercest struggles between foreign producers, five years of 'calm' without competition had allowed the refiners to amass a considerable war chest, to penetrate the commercial circuits which had hitherto been in the hand of their competitors and above all to initiate fruitful relations with the Government apparatus.

This take-off was to last for the next sixty years, culminating in the historic peak in sugar supplies entering the British food system in the 1960s.

The Sugar Commission continued to function until 26 February 1921; the next day, the two largest British sugar-refining firms merged to form Tate & Lyle – the new firm now possessed half of UK sugar-refining capacity. From a general policy of *laissez-faire*, the government now adopted policies specifically directed towards the sugar industry. From the 1920s this took the form of initiating the cultivation of beet in British soil, as discussed shortly, and increasing supplies of raw sugar cane from the empire. The last part of this policy was achieved through a system of tariffs, with sugar from the empire receiving preferential tariffs over 'foreign' sugar. Between 1919 and 1938 refined sugar imports dropped from 23.44% to 1.87% of total sugar imported and empire raw materials grew from 26.65% to 49.39%. Part of this increase was met by the entry of new suppliers; especially important from 1925 onwards were Australia, South Africa and the Fiji Islands (Chalmin 1990, p. 164).

The success of the refining industry almost caused the fledgling beet industry to die in its infancy. The first modern beet sugar factory was built in Cantley in 1912, but closed in 1916. Later, official loans and public subscriptions were used to buy land devoted to beet growing and to erect a factory at Kelham which began operation in 1921 (in 1922 the Cantley factory reopened). However, the beet industry consistently experienced financial difficulties and, in 1925, to save the industry, the government made the decision to subsidize it for a period of ten years. Table 5.2 shows the increase in home-produced sugar for this period.

The basic idea behind the subsidy was to grant the sugar factories a large enough sum of money to enable them to pay farmers prices that would make it worthwhile for them to grow sugar beet – by the 1930s this involved 46,000 farmers growing beet on 404,000 acres. The subsidy was supposed to diminish gradually and end finally after ten years. By 1928 the eighteen operating beet factories were owned by five financial interests, each linked to one or other aspect of the sugar chain: equipment manufacture, refining or trade, for example.

Many of the beet factories did their own refining of home-grown raw sugar and some, in competition with Tate & Lyle, reduced their overhead costs by importing raw sugar for refining in the off-season. This created a

Table 5.2 UK production of centrifugal sugar from beet 1905–40

Years	Tons (in thousands)
1905/6–1909/10	0
1915/16–1919/20	2
1920/21–1924/25	12
1925/26–1929/30	195
1930/31–1934/35	420
1935/36–1939/40	467

Source: Chalmin (1990, p. 142)

large surplus of refining capacity in the United Kingdom (Hammond 1962, p. 5). This potentially disastrous overcapacity of sugar production and the conflict between beet and cane interests were settled by the government when, in 1933, the Ministry of Agriculture induced refiners to enter into an agreement with beet processors which allocated beet factories a quota of 500,000 tons of sugar in the UK market, by now of 1.9 million tonnes.

At the end of the ten-year period, the Greene Committee was appointed in 1935 to determine the future of the beet industry and advised that assistance to it should be abolished. However, the government adopted a minority recommendation that assistance should continue without time limit and passed the Sugar Industry (Reorganisation) Act of 1936. Under this Act the eighteen beet factories were amalgamated to form the British Sugar Corporation Ltd, and financial assistance was to be provided to growers for the production of the equivalent of 560,000 tons of white sugar per annum. An outstanding Treasury loan was converted to a 15% shareholding (Monopolies and Mergers Commission 1981, p. 4). In effect, a *de facto* nationalization of the sugar beet industry had taken place, Chalmin (1990, p. 178).

The UK beet industry was established and survived as the direct result of government subsidy, amounting to around £700,000 a year; the benefits largely accrued to a small group of East Anglian farmers (Hammond 1946). Chalmin gives the figure for the total government subsidy between 1924/5 and 1935/6 as being £36.8 million with a tax preference of £15.8 million, giving total assistance amounting to £52.6 million. In addition, the quota system that was introduced enabled competition between sugar refiners and sugar factories to be regulated, together with a preferential duty on empire raw sugar against foreign competition. Sugar beet, a completely new crop, quickly became, together with beef and corn, a powerful vested interest. As Hammond (1946, p. 14) observes: 'sugar-beet . . . had overnight become an indispensable feature in (crop) rotations, and sugar-beet tops essential to the maintenance of milk supplies'. It was, therefore, during the inter-war period that the characteristics of sugar's second SOP were formed.

Of obvious importance was the establishment of a British sugar industry using home-grown sugar beet as the raw material. At one level this can be seen as the extensification of agricultural production to supply a growing market for refined sugar. At another, it can be seen as temperate farmers' interests competing with those of tropical growers. It is these forces that Friedmann and McMichael (1989) try to capture in their description of the first food regime and the two simultaneous and contradictory movements taking place in agriculture before the Second World War which they conceptualize as the culmination of colonialism and the rise of the nation-state system.

Sugar beet as a rotation or break crop may have also served to increase the profitability of farming. Berlan (1992) describes how, in the United States, with increasing mechanization and the development of power farming in the 1930s, the need for a new rotation crop became crucial for continuous farming. There, the solution proved to be the development of soya beans. Sugar beet may have served the same purpose in the United Kingdom, although this is a suggestion that warrants further empirical investigation.

Learning to consume sugar[8]

These considerable efforts, through supports to refining and factory pro-duction, produced hundreds of thousands of tons of sugar. Remembering that the widespread availability of sugar was still something of a novelty, this begs the question of how the British population learnt to use such quantities in their diet. Table 5.3 shows that per capita consumption of sugar increased by nearly 50% between 1880 and the late 1930s (with falls in the 1940s due to rationing, with consumption again increasing in the 1950s.

Mintz (1985) describes in considerable detail the use and consumption of sugar in Britain: from its early days as a spice and medicine, and its luxury use on ceremonial and royal occasions, to its essential use by more and more sectors of the British population in the 1800s. He suggests two concurrent (but contradictory) processes to describe the spread of sugar as a foodstuff throughout society – 'intensification' and 'extensification'. For the former, sugar usage is linked to the past with its attachment to (upper-class) ceremonial occasions and the emulation of these by more and more people lower down the economic stratum, often in new or modified rituals and ceremonial contexts. With extensification, the familiar and regular use of sugar increases consumption which, in turn, reduces sugar's status as a glamorous luxury and precious good.

Lloyd (1936, p. 90) describes the fivefold increase in sugar consumption between 1836 and 1936 as the 'most significant change in the nation's diet during the last 100 years'. He attributes this to the fall in price. In the 1830s, sugar cost 6d per lb; in 1936, less than half this. Sugar also was firmly

Table 5.3 UK per capita sugar supply 1880–1962

Years	lb (kg) per person per year
1880	64 (29.0)
1909–1913	79 (35.8)
1924–1928	87 (39.5)
1934–1938	96 (43.5)
1941	67 (30.4)
1944	71 (32.2)
1947	82 (37.2)
1950	84 (38.1)
1953	98 (44.5)
1956	109 (49.4)
1959	111 (50.3)
1962	111 (50.3)

Source: Greaves and Hollingsworth (1966)

established as an important source of carbohydrate in the diet by the 1930s, in combination with wheat and potatoes. Altogether these furnished 78% of the total supply of carbohydrate in the period following the First World War (Flux 1930).

However, it is not exactly clear how sugar was eaten. Putting it crudely, most people do not sit down to a plate or bowl of just sugar, or a meal, say, of meat and two vegetables, one of which is sugar. Sugar consumption from the late 1800s onwards was increasingly the result of sugar being added to something else for final consumption. In this sense, the organic properties of sugar as an ingredient is the key to the successful diffusion of sugar throughout the British food supply, especially when used as an industrial input to produce other foodstuffs. Sugar's sweetness together with its other organic properties, when used in food processing, led to its innovative use in helping to produce many new manufactured food products (for example, sugar confectionery and canned products). Sugar was able to transform industrial food supply, aided and abetted by a cocktail of vested interests from cane and beet production which set themselves to deliver a mass-produced, standardized product into the distribution system.

During this period sugar consumption was skewed in favour of higher-income groups, although by the 1930s weekly amounts purchased for home use by five social classes were remarkably uniform – 17.6 oz class in AA to 15.2 oz in class D, with an average national figure of 16.7 oz (Crawford and Broadley 1936). To be added to these figures was sugar consumed in confectionery, cakes, biscuits, jam, syrups and other forms, which Crawford and Broadley estimated as 11.9 oz per person per week. This gives a total national figure of 28.6 oz or the equivalent of around 42 kg per person per annum with the split between retail and industrial use of sugar being 60:40 in favour of the retail market. Boyd Orr's (1937) study on food, health and income gave figures of sugar bought as such as averaging 17.8 oz per head per week, 5.2 oz for jams, jellies and syrups, and 9 oz for sugar consumed in other forms, a total of 32 oz (around 47 kg per person per year). While average per capita sugar purchased as such and in jams, jellies and syrups was fairly even across income groups (still greater in higher-income groups than lower), this relationship changes with sugar consumed in other forms, that is in processed foods, with the highest income group consuming around 46% more sugar in this form than the lowest income group.

By the 1930s, on these calculations, 40% of sugar entering the food system was used for the industrial production of foods – many of them familiar and even household names.[9] By 1900, for example, Huntley & Palmer were already producing more than 400 different varieties of biscuit, and Peak Frean more than 200. The 'new-fangled breakfast foods' (Lloyd 1936, p. 91) were growing in popularity with more than 60 different brands of proprietary cereal foods recorded in 1912 (Dr Kellogg had only invented the cornflake in 1899!). The cereal market expanded when a number of leading American firms established manufacturing plants in the United Kingdom.[10] In the 1870s, the first milk chocolate appeared, and by the early 1900s British manufacturers had successfully started to produce it. Also important were syrups – especially Lyle's Golden Syrup (Chalmin 1990), cheap jams (Burnett 1989) and products like tinned condensed and sweetened milk.

Lyle (1950) gives a detailed breakdown of sugar use in the United Kingdom for 1938 (see Table 5.4) which clearly demonstrates the importance of sugar in UK food manufacture – nearly half of total supply (46.34%). But the rise of sugar to such prominence was not met without resistance, in particular in view of its role in the nation's diet. During the early decades of the century there was a shift in nutritional thinking. With the discovery of vitamins, amino acids and mineral elements, food quality came to be recognized as being just as important as quantity. Research in the new science of nutrition was increasingly being organized to examine nutrition-related diseases such as rickets. This new knowledge of nutrition showed that, while the working-class population as a whole appeared to be getting enough to eat, many families were living on levels of nutrient intake below those now being thought essential for health. In particular, it was found that a large proportion of the low-paid and unemployed could not afford sufficient quantities of the 'protective foods', that is, milk, fresh vegetables, meat, fish and fruit. In scientific circles it was felt that enough was known about protective foods by the 1930s for the principles of the

Table 5.4 The industrial and retail supply of sugar 1938

Sugar use	Tonnes
Domestic	1,100,000
Catering establishments	110,000
Total	*1,210,000*
Manufacturing	
Chocolate and sugar confectionery	296,400
Bakers' flour, confectionery and cakes	184,000
Jams and preserves	162,400
Brewers	76,600
Biscuits	60,000
Condensed milk and crumb	50,600
Soft drinks	50,200
Syrup and treacle	45,000
Bakers' prepared materials	19,700
Ice cream	17,300
Table jellies	17,200
Medicinal	9,400
Bottling and canning	9,300
Candied peel	8,200
Cider	5,800
British wines	5,700
Bee feeding and synthetic honey	5,800
Pickles and sauces	4,500
Coffee essence	4,300
Cake, pudding and sponge mix	3,500
Vinegar brewing, home brewers and herb beer	3,200
Infants' and invalids' foods	1,000
Breakfast cereals	–
Miscellaneous	5,000
Total	*1,045,100*
Total home sugar supply	**2,255,100**

Source: adapted from Lyle (1950)

new science of nutrition to be put into practice on a wide scale. Bodies like the Medical Research Council wanted the government to tell people about the 'newer knowledge of nutrition' but as Mayhew (1988, p. 447) notes: 'The practical application of many of the principles of the new science had far-reaching economic, social and political implications, which proved bitterly controversial in Britain during the 1930s.'

Sugar consumption had also been singled out as a growing nutritional problem. The substitution of sugar (largely in the form of confectionery and as an ingredient in cakes, etc.) for bread was noted as the most conspicuous change in food habits by the government's Advisory Committee on Nutrition in 1937; they (and the League of Nations' nutritional experts) also regarded it with a certain alarm, since sugar, unlike even white bread, is wholly devoid of minerals and vitamins (Hammond 1946, p. 13). Experts also condemned its effects on children's teeth (Burnett 1989, p. 283). This countertrend, based on sugar's (poorer) organic properties, coincided, therefore, with the changing final use of sugar in the food supply. These societal changes in diet and the contribution of sugar in shaping and meeting these was rudely interrupted by the crisis of war.

Sugar supply during the second world war[11]

The underlying structure of the British sugar system did not change in any significant way with the outbreak of war. Naturally the constraints of food control and the severity of wartime conditions caused supply shortages and other restrictions which for many years disrupted the extent of sweetness in the diet. The main thrust of wartime strategy regarding sugar was the procurement of adequate supplies and the series of complex financial arrangements associated with this supply.

Rationing (12 oz per person per week initially) was introduced on 8 January 1940 and did not end until September 1953. Wartime control measures (taken from the outbreak of war) were given statutory effect by the Sugar Industry Act of 1942, with day-to-day control undertaken by the Sugar Division of the Ministry of Food. Food manufacturers were given percentage allocations of sugar calculated on the basis of their previous use over the year prior to war and on the nutritional significance of their products. So, for example, condensed-milk makers were allocated 75% of the amount that they had used over the previous year, sugar-confectionery makers 60%, etc.

Other wartime problems for sugar supply included developing and maintaining home sugar-beet production in the face of competition from other crops. This included arranging suitable incentives for farmers to grow sugar beet. For example, at one stage potatoes were a more attractive crop than beet to farmers because potatoes became more profitable to grow; the beet harvesting campaign produced problems in securing adequate labour and provisions were made to recruit prisoners of war; a zoning arrangement for the supply of sugar was put into force relating to the geographical location of beet factories and refiners to economize on transport and distribution costs, etc.

An example of the adjustments to the existing sugar structure that the crisis of wartime caused was the complex financial formula agreed between the refiners (after a proposal by Tate & Lyle) and the government. This was to enable refiners to be compensated for the monetary losses that they forecast as a result of complications arising from the Refining Agreement made in 1937 (later modified by the 1942 Sugar Industry Act).

Under the 1937 Industrial Agreement, the government had allocated the British Sugar Corporation quota rights to 720,000 tons of sugar a year. Of these rights, part of the agreement was that 220,000 tons would be bought by refiners at an agreed price. In other words, the refiners would pay a levy to the Corporation (thereby helping to relieve the Exchequer of a part of the cost of maintaining the home-grown sugar industry) which, in turn, allowed refiners to maintain their then present turnover. They had been able to achieve this with the help of duty protection granted in 1928 (that is, preferential duty on raw empire sugars in relation to foreign sugars) and this, enabling a much greater refining capacity, was the principal source of refiners' increased profits.

With the outbreak of war, however, rationing reduced home sales, and the export trade was virtually eliminated, thus reducing refiners' sugar production. The formula agreed between government and refiners compensated the latter for this reduction in markets on the basis of adjustments to their refining margins, taking into account three elements of commercial overheads (Hammond 1962, p. 104). This arrangement, brought about by wartime crisis, clearly demonstrates the already complex and intricate relationships that had developed between the refining industry, the newer beet industry and government and the importance of these relationships for the profitability and financial success of these businesses. These relationships, together with those of other vested interests including British farmers, colonial suppliers and the food industry, swinging one way and then another, set the pattern for the more recent history of the British sugar system and the resolution of periodic crises that have taken place in sugar's SOP for this period.

The peak in UK sugar supply: The 1950s to the 1970s

General food supply in the years immediately following the Second World War was more difficult than during the war period (Hollingsworth 1985). In 1946 sugar supplies entering the food system stood at 79% of pre-war supplies, but recovered to 83% in the period 1946–48. One area where the British government failed fully to recognize pent-up demand was for chocolates and sweets. These were taken off the ration in April 1949, but the desire for sweets was such that they had to be rationed again, this time until February 1953 (Hollingsworth 1985, p. 266).

In the late 1950s sugar entering the British system reached what has proved to be an all-time high. Supplies peaked at 52.4 kg per person per year (115.5 lb); around 2,600,000 tons (this includes sugar content of imported manufactured foods and sugar used in the production of alcoholic drinks). The table in Appendix I details the disposal of sugar used for food in the United Kingdom between 1934 and 1990 together with this converted to sugar available per head of population (in kg). These should be regarded as ballpark figures in that they do not represent final human consumption nor take into account such variables as, for example, wastage or food stocks. They do, however, give the best available picture of the supplies of sugar entering the UK food system taken as a whole. The data in Apppendix I show a decrease in supplies of around 21% during the thirty year period from the late 1950s to the 1980s.

However, an early post-war crisis for Tate & Lyle was the inclusion of sugar in the new Labour Government's nationalization programme. The 1945 Labour Government came to power with some level of commitment to collective ownership as the guarantee for the pre-eminence of national interest over private need. The sugar industry – in practice Tate & Lyle – was included in the second wave of nationalization plans drawn up in 1949. Tate & Lyle responded to this threat with a vigorous defence. This involved two strategies: first, a scheme to protect the interests of share-holders should the nationalizers have their way and, second, a campaign to stir up public opinion against nationalization at all levels.

To tackle the first problem, a hiving-off scheme was devised to group all assets not directly linked to refining in Britain in a holding company which would escape nationalization. By means of a complex process involving the movement of shares, two companies were created (Tate & Lyle Investment Ltd and Silvertown Services) which resulted in each original shareholder in Tate & Lyle becoming a shareholder of three legally independent com-panies. In this way, as Chalmin (1990, p. 241) describes:

> About £5 million worth of assets were 'saved' for the benefit of shareholders who, in the event of nationalisation, would in any case have been able to keep their shares in Tate & Lyle Investment Ltd and Silvertown Services since there was nothing to justify the national-isation of these two companies.

The attempt to stir up public opinion involved a wide-ranging campaign using publicity and public relations techniques. Perhaps the most well-known of these was the use of the company's sugar packets to get the message across. This began on 26 June 1949 when the first packages began leaving the factory printed with the slogan 'Tate not State'. The tactic took a dramatic and extremely successful turn with the invention and intro-duction of the 'Mr Cube' character (whose first public appearance was on 28 July 1949). The public anti-nationalization campaign lasted for more than two years and, with the defeat of the Labour Party in the October 1951 election, saw the end of the nationalization threat. Ironically, with the campaign and Mr Cube, Tate & Lyle and sugar had become household institutions in more than food alone. Paradoxically, state ownership was beaten off even though what was already extensive state intervention was to be sustained and even deepened over the post-war years.

For the state took on a larger role in coordinating and organizing the framework in which the whole sugar industry operated. The procurement of sugar after the Second World War was organized by the 1956 Sugar Act which saw the setting up of the Sugar Board. Its job was to regulate the supply of sugar to the British Sugar Corporation and to make new provision for the sugar-refining industry in the importation of sugar and related goods into the United Kingdom. The organization of the supply of sugar drew heavily on wartime experience. The Sugar Board continued to purchase Commonwealth sugar in line with the Commonwealth Sugar Agreement (CSA) signed in December 1951 by the Ministry of Food, as the importing party, and Commonwealth sugar industries as the exporting parties – the original signatories being the Queensland Sugar Board, the South Africa Sugar Association, the British West Indies Sugar Association, the Colonial Sugar Refining Company (Fiji) and the Mauritius Sugar Syndicate. The CSA, which ran from 1951 to 1974, allocated volume quotas (known as overall agreement quotas or OAQs) to individual countries as well as negotiated price quotas (known as NPQs) for raw sugars (the equivalent of around 1.8 million tonnes of raw sugar per year). The CSA, therefore, not only gave a guaranteed, preferential long-term market in the United Kingdom for volume sales, but also a guaranteed price for a certain proportion of this volume. For example, the West Indies and Guyana were allocated an original OAQ of 900,000 tons and an NPQ of 640,000 tons.

From 1956, the British market was also divided into zones between the refiners, that is, cane and beet supplies. In exchange for this deal Tate & Lyle refined 225,000 tons of beet sugar from British Sugar, and the land cultivated for beet was strictly controlled. Tate & Lyle continued to promise to the Exchequer that it would restrict its refining margins (profits) and would only change these according to variations in a number of cost parameters (Chalmin 1990, p. 479). Commenting on this arrangement and its impact on refining Chalmin says:

> [Sugar refining was] an activity which was perfectly risk-free: guaranteed margins, lack of competition and reliable supplies (of raw sugar) eliminated almost all risk in the management of sugar firms . . . for Tate & Lyle sugar refining in the United Kingdom thus provided an excellent source of regular profits. (pp. 479–80)

Under these arrangements the beet industry also continued to develop and expand with production between 1956/7 and 1971/72 rising from 698,000 tonnes of white sugar equivalents to 1,086,000 tonnes. Southgate (1984, p. 31) neatly sums up the state-run sugar market under the Sugar Board: 'The Sugar Board deserves far more notice than it has received as a model for reconciling, with a small staff and very little paper work, the regulation of trade by government with the mechanism of the free market.'

Between the 1950s and the 1970s, links with tropical empire sources of supply were strengthened or re-established while the production of sugar from home-grown beet was strictly regulated and controlled – contrary to the generalized argument of Friedmann and McMichael (1989). They argue that advanced capitalist countries, during what they describe as the second food regime, experienced a decline in markets for tropical exports, notably sugar, through import substitution. At the start of their second food regime, the United Kingdom is, therefore, an exception which can possibly be explained by historically contingent but longstanding reasons, that is, Britain's colonial links with cane producers and the political interests associated with sugar produced from cane.

THE THIRD SOP: 1973 TO THE PRESENT DAY

From 1973 to the present day the distinguishing feature of the sugar industry has been the new-found dominance of the industry based on sugar beet. The transition between these two sugar systems, that is from cane to beet, has been more ordered and gradual than that associated with the rise of cane over beet from 1914 onwards. The end of cane's sixty-year domination resulted in part from a dramatic restructuring of the UK industry when Britain joined the EEC and became part of the EC Sugar Regime within the CAP. Britain's beet industry then found itself allied with Europe's and, at first, beet interests threatened to wipe out the UK cane industry completely until a compromise was reached on the back of an exceptional peak in world sugar prices. However, as described in more detail in the next section, the next two decades were to witness considerable disruption within the UK sugar system, with cane interests as represented by Tate & Lyle, on two occasions in particular, coming close to regaining the upper hand.

The highly regulated production of sugar in Europe, which now included a restricted supply of sugar refined from cane, has forced major restructuring of the cane industry, but has also witnessed the expansion of the British beet industry to conform more closely with other EC countries. Ironically, this restructuring has allowed Tate & Lyle to become a monopoly refiner of cane in the United Kingdom, and the company has attempted on two occasions to buy British Sugar (the United Kingdom's beet monopoly) to make it the single sugar producer in Britain.

As well as the refining and processing industries polarizing into monopolies, the food industries using sugar as an ingredient have also become more highly concentrated. Supplies of sugar have been pushed further into the role of an industrial input with a large decline in household purchases. However, the total market for sugar has only declined slowly, from around 2.4 million tons in the mid-1970s to an average of 2.25 million tons throughout the 1980s. A major countertrend to sugar's declining nutritional status in the nation's diet has developed over the past decade, based on the organic role of sugar in food supply. Healthy eating messages have attracted widespread media coverage and have caught the popular imagination. One of the cornerstones of this appeal has been a reduction or moderation in the consumption of sugar. These three parts of sugar's SOP from 1973 – that is, the restructuring of the industry under the EC Sugar Regime, the industrialization of sugar and growing industry concentration, and sugar, nutrition and healthy eating – are discussed in more detail below.

The new sugar regime: The rise of sugar beet and the decline of cane

The most important recent act of restructuring of the sugar system involving the state was Britain's entry into the EEC in 1973. One consequence of this was protracted negotiations around the absorption of the British sugar market into the Sugar Regime of the CAP (see Appendix II for a description of the EC Sugar Regime). The conflict arose because the prize for the European beet industry was the prospect of taking over the part of the UK market then supplied by imported cane. This outcome would have presented a severe setback for Tate & Lyle and a possible disaster for Third World cane sugar producers. Extraordinary and difficult negotiations took place over who was to supply Britain's (deficit) market,[12] a major principle of the EC Sugar Regime being the protection of markets from imports, and home consumption to be supplied from EC-grown sugar.

At one stage an uncompromising stand-off was reached between beet and cane interests and it took the world-wide commodity crisis of 1972–74 for a compromise to be finally sealed. The agreement achieved was in part due to both sides looking to take advantage of the then record world prices for sugar. Factors that contributed to these price rises were the exceptionally bad weather and poor crops throughout the world and the large Soviet purchases which helped to exhaust stocks.

A compromise was reached in June 1974. EC beet growers agreed not to oppose separate negotiations for cane sugar to enter the EC under guarantee, and the Commonwealth sugar exporters agreed not to seek to restrict the domestic production of EC sugar in the absence of an international sugar agreement to which the EC adhered. In short, this meant the EC, a beet producer, introduced provisions for a third-country agricultural crop (cane sugar) to be imported into the EC with price and volume guarantees – an unprecedented arrangement for any part of the CAP. This agreement was incorporated in Protocol 3 of the Lome Convention signed in 1975; it allowed, for an indefinite period, up to 1.4 million tonnes raw value of sugar at a guaranteed price for a number of African, Caribbean and Pacific countries. Virtually all of this raw cane sugar is refined in the United Kingdom and destined for the British market.[13]

The first casualty of this agreement was Australia (a cane producer), overnight losing its UK market of around 330,000 tonnes (in white sugar equivalents – WSE) which had been guaranteed by the CSA. Second, Tate & Lyle was faced with massive refining overcapacity with no way of remedying this due to control over imports of cane raw materials into Europe. This heralded a period of restructuring in the cane-refining industry (including continued diversification by Tate & Lyle at a global level, an issue not discussed here). In 1976, Tate & Lyle took over Manbre & Garton, Britain's only other remaining refiner and, between 1977 and 1981, four refineries, with a total capacity of 950,000 tonnes, were shut. This left the United Kingdom with two remaining refineries (Thames, Silvertown and Westburn, Greenock), both owned by Tate & Lyle.

Britain's beet industry, however, received a substantial boost with an 'A' quota of 1,040,000 tonnes WSE and a 'B' quota of 286,000 (see Appendix II for an explanation of 'A' and 'B' quotas). The British Sugar Corporation responded with a programme of expansion on three fronts: (1) to expand and modernize both its beet-slicing and white-sugar processing capacity; (2) to increase the area of beet grown by UK farmers; and (3) to expand its sales into those parts of the British market that traditionally had not been part of its marketing zone. A major investment plan was undertaken over the five year period 1976–1980 which cost £150 million (at 1975 prices) (Harris 1984). The development of beet was also very much in tune with the British government's overall policy of home-based agricultural expansion outlined in such papers as 'Food from Our Own Resources' (1975) and the White Paper 'Farming and the Nation' (1979).

During the 1980s many of the consequences arising from the restructuring of the British sugar system caused by the EC Sugar Regime became apparent. In Britain, the market for beet increased from one-third to half of British supplies. In addition, the British market was liberalized in the sense that the British government's direct control ended, together with the market sharing (zoning) arrangements between beet and cane. It also became apparent that, under the Sugar Regime's financial structure, the refining margins on cane worked out less favourably than those for beet processing. British Sugar used this position to start a price war in the mid-1980s but, since then, British Sugar has abandoned its aggressive price strategy, and the profitability of both itself and Tate & Lyle has increased substantially (Monopolies and Mergers Commission 1991).

Today, Tate & Lyle's Thames refinery at Silvertown is the world's largest with a capacity to process one million tonnes of raw sugar a year (Greenock has a capacity of 145,000 tonnes). By 1990, Tate & Lyle Sugars (TLS), the unit carrying on sugar-refining operations in the United Kingdom, only contributed 14% to the group's turnover and 16% of its operating profit. Meanwhile, British Sugar has become the third largest producer of sugar in Europe, converting 9 million tonnes of beet into 1.3

million tonnes of sugar and 700,000 tonnes of animal feed in its twelve factories. Between them, Tate & Lyle and British Sugar produce more than 90% of Britain's sugar (the rest comes via sugar merchants/brokers and is supplied in accordance with the EC Sugar Regime) – a market of around 2.3 million tonnes, worth nearly £1 billion.

However, this apparent strength and stability in the current sugar-processing industries glosses over more than two decades of turmoil. The period between 1970 and 1980 saw the transition from the cane sugar system to the beet sugar system. The key point here is that Tate & Lyle successfully preserved its cane operations through negotiating a phased restructuring – the company publishing, for example, its proposals in March 1977 as the 'Cane Sugar Rationalisation Plan'.

During the 1980s British Sugar became the real focus of attention and speculation in the domestic market with a series of successful and un-successful take-over bids. The first of these bids, in this case unwelcome, was by S. & W. Berisford initiated in April 1980. Berisford was a holding company for an international group of companies, with a wide range of activities including its being the largest sugar merchant in the United Kingdom. It handled almost half of all sugar sold by British Sugar and around a third of sugar sold by Tate & Lyle. The total tonnage of sugar merchanted by Berisford's Sugar Division over the three year period prior to 1981 represented approximately 37% of total UK consumption (Mono-polies and Mergers Commission 1981).

As a result, the bid was referred to the Monopolies and Mergers Commission (MMC) which, reporting in March 1981, stated that they found it hard to identify any way in which the proposed merger would be likely to operate positively for the public benefit. However, the MMC suggested that this might be remedied if, first, Berisford ceased trading in Tate & Lyle sugar and sugar products and, second, if British Sugar was maintained as a separate subsidy without major changes in its activities or purposes and to publish separate annual reports and accounts with supplementary material. There was a note of dissent from one member who argued that the proposed merger should not be allowed to proceed on the basis that the merger would disrupt British Sugar's good industrial relations and Berisford had little if any experience in handling such complex and balanced relationships.

In its evidence to the MMC, British Sugar gave its reasons that it felt the merger would operate against the public interest and also argued, in what was to prove to be accurate foresight, that British Sugar would have to compete with other divisions of the Berisford group resources, and that it and the whole UK beet industry could be prejudiced severely by a downturn in Berisford's other trading operations.

With the MMC's conditional approval, Berisford announced that it would continue with its bid, which valued British Sugar at £200 million. However, the company did not hold enough shares in its own right or promises to sell from other shareholders to be successful. In June 1981 Berisford staged a stock-market raid on British Sugar's shares and managed to raise its stake to 39.56%, but this was still not enough for control of the company. It was now that government action became decisive.

The government, through the Treasury, held a 15% stake in British Sugar from its formation in 1936. This was changed in 1964 when the authorized share capital was increased, giving the Treasury 11.25% and the Sugar Board 25%, taking the total Crown holding to 36.25%. In 1977 the share capital was increased again, but the government sold its rights, reducing its holding to the 24.17% that it held at the time of the proposed Berisford take-over (Monopolies and Mergers Commission 1981). In evidence to the MMC the Ministry of Agriculture Fisheries and Food (MAFF) said that it was the government's policy to reduce the involvement of the state in industry and that it would not be the government's intention to retain its holding in British Sugar indefinitely. But no decision had been taken about how or when the government shares would be sold. The decision finally came in July 1981 when the government sold its stake in British Sugar for £44 million, ending forty-five years of involvement as a shareholder. However, the government had announced that it would only sell its own shares to an existing shareholder with more than 42.56% of the British Sugar capital. Berisford were stuck at a 40% shareholding and their take-over bid elapsed. In November 1981 British Sugar bought 14.7% of the capital of Rank Hovis MacDougal (RHM). RHM retaliated by buying 10.5% in British Sugar the next week. In July 1982, Berisford bought RHM's block of British Sugar shares and finally, after a take-over battle lasting more than two years, had acquired British Sugar.

Under Berisford, British Sugar began a period of aggressive marketing and sought to maximize productivity. Beet production, for example, was rationalized from seventeen factories in 1980/81 to thirteen in 1985/86, and British Sugar, in May 1984, launched its biggest-ever advertising and promotions campaign to promote its Silver Spoon brands. The media campaign, as part of this £2 million expenditure, centred on double-page spreads in women's magazines. It was planned to reach 80% of house-wives, each of whom would see the advertising at least ten times. A significant part of investment was earmarked to 're-educate' British house-wives to 'appreciate the usefulness of speciality sugar' (Heasman 1987).

By the end of 1985 British Sugar again became the subject of take-over interest. In the summer of 1985 Berisford and Tate & Lyle informally considered a general proposition relating to a possible merger of Tate & Lyle Sugars and British Sugar. By the end of the year, Tate & Lyle told Berisford it was interested in acquiring British Sugar outright. In the meantime the British food company Hillsdown Holdings plc had indicated an interest in British Sugar as well as the Italian company Ferruzzi. Ferruzzi, an agro-business conglomerate and Italy's third largest private concern, already controlled Eridania which held 45% of the Italian sugar market and Beghin-Say which held 33% of the French market. With British Sugar giving the company 50% of the British market, it would push up Ferruzzi's European market share from 18% to 22.5%.

During January and February 1986, considerable progress was made in formulating proposals by which Ferruzzi would acquire Berisford (and hence British Sugar). But on 4 April, Hillsdown made an all-shares bid for Berisford (valuing British Sugar at £488 million). On 30 April Tate & Lyle also announced its intention to bid for Berisford. Both proposed bids were referred to the MMC. Following the reference, Hillsdown announced on 27 May that it was not going to pursue its bid and sold its Berisford shares to Ferruzzi which was still on course to buy British Sugar. Both Tate & Lyle's and Ferruzzi's proposed bids were referred to the MMC (in July 1986). In November, before the MMC had reported, Berisford and Ferruzzi exchanged conditional contracts for sale. However, when the MMC published the results of its inquiry in February 1987, it stated that both Ferruzzi's and Tate & Lyle's bids would operate against the public interest (Monopolies and Mergers Commission 1987), and the government accepted the recommendations and stopped the proposed take-over by either company. Following the MMC report, Associated British Foods (ABF) entered the fray by building up a 23.5% shareholding in Berisford by buying Ferruzzi's stake. Its subsequent take-over bid was cleared without referral to the MMC, but the collapse in world share prices in October 1987 led ABF to reconsider and then withdraw its offer.

However, Berisford still wanted to sell British Sugar. By 1990 the successful sale of British Sugar had become crucial since the money raised would be central to the process of restructuring the Berisford group. Berisford was experiencing considerable financial difficulties following investments, principally in New York property, that had turned sour. Tate & Lyle announced its intention to make an offer for British Sugar in September 1990. In the same month the proposed bid was referred to the MMC. Subsequently Berisford entered into a provisional agreement to sell British Sugar to ABF – a bid that was not referred to the MMC. Tate & Lyle told the MMC that its offer for British Sugar had not been withdrawn and that it would wish to proceed with the offer if the transaction with ABF were not completed. So the MMC inquiry continued. ABF and Berisford proceeded with their negotiations over British Sugar, and ABF finally acquired British Sugar for £880 million in January 1991. The MMC report, published in February 1991, concluded that the merger between Tate & Lyle and British Sugar might be expected to operate against the public interest.

Sugar as an industrial input: Growing concentration

This section considers sugar as an industrial input. To put the current position into historical context and illustrate sugar's changing role, the industrial use of sugar in the 1980s is compared with those of 1938 and 1964/65.

By 1988/89 the industrial market for sugar had risen to 72%, with total tonnage entering the market at around 2.25 million tonnes. In some foods, the use of sugar in manufactured food has remained remarkably consistent. In others, there have been notable changes. Unfortunately, published sources that detail industrial sugar disposals are not directly comparable and can only be interpreted as giving orders of magnitude (Heasman 1988). However, in all cases, chocolate and sugar confectionery combined remain the most important food categories that purchase sugar as an industrial input. Using the 1938 data as a baseline for comparison, this industry accounted for around 28% of industrial supplies (296,000 tons), in 1965/66 35% (359,000 tons), in 1984/85 26% (385,000 tonnes) and in 1988/89 27% (est. 406,500 tonnes). Also consistent users over this period are manufacturers producing cakes, biscuits and flour confectionery. Direct comparisons from published data are not possible but, to give a feel for the importance of this sector, in 1938 bakers' flour confectionery, cakes and biscuits used 23% of industrial supply (244,000 tons); in 1965/66 cakes, biscuits and cereals 17% (190,000 tons); in 1984/85 baking, biscuits and cereals 16% (240,000 tonnes); in 1988/89 biscuits, baking and cereals 16% (est. 237,000 tonnes).

The major new use of sugar has been in the production of soft drinks. In 1938 less than 5% and, in 1965/66, less than 12% of industrial use was categorized for soft-drink use. By 1984/85 this had risen to 19% (275,000 tonnes) and by 1989 to nearly 23% (est. 343,500 tonnes), making soft drinks the largest user of sugar if chocolate confectionery and sugar confectionery are regarded as separate categories.

From the available information it is difficult to tell which other product categories have gained or diminished as users of sugar. Table 5.5 gives a recent breakdown of the shares of industrial uses by individual food and other industry categories for the year up to September 1989. As can be seen, the three sectors of soft drinks, chocolate and sugar confectionery account for half of all industrial sugar sales.

While industrial sales have gained in volume, retail sales of sugar for household use have fallen consistently, with an especially sharp drop after the sugar shortages and price rises of the mid-1970s. The NFS, for example, dramatically charts the fall in household purchases from 25 kg per person per year in 1966 to just under 13.5 kg per person per year by 1984 (MAFF, various years). Or, looking at household purchases recorded by the NFS from 1980, over a ten-year period it would seem that sugar consumption had halved, but in fact, as Table 5.6 shows, total sugar entering the UK food supply has remained static and even rose slightly in the late 1980s.

Table 5.5 Shares of industrial sugar sales by individual food and other industry sectors (year up to September 1989)

Sector	% share of sales
Soft drinks	22.9
Chocolate confectionery	14.9
Sugar confectionery	12.2
Biscuits	7.7
Preserves	5.6
Bakery	5.3
Bakers' sundries	5.3
Canners	4.7
Packers	4.7
Brewers/cider	3.2
Cereals	2.8
Milk products	2.5
Pharmaceutical	2.1
Ice cream	1.7
Frozen foods	0.2
Other	4.2

Note: Estimated sugar going for industrial use in 1989 was around 1,532,000 tonnes.

Source: Monopolies and Mergers Commission (1991)

Table 5.6 Sugar for food in the United Kingdom, 1980–90

Year	Sugar supply ('000 tonnes)	Equivalent per head of population (kg)
1980	2,254	40.01
1981	2,188	38.83
1982	2,317	41.15
1983	2,236	39.68
1984	2,264	40.10
1985	2,227	39.33
1986	2,233	39.34
1987	2,276	39.98
1988	2,301	40.32
1989	2,336	40.81
1990	2,320	40.41

Note: Includes sugar used in the manufacture of other foods and subsequently exported. Excludes sugar in imported manufactured goods.

Source: *Annual Abstract of Statistics* (Central Statistical Office 1992)

As well as the sugar-processing industry becoming more concentrated, the manufacturers using it as an industrial input were also changing as they sought to achieve economies of scale and the mass production of foodstuffs. A very small number of both industrial and retail customers became responsible for distributing sugar and sweetness throughout the entire food chain. In 1989 ten customers accounted for around 95% of TLS's retail business and their twelve largest industrial customers took 75% of TLS's industrial turnover. For British Sugar, ten customers again accounted for 95% of retail sales, but their ten largest industrial customers were responsible for 60% of industrial sales (Monopolies and Mergers Commission 1991).[14]

Goodman *et al.* (1987) document the growing concentration of the food industry into large oligopolistic producers with multi-plant operations and barriers to market entry typically created, not as much by product differentiation supported by high levels of advertising expenditure, as by scale economies. This description of industrial structure can be used to fit a number of well-known sweet foods such as soft drinks, confectionery and cereals for example.

Of further concern to Goodman *et al.* is product fractioning and fabricated foods. By this they mean that the breaking down of food ingredients into their constituent parts, based on proteins, carbohydrates and so on, and then the recombination of these components to extend the range and concept of products even to the point of redefining conventional notions of food (1987, p. 88). Sugar, as an industrial input, has been subject to both of these trends. Its use has been concentrated into a small number of large, mass-production industries but, at the same time, it has been used in the creation and the fabrication of a diverse range of new foods and drinks. Its organic properties in this part of the food system have, therefore, been of paramount importance. The expansion of sweetness can be traced through all parts of the food system, from processed meats to convenience foods and drinks, to such an extent that a common term to denote the use of sugar in the general UK food system is as a hidden ingredient. In addition, while early industries grew and developed around sugar's unique organic qualities, such as confectionery, its versatility has contributed to product differentiation and the modernization and reinvention of new products in these industries to adapt to changing market conditions, for example frozen desserts, dry powder mixes, new confectionery brands, breakfast cereals, etc. Concomitant with these processes has been declining home use, as in cooking. But, as packet sugar was being thrown out of the home in one form it has been brought back in again through manufactured products.

Sugar, nutrition and 'healthy eating'

In recent years, but especially from 1983 onwards, at the consumption end of the SOP, new concerns about sugar have been voiced from what can be termed non-agricultural bodies. The impact of these different and new factors on sugar's SOP has been to question the very need for there to be much sugar in the average diet at all.

The basis for this attention on the consumption of sugar is that it may contribute to a number of serious 'Western diseases of affluence'. In fact, almost as impressive as the gains and increases in sugar production and consumption throughout the world has been the research and scientific output examining sugar consumption's effects on ill health. The Report of Sugars Task Force from the United States' Food and Drug Administration, for example, which evaluated the health aspects of sugars contained in carbohydrate sweeteners, lists more than 900 references in its bibliography (Glinsmann *et al.* 1986). In Britain, while one part of government policy was (and is) concerned with securing adequate production and supplies of sugar, another was advocating limiting consumption by individuals as one of the cornerstones of UK nutritional advice and as part of a campaign to change the nation's diet to help prevent a range of diseases and illnesses.

In the mid-1980s sugar in the diet had become a major consumption issue and an arena of confrontation. This concern about dietary sugar was centred around three broad areas. First, sugar (sucrose), in the quantities being consumed, was the cause of, or contributed significantly to, certain diseases and illnesses. Second, sucrose had become a major source of refined carbohydrate, devoid of fibre, vitamins and minerals and, therefore, contributed to an unbalanced diet. Linked to this is the observation that, as income in a country rises, the proportion of energy supplied by carbohydrate decreases, but often concealed within this trend is a change from starch foods (especially complex carbohydrates) to increased consumption of sugar (Lee 1981). So, for example, in 1962 sugar in all its forms (excluding its use in brewing and distilling) provided 37% of total UK dietary carbohydrate, about twice as much as at the turn of the century (Greaves and Hollingsworth 1964). Third, putting it crudely, the 'sweet–fat' argument against sugar is that sucrose makes fat more palatable and, as used in processed food products, encourages people to eat more fatty foods and, hence, more fat than current nutritional advice suggests is beneficial.

Counterarguments to these positions also abound: for example, sugar's role in the aetiology of disease and illness is becoming more and more controversial. In addition, it is argued that while some people may fall into high-risk groups from the overconsumption of certain foodstuffs, nutrition policy should be targeted, not at the general population, but towards those sections of the population at risk. There is also the idea, for the general population, that there are no 'bad' foods as such, just 'poor' individual diets and the key to good nutrition is for individuals to adopt a more balanced diet. This view presupposes the potentially beneficial role of nutrition education and information, especially for children.

Sugar has been linked to a number of diseases and illnesses. These have included dental caries; problems of the stomach (gastric and duodenal ulcers); problems of the large and small intestine; metabolic problems, such as overweight, vitamin and mineral deficiency, diabetes mellitus, cardiac and circulatory diseases; some cancers; and the influence on and alteration of behaviour (Schiwech 1985). A recent government review of dietary sugars and human disease, however, gave evidence that suggests that sugar (sucrose) posed a limited direct threat to human health other than in the case of dental caries (Department of Health 1989).[15]

In Britain, since 1974, there have been no less than twelve reports published by authoritative bodies, including government, that give dietary advice and recommendations including information about sugar consumption (Heasman 1989). The most important, in terms of publicity and therefore impact on the nation as a whole, is the NACNE (1983) report which, for the first time in the United Kingdom, gave quantified nutritional guidelines. For sugar, its long-term recommendation was that sucrose intakes should be reduced to 20kg per person per year by the end of the 1990s – a virtual halving of then current sugar consumption. Singled out for special attention by the NACNE report was that in calculating this total, the sucrose content of snacks, sweets and drinks between meals should be limited to 10kg per person per year. This advice applied especially to sugar intakes in confectionery and soft drinks. Ironically, increases in volume and value of sales of both soft drinks and confectionery have been particularly strong throughout the late 1980s and early 1990s.

The success of soft drinks and confectionery in the marketplace (and the sugar industry itself in countering what has been a sustained period of negative commentary upon sugar) suggests that the public are selective about their beliefs and behaviour regarding nutritional advice, and other factors play an important part in determining final consumption. What is perhaps just as important as publicly available scientific advice about sugar and health is public perception and mythology surrounding the effects of sugar consumption on health and the exploitation of this, not only by the media, but food manufacturers and retailers as well. For example, in a review of a random sample of British regional newspaper cuttings between September 1987 and October 1990 that reported on sugar, diet and health, a total of twenty-five different illnesses, diseases and ailments were associated or linked with sugar consumption (Heasman 1991). These were: pre-menstrual tension, headaches, high blood pressure, diabetes, overweight/being fat, eating fads, premature death and degenerative diseases, unhealthy hair, shorter life, mood changes, lower natural fertility, high blood sugar levels, dental caries/tooth decay, allergies, heart disease, disressing menopause, sugar addiction/craving, criminal behaviour, irritability and lack of concentration, ugly legs, thrush, feeling the cold more acutely, certain cancers, raised blood cholesterol, and lowered resistance to

117

disease. Clearly, from these newspaper cuttings, scientific/medical information on sugar consumption, disease and illness took on some interesting angles when used in the realm of media information.

There can be little doubt that nutrition, diet and healthy living issues (among others) have created an unprecedented focus at the consumption end of food supply. For sugar (and other foodstuffs), there has been a continual publicity war involving all parts of the information and media system. However, while there has been little substantive change to many parts of sugar's current SOP, there have been many new opportunities, using other food systems, for accumulation in the market for sweetness. First, it will be noted from earlier tables that the vast drop in sugar supplies entering the food system occurred before the 1980s. However, it was during the 1980s that the publicity on healthy eating was at its height, and food and drink manufacturers started to fall over themselves to produce sugar-free and sugar-reduced products. Supplies of sugar had levelled off in the 1980s (see Table 5.6), but with continuing pressure on retail sales. However, the latter is consistent with longer-term market trends, and although healthy eating has an influence, other factors, such as less food production in the house, less sugar used in tea drinking, changing demographics, the move to convenience foods and eating outside the home, all play a part.

In addition, the sugar industry launched an unprecedented £12 million advertising campaign in June 1990 to promote sugar as a natural and healthy product. Tate & Lyle and British Sugar joined forces for the three-year campaign which aimed to explain that health risks associated with sugar had been exaggerated and, therefore, sought to correct the image of sugar.

Along with these factors, and of special importance to the total market for sweetness in the United Kingdom, has been the creation or further development of 'sugar-free', 'no added sugar' and 'sugar-reduced' products. Heasman (1990a), concentrating on the use of sweeteners, describes in detail trends in the development of the UK market for 'lite' products during the 1980s. Far from artificial sweeteners simply substituting for sugar in food product systems, these products run parallel to full-sugar product ranges creating a separate and distinct new food product system. The overall result is to expand the total market for sweetness – see Table 5.7, for example, which shows the volume growth in both sugar-free and full-sugar soft drinks. MacKay (1987) argues, in the case of the United States, that sweeteners have so far created new products which supplement but do not directly compete with sugar-sweetened products, although they may have prevented or impeded growth of sugar products that might otherwise have occurred in the absence of artificial sweeteners.

The long-term reduction of sugar purchases does, however, produce problems at the production end around business expansion, investment decisions and returns on capital employed (it is getting harder to justify

Table 5.7 Volume sales of low-calorie carbonates 1981–87 (million litres)

Year	1 Total carbonates	2 Low-calorie carbonates	1–2
1981	2,040	84	1,956
1982	2,180	95	2,085
1983	2,390	139	2,251
1984	2,550	185	2,365
1985	2,735	221	2,514
1986	3,075	281	2,794
1987	3,290	397	2,893

Source: The British Soft Drinks Association (1988)

increased sugar quotas when markets continue to underperform). Diet and health advice not only pushes against market growth, but attaches a negative stigma to the whole idea of sugar in the diet. More recent campaigns to limit sugar consumption, on the basis of this analysis, really hit against sugar's SOP and, from the sugar industry's point of view, represent serious threats – as in the lobbying against the advertising to children of sugar-containing foods (Young 1987).

The role of science and technology in recent years in transforming society's understanding of diet and nutrition and the impact of this new knowledge on food supply in advanced capitalist countries is not fully addressed in the food systems literature (in contrast to biotechnology!). In the case of sugar in the United Kingdom (and for other foodstuffs) this started to prove increasingly important from the mid-1970s onwards. It possibly still holds the key to understanding the future direction of food consumption trends, but the theoretical examination of sugar's SOPs suggests that for total sugar supply this needs to be modified in the light of other (more important) factors. For example, coupled with changing demographic trends (in advanced capitalist societies) the role of food as preventative health versus pleasure, enjoyment or functional use has placed sugar in an ambivalent position. Sugar is also considered a lower-class food, with the NFS showing the fastest decline in retail sugar purchases in higher-income groups. Parallel to this, the marketing of foods and drinks using low-calorie sweeteners has often appealed to higher-income groups (and is priced accordingly). Ironically, the better educated, wealthier consumer has preferred food and drink sweetened with an artificial (inorganic) chemical additive rather than natural sugar because sugar is now considered to have undesirable (organic) properties, but clearly the taste for sweetness remains.

119

CONCLUDING REMARKS

To explain sugar's SOPs this century, it has been necessary to look at the role of governments and agricultural policy in structuring and restructuring the markets for sugar, the historical dominance of the cane-refining industry, and why sugar has been able to adapt to changing eating habits and consumption patterns, not least in recent years when it has been caught in a squeeze between readily available supplies of sugar substitutes and demand trends towards sugar-free healthy eating.

Within the SOP framework, two broad analytical themes have been employed and developed to explain the persistence and the widespread production and consumption of sugar in Britain. As a result, sugar's SOPs are conceptualized through an analysis of coexisting tendencies, producing and reproducing structures, with both subject to historically contingent outcomes. From this perspective, the presence of inherent tendencies linked to the imperatives of capitalist accumulation and profitability has led historically to three distinct sugar systems in the United Kingdom: pre-1914, from 1914 to 1973 and from 1973 to the present day. Second, the persistence of sugar and the food systems to which it has been attached have been dependent upon sugar's unique organic properties and how it has materially functioned within food systems.

These two themes, that is the coexistence of tendency–structure–contingency and the organic properties of sugar, are also suggested as a more general and appropriate basis for the analysis of the sugar systems than the undoubted insights suggested by the recent food systems literature, as in Goodman *et al.* (1987), Goodman and Wilkinson (1990), Goodman and Redclift (1991a), Friedmann (1982, 1993) and Friedmann and McMichael (1989). While these approaches have many strengths, they leave a residue of anomalies in explaining sugar's persistence in the UK food system; they provide only a partial and piecemeal understanding of the sugar systems and the historical passage between them.

A study of sugar is now less important for its consumption from the packet or bowl, because an intrinsic characteristic of much industrialized food supply is its sweetness. As well as the many well-known, modern processed foods and drinks that are sweet such as biscuits, cakes, jams, puddings, confectionery and soft drinks, other food categories like dairy products, cereals, prepared convenience meals and snack foods are often sweet and successfully exploit the human innate liking for and pleasure in the sweet taste.

Remarkably the principal ingredient used as the source of sweetness in the nation's diet over the past century has been and still remains refined sucrose. At the start of this century, on average, sugar and syrups provided 14% of the UK population's calorie supplies (Greaves and Hollingsworth 1966) and, by 1987, sucrose was still providing 14% of food energy to the average diet

(Department of Health 1991). However, as has been described, over the intervening years significant changes have taken place in the production and consumption patterns of sugar and the role of sweetness in foodstuffs. Its persistence in industrial food supply stands as a testament to its versatility as a food and the ingenuity of those who have brought it to our tables.

For example, in terms of the restructuring of the sugar industry, the past eight decades has seen the United Kingdom develop its own home-produced sugar supply; marketing arrangements and the procurement of sugar have been the subject of several Acts of Parliament and other government reviews including three reports from the MMC; British sugar supply has been secured through complex state-to-state treaties and nego-tiations culminating in Britain's entry into the EEC in 1973; and sugar has become an integral part of an industrialized, highly processed and heavily concentrated foods complex. More recently the (over)consumption, nutri-tional and dietary role of sugar, especially its relation to a number of illnesses and diseases, has been fiercely contested.

Sugar serves, therefore, as an example of how choice and consumption of food are influenced by the food system in all its components. Decline in sugar consumption from the packet, for example, sees it reincorporated in the diet through other means such as soft drinks. Specific food manu-facturing industries, like confectionery and soft drinks, have grown around sugar as an ingredient and exploit its unique organic properties, including its adaptability in the production process. In the same way, sugar contributes but also reacts to changing eating habits that have developed around wider changes in society, not least working practices and the changing nature of the family and household. In this sense sugar has become divorced from its agricultural roots and has been commodified through a wide range of packaged food and drink products to supply the growing population of consumers who have become heavily dependent upon, and incorporated into, commercial food markets.

Sugar, as a refined ingredient, is a product of modern industrial food supply; the founding fathers (and sons) of Tate & Lyle, for example, did not begin their sugar-refining operations until the 1860s. For sugar the dynamic of appropriationism, that is the action of industrial capitals to reduce the importance of nature in the production process, at least as an unpredictable capricious force beyond their direction and control (Goodman and Redclift 1991a), has been a prevailing feature in each of sugar's SOPs. At the same time a countertrend has been the growing economies of scale achieved in refining and reliance upon the subsequent massive inputs from nature required to secure profitable refining margins. Further along the sugar chain, manufacturing industries have also become dependent on regular supplies of sugar as an industrial input in their food-processing systems.

The peculiarity of its organic properties has allowed sugar to gain an important role in the nation's diet as illustrated by the fact that it has

121

become such a problem in human nutrition. Sugar's organic properties have shaped consumption patterns and helped to introduce foods into the diet creating a nutrition issue by pushing the parameters of human nutrition in both positive and negative ways. This has enabled competitors in the sweetness market to make substitutionism seem more attractive to many food manufacturers, but at the same time reinforcing the sweetness of the modern diet. In the meantime healthy eating advice on sugar is countered by the sugar industry spending millions of pounds on improving sugar's consumer image. The fate of seventeen African, Caribbbean and Pacific (ACP) countries and around ten thousand UK farmers who supply Britain's sugar hinge on these important issues. But new uses for sugar are also emerging, as the sugar industry looks and lobbies for new outlets, such as becoming the feedstock for the biotechnology and chemical industries.

The current SOP for sugar has experienced almost continuous change and restructuring over the past twenty years; not so much a crisis, but the continual upheaval of underlying tendencies being played out. Munton (1992) argues that the global food system is itself being restructured and a new international food regime is emerging. He outlines three main sets of processes at work in creating the new regime: technological advance, changes in ownership patterns and the liberalization of agricultural trade. However, as argued here, for the impact of these to be examined rigorously in the context of sugar, it has to be regarded as belonging to a unique SOP with historically specific structures and outcomes that shift over time.

APPENDIX I: REFINED SUGAR DISPOSALS FOR FOOD IN THE UNITED KINGDOM 1934–1990

Year	Tons of refined sugar (in thousands)	Supplies per head of population (kg)
1934–38 average	2,113	47.1[a]
1941–45 average	1,517	31.4
1946	1,657	34.3
1947	1,781	36.2
1948	1,845	36.5
1949	1,936	38.8
1950	1,749	34.2
1951	1,930	43.1[b]
1952	1,833	41.0
1953	2,145	44.8
1954	2,365	48.1
1955	2,475	49.4

1956	2,588	49.8
1957	2,703	50.7
1958	2,410	52.4
1959	2,609	50.9
1960	2,622	51.2
1961	2,679	51.5
1962[c]	2,618	50.4
1963	2,693	50.6
1964	2,542	48.8
1965	2,661	49.0
1966	2,618	49.4
1967	2,604	48.5
1968	2,614	47.9
1969	2,653	48.4
1970[d]	2,704	48.1
1971	2,677	47.2
1972	2,692	47.8
1973	2,657	47.0
1974	2,944	47.9
1975	2,199	42.8
1976	2,445	42.9
1977	2,436	42.6
1978	2,459	42.9
1979	2,425	42.3
1980	2,254	40.01[e]
1981	2,188	38.83
1982	2,317	41.15
1983	2,236	39.68
1984	2,264	40.10
1985	2,227	39.33
1986	2,233	39.34
1987	2,276	39.98
1988	2,301	40.32
1989	2,336	40.81
1990	2,320	40.41

Notes: [a] Including sugar in all home-produced manufactured foods.
[b] From 1951, including sugar in all home-produced and imported manufactured foods and in brewing, but excluding sugar in exported manufactured foods.
[c] From 1962, including sugar in the manufacture of other foods subsequently exported.
[d] From 1970, disposals are measured in metric tonnes (1,000 kg), the equivalent of 0.984 (long) tons as measured previously.
[e] From 1980, per capita figures for sugar are not published. Figures are calculated by dividing total refined sugar disposals (tonnes) by total population figures.

Source: Central Statistical Office (various years)

APPENDIX II: THE EC SUGAR REGIME

The EC Sugar Regime, like other regimes of the CAP, is a complex mechanism of financial measures designed to support production of sugar equally across all member states. For excellent descriptions of the functioning and measures that have evolved to support sugar in the EC, also covering some of the complexities of the CAP, see the work of Harris *et al.* (1983) and Harris (1985). Also background can be found in *Halsbury's Laws of England* (Halsbury 1986).

Proposals for incorporating sugar in the CAP were not made until March 1966. The differences in pricing and trading policies of the then five producing countries of the EC made agreements on the basic principles very difficult and it did not finally come into operation until July 1968. The degree of regulation of the market in sugar is probably greater than any other sector of agriculture (Halsbury 1986). The specific features of the regime can be summarized under the following points:

1 Intervention buying (that is, national intervention agencies have an obligation to buy, at intervention prices or minimum market prices, EC produce offered to them) does not apply to the farm product (sugar beet and sugar cane), but to the processed product – raw or white sugar.
2 Intervention buying is restricted by a series of quotas (see below).
3 A system of production levies operate which means that, in principle, producers (that is, growers and processors) pay the cost of disposing of surpluses.
4 There is free trade within the EC, but a system of levies and refunds on trade with other countries outside the EC are designed to insulate the European market from fluctuations in world prices and to allow the disposal on world markets of European production surplus to consumption.
5 There is guaranteed access to the EC market for specified third-country sugars from the ACP states under the Lome Convention and from India under a similar arrangement.
6 The regime covers two different farm crops producing sugar – sugar beet and sugar cane.

Sugar quotas

Each region of the EC is allocated annual 'basic quantities' of sugar (annual quotas, prices, etc., are renegotiated at five-yearly intervals). These are known as 'basic quantities A' (A quota) and 'basic quantities B' (B quota), the difference between the quotas being the amount of production levy due (see p. 125). For each marketing year (1 July to 30 June) member states allocate A and B quota production (all to British Sugar in the case of the United Kingdom). 'C' sugar refers to any quantity of sugar produced by a processor in a given marketing year outside the sum of its A and B quotas and must be sold outside the EC. To obtain the sugar beet to fulfil their quotas, processors sign pre-season sowing delivery contracts for a quantity of beet expected to meet its quotas. In the United Kingdom, this is arranged between British Sugar and the National Farmers' Union.

The system of prices for sugar

The system of prices consists of a target price, a threshold price and an intervention price for sugar, and basic and minimum prices for sugar beet. The target price is the theoretical internal market price for white sugar from which other sugar prices are worked out. The threshold price applies at the EC Frontier and is the minimum price at which sugar may be imported from non-member countries and is designed to protect EC sugar when the world price for sugar is lower than the EC price. The intervention price is the guaranteed minimum price for white sugar. In principle, the price at which government agencies must buy sugar produced within the A and B quotas creates supply that cannot be sold in the EC and is a surplus. But, despite the Sugar Regime being essentially an intervention buyer of last resort, in practice sugar is rarely held in stocks, since any surplus is usually sold into the world market with the help of export refunds (that is, the difference between the EC price and the current world price). The effective support price is the intervention price plus storage cost levy and represents the minimum market price for sugar, as the storage cost levy has to be paid on all sales.

For sugar beet, the 'basic' price is derived from the white sugar intervention price and is based on sugar yields from sugar beet. However, it is the 'minimum' prices for beet derived from the basic price of beet that are the guaranteed prices to beet growers since they take into account the cost of production levies on A and B quota sugar.

Production levies

These were introduced as a means of recouping for the EC budget the cost of export refunds on quota sugar exports to the world market. They represent a percentage charge on quota sugar prices, small for A and larger for B. The introduction of production levies (including a later 'elimination levy') further complicates the costings of sugar production and the cost of the Sugar Regime.

It is not possible in this note to go into the full financial and production arrangements of the EC Sugar Regime. Suffice it to say that the size of quota is one of the key factors in profitability. For example, Paul Gardini of the Ferruzzi Group, commenting during the Group's proposed take-over of British Sugar in 1986, which would have pushed Ferruzzi's European market share up from 18% to 22.5%, is reported as saying: 'That does not mean I can control European policy. But it does mean I can have a stronger

125

voice in Brussels in order to influence quotas . . . my profitability is tied to quotas – the more quotas, the more profits' (*Financial Times*, 2 April 1986). The policy of 'export refunds' has seen the EC change from a net importer of sugar in the 1970s to taking, at one stage, around 25% of the world market. This policy of dumping at subsidized prices and destabilizing the world sugar market caused adverse criticism from, for example, the Consumers in the European Community Group (1983) and other consumer groups and some food industry interests.

NOTES

1 Sugar and the taste of 'sweetness' had and still has a profound cultural and social role in society with a sweet taste being preferred from early childhood (Desor *et al.* 1977). There are few individuals in the industrialized countries beyond the age of infancy who lack experience of sugar-containing foods. Sugar (sucrose) is one of the most commonly available foodstuffs in the world today. There are many 'free sugars' in nature and the five common sugars found in food are glucose, fructose, sucrose, lactose and maltose. For the purposes of this paper sugar is the processed product sucrose – extracted and concentrated from its plant source. Commonly referred to as 'refined sugar', in the United Kingdom this is sucrose extracted from sugar cane (a tropical crop) and sugar beet (a temperate crop). When sugar is discussed outside scientific circles, people invariably mean sucrose.

2 Below, as adapted from Pancoast and Junk (1980), are listed the major functional properties of sucrose:

(a) Preservative effect – sucrose solutions of high density act as a preservative against most micro-organisms.

(b) Fermentable carbohydrate – sucrose is widely used as a fermentable carbohydrate, for example in bread baking.

(c) Flavour enhancement – sucrose will serve as a flavour enhancer when used in concentrations in which the sense of sweetness will not override the flavours that are being accentuated.

(d) Bulking agent – sucrose serves as a bulking agent in a variety of formulated foods, for example, in dry mixes of various types. It also serves, along with other ingredients, to give bulk to many confectionery products.

(e) Body and mouth feel – the 'body' or 'mouth feel' of beverages may be altered with the use of sucrose by reducing the watery condition of the product.

In practice this means that, apart from 'sweetness', sugar's technical properties, for example, help to give biscuits their characteristic crunchy texture and chocolate its 'snap'; it influences the texture and freezing point of dairy products and frozen desserts; it suppresses microbiological spoilage in preserves, etc.

3 Another important issue addressed by the food systems literature, but not covered in detail in this chapter, is that food chains are becoming increasingly internationalized and global. An excellent illustration of this process is the work by Sanderson (1986) on the emergence of the 'world steer' and the internationalization and foreign domination of Latin American cattle production. He describes how cattle production has to be considered as a key element in the 'foodgrain–feedgrain–livestock complex'. Among the features of this 'complex', cattle reared in Latin America use US feedlot technology, European antibiotics

and Japanese markets for boxed beef. In addition, cattle are reared to meet international (Western) standards of consumption and trade including, for example, immunities from major contagious diseases, certain marbling characteristics of the meat and standardized cuts of beef. The structures of the world market for sugar are integrally linked between the economies of industrialized and developing countries and are international in character. However, similar 'food complex' studies on sugar that embrace the interdisciplinary features of, for example, Sanderson's research – that is homogeneous markets, the shaping of consumption and dietary patterns, the supply of inputs, labour relations, the use of investment, environmental consequences and international competition – are not currently available in the academic literature.

4 See also Busch *et al.* (1991) and Kloppenburg (1988).

5 See Deerr (1949 and 1950), Hobhouse (1985) and Aykroyd (1967) for histories of sugar. For consumption, see Mintz (1985).

6 Beets were first used in Europe as cattle feed, but in 1745 the German chemist Marggraf made a report to the Berlin Academy of Sciences on chemical experiments that he had undertaken to extract a true sugar from various plants commonly available in the countryside. In 1747 he succeeded in extracting sugar from beet and was able to turn it into a solid substance. His pupil Frederic Achard had turned sucrose extraction from beet into an industrial process by 1786. He set up several small sugar-beet factories with the financial help of the Prussian government, but production and quality was low and the price high. The British naval blockade of Europe during the Napoleonic Wars triggered sugar-beet production. Napoleon, cut off from colonial sugar, encouraged the production of European sugar beet. The French chemist Benjamin Delessert was the first to succeed in producing sucrose commercially from beet in 1811–12. By 1880 beet had displaced cane as the main source of sugar in Europe, and its cultivation had spread to the United States and Canada (Deerr 1950).

7 Philippe Chalmin's (1990) book, *The Making of a Sugar Giant: Tate & Lyle 1859–1989*, must be one of the most detailed food company histories ever written. It is a mine of information on the company in the United Kingdom and abroad. However, the extensively descriptive narrative (speaking of the English translation – the book was originally published in French) is, in parts, presented in such a detailed way that it is often difficult for the reader to see the wood for the trees. The study effectively ends at 1980 and the postscript on Tate & Lyle 1980–89 is spartan compared to what is served up earlier. Chalmin's book is worth the effort if approached with a well-defined set of reading objectives and proves especially valuable as a source of data on sugar.

8 Throughout this chapter, because we are principally concerned with industrial production, sugar 'consumption' refers to supplies available or entering the whole UK food system. These are not meant to be used or interpreted as individual, human 'consumption' figures. The supply figures are, in the main, from consumption level estimates published by MAFF and derived from deliveries to retail and industrial users by Tate & Lyle and British Sugar. Changes in stocks and other sources of supply are also taken into account.

Human consumption and individual sugar intakes are more problematic. Information on individual consumption is found in many dietary surveys which measure energy and nutrient intakes of individuals recording all foods eaten, usually over several days. It is difficult to make broad generalizations on sugar intakes from these surveys because they sample different populations often using a variety of methods. But from some recent dietary surveys reported in the literature, in all cases on average, men consume more sugar than women, and total dietary sugars account for one-fifth of total dietary energy. For sucrose only, this varies around 16% of total energy. Most dietary surveys have not differentiated between 'natural' and 'added' sugars. However, they suggest that there is a wide variability in sugar intake between individuals, but 'high' and 'low' sugar consumers do not eat fundamentally different foods, but 'high' sugar eaters ate consistently more of certain foodstuffs while 'low' sugar consumers rarely 'overindulged' in such foods.

9 This paragraph draws on information in different chapters of Oddy and Miller (1976).

10 However, the total industrial use of sucrose in cereal manufacture is relatively low – if sugar is added it is often by individual discretion from the sugar bowl, although it should be noted that many individual cereal brands are also particularly high in added sugar content.

11 Sugar supply during the Second World War is fully detailed in Hammond (1962), and the information in this section is drawn from his account.

12 See Webb (1977), Stevens and Webb (1983) and Southgate (1984).

13 The table below compares the CSA and Lome Sugar Convention quotas (tonnes of white sugar equivalents) and details the countries involved in the supply of this sugar.

Country	Final CSA quotas*	Initial Lome and related quotas
Mauritius	374,438	487,200
Swaziland	83,980	116,400
Fiji	138,036	163,600
India	24,680	25,000
Belize	19,842	39,400
West Indies and		
Guyana of which:	682,958	409,100
Jamaica	212,666	118,300
Trinidad and		
Tobago	123,630	69,000
Barbados	133,513	49,300
Guyana	180,254	157,700
St Kitts-		
Nevis-Anguilla	32,895	14,800
Kenya		5,000
Uganda	7,000	5,000
Tanzania		10,000
Total developing country CSA members	**1,330,934**	
Malawi	Not a member	20,000
Congo (Brazzaville)	Not a member	10,000
Madagascar	Not a member	10,000
Surinam	Not a member	4,000
Total ACP sugar exporters (and India)		**1,304,700**
Australia	330,165	Not a member
Total CSA members	**1,661,099**	

*Note: UK Ministry of Agriculture estimate of the white sugar equivalents of the CSA quotas which were set in raw sugar terms.

Source: Harris (1985, p. 56)

14 The Monopolies and Mergers Commission report (1991) gives more detail about these sales. For TLS there had been little change in volume of sugar sales in the United Kingdom between 1985/86 and 1988/89. The volume of industrial sales had grown from 648,000 to 739,000 tonnes – 14% up compared with growth of 11% in the industrial market. Retail sales sold by TLS had fallen 21% to 205,000 tonnes compared to an overall fall in the retail market of 16%. The prices of retail sugar had risen faster than prices charged for industrial sugar. For British Sugar, industrial sales between 1985/86 and 1989/90 had grown from 745,000 to 834,000 tonnes, up 12%, while retail sales had fallen 24% to 322,000 tonnes. The rate of increase of prices for British Sugar's retail sales was almost three times as fast as that for industrial sales (Monopolies and Mergers Commission 1991, p. 12).

15 The major concern of most policy-directed nutritional advice has been to tackle the high incidence of coronary heart disease. In particular, advice geared to this end has concentrated on dietary fats, the generalized message being to reduce total dietary energy derived from all fats, but especially saturated (animal) fat consumption. 'The Health of the Nation' (June 1991) lists the current advice on the broad changes that people should make in their eating habits:

- reduce the amount of energy from saturated fatty acids to 15% or less of their food energy intake
- reduce the amount of energy from total fats to 35% or less of their food energy intake
- eat less non-milk extrinsic sugars and eat sugary foods less often (by 'non-milk extrinsic sugars' is meant, in the main, processed sugar/sucrose)
- seek ways of eating less salt
- replace fatty and sugary foods by cereal and starchy foods
- avoid an excessive intake of alcohol

Like all sugars, sucrose is a carbohydrate (a disaccharide), and starches and sugars are almost completely digested and absorbed. The factor used for calculating their energy yields in mixed British diets is 3.75 kcal per gram of monosaccharide equivalent. The corresponding factors for protein, fat and alcohol are 4 kcal, 9 kcal and 7 kcal per gram, respectively (Department of Health 1989). This review by the Committee on Medical Aspects of Food Policy assessed the evidence relating sugars in the diet to health and recommended that, in order to reduce the risk of dental caries, consumption of non-milk extrinsic sugars (principally sucrose) by the population should be decreased and these sugars replaced by fresh fruit, vegetables and starchy foods. On obesity the Committee's panel of experts noted that dietary sugars may contribute to the general excess food energy consumption responsible for the development of obesity. They endorsed the need for the obese to reduce energy consumption and recommended that the reduction of non-milk extrinsic sugars intake should be part of a general reduction in dietary energy intake.

In the area of the metabolism Panel said that there is no evidence for a direct adverse effect in most people on blood levels of cholesterol, triglycerides, glucose or insulin when sucrose is substituted isocalorically for starch up to about 150 g per day or 25% of total food energy. They continued:

For the majority of the population, who have normal plasma lipids and normal glucose tolerance, the consumption of sugars within the present range in the U.K. carries no special metabolic risks . . . current consumption of sugars, particularly sucrose, played no direct causal role in the development of cardiovascular . . . disease, of essential hypertension, or

of diabetes mellitus . . . It further concluded that sucrose had no significant specific effects on behaviour or psychological function. (p. 43)

The more recent report on dietary reference values for food, energy and
nutrients for the United Kingdom (Department of Health 1991) endorsed the
conclusions of the 1989 COMA report and that non-milk extrinsic sugars were
a major cause of dental caries in the United Kingdom and that their consumption by the population should be decreased. However, this Panel went further
and for the first time by a Department of Health report suggested quantified
guidelines for sugar consumption: 'The Panel therefore proposed that the
population's average intake of non-milk extrinsic sugars should not exceed
about 60 g/d or 10 per cent of total dietary energy' (p. 74).

6

SUGAR OR SWEET

In Chapter 4, the theoretical problem of distinguishing between different SOPs was addressed. In this chapter, we take these arguments a stage further by empirically demonstrating the difference between two SOPs, namely the one for sugar and the one for artificial sweeteners. A cursory consideration of sugar and sweeteners might suggest both these providers of sweetness to be intricately linked. Here, we show how this is not the case.

In doing so, we will argue that the total market for sweetness in EU food and drink provision is being expanded without sugar (sucrose) being significantly displaced. In particular, far from artificial sweeteners substituting for sugar within a fully integrated SOP for sweetness, sweetener use constitutes a separate SOP from that of sugar. Both sugar and sweeteners rely upon distinct, vertically integrated SOPs. These differ in four important respects. First, their production and sourcing methods are quite separate. Second, they employ specific organic properties in their respective applications in food and drink use. Third, the state structuring of, and the regulatory policies directed towards, sugar and sweeteners are separate and distinct; more specifically, sugar is defined as a food and sweeteners as food additives. Finally, their marketing and consumption patterns can be differentiated. This has seen the recent growth throughout the EU of the market for 'lite' sweet products, incorporating sweeteners, and aimed at exploiting new food and drink markets centred on health and diet concerns in the developed world.

This chapter examines the supply of sugar within the EU and the impact upon it of artificial sweeteners.[1] In particular, the marketing of sweeteners in relation to sugar is investigated in the context of substitutionism.[2] This would suggest that sugar, an organic ingredient, would increasingly be displaced or substituted by an inorganic industrial input such as low-calorie artificial sweeteners, with a subsequent restructuring of the associated food system.

The common organic link between sugar and sweeteners is that they both deliver sweetness as part of their use in food and drink processing. This is a potential source of confusion over the integration of their SOPs and the consequential implications for substitutionism effects. Such confusion is compounded by labelling use on 'lite' products such as sugar-free or reduced sugar. While obviously attacking sugar with one hand, it designates to the consumer with the other that the product is still sweet even if sugar is not the sweetening ingredient. In short, the common property of providing sweetness is a veil that conceals radically different roles for sugar and artificial sweeteners in the food system, and in their own food systems. To demonstrate how each of their respective SOPs differs, the potential substitution of sugar by sweeteners within the EU is investigated in the context of the regulation of sweeteners.

To develop the arguments outlined above, the chapter is organized in two main sections. The first section describes the EU market for sugar in relation to alternative sweeteners and calculates from the recent EU Sweeteners' Directive the potential use of sweeteners in EU food supply. It is clear from a comparison between the EU organization for sugar and for sweeteners that different food regimes are being described. The second section considers what has happened over the 1980s in the EU, but particularly in the United Kingdom, focusing on the 'lite' market for sweeteners as a case study, thus examining the sweetness system from production to final consumption.

It is concluded that while alternative low-calorie sweeteners have possibly restricted the growth in the use of sugar, the effect in practice has been to expand the total market for sweetness. In practice this means that market analysts predict a substantial growth for the EU market for sweeteners. In the meantime, EU sugar producers, in turn, have continued to maintain and expand their production and have sought to develop new outlets for their supplies, such as the chemicals industry, as well as in maintaining exports. In particular, the EU has become a net exporter of sugar and is seen by many other sugar exporters as 'dumping' sugar on the world market. The main threat, therefore, to sugar producers is the vagaries of the world sugar system rather than substitutionism by sweeteners. In other words, substitutionism as described by Goodman *et al.* is currently seen to be conceptually blunted in a number of significant ways by an examination of the EU market for sugar and sweeteners.

SUGAR AND SWEETENER SUPPLY IN THE EU: TWO DISTINCT SYSTEMS OF PROVISION

As described in Chapter 5, within the EU there is a distinct policy environment and state structuring of sugar's SOP. This has meant that the production and use of HFCs, for example, has been politically blocked by sugar interests, when it was incorporated into the EU Sugar Regime in 1977, through the imposition of conditions making it too costly for widespread industrial use. Thus, the current EU sugar regime, through government regulation, has effectively stopped substitutionism, and sugar remains the principal bulk sweetener within the EU. The only other realistic substitutes for sugar within the current EU sugar regime, therefore, are low-calorie alternative sweeteners – potentially the very epitome of Goodman *et al.'s* thesis of inorganic inputs replacing the agricultural in food processes.

Thus, a possible example of inorganic substitutionism, at the consumption end of sugar's SOPs, is in the area of low-calorie artificial sweeteners. Before considering this in more detail, the organic properties of two widely used sweeteners are detailed. Saccharin has been available for many years, having been in commercial production from the early 1900s. Today it is extremely cheap compared to sugar. However, its particular organic properties, especially the bitter after-taste, have made it a poor substitute. Its industrial use has been restricted to products that use sugar, but where sugar content can be reduced slightly (thus saving on an expensive ingredient) with saccharin making up the sweetness, for example in fruit squashes. Like other artificial sweeteners, it has also been subject to restrictions on its use imposed by government food regulations relating to food additives.

Aspartame (developed in the 1970s), on the other hand, has a far superior taste profile – that is closer to mimicking sugar, but it is more expensive relative to saccharin. Thus, the combination of the organic property of sweetness with less calories and an acceptable taste profile together with the high EU price for sugar, has contributed to the rapid introduction and diffusion of aspartame in food products and the retail market on the back of the up-market healthy eating and lifestyle revolution in, for example, 1980s Britain (Heasman 1990a and 1991).

Many sweeteners are the products of discoveries by the chemical rather than agricultural or food industries (although many 'bulk' sweeteners, like sorbitol, are widely distributed in nature, they are also manufactured using artificial processes). Many sweeteners are not manufactured in the EU; saccharin, for example, is produced in the Far East. The Holland Sweetener Company is the only European manufacturer of aspartame; NutraSweet obtains supplies from outside the EU. Other sweeteners are produced in purpose-built factories; acesulfame K, for example, is manufactured in Germany by Hoechst A.G.

There are many potential sugar substitutes available on the market, but these, like the sugar alcohols for example, have made less of an impact on the sugar (sucrose) market (see the next sections). Substitutes like the sugar alcohols are more expensive than sucrose and have been restricted to specialist dietetic foods (an exception being sugar-free chewing gums). Other manufacturers have, in the past, been reluctant to use them in mass-produced products because they consider them to have undesirable organic properties, such as gastrointestinal discomfort and, in some instances, diarrhoea.

Biotechnologies may have immense potential to restructure and change food systems fundamentally, as persuasively argued by Goodman *et al.* However, it is demonstrated in the next sections that, in the case of the EU sugar system, substitutionism needs to be modified in the context of other factors not least the organic relationship between specific foods, the role of different ingredients in food manufacturing systems, trends in food consumption habits and state policies directed towards different commodities. The extent of sugar substitutionism is examined in more detail in the following section describing the EU sugar system.

Sugar 'substitutionism'?

Government agricultural policies in many European countries have been specifically directed to ensuring adequate support, through subsidies and protection from competition, for sugar supply. This has primarily been for sugar-beet production although for the United Kingdom, it has also involved ensuring a market for substantial supplies of sugar from cane as a result of historical and colonial links with the sugar-exporting ACP countries. To recap from the previous chapter, EU control of sugar production has been implemented through the Sugar Regime (part of the CAP) set up in 1966. The Regime operates through a series of production quotas at guaranteed prices distributed on a national basis. In addition, as well as protecting producers from competing suppliers of sugar from outside the EU through import levies, the EU support of beet production has been instrumental in turning the EU from a net importer in the 1970s to a major exporter of sugar accounting for around 20% of the world market in traded sugar.

However, recent years have witnessed the introduction and EU regulatory approval of artificial sweeteners, especially low-calorie versions such as aspartame. These, coupled with widespread government-inspired nutrition or healthy eating advice, which recommends a limitation in consumption of sugar and sugary foods, would appear to create the conditions for the substitution for sugar. This trend seems to be supported throughout the EU which has seen considerable growth in the market for so-called sugar-free, 'lite' products, although the extent and content of this market varies considerably between countries. The following section details the regulatory structuring of the sweetener system within the EU and the relationship between it and the sugar system. From this, it is suggested that each is structured and operates in a distinct way and, although in parts complementary, they are far from becoming fully integrated.

The sugar and sweetener systems of the EU

An obvious structural and organic difference between sugar and sweeteners is the fact that sugar is an agricultural crop. Around 57% of the land area within the EU is devoted to agriculture, employing 6.8% of the working population (approximately 17 million people), as against 11.3% in 1973 (Commission of the European Union 1992). The sugar-producing sector employs 2% of this workforce and cultivates about 1.5% of the EU agricultural area (1.8 million hectares) for the production of sugar beet. This crop accounts for 2.2% of EU agricultural output.

Sugar beet thrives best in a humid climate and is particularly suited to northern Europe. The best beet yields are found in France, Germany, Belgium, the Netherlands and the United Kingdom. However, due to climatic conditions, the length of growing season and aspects of sugar-beet processing, the cost of production in Belgium, Denmark and the United Kingdom are considerably lower than other European countries. For example, in Germany the costs per hectare of sugar-beet production are 1.5 times higher than low-cost countries. The refining industry within the EU is highly concentrated (over the twenty-year period from 1970/71, the number of sugar factories fell by 40%) and by the 1990s there were 188 factories and 85 sugar companies in operation. In the 1990/91 marketing year EU sugar production was 16 million tonnes (white sugar) which was 35% above domestic consumption (see Table 6.1 for a breakdown of this total figure by individual country). The surplus sugar is either stored or exported to the world market (CEFS 1990).

Table 6.1 EU sugar balance 1990/91 (tonnes white sugar)

Country	Total consumption	Production	Self-sufficiency (%)	Stocks	Exports
Belgium	473,800	1,029,816	220	116,000	
Denmark	199,100	534,544	245	36,000	
France	2,029,000	4,364,015	194	643,000	
Germany	2,785,000	4,297,761	139	257,000	
Greece	307,000	286,868	76	75,000	
Ireland	132,402	225,601	162	37,000	
Italy	1,563,000	1,458,000	91	302,000	
Netherlands	560,000	1,232,000	205	105,000	
Portugal	308,760	2,000	1	40,000	
Spain	1,122,000	952,000	85	255,000	
UK	2,091,070	1,241,000	56	249,000	
Total EU	**11,571,132**	**15,623,605**	132	**2,115,000**	**2,700,000**

Source: CEFS, *Sugar Statistics 1991*, Brussels 1992

Table 6.2 Breakdown of indirect EU human sugar consumption 1990/91

Food product	European sales	Relative sugar content of product (%)	Absolute sugar quantity utilized by sector
Soft drinks (1000 litres)	173,723,510	11	1,910,958
Sugar confectionery (tonnes)	1,327,900	85	1,128,715
Pastry, biscuits, cakes, etc. (tonnes)	3,515,900	27	949,293
Chocolate preparations (tonnes)	1,842,000	40	736,960
Confitures, jams, marmalades (tonnes)	1,906,848	34	648,312
Dairy products (tonnes)	3,958,000	10	395,800
Ice creams (1000 litres)	18,892,280	13.5	255,045
Misc. (tonnes)			584,132
Total indirect human consumption			6,609,215

Source: Schmitt, A draft doctoral thesis, Université Catholique de Louvain, 1995

While in absolute terms EU sugar consumption has increased during the last twenty years,[3] the real sugar consumption data indicate a constant decrease in all member states except Germany and Belgium. Total consumption of sugar in the EU marketing year 1990/91 was around 11.6 million tonnes of white sugar. A fifth of this was used for non-food purposes (feedstuff, the chemical and pharmaceutical industries), 23% was consumed directly (table-top) and 57% indirectly through food and beverages (about 6.6 million tonnes). Table 6.2 breaks down indirect human consumption by type of industry. This shows the dominance of the soft drinks industry as the major customer for sugar.

The apparent trend in the EU is of a stagnating demand for sugar and strong growth for sweeteners. On the basis of sweetness equivalence (that is, the sweetening power of individual sweeteners relative to sucrose), the raw-material costs for sweeteners are highly competitive with sugar. The relative sweetness of a sweetener can only be roughly estimated since its intensity is influenced not only by its concentration, but also by the temperature and other substances consumed at the same time. According to different authors, the sweetness intensity of different sweeteners in relation to sugar can be as much as 1,500 times higher for neohesperidine, 550 times higher for saccharin, 200 times higher for acesulfame K and aspartame, and 40 times higher for cyclamates. The important point to consider here in terms of the SOP for sweeteners in relation to sugar is this organic property, that is sweeteners can provide a sweetness exceeding that of sugar from 10 to 2,000 times. As such, their use in foods and drinks is restricted to small quantities. Sweeteners, therefore, are defined as food additives rather than as a food like sugar.

An important commercial advantage of intense sweeteners, and another organic quality, is their synergy effect. This means that when used in combinations, their total sweetness is greater than the sum of sweetness provided by each sweetener individually. This synergistic effect allows for lower dosage levels of sweetener. However, sugar still dominates the market for sweetness because the food industry uses sugar not only for its sweetening function. Sugar also has other organic or technological functions in food. For example, it helps to preserve food, it increases the boiling point and reduces freezing points, it acts as a bulking agent, it serves as a flavour enhancer, etc. These and other properties are of considerable importance in many types of food and drink manufacturing systems (Pancoast and Junk 1980). The substitution of sugar by sweeteners is, therefore, limited by a number of organic factors such as food production and processing technology, taste requirements, health aspects, legislative restrictions and economic efficiency.

However, what in principle is the potential substitution of sugar by sweeteners? In 1986, UK sugar refiner Tate & Lyle estimated a general technical substitutability of sugar in food and drink products. This ranged from 100% for soft drinks, ice cream, yoghurt, frozen confectionery, gelatin desserts, canned fruit, pickles, baked beans, sauces and meat products; 50% for other canned products; 10% for sugar confectionery; and 5% for biscuits, chocolate, pie fillings and jams (Heasman 1988). Based on this assessment and applied to the indirect sugar consumption figures (see Table 6.2), the food industry could theoretically have replaced about 24% of total sugar consumption for 1990/91 (2.8 million tonnes).

EU policy on sweeteners and the eventual regulatory structure were given a framework for harmonization throughout the EU with the publication at the end of 1990 of a Draft Sweeteners Directive.[4] This in effect lays out the future legal structuring of the sweetener system of provision within the EU. Underpinning the directive is that sweeteners may only be considered for use where they have a demonstrable advantage to the consumer and where they do not present a hazard to health. The directive is designed to allow for the Europe-wide use of the sweeteners acesulfame K (EU food additive number E950), aspartame (E951), cyclamate (E952),[5] saccharin (E954), thaumatin (E957), neohesperidine (NHDC) (E959) and the polyols, sorbitol, mannitol, isomalt, lactitol and xylitol at acceptable daily intake (ADI)[6] levels determined by the Scientific Committee for Food (SCF). The SCF was set up in 1974 to aid the Commission in questions relating to health in the food sector. The evaluations on the intake limits for the safe consumption of sweeteners prepared by the SCF are largely based on summary reports carried out at national level. These are detailed in Table 6.3.

Table 6.3 Summary of the SCF examination of sweeteners

Acesulfame K	0–9 mg/kg body weight
Aspartame	0–4 mg/kg body weight
Cyclamate	0–11 mg/kg body weight
NHDC	0–5 mg/kg body weight
Saccharin	0–2.5 mg/kg body weight
(Thaumatin)	(acceptable)

Source: SCF 1987

Based on the assumptions for sweetness intensity and the EU/SCF assessment for the safe consumption of sweeteners, the annual upper intake limit for the whole of the EU population would convert to the equivalent of nearly 72 million tonnes of white sugar – more than six times the total sugar actually consumed within the EU![7] This is, in effect, a carte blanche for the sweetener and food industries to develop artificially sweetened products at will. Table 6.4 details a conversion of these figures into a maximum amount of sweeteners that could have been employed in 1990/91 food production under the Sweeteners' Directive guidelines, thereby giving an estimate of the regulatory limit of the EU sweetener markets.

Using this maximum theoretical use of sweeteners in EU food production would convert to more than 14 million tonnes of white sugar equivalent in 1990/91. Weighted on the basis of relative sweetness intensity,

Table 6.4 Maximum quantities of sweeteners which could have been employed in 1990 food production according to the EU Sweeteners' Directive (tonnes)

Food product	Acesulfame	Aspartame	Cyclamate	Saccharin	NHDC
Soft drinks	6,090	10,440	6,800	1,392–1,740	522–870
Sugar confectionery	650–1,300	1,300	2,600	650	390–1,040
Chocolate preparations	900–1,800	1,800	3,600	900	540–1,440
Pastry, biscuits, cakes, etc.	1,230	1,750	875	350	–
Confitures, jams, marmalades	1,900	1,900	1,900	380	95
Dairy products	1,400	4,000	1,000	400	200
Ice creams	1,520	1,520	475	190	95
Total used	**14,465**	**22,710**	**17,250**	**4,436**	**2,791**

Source: Schmitt, A., draft doctoral thesis, Université Catholique de Louvain, 1995

Table 6.5 Actual consumption of intense sweeteners in the EU 1992 (tonnes sugar equivalent in '000s)

	Saccharin	*Cyclamate*	*Aspartame*	*Acesulfame*	*Total*
Belgium	31	0	3	1	35
Denmark	18	0	5	2	25
France	60	1	29	7	97
Germany	261	35	36	4	336
Greece	2	0	3	0	5
Ireland	18	1	9	1	29
Italy	68	0	6	2	76
Netherlands	45	11	11	1	68
Portugal	10	0	1	0	11
Spain	170	15	4	0	189
UK	330	1	129	12	472
EU total	**1,013**	**64**	**236**	**30**	**1,343**
% of total sugar consumption	**8.73**	**0.55**	**2.02**	**0.3**	**11.6**

Source: Schmitt, A., *op. cit.*, 1995

these legal dosages would correspond to about 2.9 million tonnes sugar equivalent from acesulfame, 4.5 million tonnes from aspartame, 2.4 million tonnes from saccharin, 0.7 million from cyclamate, and 4.2 million tonnes from neohesperidine. These amounts would translate into a surplus of 27% over actual consumption and thus the Sweeteners' Directive theoretically allows for the complete substitution of sugar in foodstuffs by sweeteners. This legislative framework clearly allows for the development and harmonization of a distinct source of sweetness for foodstuffs. Yet actual sweetener consumption in the EU 1990/91 marketing year was around 1.3 million tonnes white sugar equivalent or about 14% of total human consumption. Most of this was indirect consumption through food and beverages. Table 6.5 breaks down actual sweetener consumption by member states (converted as white sugar equivalents). The next section considers the consumption of sweeteners in practice within the EU.

THE MARKET FOR 'LITE' PRODUCTS AND SUGAR SUBSTITUTION

Concentrating in particular on the United Kingdom, this section examines the substitution of sugar by other sweeteners in practice by considering the market for so-called 'lite' products using artificial sweeteners during the 1980s. In the late 1980s, the products showing the most dramatic growth across Europe were those formulated, packaged and promoted on some form of health platform such as low calorie, low fat and sugar free (ISA 1987). Acceptance of these 'healthy' foods varied considerably by country. For example, Germany, Switzerland and Scandinavia showed slower growth rates compared to the United Kingdom, while in countries like France, Italy and Spain the healthy-eating movement was still to take off.

Value and volume growth in all 'lite' foods (low fat as well as sugar reduced) has been significant. In the United Kingdom in 1986 sales of low-calorie foods and drinks were estimated as exceeding £800 million with a growth rate of around 5% per annum. A more recent calculation of the UK 'lite' market, including reduced alcohol and caffeine products, valued it at around £1.9 billion. 'Low' and 'lite' products accounted for 3.5% of total United Kingdom food and drink expenditure (Young 1990).

In terms of all sweeteners Europe makes up the third largest market (with roughly 15% of global consumption in 1988), after Asia (China, Japan, Thailand, Indonesia, South Korea and India) with 36% of world consumption, and North America, Canada and Latin America accounting for 49% of global consumption. Growth in the European market for sweeteners has been in the region of 9% per annum since 1980, and the United Kingdom, West Germany and Switzerland are the largest markets for sweeteners. Although actual experience of sweetener consumption among consumers is still relatively limited, it is estimated that products based on saccharin are consumed by 56% of Europeans, followed by aspartame (22%), with acesulfame K a poor third (4%).

However, the most important new sweetener for the 'lite' market for sweet products is aspartame. The number of products in Europe sweetened with aspartame, and marketed as NutraSweet, grew from 8 in 1983, to 451 in 1985, 784 in 1987 and 1,460 by 1989. In 1990, the market for aspartame in Western Europe was about 1,000 tonnes (around 200,000 tonnes white sugar equivalent). The soft drinks market accounted for around 60% of this, while table-top sweeteners represent around 25%. All other uses, such as desserts, confectionery and dairy products, amounted to 15%. The European market is forecast to double or even triple by the year 2000. The relative significance of soft drinks/table-top/other foods is not expected to change in the short term.

The UK market for 'lite' foods and drinks

In the United Kingdom one of the major technological changes in food products during the 1980s has been the development of lite foods and drinks. More important, these products have now become regular items of purchase and acceptance in the UK diet. However, the marketing of 'lite' products has been aimed at higher-income levels and particular sections of the population. Part of the growth in the consumption of 'lite' products has been stimulated by growing consumer awareness of diet and good nutrition, as well as concerns over fitness and changing consumption patterns – the demand for greater convenience, for example.

However, technical progress in this area has also been driven by other influences on the food system. The food industry has sought gains in productivity in a relatively inelastic market. There has been a rapid diffusion and transfer of food technology, both geographically and throughout product ranges. Government regulatory processes, though slow, have successfully influenced technological change by establishing standards for safety and by unilaterally introducing new ingredients into the food chain through regulatory approval – not least artificial sweeteners. Finally, technological change in the food industry has been driven by the opportunities for large profits. Despite the apparent drawbacks of rapid growth in development costs, lengthening lead times and the uncertainty of market performance, innovators often reap large rewards. Many sugar-free products and ingredients have enjoyed considerable commercial success.

Much nutrition information on diet published in the United Kingdom (and similar dietary advice in other parts of Europe) has included sections on restricting or not increasing consumption of sugar and sugary foods. The NACNE Report, published in 1983, for example, included among its long-term recommendations an eventual halving of sugar consumption from around 38 kg to 20 kg per head per year. By coincidence, 1983 also saw the approval of a batch of intense and bulk sweeteners for use in beverages, food and table-top applications following a five-and-a-half-year government review. Use of approved sweeteners was not restricted to specific areas, as in the case in many other EU countries, but was allowed across all foods and drinks apart from those manufactured specifically for babies and young children. This approval made the United Kingdom one of the most liberal legislators in this area. Up until this time, saccharin was the only high-intensity sweetener permitted. The new regulations introduced two new sweeteners to the United Kingdom food system: aspartame and acesulfame K.

The introduction of these sweeteners, especially aspartame, has helped to transform the 'lite' market in the sugar-free and sugar-reduced product categories by providing superior sweetening ingredients compared to saccharin. Of importance, up until this time, saccharin was mainly considered as a low-cost or strategic substitute for sugar. With the new sweeteners, manufacturers sought to develop products and markets providing low-calorie alternatives, rather than simply targeting strategic alternatives to sugar. In terms of market impact, aspartame, as marketed by NutraSweet, has been the driving force.

In the United Kingdom, between 1985 and 1987, NutraSweet spent £3.5 million on advertising and promoting aspartame, partially as an ingredient for the products that contain it. The media used included television, cinema, press and door-to-door. The marketing was aimed principally at women aged 16 to 54 years old who are the primary purchasers and users of products such as diet cokes, yoghurts and table-top sweeteners, these markets being especially important in the summer months. NutraSweet developed what they call a 'branded ingredient strategy' which aimed to make their name stand for 'sugar-free, great taste, not saccharin, safe and good for the whole family' (Currie 1987).

Aspartame has been used in one of the most dynamic categories of 'lite' markets, namely soft drinks. Pepsi and Coca-Cola, for example, went over to using 100% aspartame from aspartame/saccharin blends in their diet soft drinks in 1987 and 1988, respectively. By 1989, total low-calorie carbonate sales in the United Kingdom accounted for just over a quarter of all carbonates sold (in thousands of litres), up from 13% in 1985. Annual trends of low-calorie carbonates through grocers, off-licences and cigarettes, tobacco and newspaper sellers (CTNs) grew by 35% in 1986, 39% in 1987, 20% in 1988 and 34% in 1989. Total regular (sugar) carbonate sales also grew by 7%, 12%, 0% and 11%, respectively, over the same years. Diet or low-calorie soft drinks have generally been sold at the same price as regular soft drinks. For other 'lite' products, one survey found that prices were between 30% and 100% more expensive than the equivalent standard product. There is widespread optimism in the growth of the market for sweet 'lite' products among both manufacturers and sweetener suppliers with many expecting continuing development and expansion throughout the 1990s (Heasman 1990a).

However, despite the rapid growth in sweet-tasting 'lite' products during the 1980s, sweeteners accounted for less than 10%, in white sugar equivalents, of the total United Kingdom retail and food and drink manufacturers' purchases of all sugars and sweeteners. Table 6.6 is an estimate of the breakdown of the total United Kingdom sugars and sweeteners market. Since the figures are derived from a variety of sources, some less accurate than others, they must be treated very much as an approximation. However, it is clear that sucrose is still the dominant sweetener in the United Kingdom holding 82% of the market. Other nutritive sweeteners – that is sweeteners derived from starch, the glucose syrups and isoglucose – represent 11% of the total and for artificial sweeteners around 7%. Despite nearly a decade of healthy eating, sugar supplies entering the United Kingdom food system have remained virtually static at around 37–38 kg per person per year. In other words, the use of sugar substitutes has grown, but the total sugar (sucrose) market has held its own. This implies that the total sugar and sweetener market has expanded. By 1990 the sweetener share of the total sweetness market had grown to around 10% with the other sources of sweetness remaining the same relative to sweeteners. Ironically, total supplies of sugar entering the United Kingdom food system also started to grow, albeit slightly, in the 1990s.

Table 6.6 Estimated UK sugars and sweeteners market

	Tonnes (WSE)	*% of total*	*kg/person/year*
Sucrose			
Retail	750,000	27.4	13.21
Industrial[b]	1,500,000	54.7	26.57
Total sucrose	2,250,000	82.1	39.78
Sweeteners from starch			
Isoglucose	37,000	1.4	0.65
Glucose syrups[c]	266,000	9.7	4.69
Total starch sweeteners	303,000	11.1	5.34
Artificial sweeteners			
Saccharin (75%)[d]	160,000	5.8	2.82
Aspartame (20%)[e]	28,000	1.0	0.49
Total artificial sweeteners[f]	188,000	6.8	3.31
Total UK sugars and sweetener consumption	2,741,000		48.43

Notes:
[a] WSE = white sugar equivalents.
[b] Sugar used in the manufacture of foods and drinks.
[c] Assumes sweetness relative to sucrose of 0.7.
[d] Assumes sweetness relative to sucrose of 300.
[e] Assumes sweetness relative to sucrose of 200.
[f] The total includes 5% others, data not available.

Source: Heasman 1990a

Growth in total consumer demand for food is limited or static in many years. However, market activity in the diet and health sector illustrates how the food industry uses innovations in technology, new ingredients and the commercial exploitation of consumer tastes. This has seen the creation of a multi-million pound added-value lite sector in a static market. In this respect, United Kingdom retailers have played a prominent role in this area – not only in promoting healthy eating including specifically sugar-free products, but in actually giving shelf-space to low-calorie versions next to traditional products. Equally important has been the role that retailers play in product innovation in terms of their own brands and in responding rapidly to changes in consumer attitudes. For example, by 1986, own brands in the United Kingdom already accounted for more than 30% of market share of packaged groceries in the large multiple food retail groups.

The attraction to food and drink manufacturers of the development of new product ranges using a 'lite' ingredient can be partly explained by the creation of a monopoly position. For an ingredient this advantage accrues in two forms. First, the innovating manufacturer creating a 'lite' product has a monopoly position in its niche market. The second form is the usual patent protection but, as MacKay (1987) points out, monopoly is also afforded through regulatory clearances for safety and designated product applications. That is, before any competitive ingredient can enter the market, for example a competing sweetener to aspartame, it has to go through a lengthy regulatory and approval process. This obviously has a bearing on future developments in the sugar-free 'lite' market, with uncertainty over the introduction of new ingredients and then their ability to compete in a well-defended marketplace, let alone their possible substitution effects.

While nutrition advice continues against sugar, this will add fuel to the sweet 'lite' market as a spur to product development. For example, in a survey of United Kingdom food and drink manufacturers using 'lite' ingredients carried out in 1990, only 9% of respondents agreed that terms like 'sugar-free' and 'sugar-reduced' were becoming less relevant in the marketing environment of the 1990s (Heasman 1991). The United Kingdom's Department of Health Report (1989) on dietary sugars and human health makes clear that sugar still has a case to answer as far as dental disease is concerned. It also recommends that food manufacturers produce low-sugar or sugar-free alternatives to existing sugar-rich products, particularly those for children. However, there is little evidence that sugar-free alternatives have had any depressing effect on per capita consumption of sugar, although in their absence it would seem likely that sugar versions might have increased their per capita consumption at a greater rate than experienced.

CONCLUSION

This chapter has argued that substitutionism as outlined in its pure form by Goodman *et al.* in their theory of agro-industrial development is not taking place in the use of sweeteners replacing sugar in the EU. With sugar and sweeteners being analysed as separate and distinct SOPs, reasons for this blunted form of substitutionism are suggested in terms of the (lack of) integration between the sugar and sweetener SOPs. This has been demonstrated in the area of the organic properties of sugar and sweeteners and their respective applications and uses in food and drink manufacturing, the EU regulatory structure of sweetener and sugar supply, in which sweeteners are food additives while sugar is a food, and in the marketing and consumption patterns of foods and drinks using artificial sweeteners. While it has been shown that the current proposed legal EU definitions for sweetener application and use in the food system would more than allow for the complete theoretical substitution of sugar, actual use, as illustrated by reference to the UK 'lite' market, would suggest that, in the first instance,

144

the total market for sweetness in food and drink provision is being expanded without sugar being significantly displaced.

NOTES

1 By artificial sweetener is principally meant the 'low-calorie' sweeteners. Especially widespread in EU food and drink applications are aspartame, saccharin, acesulfame K, cyclamates and neohesperidin (NHDC). Other artificial sweeteners, the 'bulk' sweeteners, are also approved and used in food and drink applications. These include hydrogenated glucose syrups, isomalt, mannitol, sorbitol and xylitol.
2 As proposed by Goodman *et al.* (1987); see Chapter 4.
3 This increase must be attributed, however, to the enlargement of the EU which has grown as follows: six member states in 1973, nine member states until 1981, ten member states until 1986, and from twelve to fifteen member states in 1994.
4 Since its publication in September 1990 the Sweeteners' Directive has experienced a long delay. The reason is that in May 1992 the European Parliament rejected the Common Position (a very rare occurrence) on the EC's proposal for the Sweeteners' Directive due to political rather than scientific reasons. It is believed that the framework of the directive will not be fundamentally changed, however, until passed and converted into national legislation. Consequently, the future of the EU Sweeteners' Directive continues to remain unclear and the existing national legislation on sweeteners remains in force.
5 Perhaps the most notable inclusion on the directive list in view of the history of the national regulation of sweetener use is the appearance of cyclamate and neohesperidine DC. The use of cyclamates has been banned in the United Kingdom from the mid-1960s. It will be interesting to see how the United Kingdom responds to the obligation to accept cyclamate in foods destined for European consumption if the directive is given approval in its present form.
6 The ADI has most recently been defined by the World Health Organization as 'an estimate of the amount of food additive, expressed on a body weight basis, that can be ingested over a lifetime without appreciable health risk' (WHO 1987, p. 1).
7 Calculated by the equation: EU population × body weight average × ADI/day × 365 days (ADI: mg/kg weight/day: acesulfame – 9; aspartame – 4; cyclamate – 11; saccharin – 2.5; NHDC – 5).

7

THE POVERTY OF FOOD ECONOMETRICS

INTRODUCTION

Over the past decade or so, there has been an explosion of interest in consumption across the social sciences. The topic has emerged to prominence in the separate disciplines, often following a common pattern. It is often pointed out that consumption has previously been neglected because it has fallen under the shadow of production which has been presumed to be a more fundamental determinant. Initially, academics have extended existing theories to consumption – as in the notion of forging identity through consumption rather than through work, for example. This has been followed by theoretical and conceptual innovation around consumption itself – most notably in the range of interpretative analysis associated with post-modernism.

It is striking how little orthodox economics has been touched by these characteristic changes within other disciplines. It is arguable that economics is certainly not bereft of theoretical innovation at the moment, especially around the microeconomic and macroeconomic implications of access to information for instance, but it has evolved in a world of its own, unconscious of the dramatic impact of post-modernism upon other social science disciplines. Even within political economy, where post-modernism is acknowledged in the emergence of post-Fordism, the attention to consumption is, paradoxically, extremely muted. With whatever empirical validity, it is presumed that the age of mass consumption is confined to the past, and production, design, contracting, retailing, and products themselves must be geared towards the flexibility associated with market niches. However, the source of the correspondingly sophisticated consumers tends to remain unexplored; they are as restlessly insatiable for quality and variety as they were previously for quantity and uniformity.

Why should economics have been so immune to these fashions which have swept through other disciplines like a bush fire? One important reason is the isolation and cushioning of economics both from other social sciences and the concerns of their subject matter. Closely related to this is the potential claim that consumption has not been unduly neglected within economics. From a conceptual point of view, it has occupied an equal position with production, with one corresponding to demand and the other to supply, respectively. Accordingly, the pressure to innovate, because of cumulative attention to consumption across the social sciences, would not be felt by economics both because of its insulation from interdisciplinary ricochets and because of its pre-existing account of consumption.

Of course, from the perspective of the other social sciences, whether in old or newer versions, economics has depended upon a peculiarly unacceptable theory of consumption. Most obviously, underlying preferences are taken as given along with the world of goods over which they are exercised, and consumer theory is reduced to the maximization of utility subject to budget constraints. It is worth briefly running over what have long been recognized as the deficiencies of this approach. First, preferences cannot be taken as fixed; however much they are stable over time, it is important to understand how preferences are formed. Second, consumption cannot be reduced to a single decision over what to purchase; consumer behaviour rests upon a range of motivations and determinants which may be systematic even if dubbed irrational by economics. Moreover, consumption involves a range of activities over and above deciding what to purchase, within which other determinants are prominent (and the focus of other social sciences – consumption as emulation and distinction, as exercise or reflection of power, as symbolic or ritualistic, as expressing or forming self-identity, etc.). Third, consumption goods themselves cannot be reduced to a presumed set of fixed physical or other properties from which utility flows; goods have socially determined properties which define them historically and culturally – as is most apparent in the use made of advertising which endows products with all sorts of fantastic, socially constructed, properties.

In short, the theory of consumption associated with neoclassical economics is distinguished by its debasement of human rationale to the level of an individualistic and calculated hedonism; significantly, production and consumption share common analytical principles, with the latter equivalent to a self-employed firm manufacturing 'utils' at minimum input cost.[1] Consumer theory within economics is properly construed as an analysis of derived demands to maximize utility. Where it differs from supply is that the latter is based on more or less competition between firms from which can be derived an industrial structure with potential variation in response to exogenously given parameters (such as technology, endowments and preferences). In other words, there is no entry and exit for consumers (or profit or seriously considered survival constraint) and this, despite its formal equivalence with producer theory, has meant that consumer theory within economics has remained particularly unchanging – not only over the most recent period of turbulence within consumer theory across other disciplines, but also since the period of the marginalist revolution.[2]

Moreover, the orthodoxy's preoccupation with equilibrium has rendered it especially vulnerable to the introduction of approaches in which preferences become endogenous, for this tends to lead to multiple or ill-defined equilibria. Does it make sense to have rational economic agents choosing in advance the endogenous preference paths that lead to the highest levels of utility over time? This would appear to be a poor basis either for the description of, or the prescription for, addictive or habit-forming behaviour (Fine 1995d).

It would be a mistake, however, to consider that consumer theory has stagnated within economics for, if anything, it has experienced a considerable revival over the past decade, although the analytical origins for this revival are more longstanding. It has done so, not through addressing its continuing and deep-rooted conceptual inadequacies, but by prodigious progress in what has always served as a 'cover-up' for these inadequacies, namely statistical investigation in the form of econometrics. Two developments, in particular, have been prominent.[3] One has been in the theoretical specification of demand systems so that the available forms and internal consistency of the equations to be estimated have been enhanced.[4] Here, of course, consistency refers to the mathematical properties of demand systems that must hold if they have been derived from utility-maximizing individuals with given preferences (and facing given prices for uniquely specified goods). These are the homogeneity, concavity and symmetry conditions for the Hicksian demand functions. They provide the logical basis upon which restrictions are imposed or tested on the data.

This has been accommodated by the second development, the enhanced capacity with which econometrics has been provided in the wake of the (personal) computer revolution. The availability of large data sets and a range of techniques, that can be easily, widely and cheaply employed, has promoted such empirical analysis at the expense of conceptual growth or, more exactly, as the driving force behind conceptualization on an extremely narrow basis. In particular, the economics of consumer behaviour has continued to be founded on the same principles as previously outlined, but it has incorporated a number of other features which give rise to more complicated mathematical models and econometrics. These include, for example, the presence of corner solutions (where marginal conditions are not satisfied because not all goods are purchased by each individual) and the optimization of consumer behaviour over time (with lags, sequencing of purchases, and discounting of utility). The neat combination of more complex mathematical models, the availability and use of large data sets, and the computability of more complex models and functional forms have allowed consumer theory to sustain, and lend a new lease of life to, its previous methodology and conceptual framework by combining given preferences with a more sophisticated mathematical and statistical investigation of their empirical implications.

It is worth speculating, in this light, on the impact that the development of computer technology has had upon theory across the social sciences. The way in which it has been employed seems to be quite different from discipline to discipline. Outside economics, a major impetus has been given towards greater detail in the descriptive account of socioeconomic categories – as in geographical information systems (GIS) and computer mapping, for example. In economics, on the other hand, progress in the capacity to undertake statistical enquiry has not primarily strengthened what has always been a spurious commitment to empiricism in practice. Rather than directing theory through the enhanced powers of empirical verification (or non-rejection), the personal computer (PC) revolution has induced, or permitted, the emergence of theories (such as rational expectations, for example) despite their apparent distance from day-to-day descriptive reality and because of the technical skills required to achieve them. In this way, economic theory has become more entrenched in its bizarre assumptions concerning economic rationality, while establishing both a dynamism and, of its practitioners, an increasingly demanding set of technical skills of the trade.

In other words, the computer has had a remarkable impact upon theoretical development, both within economics and, in other ways, upon other social sciences. This raises the more general issue of the way in which the means of production of knowledge have an influence upon that knowledge itself. An obvious example is provided by scientific equipment which may create anomalies, in the Kuhnian sense, that require theoretical change. The analogy to be lightly pursued here, however, is with the significance of the telescope for astronomy in the context of the persistence of geocentric theories of the solar system. Its enhanced observational powers led to an ever more intricate explanation of heavenly movements through systems of shifting spheres in a desperate attempt to ward off, ultimately unsuccessfully, the mounting wealth of evidence for the simple alternative – that the earth revolved around the sun rather than vice versa.

The treatment of consumption by neoclassical economics occupies a comparable position. The notion, in particular, that consumer preferences are given, directed towards utility maximization, and served by a more or less independent system of supply, is the basis on which empirical evidence is confronted; and this core starting point, far from being questioned by the evidence to the contrary, persists through the improvement of econometric techniques for handling it. These become more and more Byzantine relative to the simpler alternative of accepting the unacceptable – that preferences are not given, etc.

THE NFS AND THE DEMAND FOR FOODS

The above points will be illustrated by following the demand analysis that has been used with the NFS. The NFS is a continuous inquiry into household food consumption, expenditure and nutrient intake in Great Britain. Broadly comparable data have been collected since 1952, and data are available in magnetic form from 1979. The sample size in each year is approximately 7,000 households (after taking account of an effective response rate of about 50%). In each household a diary keeper, the 'housewife' whether male or female, records details of the description, quantity and cost of the foods entering the home over a period of seven days. The survey classifies the food entries into about 200 food codes. Data are also collected on the number of meals eaten outside the home although not on the content or cost of those meals. Until 1992, no data on alcoholic drinks and confectionery were recorded.[5]

In following the evolution of demand analysis as presented in the NFS reports (subsequently referred to by the year of the survey rather than the later year of publication), it is necessary to recognize that a number of different influences are at work. There is the changing content of econometrics as a discipline and the varying degree of skill with which it is employed and displayed within the NFS, itself dependent upon the nature of the data. The reports, and presumably the analysis underlying them, also seem to suffer from a degree of inertia, with the ways in which matters have been handled and presented in the past being carried over from one year to the next. Possibly some changes are arbitrary and others the response to unidentified pressures or objectives. As already indicated, the purpose here is to read how the issue of relying upon given preferences is handled despite the apparent evidence to the contrary. But it is certainly not presumed that this is the only influence constraining the NFS demand analysis, nor necessarily its most important determinant. Nor, of course, is demand analysis the only (economic) use to which the NFS is put.

Paradoxically, although the NFS demand analysis is based primarily upon the principle of given preferences, it explicitly recognizes that preferences do change over time. This is because demand estimated on the basis of given preferences gives rise both to shifting parameters over time and to unexplained residuals which are too large to be accounted for by random variation. Indeed, one part of the NFS analysis divides changes in demand into two components – those due to changes in prices and incomes, which are estimated first, and those due to everything else, and assigned primarily to shifts in taste, which are calculated as the changes unexplained by the first step. It is immediate that the theory as a whole cannot be rejected, although statistical significance for parameter estimates is possible. For whatever residual is unexplained is assigned to changing preferences. In other words, when we say that the NFS demand analysis depends upon given preferences, it will mean that the effects of prices and incomes on purchases are first estimated as if preferences are fixed (leaving, as a residual, what is not statistically explained – and which the NFS frequently refers to as underlying shifts in demand even though they may be due to shifts in supply).

It also follows, because of the priority accorded to given preferences, that the NFS estimates of elasticities on the basis of given preferences necessarily pick up the changes due to shifts in preferences to the extent that the two are statistically correlated. For example, suppose that prices decrease in exactly the same direction as a shift in tastes, then price elasticities will be estimated at more than their actual values, and the residual, calculated as due to shifting tastes, will be correspondingly underestimated. The method is described in the bluntest way in MAFF (1984):

> Attempts have been made . . . to assess how much of the variation in annual average purchases of specific foods is explained by changes in real prices and incomes. The Survey elasticity estimates were used to estimate the effects of these changes which were then removed. This leaves the variation in purchases due to shifts in consumers' tastes and preferences (and any residual estimation error) caused by advertising pressures and other environmental changes, and by advances in food technology. (p. 177)

This problem arises because two factors, shifts along the demand curve and shifts of the demand curve, are initially being estimated as if they were just one factor, as in the classical identification problem. The significance of this is different for the different types of demand analysis that have been undertaken by the NFS. These have fallen into three types – income elasticities, own-price elasticities, and cross-price elasticities – although, to be exact, there are three different methods of analysis with each most closely, but not exclusively, attached to the estimation of one each of these sets of parameters. There is also a conflation in practice between estimating shifts of, and along, the demand curves and shifts of the conditions surrounding supply (how competitive these are, for example). Thus, what is not explained by price and income effects is dubbed a residual and imputed to shifts in demand. But the residual will pick up all other changes in supply and demand, and their contribution will be inappropriately estimated to the extent that they are correlated with prices and income into which their effects will be incorporated. This procedure is unwittingly made explicit, with no reference at all to supply, in one of the most recent analyses undertaken in the NFS reports (Ritson 1988, p. 27):[6]

> Statistical analysis of time series of NFS data allow us to identify that part of the past change in the consumption which can be ascribed to

changes in prices and incomes. The implication is that the remaining change (the residual), known as 'the underlying trend in demand' must be attributable to other factors – probably associated with more fundamental changes in consumer behaviour and attitudes with respect to food products. In some cases, where the changes in the economic factors would have implied a change in consumption in one direction, but actual consumption has moved in the opposite direction, the implication is that the underlying trend in demand is greater than the actual trend in consumption. In other words, the underlying trend in demand shows *what would have happened to consumption* if prices and incomes had remained stable in real terms.

Income elasticities of demand for food expenditure as a whole, and for individual foods, were first presented in 1955, although they were calculated separately for each of the years from 1952 until 1955. The method for doing so was as follows. First, where the data were fully available, the sample was restricted to, and divided into, eleven different types of households according to the number of adults and children with some account taken of age (couples without children with at least one of them over 55 were treated as a separate group). Each household type was then partitioned by quartiles of income, and averages taken over the quartiles. Elasticities were calculated for each household type from the four observations by regressing logs of quantities on logs of income.

The reason for averaging over quartiles before undertaking the regressions is because of the possibility of zero expenditures on many of the foods by many of the households.[7] These observations would not be compatible with the assumed functional (constant elasticity) form for demand. This, then, allows the (extremely frequent) problem of non-purchase of foods to be set aside with an implicit assumption that each household of a particular type enjoys identical preferences but goes through a cycle of purchasing the various foods in sequence (or with uniform probabilities). As the 1967 report puts it:

> To exclude the households which did not record a purchase (whether this is due to the households never buying the food or buying it only infrequently) would give averages relating to the average size of purchase made by *households which made a purchase during the Survey week* and not average purchases by *all households* . . . it would therefore not produce income elasticities of average quantity purchased but of average size of purchase, and the latter would have limited practical value unless they were supplemented by an income elasticity of the proportion of households buying. (p. 148)[8]

This is an extremely revealing rationale. It just about recognizes that households of the same type may have different preferences (since some may never purchase a food). It might be thought, then, that the issue of what determines whether a household purchases a food or not is of importance (and even indicative of preferences that are not the same across households). This, however, is set aside by the NFS as of limited practical value unless reduced to an estimated income elasticity of proportion of households purchasing a food (which never appears to have been broached in practice). This carries the implication that the proportion purchasing is, for all intents and purposes, determined by income alone (and is made equivalent, again, to the assumption of identical households with the same greater or lesser probability of purchasing depending upon income).[9] In short, either it must be assumed that households have the same preferences (which is empirically demonstrated to be false) or they do not, in which case the reasons for this ought to be theoretically and empirically examined.

For the four years from 1952 to 1955, the income elasticities of food expenditure for each household type are fairly constant and close to one another, approximately equal to 0.3. There is an exception for childless couples under 55. This is explained by their greater reliance upon meals taken outside the home, although it is equally observed in 1958 that single women adjust in the opposite direction because those with more income entertain more visitors (p. 27). For both 1956 and 1958, taking account of meals eaten outside the home has the effect of raising the weighted average income elasticity for all households from 0.28 to 0.32 (p. 27 of the 1958 report).[10]

While it seems reasonable to adjust for meals taken outside the home (and extra ones provided within it), two crucial steps are taken in doing so. First, the econometrics is operationalized by imposing the same preferences on all households of a given type (in order, in the absence of longitudinal data, to generate separate observations for estimation). By the same token, it is accepted that households of different types have different preferences. At least four variables are involved in various ways – age, gender, presence of children, and overall numbers in the household. In other words, as households vary over these variables, so their preferences are deemed to differ and are estimated as such. There is an implicit understanding that these socioeconomic variables influence preferences, although why and how is rarely ever discussed (nor why these types of households should be considered rather than those partitioned by other criteria such as education, region, occupation, etc.).[11] Thus, in order to estimate income elasticities on the basis of a theory of given preferences, it is assumed that preferences are not fixed but vary quite systematically according to a set of socioeconomic characteristics.

Second, however, it could even be assumed that preferences were uniform across the population but that different household compositions offered separate comparative advantages in the purchase and use of food. It is easier, not necessarily more preferred, to eat out as a childless (heterosexual) couple (or proportionately more meals might be taken at work). Or, as is more plausible in accounting for the reverse effect for single women, another joint activity is incorporated with eating out – entertainment. This raises the more general issue not only of the complementarities of consumption (across foods and other consumption) but also of the activities associated with it. These include much more than eating out – shopping and cooking, for example. Developments in the supply and price of food are complemented, and substituted for, by fast-food outlets, changing forms of retailing (supermarkets) and domestic technology and organization (with new, convenient foods, and the means with which to use them through freezers and microwaves, and with women going out to work). Of course, such matters can be accommodated within the new household economics. But to do so, irrespective of its own dubious merits,[12] sheds doubts on the division between supply and demand (as production and consumption, now both take place within the home) and renders more complex the statistical independence of price and income effects and residual changes in underlying preferences (as these reflect wage rates and decisions over the labour market also). As is acknowledged in the 1969 report:[13]

> Consumers collectively (as well as individually) can and do change their ideas of relative values from one point in time to another. Even in a comparatively short period they are subjected to changing pressures from the advertising industry, from manufacturing and agencies who provide new products and services, and from a host of environmental changes, including changes in the value of money [a reference to money illusion?]. The condition about 'other things being equal' is rarely realized in practice, and for this reason it is an over-simplification to attempt to estimate the demand function by fitting a regression to a set of observations of income and expenditure only taken at different points in time (time-series analysis), even when deflated since the locus of such points may trace out *shifts* in the demand function rather than the demand function itself. Indeed, a demand relationship estimated in this way would not satisfy the condition that demand may change even though there may be no change in incomes. Moreover, it would imply that any response to a change in income would be instantaneous when in practice there is likely to be a lag. (pp. 177–8)

In short, the NFS appeals to the variability of preferences and the circumstances in which they are exercised as a rationale for using cross-section rather than time-series analysis, at least for estimating income elasticities, a matter to be discussed immediately below.

These methods for estimating income elasticities were continued, with minor modifications, until 1985 – pensioners were separated out, to make twelve household types, and octiles in place of quartiles were used from

1965. As is apparent, the income elasticities are estimated as constants. This is despite the recognition in 1958 (p. 27) that the overall elasticity for food had fallen from 0.4 to 0.3 between 1937–39 and twenty years later, the earlier estimates having been made by Stone *et al.* (1954). In 1960, it is acknowledged that the elasticity is not constant, even if estimated as such:

> Although elasticity of demand is not the same at all income levels, often declining as income increases, for most foods it is found that a logarithmic transformation of the original data results in a linear relationship, giving a constant elasticity over the range of incomes considered. (p. 157)

In 1967 (p. 146), it is 'found preferable to demonstrate' the declining elasticity with income by use of the annual estimates rather than cross-section for a single year because of 'the consequences of the income effect being confounded with the purely social class effect are greater'. It is not clear what this means since the NFS had defined social class by income level! Presumably, it is intended to eliminate non-income class effects, loosely correlated with income, which affect elasticity within years but not the trend between years. This is made explicit in 1969 by reference to 'the consequences of the income effect being confounded with occupational and other non-income effects [which] are greater' (p. 177). Further, 'It has been found in practice that the fitting of demand functions which allow the elasticity to vary with income is rarely justified owing to the variability of the data.' Thus, it is found that a constant elasticity works statistically within years, so it is adopted even though it is found to decline between years. This is put down to other, more influential socioeconomic determinants which are not investigated for their effect, but which are presumed to be neutral from one year to the next. As discussed earlier, the evidence is equally consistent with a time trend in the neglected determinants with the income elasticity remaining the same.

Meanwhile, by 1965, correction for meals eaten out was no longer reported, and the overall income elasticity had fallen to 0.23. It was 0.20 in 1967 and eventually fell, though not continuously, to 0.15 in 1975. At this point, meals eaten out were restored (increasing elasticities on average by 0.05), because it was found that income elasticities for all food for some household types had become negative. In 1985, partly as a contribution to the general pruning of the report, just over 40 income elasticities were displayed, most significantly different from zero. This compares with the coverage of 200 or so foods in the preceding reports. The section on demand analysis closes with the information that 'efforts are being made to refine and develop the statistical techniques for estimating the demand parameters' (p. 52).

While the exercise of the previous year is repeated in 1986, it is accompanied by a statement of doubt concerning the method employed:[14]

'Recent investigations suggest that, for the purposes of estimating income elasticities this (constant elasticity) specification may be lacking in some respects' (p. 46). Income elasticities in 1986 are also calculated using the Working-Leser specification adopted by Deaton and Muellbauer in their almost ideal demand (AID) system, in which share of income spent on a food is a linear function of logarithm of household income (and hence of variable elasticity).[15] Quite apart from now allowing for variable elasticity, the new specification has the advantage of being able to use those observations with zero expenditure (as it allows for an income level at which this occurs). Consequently, even for individual foods, the elasticities can be calculated using all of the data directly, and without averaging it within eight percentiles.

It is not known why the methods for calculating and presenting the elasticities were changed. It might have been increasing dissatisfaction with the empirical results or the adoption of the new techniques that had emerged in the 1980s. As Chesher and Rees (1987, pp. 435–6) put it:

> The procedures [previously] used to obtain these elasticities were for the most part formulated in the late 1950s. Throughout, use is made of a constant elasticity model of households' demands . . . These estimates convey valuable information and provide a useful summary of the data. However, they are obtained using methods designed with the relatively limited computing power available in the 1950s and 1960s in mind, and they do not, of course, exploit the advances in understanding of models of consumers' expenditure that we have seen in the last twenty years.

Whatever the reason for the shifts in the NFS demand analysis, it was to remain consistent with the same conceptual basis – even if with variable elasticities and more efficient use of the data. Nor does it seem to have been successful. In 1989, demand analysis was presented for the last time. It did not figure in the 1990 report. Although this was a fiftieth anniversary issue, with many special features that may have crowded out demand analysis, it was not resumed in 1991. Nor does it seem to have been successfully carried out, since the more specialized catalogue of available statistics for 1992 only offers elasticities up to 1989 for sale.[16]

The estimation of price elasticities, first appearing in 1958,[17] necessarily differed through employing time-series data in order to generate variability in price – taken as the dependent variable and regressed upon *average* per capita quantity purchased over the entire population. Consequently, data at the household level are eschewed without comment, and it is implicitly presumed that price elasticities are common across all household types even though these are estimated to differ in income elasticities. The data are generated on a monthly basis over a five-year period,[18] and a simple regression, subject to one proviso, discussed below, is run on logs of deviations from average values over the same period. Only once, in 1958, is the identification problem acknowledged (p. 28):

> Strictly speaking, the technique used assumes that the price at any given time is fixed, while the supply is completely elastic in the short run, short term changes in demand being met by diversion of supplies from or to alternative uses or by stock adjustments. For some perishable products the supply is completely inelastic in the short run and such adjustments are impossible, so that it would be more accurate to take q rather than p as the independent variable. In the intermediate case, where the current supply is neither completely elastic nor completely inelastic, the demand relationship is logically indeterminate without further information on the supply side.

The proviso concerns the test for seasonal and annual shifts in demand, both for elasticity itself and for the constant term in the regression.[19] Two points correctly stand out from the commentary upon these regressions. First, 'no precision can be claimed for such estimates, most of which are smaller than their standard errors' (1958, p. 29). Second, where seasonal and annual shifts in demand parameters are found to be significant, these are freely explained by reference either to supply or to demand (1958, p. 29):

> The pattern of the monthly constants which measure seasonal shifts in the demand curve may arise from regular seasonal changes in the supply of the commodity in question or in its quality, or in the supply or quality of other commodities which are alternative or complementary to it. . . . Annual shifts may arise from changes in supply conditions and from improvements in the standard of living, associated with improved facilities for cooking and storage. Long term changes in taste, especially the steadily increasing demand for [and not supply of?] 'convenience' foods, also give rise to annual shifts in demand.

Such estimates are reported for ever larger numbers of foods for a number of years between 1958 and 1972, and for every year from 1973 until 1984. For each food in each year, it is indicated whether price is dependent upon annual and/or seasonal shifts in demand. On a rough count over the years, three-quarters (1,500) of the estimates exhibited an annual shift; there were negligible numbers without either annual or seasonal shift; and at least a half of the estimates suggest both annual and seasonal shifts. In 1978, for example, 102 foods were indicated as exhibiting both annual and seasonal shifts in demand.

Thus, the empirical analysis is based on given preferences even though the statistical results are generally insignificant and do, in any case, reveal that the vast majority of foods are subject to annual or seasonal shifts in demand (unconnected to price) and often to both. None the less, the actual shifts in demand for foods over time are broken down sequentially into separate components – those due to price changes, those due to income changes, and the residual due to everything else. The number of price elasticities presented was drastically reduced in 1985. From 1986 until 1989, this lower number was maintained with the comment that similar methods were being developed for the price-elasticities as had been introduced for the income elasticities in 1986.[20] In 1990, as observed, estimates for both disappeared altogether!

The NFS has also estimated a number of cross-elasticities. It has done so using the same method as for own-price elasticities but adding the prices of what are judged to be close substitutes (or complements) for small groups of foods (and also adding income in later years): these are carcass meat and poultry; carcass meat and fish; butter, margarine, and bread; tea, instant coffee and other drinks; fresh, canned and frozen vegetables; and oatmeal products and cereals. In general, the results are 'disappointing' with poor *t*-tests. Even so it is claimed that the inclusion of cross-prices improves overall explanatory power. Further, it is observed that butchers level out price fluctuations and induce customers to purchase what meat is most readily available – an explicit, if limited, acknowledgement of the endogeneity of preferences.[21] Significantly, in view of earlier comments concerning the conflation of price and income effects with changes in underlying demand (with the latter treated as a residual), the following account is given in 1970/71 of the rise of chicken purchases (p. 17/8):

> Much the greatest relative change was in average purchases of broilers, which increased by over 80 per cent between 1964 and 1970. Nearly three-fifths of this increase was due to the fall in their real price over the period, while changes in income and in the average price of carcass meat (principally beef) together accounted for about a tenth, the remainder (about a third) being due to the continued widening of the market and a strengthening of the underlying demand.

Quite clearly, both the price effect (with that of chicken dropping by 30% over the period, with that of substitutes only changing marginally) and the residual shift in demand effect are pushing in the same direction and both are found to be quantitatively significant. Is it reasonable to treat preferences as given to estimate the price and income effect, when the implication is that a third of an 80% change in quantity purchased is due to an unexplained shift in demand? Nor is there any reference to the shifting conditions of supply (other than through the observed price effect) in which the rise of battery methods of production and supermarket methods of retailing have proved so important.[22]

CONCLUDING REMARKS

In a talk before the Royal Agricultural Society, Brown (1958), who served as the chief architect of the NFS's demand analyses, was suitably modest about what could be achieved and, in calling for frequent re-estimation of demand functions, was recognizing that neither preferences nor supply conditions would remain fixed for long (p. 229):

> There are indeed grounds for thinking that, even within the area of food purchases, the rate of change of market conditions will be greater over the next twenty years than it was during the inter-war period: already the years since the war have seen the innovation of quick-frozen foods, an increasing variety of processed and semi-processed and pre-packed foods, and a considerable development in the utensils, such as pressure cookers, refrigerators and automatic cookers, with which housewives are equipped. There is, therefore, every reason to attempt frequent measurement of demand reaction in these changing conditions, even though individual results must be regarded as provisional, inconclusive, or subject to a fairly wide range of error.

He concludes (p. 339):

> For the purpose of predicting the future trend of demand or prices of individual commodities any mechanical application of the income and price elasticities here presented would involve the risk of appreciable error. For such a purpose purely econometric studies of past periods form but a small part of the information available to the forecaster, and should perhaps be regarded as the one-tenth of the iceberg which appears above the surface of the water.

Unlike an iceberg, however, whose volume, if not shape, can be calculated with precision from its tip (and the surrounding environment), the same does not apply to the determinants of food purchases and consumption. Interestingly, this is implicitly recognized in the questioning of Brown following his presentation; there are raised the issues of differential oligopoly across food provision and over time, with different profit margins at the various stages between agriculture and final consumption. In response, Brown himself points to the 'increasing service and processing content of food' and suggests study 'in order to separate the income elasticity of demand into two components, one of which would be relevant at the farm-gate and the other in the retail market' (p. 248). There is, however, no reason to presume that such elasticities will be common either across all foods or within the vertical chain of activity between the two extremes of economic activity for any individual food (and Kalecki-type analysis suggests that the degree of monopoly margins is dependent upon elasticities).

Ironically, commenting on the demand for food during the decade following on after Brown's anticipated twenty years of more rapid change, and in the fiftieth anniversary festschrift for the NFS, Ritson (1991b) suggests that it is characterized by a fifth decennial phase in which shifts in underlying demand are the dominant feature of a 'consumer revolution' in food purchases.[23] This is because of the increasing reliance upon the residual to explain shifts in food purchases, its being termed the 'underlying trend in demand' and seen as 'attributable to a large number of other economic and social factors (than prices and income) such as consumer tastes and household characteristics' (p. 41). In other words, even though the residual measures all changes in supply conditions other than price, it is not acknowledged as such except in the way and motives with which the household organizes itself – with reference to health and convenience, fast food within and outside the home, shifting meal patterns involving limited preparation time, and the needs of working women.

How are these conundrums associated with the explanation of food purchase to be addressed? One route would be to dig deeper into a more sophisticated economics and econometrics without changing the basic conceptual apparatus. Such is the source of the resurgence of demand theory within neoclassical economics. It would include the following elements:[24]

1 Food demand is obviously highly dependent upon certain non-food purchases or patterns of ownership, such as microwave, freezer, etc. (and non-consumption activities such as degree of labour market participation and number and care of children). In the short run, it might be acceptable to take ownership of such durables as exogenous (although some selection bias may be involved). But, for the long run it is preferable to endogenize such durable ownership and adopt a two-stage estimation procedure – as in Heckman (1979).

2 In allowing income elasticities to vary with income, it has been usual to assume that Engel curves are linear in the logarithm of total expenditure. This can be an unnecessarily restrictive assumption in that it presumes that goods are either luxuries or necessities over the whole range of income. This may not be so – for cream, for example, which is an indulgence at low levels of income but a necessity at high levels (with the matter further complicated by the popular notion of a cream as both a luxury and an unhealthy product). Banks *et al.* (1993) have estimated quadratic Engel curves and have found these to be significant for certain consumption goods, if not food as a whole. But the issue should be investigated within food groups, where some meats, for example, are necessities and others are luxuries.

3 One of the major issues underlying healthy eating is the avoidance of excessive consumption of particular foods or groups of foods that contain, for example, high quantities of fat, sugar and salt. To some extent this is realized by individual consumers by the total avoidance of such foods. Obvious and empirically significant examples are the

substitution of skimmed milk, margarine and brown bread for their more traditional alternatives. Estimation of food demand from the NFS has, however, been restricted by the form taken by the survey in which only within-week purchases are investigated. As some goods are purchased less frequently – either because they are used less than once per week or because they are bought in bulk and consumed more or less continuously – it is impossible to distinguish between such sequencing of purchases and the non-purchase of some commodities altogether (the presence of corner solutions). This has not proved a problem for demand estimation for food as a whole, since all must spend something on food. It has been addressed as a problem, however, in the context of alcohol and tobacco (though not possible in work on the NFS data sets). As observed, in estimation from the NFS for individual foods, the procedure has been adopted of assuming that all foods are evenly purchased in the sense that, within socioeconomic groups, non-purchase in one week is explained by a common, but non-synchronized, sequencing of purchases across weeks. Thus, there are no corner solutions permitted.

This is also the procedure adopted by Meghir and Robin (1992) in their estimation of seven foodstuffs from French household data (even though one of these foods is an overall meat group, biasing the results in the presence of vegetarians – although the meat groups includes eggs). Otherwise, their approach is extremely general, for it deals with non-linear Engel curves, two-stage estimators and a model of frequency of purchase. For the latter, motivation is provided by the idea of storage costs and indivisibility in consumption. Clearly, this needs to be supplemented by consideration of shopping patterns associated with the rise of the supermarket and superstores. In addition, they show that data on how often foods are purchased are necessary to obtain consistent estimators even when corner solutions are excluded, thereby extending the work of Keen (1987).[25]

The problem of corner solutions is a crucial one, not only for estimation purposes but also for policy. The NFS data do include frequency and quantity of purchase *within* the survey week, although this information does not appear to have been used. And, from these, it is unreasonable to assume absence of corner solutions. For whole milk, for example, non-purchase over a week is more likely to suggest no purchase at all than a similar lack of purchase in a week for salt or sugar. This is particularly important for shifts to skimmed milk.[26] Even if there are problems in identifying the difference between non-consumption and infrequency, this can be allowed for through prior knowledge or models built upon the basis of belonging to a consuming or non-consuming cohort (possibly estimated as a random variable). At the very least, the methods of Meghir and Robin can be reproduced for the NFS for appropriate (no corner solution) food groups, since previous estimates have not employed the within-week data.

4 Although frequency of purchase has been addressed in the previous heading (in its relation to corner solutions or non-consumption), it is an issue worthy of attention in its own right, given the importance of the relationship between food choice and shopping behaviour (for which storage costs, freezers, etc., apart, are probably less important than developments in retailing). Between 1979 and 1989, the number of purchases of goods that are only made once a week has risen from 74.3% to 76.3% so that the pattern of the weekly shop already seems to have been established at the earlier date.[27] However, there have been particular changes for particular commodities, and there are continuing differences between households with different socioeconomic characteristics. Here, the analysis of purchase behaviour could be more fully integrated into a model of sequencing of purchase and consumption, for which there are many modelling precedents, not least in the demand for cash in the light of the cost of trips to the bank, and in the analysis of count data (Cox 1970), as applied to patents by Hausman *et al.* (1984).

5 Traditionally, as previously stressed, results for demand analysis from the NFS have been interpreted as reflecting price and income effects from given preferences with poor test statistics and shifting parameters over time being explained by changes in preference. This is clearly unsatisfactory, in part because it is tautologous and in part because the two determinants are not being estimated simultaneously but with one left as the residual unexplained by the other. It is essential, then, that trend parameters be included in the functional forms in order to allow for shifting preferences, as in Baker *et al.* (1990), for example – again, a crucial issue both for estimation as well as for drawing policy implications for whose preferences by socioeconomic group are open to change and to what extent (i.e. where policy targeting is most needed and might be most effective).

6 Related to 5 is the possible use of dynamic specifications to estimate shifting demand functions over time even in the context of using cross-section rather than time-series data. This may be attempted by generating a quasi-panel data set along the lines of the precedent set by Deaton (1985). It would then be possible to draw upon the work of Pesaran and Smith (1992) to introduce dynamic effects in the estimation of income and price elasticities on the basis of quasi-panel data.

Thus, there are many options open within the orthodoxy to develop demand analysis beyond even the AID model whose full application appears to have been stillborn within NFS reports for almost a decade. But the conceptual and interpretative shortcomings of the given approach, even with greater sophistication in application, would remain unaddressed. An alternative approach is offered throughout this book. It differs in part by setting aside the idea that there can be a general theory of the demand for food. Greater emphasis is placed on the distinct ways in which different foods are produced and consumed in the passage from agriculture to digestion. Rather than generalizing across foods from the impact of prices and incomes on given preferences, with the latter's change regarded as a residual in explanation, focus should be placed on the vertical (dis)integration of the processes involved in the provision of foods, and how they relate (in serving, reproducing and undermining) the material culture – or tastes – associated with food.

In short, economics appears to be presented with a sharp choice. It can continue in the same way as before, analysing more or less satisfactory data as if they were generated by optimizing individuals, exercising given but shifting preferences in response to prevailing prices and incomes, treating all foods as if they were undifferentiated objects of consumption (apart from some *ad hoc* concessions to substitutability and complementarity), and allocating unexplained residuals to underlying changes in everything else. As outlined above, the scope of theory and statistical techniques available have created a vast virgin territory for orthodox economics and econometrics to occupy. Alternatively, foods can be understood as distinct, vertically organized structures of provision subject to a wide range of socioeconomic and cultural forces which have complex and contradictory outcomes. It is only possible to be pessimistic about the option that is liable to be adopted.

NOTES

1 Hence the formal, and diagrammatic, equivalence between the minimization of cost to attain a given isoquant and the minimization of expenditure to attain a given indifference curve. Note also the formalism of such analysis, in which the ideal designation of goods, whether inputs or outputs, by mathematical symbols detaches them from connection to any specific act of production or consumption. The theory is the same irrespective of the nature of the goods or activities concerned.

2 This is not to suggest a complete absence in economics of theoretical innovation for consumption. Ironmonger (1972), Lancaster (1966) and Pearce (1964) have been variously concerned with hierarchies of wants, (shifting) characteristics of goods, diffusion of tastes, etc. And Becker (1981), in the new household economics, has integrated consumer with other household decisions. But these innovations are most notable for their continuing limitations in scope and/or their total lack of plausibility.

3 For the first stage post, encapsulating these developments, see Deaton and Muellbauer (1980), but also Brown and Deaton (1972) and Blundell (1988).

4 Other significant developments in demand theory which, even if in a more complex fashion, continue to function within the given framework, are discussed in the concluding remarks.

5 Apart from the NFS Reports themselves, see Slater (1991) and Frank *et al.* (1984) for accounts of the NFS. Some aspects of our use of the data are outlined in the methodological introduction to the following Part of the book (Chapter 8).

6 See also Ritson (1991b).

7 As all households make some expenditure on food, as opposed to individual foods, it is not necessary to go through the quartile procedure to estimate the income elasticity of food expenditure as a whole. This is first acknowledged in practice in 1965.

8 See also report for 1981, p. 187.

9 See also Chesher and Rees (1987). The issue of being of limited practical value cannot be left without comment given the serious neglect of the NFS of the issue of who does or does not purchase foods in contexts other than demand analysis (such as the study of the incidence of healthy diets on the basis of averages across households). See Chapter 10, for example, where the issue of 'core' eaters of particular products is raised. Also consider the same issue in the context of smoking or drinking, and whether it is worthwhile estimating the income elasticity of size of purchase for these products – rather than assuming identical preferences across all households to a particular type.

10 See also reports for 1960 (p. 159) and 1962 (p. 115); and Chesher and Rees (1987).

11 Frequent reference is made to economies of scale in household production/consumption of food in order to explain declining per capita purchases with household size.

12 On which see Fine (1992), for example.

13 See also report of 1981, p. 185.

14 In 1987 this is strengthened to the following: 'Recent investigations suggest that this specification may not be valid' (p. 41). In 1988, constant elasticity is simply referred to as the 'model which was previously used' (p. 40).

15 See Deaton and Muellbauer (1980) and Appendix C to the 1986 report. If the coefficient on household income is negative, then elasticity is always less than one and is negative at high levels of income. This is found to be the case for most foods. See also Chesher and Rees (1987) and Chesher (1991). In addition, rather than partitioning the households into different types to be estimated separately, the demand equation is supplemented by variables for household characteristics, such as age (of housewife), number of earners, number and age of children and number of adults. Otherwise, the separate gender effect seems to have been dropped from the specification.

16 The reason given by MAFF for this is that it has moved to a new computer system and there have been pressures generated by other work, such as taking greater account of the impact of eating out. Ironically, Frank *et al*. (1984) argue, in a critical assessment of the NFS as a survey, that it has been increasingly oriented towards economic analysis (i.e. demand) as opposed to nutritional concerns. This is precisely at the point where the demand analysis was about to be diminished in prominence.

17 To allow, for the purposes of time-series estimation, a decent passage of time from the ending of rationing in 1954.

18 In 1963, the elasticities are estimated over the periods from 1956 to 1963, and from 1958 to 1963. The length of period varies in subsequent years also. Further, in 1963 (p. 33), these elasticities are termed 'short-run', presumably reflecting the conceptual basis on which they are calculated rather than any belief that everything else affecting supply and demand remains the same over such lengthy periods!

19 For details of the technique used to identify annual and seasonal demand shifts, see the report for 1958 (pp. 28–9), and many subsequent reports.

20 For 1986 (p. 49), repeated in 1987, 'such a model does not allow the best use to be made of all the information bearing on food purchases. With this in mind,

efforts are being made to refine and develop the statistical techniques for estimating price elasticities on a similar basis to that described for income elasticities'. For 1988 (p. 41), repeated in 1989, 'The Almost Ideal Demand model is currently being developed in order that price elasticities for food can be evaluated on a similar basis to that described for income elasticities.'

21 This is frequently commented upon in the reports. In 1966, it is more seriously recognized, albeit in a footnote (p. 20):

> From a purely econometric viewpoint the practice of levelling out prices excludes from that data much of the variation that is necessary in order to be able to measure the price/quantity relationships, while evening or averaging of prices for the different varieties of meat contributes to multicollinearity in the explanatory variables.

In 1969, the NFS undertook a special study of the role of different meat retailers. The friendly, but statistically disruptive, independent butchers were then responsible for two-thirds of meat sales, although two-thirds of other groceries were purchased from self-service stores. This is at a time of the growing role of supermarkets, whose impact is also uneven across meats with their taking, for example, 50.1% of meat sales in 1992 compared to 27.8% for independent butchers. But, for chicken, the respective shares were 57.2% and 15.4% – see MLC (1993). The 1969 survey did not report on sales by different meat products.

22 In the quotation above, the appeal to the widening of the market presumably refers to the larger proportion of households purchasing chicken and the strengthening of demand to increases in the quantities purchased, although the former is not generally distinguished in the NFS analysis. Here, then, is an implicit acknowledgement of the importance of more households purchasing at all (rather than this being of no practical significance as discussed earlier). This is itself dependent, of course, not only on price, income and demand shifts, but on availability in supermarkets in a variety of convenient forms.

23 The other phases are those of austerity and rationing (1940–59), return to normal diet (1950–60), income effects (1960–1970) and price effects (1970–80). See also Ritson (1991a).

24 To complement assumptions around the integrability and separability of household demand functions, and taking account of shifts in supply conditions. In addition, the recognition of the impact of different socioeconomic variables needs to be extended (although this is limited by the data); see Lund and Derry (1985). For example, Baker et al. (1990) find that car ownership and smoking are crucial distinguishing characteristics for consumer purchase (for total food expenditure in their work), and other work shows that the same holds for alcohol consumption. Unfortunately, these data have not been collected for the NFS.

25 See also Pudney (1989).

26 From very low levels, skimmed milk has taken up over 50% of quantities purchased over the past fifteen years.

27 Figures calculated from NFS data. Of course, there could have been a number of shopping trips during the week to buy a smaller number of the different goods on each occasion.

Part IV

WHAT WE EAT AND WHY

8

FOOD NORMS: METHODS AND DATA

Each of the other four chapters in this part is based upon statistical analyses of data drawn from the NFS. The purpose of this chapter is twofold. In the first section, the method of statistical analysis that we employ is explained, predominantly in a technical sense. It is an unusual method and, hence, will almost certainly be unfamiliar in itself and open to uncertain interpretation by the reader. Paradoxically, this is more likely among those who are already acquainted with empirical research involving the NFS or other food data sets, since these earlier analyses will have depended upon different methods and concepts with which ours should not be conflated.

Our empirical work also involves particular use of terminology which has proved confusing to some in previous presentations of our results. Accordingly, we provide here an explicit definition of the terms that are to be used. None the less, the methods that we employ are refined in later chapters as required. This leads to some limited repetition of the material covered in this chapter but has the added advantage of allowing these chapters to stand alone for those who feel comfortable with the methods outlined here. Later chapters, especially the next, also offer considerable motivation for the alternative methods that we adopt. But this is not the main aim here which remains primarily confined to a technical exposition.

The second purpose of this chapter, covered in the last section, is to provide some information on the NFS as a data set and how we have used it. Again, some readers may prefer to take this for granted, simply relying upon empirical results as presented. But others may wish to examine more closely what is meant by a particular category of food or a particular socioeconomic grouping.

THE MODE OF STATISTICAL ANALYSIS

Our empirical work adopts methods previously employed to identify consumption norms in the ownership of consumer durables.[1] First of all, what do we mean at a very general level by a (consumption) *norm*? It has two components – one is the common pattern of behaviour across a sample of the population. In principle, this could be measured in a number of different ways, by an average or some other measure of central tendency. The problem with this is that it tells us very little about the variation of consumption across the population. Two different samples might have the same average or whatever but exhibit a very different pattern across individuals. If consumption were highly differentiated across a sample, as measured by variance for example, we might be tempted to deny the presence of a norm at all.

This is not the attitude that we adopt because of what we interpret as the second component of our consumption norm. This is motivated by the notion that one section of the population may have consistent consumption patterns but which differ markedly from another section of the population which itself is consistent in its patterns of consumption. Thus, it might be considered *normal* for the popularity of the most recent pop music to decline with age after adolescence. We wish to capture such patterns in our definition of consumption norms. Accordingly, a norm is made up of the patterns for the population as a whole, together with consistent, possibly different, patterns for subsections of the population.

What if there are no such patterns at all – either for the population as a whole or for subsamples of it? It would be tempting to deny the existence of a norm altogether. Although this is merely a terminological matter, we will continue to understand this as a norm. This is partly because, whether behaviour is common or not, the statistical methods will still yield results which can be reported as the norm. In addition, it is possible to interpret what might (appear to) be random behaviour as a norm itself, characteristic of the population. Thus, the norm for whether individuals are left- or right-handed may have no socioeconomic basis at all and could be interpreted as such.

In short, what we mean by a norm is the common or divergent patterns of consumption that can be identified. It follows that the norms exist even where there are no common patterns – this, as it were, being the pattern. In the chapters that follow, we will identify such norms, searching for commonalities and differences across the population by socioeconomic characteristics. What we do not do, however, is investigate the extent of variation within the subsamples that we construct.[2]

This gives a very general idea of what is meant by a consumption norm. It is a way in which standard, and possibly familiar, calculations from the NFS can be interpreted. Attention is given to the average *quantities* consumed by households of specific products or specific nutrients distributed across those products. Differences might well be highlighted between different sections of the population by socioeconomic classification.

Our method is entirely different and does not deal in (average) quantities purchased at all. Rather, our estimation of food norms focuses on the issue of whether a food is purchased or not, at least once within the survey week. By the term *absolute frequency of purchase*, we will mean the proportion of a sample who buy a food at least once during the week. At times, when clear in meaning, the qualification by 'absolute' might be dropped for brevity. *Absolute* frequency of purchase, however, is to be contrasted with *relative* frequency of purchase by which is meant whether one food or another has a higher absolute frequency. In each case, the reference to frequency has nothing to do with how often a particular household purchases a particular food during the survey week, but it refers to what proportion of the sample purchases a food at least once during the week.[3] Should one food have a higher absolute frequency of purchase than another, it might be referred to as having a higher *ranking*.

This is because of the way in which the food norms are calculated here. For the sample as a whole, the food norm is initially defined in terms of its ranking of the foods by absolute frequency of purchase across the population. In other words, the foods are simply ranked in terms of their popularity, measured by whether they are purchased or not (and not by how much might be purchased). The corresponding norm or ranking gives an indication of consumption patterns for the population, or sample, as a whole. It is the analogue to the first component of a norm, discussed above as an average. In order to investigate the second component of the norm, how patterns are common or different within the population, it is natural to examine this first component of the norm, or the ranking by absolute frequency of purchase, for subsamples of the population. These can be defined by socioeconomic variables, such as age of head of household.

Suppose, then, we partition the population by some criterion.[4] Each of the subsamples of the survey defines its own food norm which will, in general, differ from that for the sample as a whole. By comparing the two rankings, we obtain the second component of the food norm – the extent to which the rankings for a subsample differ from those for the sample as a whole. In particular, each subsample norm can be compared to the sample norm by recording the upward or downward shift in the ranking of each food. Necessarily the sum of the differences in the subsample's rankings must be equal to zero as the shift up for one food in a ranking must lead to a corresponding downward and equal shift in other foods.

In summary, our food norms are defined by the ranking of foods by absolute frequency of purchase for the sample as a whole, together with the divergencies in rankings for various socioeconomic partitions of the sample. What follows does not contribute to this definition further, but it does offer a particularly convenient way of providing an exposition of the empirical results.

The application of these definitions in practice will be illustrated by a particular example drawn from our work with the NFS. So, in Table 8.1, for a range of meat products and for a partition by age of head of household, let the foods, listed horizontally, define the rows of a matrix (or table), and let the socioeconomic partition define the columns of the matrix, as shown. Now, the entries in the matrix can be defined by the subsamples' shifts in rankings of the foods relative to the rankings of the population as a whole. Looking across this matrix, dubbed the 'dramatrix', it is possible to see how the ranking of a particular food (by frequency of purchase) shifts in response to a socioeconomic variable (such as age); and looking down the dramatrix allows us to see whether a particular socioeconomic variable has a major impact upon the rankings of the foods. The definition of a food (consumption) norm is now refined to incorporate not only the ranking of foods across the sample as a whole but also the presence or not of systematic patterns in the dramatrices defined by a variety of socio-economic variables. Thus, the notion of food norm, as outlined in the previous paragraph, is easily illustrated by presentation of corresponding dramatrices, of which Table 8.1 forms an example.[5] Thus, the food norm, as represented in the dramatrix, is a descriptive device and does not imply, as might be presumed, normal, common or uniform behaviour across the population although this might be found to be present. Either common or divergent rankings, or combinations of them, make up the norm. Hopefully, the notion and usefulness of this notion of food norms will become sharper in the subsequent presentation of results in the following chapters.

Table 8.1 Aggregate dramatrix by age

Age	<25	25–34	34–44	45–54	55–64	65–74	>75
Beef	3	2	0	0	−1	−1	−1
Uncooked bacon	−4	−2	0	0	1	1	−1
Cooked bacon	−4	−1	1	0	1	−2	−1
Sausages	0	0	−2	−2	0	0	−1
Chicken	3	3	3	1	−1	−4	−4
Pork	−1	0	1	0	1	2	−2
Lamb	−28	−15	−8	0	0	6	9
Meat pies	6	1	3	−1	−3	−4	−6
Corned meat	−8	−5	0	1	5	−2	−4
Cooked meat	−14	−10	−10	0	1	4	4
Canned meat	13	11	1	−6	−10	−7	−5
Other frozen	22	11	6	−3	−4	−4	−4
Deli/pâté	5	21	15	3	−4	−3	0
Cold pies	−6	−6	−4	6	5	6	5
Liver	−11	−12	−9	2	12	15	16
Burgers	16	7	3	−4	−4	−3	−4
Ready meals	15	5	3	−3	−3	−6	−4
Cooked poultry	0	0	1	4	5	5	9
Turkey	1	1	0	1	1	2	0

Note: No separate category for frozen burgers in 1979.

One of the advantages of the food norm as defined here is that its corresponding empirical representation in the form of the dramatrix can allow relationships between foods and socioeconomic variables to be readily revealed. For the dramatrix often presents consistent, monotonic patterns as the subsample varies across a socioeconomic factor. For example, Table 8.1 is constructed for a selection of meats from the dramatrices for each of the four years 1979, 1984, 1986 and 1989. The four dramatrices have simply been added together. Thus, the first entry (for beef, for head of households of less than 25 years old) shows that on average over the four years, beef has been ranked three places above the norm for the population as a whole. More dramatically, lamb has been ranked twenty-eight places lower.[6] What the table shows is how there is a skew in ranking towards the young for frozen burgers, canned meat, other frozen foods, ready meals and deli/pâté (other than the under-25s), and skews to the old for lamb, liver and cooked meats.

In the following chapters in this Part, similar methods are used for different foods and for different partitions of the population. In each case, for the results presented, as well as for many that have not been presented, it is possible to examine the dramatrices for the consistent patterns of socioeconomic variation that correspond to the food norms as we have defined them.

THE USE OF THE NFS DATA

The data sets used throughout our empirical research were those of the NFS for the years 1979, 1984, 1986 and 1989 (the latest available at the time that the research began); otherwise, apart from evenness of the gap between the years, these were chosen to reflect convenience given the shifting content of the data in terms of the way in which the foods were included (see next section). Taking a selection of foods, for which major dietary changes had occurred or were occurring, these were ranked by absolute frequency of purchase, both across the survey population as a whole and for a wide variety of subsamples defined by socioeconomic variables, such as age, income, class, household composition, etc., as well as by subsets of these subsamples obtained by combining their associated variables together (the influence of age with household composition, for example). Usually, the definition of foods followed those employed by the NFS but, at times, our own definitions were used by aggregating over the NFS codes. Similarly, at times, we used the NFS definition of socioeconomic variables, but more often than for foods, our own variables were generated from the raw NFS data. Details for these procedures are outlined below, and they are remarked upon elsewhere in the book where considered relevant.

The methodology for identifying consumption norms, as described in the previous section, had been developed for a previous research project when applied to consumer durables for data from the National Readership

Survey (NRS) and General Household Survey (GHS). The empirical analysis of the NFS data necessitated developing new, as well as adapting existing, computer procedures to allow the adoption of this method.

The NFS is a continuous inquiry into household food consumption, expenditure and nutrient intake in Great Britain. Broadly comparable data have been collected since 1952, and data were at the time of our research only available in magnetic form from 1979.[7] The objective of this project was to analyse the data from a selection of years appropriate to the food systems under investigation. The sample size in each year is approximately 7,000 households. In each household a diary keeper, the 'housewife' whether male or female,[8] records details of the description, quantity and cost of the foods entering the home over a period of seven days. The survey classifies the food entries into about 200 food codes. Data are also collected on the number of meals eaten outside the home although not on the content or cost of those meals. Until 1992, no data on alcoholic drinks and confectionery are recorded.

The data available on the survey contain information about: the *household*, including discrete categorical variables such as region, income group of head of household, age of housewife, number of adults and children, etc.; the *persons in the household* including variables such as age, sex, whether they are working or not; and *foods that enter the household in the survey week* with information on whether it was a normal purchase or, for example, discounted (from employer) or free (from garden or allotment), the quantity and price and the allocated food code.

There are some important points to note about the NFS. First, the survey records only purchase and not consumption. In addition, only household, and not individual, purchase of food is identified.

Second, because the survey records purchases for a sample household only in one single survey week, bulk purchasing behaviour may skew the results, by reflecting more or less than is typically consumed by the household. It is generally assumed, even if implicitly, in the NFS's own presentation of its results, that bulk purchasing averages out over all the households to produce a representative sample, but it is still an aspect to be borne in mind for small subsamples and especially for individual households. The incidence is also necessarily different for different foods; infrequent purchase *can* indicate foods consumed infrequently, for example long-life milk, or those consumed frequently, such as tea bags and coffee. This *may* correspond to the perishability of foods. There is, therefore, some interplay between shopping patterns, consumption behaviour *and* the nature of the food being investigated. It also raises the related question of perishability and what foods are convenience foods – and what is the definition of 'convenience'.[9]

Third, all foods purchased are allocated to one of the 200 food codes, and the content of these varies in scope. For example, fresh peas are identified by one food code, clearly corresponding to a particular food, whereas all breakfast cereals are coded within a single food code.[10] This has implications for identifying, for example, healthy or other eating trends since no differentiation concerning nutrients can be made between low-sugar cereals and those laden with sugar.

Fourth, there is some incompatibility between comparing different years, as some foods are not recorded separately in some years. This usually corresponds to the introduction of 'new' foods not available earlier or not purchased in large quantities before – such as semi-skimmed milk or low-fat spreads.

CHOICE OF YEARS AND OTHER ISSUES

In order to carry out empirical analysis, it was decided to investigate a selection of years from the NFS data. The following describes our strategy for doing so for dairy foods (the first study undertaken even though it appears as the last in the book). Greater details follow for dairy foods than for the others. Having set up the data for use from appropriate years for the dairy foods, there were advantages in carrying these years over for the other foods even if these years would not have been chosen for these foods if starting from scratch.

The years that were chosen for dairy foods to be analysed were the first and last years of the survey available at the start of the research (1979 and 1989) and two intermediate years, 1984 and 1986, which were chosen in part because of changes in the way of recording 'dairy' foods in the survey. A full description of foods included in the results is to be found below, but the main changes throughout the period are noted here.

Whole-fat liquid milk alone was recorded separately in 1979; new categories were introduced for skimmed milks in 1984 and semi-skimmed milks in 1986. Because of interest in the (reported) decline in butter consumption and the availability of other 'spreads', margarine and other butter substitutes are included in our 'dairy' analysis. In 1979, 'other fats' are considered although this category includes a variety of possible foods; 'low-fat' spreads are introduced in 1984 and 'reduced-fat' spreads in 1986. Margarine is recorded separately throughout all the years.

In order to give some indication of the increase in frequency of households purchasing the foods, 'other fats' and 'other milk' were added to the 1979 analysis, although it must be noted that these codes contain a broad range of possible foods purchased. Yoghurt and cream were included, as well as the liquid milks and 'spreads', in order to identify what were previously assumed to be foods undergoing changes in patterns of consumption.

DAIRY FOODS USED IN THE RESULTS

NFS code	Food name in our analysis	Description
		1989
3	Whole milk	Other liquid milk, full price (includes pasteurized and homogenized *but not* UHT or sterilized)
13	Yoghurt	Includes fruit yoghurt and flavoured yoghurts.
14	Skim milk	Fully skimmed milk; e.g., Trimilk, Unigate Balance, etc.
15	Semi milk	Semi and other skimmed milk, e.g. Light Gold, and Vita Pints includes long-life.
17	Cream	Fresh or bottled or frozen, processed or canned, but excluding substitute and imitation cream.
18–23	Any cheese	Cheese, any in the range of:–
18		natural, hard cheddar and cheddar type;
19		natural, hard other UK varieties or foreign equivalents;
20		natural, hard Edam and other continental;
21		natural, soft;
23		processed.
131–4	Any butter	Any butter:
131		butter – New Zealand;
132		butter – Danish;
133		butter – UK; or
134		all other butter.
136–7	Any marg	Any margarine, either:
136		soft margarine; or
137		other margarine, includes margarine containing a proportion of butter.
145	Reduced fat	Reduced-fat spreads, e.g. Clover, Kerry Gold Meadow Cup.
146	Low fat	Low-fat spreads, e.g. Outline, St Ivel Gold, Sainsbury's Low-Fat Spread, Weight Watchers.

1986

As 1989.

1984

As 1989 except:

1 Food code 14, *skimmed milk*, was available for the first time, and it also included *semi-skimmed milk* which was *not* recorded separately until 1986.
2 Food code 146, *low-fat spreads*, was available for the first time, but reduced-fat spreads were *not* recorded separately until 1989.

1979

As 1984 except:

1 *Whole milk* (food code 4) included UHT, sterilized and long-life milk, which were not included in the whole-milk codes in years 1984, 1986 and 1989.
2 *Other milk* (food code 14) was used in the results for 1979 to give some indication of frequencies of households purchasing semi-skimmed (if available) and skimmed milks which were included in this foodcode for 1979 but not recorded separately. However, it should be noted that although this gives some indication of these purchases, the code also includes 'other milk' products – 'goats' milk, sour milk, fresh cream desserts containing cream, milk or skimmed-milk solids' – and cannot be a direct comparison with the later 'skimmed and semi-skimmed milk' foodcodes.
3 Similarly, *other fats* are used in the results for 1979 to show the extent of households purchasing low-fat spreads which were included in this code (foodcode 148) in 1979 although 'other fats' also include suet, dripping, and 'substitute' and 'imitation' cream.

OTHER FOODS USED IN THE RESULTS

In lesser detail, for another group of foods with which we dealt (those associated with major trends), the following are those corresponding to a single food code, indicated in brackets, from the NFS of 1989. If asterisked, they are made up of a number of different products even if allocated a single food code by the NFS:[11] whole milk (3), yoghurt (13), frozen burgers (86)* which was grouped with frozen convenience foods in 1979, ready meals (92),* eggs (129), sugar (150), crisps, etc. (200),* frozen chips (205),* fruit juice (248),* breakfast cereals (282)* and ice cream (332). The following foods were made up by combining the NFS food codes as indicated (each of which may have included a range of commodities): skimmed milk (14–15) with some change in definition over the years, chicken (73–4), butter (131–4), margarine (136–7), less-fat spreads (145–6) with some change in definition over the years, potatoes (156–61), white bread (251–4), brown bread (255–6), and biscuits (274–7).

177

A variety of meat products were also analysed. The products are all composites whether amalgamating more than one food code or not. The codes from NFS for 1989, not already covered, are as follows: beef (25–30), lamb (32–5), pork (37–40), liver offals (42–51), uncooked bacon (52–4), cooked bacon (58), cooked poultry (59), corned meat (62), cooked meats (66), canned meats (71), turkey (75–6), sausages (79–80), cold pies (81–2), other frozen convenience (87) including burgers in 1979, deli/pâté (89–90), and meat pies (91).

SOCIOECONOMIC VARIABLES

There are a range of socioeconomic variables available in the NFS. Those that were used in analysing the whole survey population and subsamples of the population for the four years under consideration are listed below. Following initial results, we undertook to create new variables and modify existing ones in order to identify subsamples of the survey population that were not recorded separately in the data. These could be used in combination to provide nests of subsamples for the purposes of calculating food norms. Details are provided below for the dairy foods. Similar, but not always the same, procedures were used for the other results.

The variables that were adapted for our purposes included *region* where the category 'GLC and East Anglia' was split using the 'type of area or sample class' variable to produce the two regions separately. The order of some categorical variables was recoded, such as *household composition*, *tenure* and *microwave/freezer/fridge* ownership so that the results could be interpreted monotonically as far as possible. Two 'continuous' variables in the NFS data – *total family income* and *total expenditure* in the survey week – were used to create two new categorical variables, dividing all households into one of the six percentile categories. The total family income data were not available for all households (no total family income data for 37% of households in 1989). A new categorical variable was created in order to identify those households where there were *children* present, by age of children. Some categories in this variable were so small that they were aggregated with others for the subsample populations in order to give reasonable sample sizes. In the NFS variables, social class and socio-economic class both lump together all households where the head of household is not in an occupation, so another variable 'occupation code' was used to produce separate categories for the unemployed, and the senior citizens or the retired. In the social class category, armed forces were also separated out of the 'not economically active' group.

Subsamples were created by selecting from the survey by one of the categorical variables – for example, *all* single adult households were extracted by using the household composition variable. In addition, a new subsample was created using data on the people in the household to eliminate male-only households. This produced a subsample of females for which it was possible to analyse the working code variable – i.e. full-time, part-time, housewife, etc. Again the working code was refined using the occupation code in a similar way to social class and socioeconomic groups so that housewives could be identified separately from the senior citizens or the retired and the unemployed. The following pages list our use of socioeconomic variables in our analysis of purchasing of dairy products. The full implications of using these variables and associated subsamples will become clear in the detailed presentations of results that follow in the next four chapters.

SOCIOECONOMIC VARIABLES AND SUBSETS USED IN THE DAIRY RESULTS[12]

Whole (survey) population

Variable   Categories (or partition)

Region   Wales, Scotland, Northern, Yorkshire and Humberside, North West, East Midlands, West Midlands, South West, GLC, East Anglia, rest of South East

Area type   1 Greater London

2 Metropolitan districts and the Central Clydeside conurbation

Local authority districts with an electoral density of:

3 Seven or more electors per acre
4 Three but fewer than seven electors per acre
5 Fewer than seven electors per acre but more than 0.5
6 Fewer than 0.5 electors per acre.

The numbers 1–6 indicate a different socioeconomic variable.

Social class

*Occupation inadequately described/no information; *armed forces; professional occupations; intermediate occupations; skilled occupations; part-skilled occupations; unskilled occupations; *unemployed; *senior citizens or retired

*Registrar-General's social class categories are defined in terms of occupation of the head of household. The categories asterisked were composite in the NFS data and separated for the purposes of this analysis using the NFS occupation code.

Socioeconomic group

Occupation inadequately described/no information; member of Armed forces; employers, managers and own-account workers (other than professional non-agricultural); professional workers, self-employed; professional workers, employees; intermediate non-manual workers; junior non-manual workers; personal service workers; foreman and supervisors; manual; skilled manual workers; semi-skilled manual workers; unskilled manual workers; farmers, whether or not employing non-family labour; agricultural workers; unemployed; senior citizens/retired

Tenure

Rent free; furnished rented; unfurnished, rented other than council; unfurnished, council rented; owns with mortgage; owns outright

Micro/Freezer ownership

Owns both; owns microwave only; owns freezer only; owns neither

For 1979 to 1986 this variable was fridge/freezer ownership.

Housewife age

Less than 25 years; 25–34 years; 35–44 years; 45–54 years; 55–64 years; 65–74 years; 75 years plus; or age unknown.

Head of household age as above.

Household composition

Single adult; two adults; three adults; four adults; one adult plus one or more children; two adults plus one child; two adults plus two children; two adults plus three children; two adults plus four or more children; three adults plus one or two children; three adults plus three or more children

Children

A new variable was created as follows from the NFS variables 'number of children aged 16–17; 12–15; 8–11; 5–7; 1–4; infants (i.e. <1 year old)', and used with other unmodified NFS variables.

Households with:

No children; infants only; infants and children aged 1–4; infants and children aged 5 or over; infants and children of both under and over 5 years; children aged 1–4 only; children aged 1–4 and 5 or more only; Children aged 5 or more only.

Number of pregnant women in the household

Number of senior citizens or retired people in the household

Number of males in the household

Number of females in the household

Number of earners in the household

Benefit

Income support only; Family Credit only; both; neither

Income of head of household or principal earner[13]

Gross weekly income of the head of household or principal earner.

	1989	1986	1984	1979
With one or more earner in the household:				
A1	£560 or more	£430 o.m.	£355 o.m.	£200 o.m.
A2	£420–559.99	£335–	£270–	£145–

B	£230–419.99	£165–	£140–	£90–
C	£120–229.99	£90–	£83–	£56–
D	<£120	<£90	<£83	<£56

With no earner in the household:

| **E1** | £120 or more | £90 o.m. | £83 o.m. | £56 o.m. |
| **E2** | Less than £120 | <£90 | <£83 | <£56 |

OAP single person*
OAP couple*
OAP other*

*Pensioner households (in which at least three-quarters of the total income is derived from National Insurance retirement or similar pensions and/or paid in supplementation or instead of such pensions). Such households will include at least one person over retirement age.

Total family income

This is a new variable created from the continuous variable total weekly net family income in £s. Note a high percentage of households in each year do not have record of total family income. The values were used to divide all households into one of the six percentile categories: high to low total family income, with an 'unknown' category.

Food expenditure

In the same way as the variable above, the total value of all foods purchased in the survey week for each household was used to create a six-category variable from high to low total household expenditure on food.

Month

January to December.

Subsamples of the population

'Females' subsample

  Workcode

  Unknown; full-time; part-time; unemployed; sick; not working and pregnant; full-time and pregnant; part-time and pregnant; unemployed and pregnant; sick and pregnant; senior citizen/retired; housewife

Household type and income subsamples

The following subsamples were selected from the categorical variables described above:

1 Single households
2 Two-adult households
3 Two-adult households with one or two children
4 Adult households only (any number)
5 Households where (any age or number of) children are present

Households where the head of household income is in category:

6 A1 or A2 (see above for values)

7 B

8 C

9 D or E2

10 OAP income groups (single, couple or other)

For each of these subsamples the categorical variables described for the whole (survey) population were analysed:

Social class

Housewife age

Household composition (for income subsamples)

Children recoded into four categories:

No children

Pre-school children only

Pre- and school-age children

School-age children only

Number of:

senior citizens/retired

males

females

Income of head of household (for household subsamples)

Total family income (with percentile values recalculated for each subsample of the population)

Total household expenditure on food in the survey week (with percentile values recalculated for each subsample of the population).

CONCLUSION

With the methods described in this chapter and our manipulation of the NFS data, we now turn to a detailed analysis of household purchasing behaviour. These investigations are, in turn, related to the food SOPs attached to the chosen food categories. Thus, for example, we examine food choice over dairy or meat products as well as the food systems that serve those choices.

NOTES

1 See Fine *et al.* (1992a–e and 1993) and Fine (1983).
2 This is because the weight of work involved did not appear to be justified by the results that might be obtained, given that the norms are calculated on the basis of purchase or not without reference to quantities purchased. Within subsample variation has, however, been measured in the earlier work on consumer durables (see note 1), using notions of 'uniformity' and 'conformity'.
3 With minor exceptions, no account is taken of how often each household purchases a food during the survey week.
4 Note that the partition might not be complete in the sense of including the whole of the original sample. This might be due to lack of data on the

partitioning criterion, or for convenience. If investigating the effect of presence of children, for example, we might exclude single households.

5 Note, as discussed in the next paragraph, that the dramatrix in this case has been aggregated over four sample years in order to highlight the results involved.

6 Note that the sum of columns is not always zero because of occasional ties in rankings. The sum across rows does not have to be zero, especially if the subsamples do not make up the entire population for some reason.

7 Electronic data have been prepared for all years back to 1972 and are to be lodged at the ESRC Archive.

8 In the most recent surveys, not covered by our results, the term 'housewife' has now been replaced by 'main diary keeper' ('the person, male or female, principally responsible for domestic food arrangements').

9 See next chapter for some further discussion of the issue of bulk purchase and the presumption that all households within a socioeconomic group follow the same sequence of weekly shopping but lagged relative to one another.

10 This code was subdivided in 1992 into muesli, other high-fibre cereals, sweetened cereals, and other cereals. This clearly reflects health concerns which, accordingly, cannot be interrogated to the same extent for earlier years.

11 But note that even this is not so simple, for yoghurt for example, treated as unasterisked, includes fruit and flavoured yoghurts.

12 Note that not all of the socioeconomic variables reported below figure explicitly in the results presented in the text. They are included here for the sake of completeness. Their omission in the text, for example the effect of form of housing tenure, can be for a number of reasons – that there were no significant results, that they were not investigated in depth, or that they did not reflect themes that we chose to explore further.

13 For convenience, some of the definitions below are laid out differently than above.

CHILDREN, LOW INCOME AND THE SAUSAGE SYNDROME

This chapter is concerned with the effect of the presence of children on food choice and with the joint effect of the presence of children *and* the level of household income. In other words, where children are present, does this affect food norms? And do the associated patterns of food choice for the presence or absence of children differ according to the level of income? This is of obvious relevance to the issue of healthy eating for it broaches the question of whether the worse-off can not only afford less but also choose differently in what they can afford. However, before undertaking this exercise, and in part as a preliminary to the remaining chapters in this part, we begin by outlining some of the weaknesses of the NFS as a data set from our perspective.

SURVEYING THE NFS

It is over a decade since Frank *et al.* (1984) made an assessment of the merits of the NFS. Much has changed over the intervening period, not only in the conduct of the survey itself but also in the world of food and how it has been understood within academia. This commentary does not seek to undertake a comprehensive nor even a balanced review of the NFS but, rather, focuses upon a few selected issues. These arise out of the practical and detailed use of the raw data derived from NFS data tapes for selected years between 1979 and 1989, the results of which follow throughout this part of the book.

First, though, consider briefly those reservations about the data expressed by Frank *et al.* which are difficult to remedy. These include a poor response rate, of approximately 50%, for which non-respondents are not liable to be proportionately representative. Moreover, households are identified by the electoral register, thereby tending to exclude, for example, those living in an institutionalized or unstable household setting. In short, the survey is almost certainly biased by language, literacy, education, domestic stability, social class and availability of spare time. The intrusion of the survey is itself liable to bias behaviour, and the questionnaire is dependent upon subjective interpretation by interviewers. There are differences between purchase and ingestion, not only in waste but also through the intra-household distribution of consumption.[1] Each of these drawbacks may be difficult to rectify on a regular basis, but they are each worthy of an occasional special analysis to gauge the order of magnitude of their significance.[2]

It is also worth examining what has been done to rectify what had been identified as deficiencies in the survey. The most important have been the greater account taken of meals eaten outside the home and the inclusion of alcohol, soft drinks and confectionery. Previously, some correction had been made for the number of meals taken outside the home, treating them as if they were of the same nutritional content as those eaten in the home. But with the rise of fast-food outlets and of dining out, always more significant for those on higher incomes, such a presumption is no longer tenable and the content of meals taken out of the home is worthy of analysis in its own right.

In the past, data for soft drinks were collected but were not presented in tables in the main body of the annual report that accompanies each year's collection of statistics. Data for sweets and alcohol were not collected at all on the grounds that they would be unreliable in the light of the high proportion of consumption taken outside the home. Of course, there is a tension here. For, if consumption out of the home is so great that the survey would be misleading, this makes the case even stronger for collecting data on extra-household, in addition to intra-household, consumption rather than collecting neither. From 1992, eating out has been more fully covered, and data on alcohol and confectionery has been collected and, together with soft drinks, has been reported upon in the main body of annual reports.

While some problems have now been resolved by adding more items of such consumption to the survey, a deeper analytical point is involved. At the very least, the motivation for collecting extra-household consumption (and also intra-household consumption even where it is dominated by the former) is to give a fuller picture of the totality of food that is purchased by members of the household. However, there are other reasons for wanting such data in order to be able to investigate their indirect impact upon diet. Thus, alcohol is consumed and statistically is an important determinant of dietary differences. The impact of its levels of consumption upon purchase of other foods is worthy of investigation. By extension, this opens up the possibility of including other variables which have an important impact upon food purchase, even if they are not foods themselves. A most obvious example is 'slimming' foods, or questions concerning whether household members are dieting or not, but we would also emphasize the potential impact of smoking upon food consumption.[3] In other words, while it is recognized that household composition, age, income, occupational class, etc., are liable to affect food purchase, less attention has been attached to other determinants such as a 'lifestyle' associated with alcohol and/or smoking. Equally important are factors such as the presence of a car, and its influence upon, and the impact of, shopping patterns.

This discussion necessarily draws upon *a priori* views of what are the important determinants of food consumption (and how these can be identified through household behaviour). Frank *et al.* identify two competing analytical thrusts in the NFS reports and so, presumably, in the thinking that informs the conduct of the survey itself. On the one hand, economic analysis is employed in order to estimate demand as a function of income and prices (and household characteristics). On the other hand, there is a nutritional or health concern, examining the nutrient content of diets and, implicitly, motivated by the idea that there is some (minimum) dietary norm that more or less rational households acknowledge and meet to a greater or lesser extent (according to socioeconomic characteristics).

Frank *et al.* deplore what they identify as an apparent shift from a nutritional to an economic balance in the evaluation of the survey results. In the event, the timing of their article could not have been more unfortunate. For, over the next few years, the estimation of price and income elasticities was to be drastically reduced and ultimately dropped altogether in deference to the development of more sophisticated methods. There also seemed to be an increasing recognition that the significance of such elasticity estimation was being undermined by the growth of the unexplained 'residual'.[4]

From our perspective, correcting the balance between the nutritional and economic evaluation of the data is less important than recognizing the inadequacy of each. The nutritional approach essentially views food purchase as arising out of the reasons that particular dietary guidelines are met or not, whereas the economic approach considers that the determinants of food choice are primarily derived from the impact of changing prices and incomes on given consumer preferences. Each approach is rooted in the original motivation for the NFS, the adequacy of working-class diets during the war – continuing the earlier Rowntree tradition, are poor households eating the right foods and can they afford them?

Irrespective of the validity of the approaches for this purpose, they have long since been superseded by the extent to which food purchase is dictated by affluence (and its associated diseases) and, thereby, a range of socioeconomic determinants that supplement, if not swamp, nutritional and cost factors. This is precisely the thrust of recent academic research on food (and the determinants of consumption more generally), as symbolized by the setting up of the ESRC programme to research the 'Nation's Diet', of which this study forms a part.

For, what the two approaches have in common analytically is the idea that the household is a decision-making unit which responds to the external world by making food purchases. This borders on the tautologous, but it permits different patterns of food purchase to be correlated with socio-economic variables. Not surprisingly, if not of necessity, this has entailed the use of each household as if it were a representative of all households of its type. For example, households of higher income are taken as a group with a common purchase behaviour distinct from those of lower income, with the implication that income is the cause of such difference. In particular, all the households in a subsample identified by socioeconomic characteristics are treated as if they share in common the behaviour of them all averaged across the group.

FROM THE NUTRITIONAL/ECONOMIC TO THE SOCIOECONOMIC

Our analytical framework is very different. Possibly it can be taken as an example of, and, at best, an imperfect representative of, the increasingly sophisticated approaches taken to food and consumption across the social sciences. It starts from the notion that socioeconomic factors do not simply delineate households from one another but signify forces acting across and through society in complex ways. Specific to our stance is the creation of food systems, chains of activities linking production to consumption and generating, and responding to, the material culture surrounding food. In this light, we attempt to identify food norms, common *or* distinct patterns of consumption, defined in terms of the rankings of foods by the pro-portion of households purchasing them at least once during the survey week rather than by average quantity purchased across a group of house-holds, as discussed in the previous chapter.

The point can best be illustrated by bringing out what is a drawback in the NFS approach from our perspective. Because of its concern with average consumption across socioeconomic subsamples, the NFS has been preoccupied with average quantities consumed across similar households. This poses two problems which arise not only out of the need to confront the limitations of the data but also out of the way in which those limitations are handled. First, of practical necessity, different foods are aggregated into common food codes. Sometimes these are relatively narrow categories, such as fresh peas. At other times, individual food codes incorporate a wide and changing variety of different products, such as cereals (which includes cornflakes, Weetabix, Shredded Wheat, Rice Krispies, Sugar Puffs, Bran Buds, All-Bran, Ready Brek, Instant Quaker Oats, Puffed Wheat, Special K, mueslis, etc). For the latter, the use of average nutritional content across a food code is potentially extremely misleading.[5] For the nutritional content of cereals is particularly variable – with some, for example, containing a very high proportion of sugar and others being sugar-free. To the extent that households, or individuals within them, rely upon a single cereal or actually respond to the health message by avoiding those with a high sugar content, then it is entirely inappropriate to treat all households within a subsample as if they were consuming an average of the nation's composite cereal bowl.

Ideally, in order to handle this problem, a finer division, or possibly a redefinition, of the food codes would be used, although this ultimately depends upon the mix of motives underlying the formation of the codes (for example, each of nutritional and economic analyses on their own might require different codes).[6] Alternatively, a special, possibly smaller, survey could be periodically undertaken in order to assess the variability of purchases within food codes. At the very least, an analysis should be undertaken of the potential variability of nutritional intake under different assumptions concerning the distribution of 'within food code' consumption. To give an extreme example: suppose there are two cereals, one with no sugar, and each equally purchased across the sample. Then, on the assumption that each household only purchases one of the cereals, the distribution of sugar consumption is half of the sample consuming the average sugar content of the one cereal, and the other half consuming no sugar. This contrasts with the NFS procedure which would suggest that each household would purchase each cereal half of the time and hence consume half of the sugar content of the sugar-containing cereal. More generally, more complex calculations of the margins of errors in nutrient analysis could be made, taking into account consumption both within *and* across food codes. It might be suspected, for example, that those eschewing sugar in cereals will also do so in other products such as yoghurt.[7]

This would be particularly important for those food codes for which sugar, fat and salt are both significant and variable ingredients, since these are the focus of advice for healthy eating. Relying upon averages across food codes has the potential of concealing the incidence of unhealthy diets (whether through under- or overconsumption) even if each household of a subsample does in fact consume the same quantity from each aggregate food code.

THE BULK PURCHASE SYNDROME

Of course, this is not the case as some households purchase and some households do not purchase at all from particular food codes. Vegetarian households, for example, will not normally purchase from meat codes at all. As they make up something of the order of 5% of households, this implies that the average quantities purchased by other households should be supplemented by the same percentage.

That this is not done, either for meat or for other, less clear-cut examples of the incidence of purchase/non-purchase behaviour, is indicative both of the commitment of the NFS to (average) quantity analysis and of the limitations of the available data. For there are reasons other than total abstinence that certain foods might not be revealed as purchased by the survey. This is due to what we term the 'bulk purchase' syndrome. Suppose that all households do have the same purchasing behaviour but that it has a cyclical pattern over a period longer than that covered by the survey (one week). The implication is that foods are consumed from store over a longer period than that for which purchases are recorded. It might also be that some items are purchased less regularly than weekly even if for immediate consumption, what we term the 'treat syndrome'. Now, effectively, the NFS proceeds as if intra-week differences in food purchases are entirely explained by the bulk purchase syndrome – as if all consumers were the same other than their position on a cycle of purchase.

As already indicated through the example of vegetarianism, this procedure is far from satisfactory, especially if one point of the exercise is to identify those lying at the extremes of the distribution of consumption (whether in over- or undereating of certain foods or nutrients). While it is appropriate not to be satisfied with analysis based on the average diet of the nation as a whole and to correct for difference across socio-economically differentiated households, the same applies to the differences in diet associated with the extremes generated by purchase and non/ purchase within socioeconomic subsamples. There is evidence to suggest that, while bulk purchasing has become more important over time, it is both unreasonable and potentially dangerously misleading to rely upon it as the basis for calculating food consumption patterns in order to assess the healthiness of the nation's diet.

Consider, in particular, what we have termed the sausage syndrome. In line with health messages concerning fatty meats and with the availability of a wider range of meat products, whether healthier or not, the proportion of households purchasing sausages has fallen from 53.87% to 34.82% between 1979 and 1989, and the average quantity of sausages purchased per person per week has also fallen from 3.29 to 2.53 ounces, or by 23%. This is, however, less than the percentage by which the number of households purchasing sausages has fallen. The result is that the quantity of sausages being purchased by those who do purchase has been increasing, by 19%. Now, of course, in principle, this could be explained entirely by less frequent bulk purchase or the treat syndrome. Neither of these is sufficiently plausible for sausages, and it must be presumed that a core of sausage eaters is emerging whose average consumption is actually increasing, against the trend of others to give up sausages almost altogether or to purchase them very much less frequently.[8]

Table 9.1 shows corresponding data for a selection of products. Biscuits, margarine and frozen burgers all exhibit the sausage syndrome (falling number of purchases but increasing size of purchase). The mirror image of growing popularity but smaller portion sizes only characterizes ready meals

Table 9.1 Changes in frequencies and quantities purchased

	Overall % of those purchasing		% change in quantity purchased*
	1989	1979	
Whole milk	69.92	97.79	−21.6
Potatoes	64.90	71.64	−9.9
Biscuits	61.79	70.81	9.0
White bread	59.54	78.25	−12.8
Eggs	53.09	77.20	−14.2
Brown bread	47.38	39.00	31.6
Cereal	42.36	39.89	24.0
Skimmed milk	39.54	4.04	14.4**
Sugar	36.07	58.80	−8.8
Margarine	35.77	45.65	22.0
Crisps	34.95	28.56	60.8
Chicken	33.60	32.09	5.3
Yoghurt	31.36	19.71	43.7
Fruit juice	29.14	15.47	81.5
Butter	27.35	60.96	−12.4
Spreads	22.36	9.76	34.6
Ice cream	19.29	15.61	24.4
Frozen chips	16.16	5.92	29.1
Frozen burgers	11.03	18.08	12.1**
Ready meals	10.54	5.40	−7.0

Note: *By those purchasing.
**These foods have a shifting composition over time; for details, see Chapter 8.

(with those products most recently targeting single households presumably having become relatively more important). Otherwise changes in popularity and size of purchase move consistently with one another, whether increasing or decreasing. However, some of the changes in quantities purchased are so large as to suggest that more than bulk purchasing is involved, and concentrated patterns of consumption are almost certainly involved.

TO BUY OR NOT TO BUY, IS THAT THE QUESTION?

Analysis in NFS reports and elsewhere tends to neglect the issue of the proportion of households purchasing (implicitly assuming average cyclical, bulk purchase behaviour). In 1967, for example, the issue was addressed directly but only to set it aside as not contributing usefully to the estimation of income elasticities, as described in Chapter 7. In other words, the problem of who purchases or not has been neglected because it is an obstacle in calculating demand parameters on the assumption that all households of the same type do purchase. In earlier reports, data for proportion of households purchasing were given for a selection of foods, apparently motivated by the wish to reveal some seasonal effects. Such data were given for all products for the previous five years in 1971, 1975 and 1980. And the data have been given annually for all food codes from 1985. However, apart from a recognition of the difference between the growth of the demand for chicken through the breadth of the market as opposed to its depth (how many purchase rather than how much they purchase), the overwhelming emphasis has been on average quantities purchased over subsamples, taking those who purchase together with those who do not.[9]

Our approach lies at the opposite extreme to that implicitly adopted by the NFS. It can be interpreted as addressing the issue of whether a food is purchased or not and, in the first instance, without even paying attention to the quantities involved. This is done through ranking foods according to the proportion of households purchasing the foods at least once during the survey week.

The original motivation for, and derivation of, consumption norms defined in this way was provided by social choice theory. In undertaking the calculation and interpretation of food norms, it is possible to abandon these analytical origins completely. However, they are briefly recalled here to add another interpretative dimension to the analysis. Social choice theory is concerned, usually normatively, with the selection or ranking of alternative states of the world (possible electoral candidates, for example) on the basis of the individual rankings of the candidates across the population. In other words, social choice theory can be seen as a way of representing aggregated individual choices. It follows that the overall social choice may be more or less strongly supported by the population as a whole and that subgroups of the population might elect very different candidates from one another. Further, social choice is solely concerned with the translation of the individual choices into an overall choice or ranking of candidates; it does not seek to explain why the patterns of preferences are the way that they are – over the group as a whole or between subgroups – although it may be able to reveal those patterns.

A strict analogy can be drawn between social choice theory and the calculation of consumption or, as here, food norms. Information about the population's (food) choices can be translated into an overall ranking that is representative of them. As in elections, this overall representation may or may not be extremely popular or conceal differences across subgroups (which can be revealed). It is as if the population is voting for foods, and we are responsible for determining the electoral outcome. This means, of course, that this is not an empirical estimation of demand, even if socioeconomic variables are used to divide the population into subgroups that could also be, and often are, used for demand analysis. In other words, the calculation of a norm does not necessarily mean that this is the predicted order of ranking of choices. Nor is it necessarily the case that the norms should be calculated by ranking by absolute frequency of purchase; there are other ways of calculating norms just as there are a range of voting systems – from majority rule to single transferable votes, etc. However, although it need not detain us here,[10] the use of ranking by frequency of purchase is unique in incorporating extremely desirable properties in, democratically as it were, projecting the individual choices into social norms without discriminating against specific consumers and foods (voters and candidates).

THE JOINT IMPACT OF CHILDREN AND INCOME

The remainder of this chapter is concerned to apply the methods outlined in the previous chapter to examine the joint impact of income and presence of children upon food choice. First, though, observe that the relative rankings of the foods revealed in the dramatrices do not necessarily provide an accurate index of absolute frequencies of purchase for two separate reasons. First, if a subsample purchases large quantities of the foods overall, then a lower ranking (or negative entry in the dramatrix) will not necessarily mean a below-average frequency of purchase. Households with more members tend to purchase more foods irrespective of their ranking of them. Second, however large is a shift in ranking, which gives rise to a non-zero element in the dramatrix, it may reflect a very large or a very small shift in absolute frequency depending upon how close are the absolute frequencies in the rankings for the sample as a whole. If, for example, two foods are ranked very closely (far apart), then a small (large) shift in frequencies in subsamples may produce a large (small or no) shift in the dramatrix.

For these reasons, in the results that follow, we present dramatrices aggregated over the four years, generally strengthening the absolute magnitude of the non-zero elements, together with absolute frequencies for 1989. It is worth reiterating that the intention cannot be to give a full explanation of purchasing behaviour, for which fuller presentation of results would be necessary, including a complementary analysis of quantities purchased. Rather, the purpose is to reveal that there are differences by income/children and to make the case in principle for further investigation of the decision to purchase or not in conjunction with decisions on how much is purchased.

Results are drawn from two sets of foods: the meats previously indicated in Table 8.1 and also from a selection of foods, predominantly subject to major change over the decade 1979 to 1989 – see previous chapter for details. Subsampling has been taken one stage further than previously described, with an initial restriction to households with couples; this is then broken down into four income groups,[11] and even further by the four categories of absence of children, and the presence of pre-school children, post-school children or both.

For the meats, the results for six of the products are selected, those for which there are the most striking outcomes. In each case, it is apparent that lower levels of income (C and D/E2) give rise to strong child effects (often different according to the sort of children) which do not emerge so strongly for the higher incomes. This is all the more remarkable since income effects in the absence of taking account of the presence of children are relatively mild across the population as a whole, when compared to class effects for example, which persist even when correcting for income (see Chapter 11). It is also important to bear in mind that the overall purchase of meats has become absolutely more important for those on lower incomes, often exceeding purchases of those on higher income, both in variety of products and quantities of meat.[12] Figure 9.1 shows how much more important meat has become to those on lower income.

Table 9.2 covers liver and lamb, two products for which there is strong negative skew for the presence of children. While the difference in absolute frequencies are small, those on low income have a much stronger antipathy to these meats (in line with trends over the decade). Thus, those on lower incomes are sustaining their frequency of purchase of these meats relative to those on higher incomes, but are ranking other meats much more highly.

As shown in Table 9.3, these meats are frozen convenience, sausages, canned meat and frozen burgers (although the latter is high for A1/2 where both pre-school and school children are present). In other words, the taste for meat among those on lower incomes is being satisfied through an increasing commitment to cheap and convenient products; there seem to be reasons for health concerns both in terms of the sorts of meat relatively more preferred and in overall consumption of meat. However, it is imperative to recognize that these are rankings and absolute frequencies across the subsample groups, and the distribution of these consumption patterns is liable to be more heavily skewed towards a core set of households – even if some of these products are more open to bulk purchase than others.

Table 9.4 repeats the above exercise for a range of products, picking out some of those, other than meat products already considered, for which the effect of children and income together are particularly pronounced.[13] The absolute frequencies are not, however, covered. This is because the overall frequencies of purchase across all the products is similar for the subsamples, and there are small and even gaps for the products between the absolute purchase frequencies. Accordingly, the aggregated dramatrices give a roughly accurate indication of the absolute movement in absolute frequencies, if not their absolute levels.

193

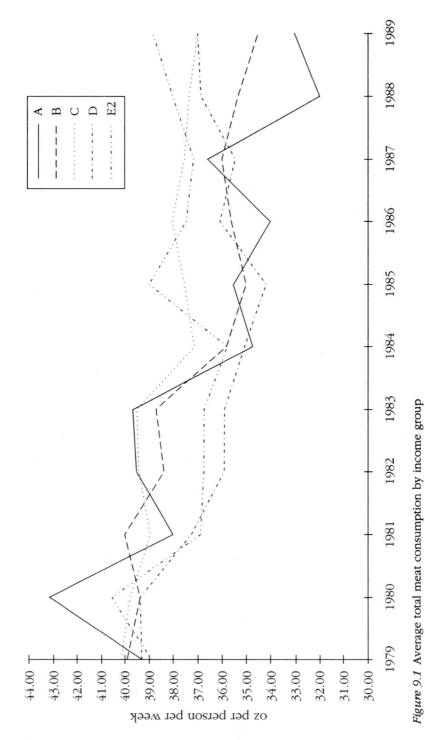

Figure 9.1 Average total meat consumption by income group

Source National Food Survey, Annual Reports

Table 9.2 Purchasing by income and presence of children

	Lamb			
	Absolute frequencies for 1989			
	None	Pre	Both	Schl
A1/2	21.25	23.08	16.00	21.93
B	22.56	16.81	16.67	22.27
C	21.97	22.45	24.36	26.71
D/E2	25.54	15.31	22.83	24.05
	Aggregate dramatrix			
	None	Pre	Both	Schl
A1/2	2	2	1	–3
B	4	–9	–8	–6
C	4	–20	–11	–7
D/E2	3	–21	–18	–14

	Liver			
	Absolute frequencies for 1989			
	None	Pre	Both	Schl
A1/2	11.88	3.85	8.00	11.40
B	10.45	9.05	10.94	8.22
C	11.78	5.10	10.26	10.33
D/E2	12.05	7.14	7.61	11.81
	Aggregate dramatrix			
	None	Pre	Both	Schl
A1/2	10	0	–7	–7
B	7	2	–4	–3
C	6	–1	–4	–1
D/E2	6	–9	–8	–7

Table 9.3 Purchasing by income and presence of children

	Frozen convenience food			
	Absolute frequencies for 1989			
	None	Pre	Both	Schl
A1/2	14.38	12.82	18.00	18.86
B	17.42	21.12	26.04	21.23
C	15.62	28.57	38.46	26.12
D/E2	11.69	24.49	32.61	24.47
	Aggregate dramatrix			
	None	Pre	Both	Schl
A1/2	1	2	3	–2
B	–3	1	5	0
C	–5	15	14	2
D/E2	–2	20	14	10

Table 9.3 Continued

Sausages

Absolute frequencies for 1989

	None	Pre	Both	Schl
A1/2	20.94	41.03	38.00	34.21
B	27.88	33.19	41.67	40.66
C	33.25	36.22	57.69	46.39
D/E2	32.19	43.88	55.43	45.99

Aggregate dramatrix

	None	Pre	Both	Schl
A1/2	−2	2	2	0
B	−1	−1	2	−1
C	−1	1	8	1
D/E2	0	7	8	2

Canned meats

Absolute frequencies for 1989

	None	Pre	Both	Schl
A1/2	8.75	20.51	8.00	12.72
B	14.23	29.74	23.44	19.93
C	18.13	30.61	31.41	26.32
D/E2	12.41	30.61	42.39	25.74

Aggregate dramatrix

	None	Pre	Both	Schl
A1/2	−2	5	8	1
B	−7	5	9	0
C	−3	15	14	5
D/E2	−3	9	11	2

Frozen burgers*

Absolute frequencies for 1989

	None	Pre	Both	Schl
A1/2	5.31	7.69	16.00	12.28
B	7.55	16.38	19.79	14.80
C	9.61	20.41	24.36	22.22
D/E2	7.46	23.47	27.17	22.36

Aggregate dramatrix

	None	Pre	Both	Schl
A1/2	−5	7	18	2
B	−7	1	11	2
C	−5	12	11	4
D/E2	−6	20	12	8

*This is an average over three years only as burgers included in frozen convenience in 1979.

Table 9.4 Select aggregate dramatrices

	None	*Pre*	*Both*	*Schl*
		White bread		
A1/2	–6	–6	–2	2
B	–3	–2	–2	4
C	–2	0	2	2
D/E2	–3	6	6	7
		Cereals		
A1/2	–9	4	14	5
B	–9	0	6	2
C	–6	5	7	2
D/E2	–5	8	11	6
		Yoghurt		
A1/2	–1	11	11	–4
B	–3	19	5	2
C	–1	12	7	0
D/E2	1	8	0	0
		Butter		
A1/2	8	–1	–11	–4
B	11	–6	–6	1
C	6	–10	–12	–3
D/E2	5	–7	–8	–9
		Brown bread		
A1/2	5	–8	–9	–11
B	6	–6	–10	– 6
C	5	–12	–19	–10
D/E2	7	–26	–14	–13

Table 9.4 Continued

	Crisps			
	None	*Pre*	*Both*	*Schl*
A1/2	–12	9	7	11
B	–15	1	8	8
C	–7	8	10	9
D/E2	–4	11	12	13

	Skimmed milks			
	None	*Pre*	*Both*	*Schl*
A1/2	7	–3	–3	–3
B	6	–6	–4	–3
C	5	–5	–9	–2
D/E2	6	–13	–9	–5

	Biscuits			
	None	*Pre*	*Both*	*Schl*
A1/2	–9	–1	1	0
B	– 5	3	0	2
C	–2	3	3	3
D/E2	0	2	0	2

The increasing skew against brown bread for the presence of (pre-school) children is striking and stronger at lower incomes. It is reflected as a mirror image, but much less strongly, for white bread. On the one hand, the commitment to cereals (healthy, leaving aside sugar and salt content, and convenient) and crisps (unhealthy and convenient) for the presence of children is much more even across income. In the presence of children, higher-income households rank yoghurt more highly, and skimmed milk much less lowly (the latter presumably reflecting the commitment to whole milk for the health of children and skimmed milk for the health of adults, but an income constraint on the purchase of both). Finally, for butter (unhealthy) and biscuits (unhealthy but convenient), the patterns for children are clear but opposite and not strongly reflected by income.

CONCLUDING REMARKS

Leaving aside the merits of the NFS for the moment, the results reveal that the determinants of purchase or not across a variety of foods is affected by

198

income and the presence of children in complex and varied ways, apparently depending upon the character of the foods (healthy, convenient, rewards, etc.). We believe that this casts some doubts upon the efficacy of relying upon health messages alone to shift the nation's diet in healthier directions. This is partly because the division of foods into healthy and unhealthy can make the latter more attractive as a form of gratification (and even a reward for consuming healthy foods),[14] especially when they are cheap. It is also because of the influence of the food system, from production through to purchasing, on the availability of foods. Crudely, the industry's output will find its way to our tables in various forms, given the expanding range of processed products, so that health messages serve in part to redistribute who eats what and how.

This makes even more imperative a fuller investigation of the incidence of purchase/non-purchase. With such significant differences across socio-economic groups, by age, children and income, for example, it seems inevitable that intra-group patterns of purchase will be far from uniform, with some incidence of core purchasing of healthy and unhealthy products. This is liable to be compounded by skewed consumption within food codes and households. It is essential that the NFS data collection be modified to take account of these factors in exploring the extent and incidence of (un)healthy food purchasing. More generally, as indicated, there are implications for a well-founded healthy food policy, a matter taken up in more detail in the second volume.

NOTES

1 Frank *et al.* seem to consider that this renders it impossible to investigate individual consumption within a household. This is, however, possible through indirect methods, as ingeniously devised by Chesher (1991) for nutrient analysis, which divide the net effect of extra household members into individual and compositional effects. This work does, none the less, suffer considerably from the averaging over food codes and households, discussed in greater detail in the next but one section.

2 As is recognized in practice, for the representativeness of the sample for example.

3 It is remarkable how often such issues continue to be neglected in dietary surveys even though they are common-sense determinants of food choice.

4 For a fuller account and critique, see Chapter 7.

5 Nutrient content of food codes is derived from the various editions of McCance and Widdowson's *The Composition of Foods*. Note that the average commodity represented by a food code will also shift according to the composition of foods within it, including the addition of new products. The NFS takes this into account in nutritional analysis.

6 Thus, an economic analysis of the trend in demand towards breakfast cereals could to some extent rely upon a single category, whereas a nutritional analysis would need to disaggregate.

7 At the very least, a calculation of standard deviations of nutrient consumption could be made on the basis that between and across food-code consumption

were independent of one another. Of course, it is possible to assume otherwise, that households seek a balanced or average diet of nutrients by compensating with one food where they deviate in others. Significantly, research is done for the danger of contamination through core purchase of foods at risk.

8 More details for some of the other meat products are to be found in Chapter 10.

9 The NFS data do provide information on how many times a household buys from a food code within a week. This might be used to infer something about non-purchase of some products – although over 75% of foods are only purchased once per week. But, for whole milk, for example, non-purchase during a week might suggest non-purchase altogether rather than bulk purchase, given the frequency with which whole milk is purchased during a week. A broad and crude check on bulk purchasing could also be made by comparing the previous week's aggregate expenditure on food, estimated by respondent, with the survey week's expenditure.

10 See Fine (1983).

11 These income groups are taken from the NFS; they run from high to low income for A to E, but some of the income subsets have been aggregated to guarantee adequate subsample sizes, A1 and A2.

12 It is worth repeating that this leaves aside meals eaten outside the home.

13 For more details of the products involved, see later chapters. Once again, but from the results not shown, the effect of income on its own across the whole population tends to be quite limited.

14 See Heasman (1990a).

10

THE MEAT SYSTEM

INTRODUCTION

Apart from the previous chapter, the book has so far been concerned with elaborating the notion of food systems and their implications in a variety of contexts. In contrast, the last chapter focused much more directly and narrowly upon the identification of food choice itself – through the definition of food norms and their calculation for shifting income and presence of children. This and the next two chapters attempt to bring these two separate sorts of analysis together; they seek to examine how food systems influence the formation of food norms (or how *and* why we 'vote' for foods in the way that we do).

MEAT SYSTEM OR SYSTEMS?

The definition of an appropriate SOP is the context within which we address the meat system. We begin by picking up from the discussion in Chapter 4, where it was argued that an SOP, or food system, is distinctly delineated according to the strength of linkages across its constituent activities other than at the level of consumption itself. Is it appropriate to differentiate between the separate meats as SOPs – the poultry, beef, pork and sheep systems[1] – or do these constitute a single SOP with the separate components incorporating an increasing variety of meat products? In this respect, there is a paradox within much of the literature.[2] For, as will be briefly shown, individual contributions tend to treat meat as if it were a single homogeneous category with the differentiation between meats considered of secondary importance, or implicit rather than primary. On the other hand, particular studies generally do have greater purchase over particular meats – applying to some more than to others – and the consequence of putting all meat studies together is, therefore, to bring out the heterogeneity across meats.

Discussion of vegetarianism illustrates the point. It is generally acknowledged that vegetarianism is increasing, although it only affects 5% or so of the UK population at any moment and tends to be concentrated among the young.[3] As an aversion to eating meat, vegetarianism is initially perceived as reflecting a late twentieth-century commitment to animal rights and welfare and to a healthier diet.[4] It is often understood as an underlying shift in demand away from meat, particularly among the wealthy for whom it was previously anticipated that consumption would continue to increase with income.

However, vegetarianism itself differentiates between meats, from red to white, from fish, and from animals to animal products. And vegetarians themselves are often described, whether humorously or bitterly, as competing with one another over being more vegan than the next.[5] This implies that vegetarianism is a socially constructed ideology, not only in the sense of what products are or are not acceptable (and in what circumstances – the vegetarian guest offered meat has to set politeness against principle), but also in practice in terms of what products are or are not eaten.[6] Given the variety of meat products available and the variety of motives and factors associated with eating, it is hardly surprising that vegetarianism is compromised by a multitude of influences varying from convenience to fashion. This will be shown in the empirical results to follow, for example, that as putative vegetarians the young tend to eschew some but not all meats. It implies that the impact of vegetarianism upon meat cannot treat the latter as an undifferentiated category.

Similarly, for sociological and anthropological studies of meat, there is a tendency to overgeneralize. For Charles and Kerr (1986a and b, and 1988) and Kerr and Charles (1986), (the distribution of) meat (consumption) signifies the exercise of power within the household. But, as they duly recognize, this is differentiated across and within (the quality of) meats – steaks as opposed to burgers, for example. Are children exercising power when their households exhibit an aversion to liver and lamb? Similar considerations apply to notions of a proper meal (Murcott 1983a), even if its significance and meaning are being eroded,[7] where meat and two veg refers to a roast to the exclusion of most other meat products.

From this cursory overview of the literature on meat, it follows that, as a category, meat is heterogeneous, not simply in its products, but also in the meanings and significance attached to them. This implies, especially from a horizontal perspective that also recognizes SOPs, that each meat ought to be construed as belonging to a separate SOP. As argued, we disagree since differentiation and articulation are possible between all consumer goods. Paradoxically, then, while criticizing the existing literature for homogenizing meat at the level of consumption, we hypothesize that the consumption of meat should be examined against the shifting nature of a single SOP, encompassing a variety of meats and meat products. Further, this is an important preliminary to understanding the heterogeneity of meat at the level of consumption.

A CENTURY OF MEAT: TWO DISTINCT SOPS?

In this light, it is easier to recognize differences between meat systems when they are viewed historically over a long period of time. The UK meat system over the past 100 years can be conveniently divided into two broad-brush SOPs separated by the Second World War. Each of these separate 'meat systems' can be differentiated in terms of the changing importance of different meats constituting each system, the sources and production methods of the different meats, the distribution and retailing of the meats in each system, the technologies employed, and the forms and preparations of meat for final consumption. Allied to the latter are cultural and social changes in the role of meat in the UK diet and its conceptualization as part of a 'proper' meal.

In both the pre- and post-war meat systems the essential 'organic' qualities of different meats are crucial in the chain from production to final consumption. Especially important is the need for meat to be first 'fattened', then 'slaughtered' and finally 'prepared' and distributed for consumption, whether as cuts/joints of meat or to be incorporated into meat products ranging from sausages to ready meals, or as 'fast-food' burgers as opposed to a pride of place in haute cuisine.

In both meat systems, beef has been the core meat. In the 1840s Britain was virtually self-sufficient in meat supply, but over the next few decades experienced a rapid expansion in meat consumption from around 80 lb per head mid-century to a peak of 132 lb per head in the early 1900s (with only a slight decline in the period leading up to 1914) (Perren 1978). This expansion in meat supply was met predominantly from meat imports and not from home production.

The turning point for the rise in imports started in 1882, but these grew especially during the 1890s, when refrigeration (first invented in 1861) was developed, making it feasible to import carcass meat from almost any country in the world (together with the application of steamship and railway technology to the meat chain). Refrigeration made Argentina a prime source of beef imports into the United Kingdom and New Zealand the principal source of lamb. In 1905–9 only 53% of beef, 52% of mutton and lamb and 36% of pig meat moving into consumption in the United Kingdom was home-produced, and by 1924–7 these had fallen to 43%, 44% and 32%, respectively. In the 1930s, the proportion of home-grown beef rose to 49%, not because home production increased but because imports fell. For lamb, the decline in British farmers' share of the market continued, although for pork UK producers supplied 78%, if only 29% of bacon (MAFF 1968).

The distribution and retailing of meat reveals significant differences when the pre- and post-war meat systems are compared. In general, the trade in cattle and sheep produced in the United Kingdom, has seen distribution flow from north to south and from west to east and from the hills to lowland fields. In the lowlands, livestock would be fattened, having been walked to be close to the main (and the cattle's final) centres of meat distribution (Whetham 1976). The localized pre-war character of meat distribution is succinctly captured by Jones and Makings (1931) in their 1930 study for the town of Loughborough. The majority (86%) of home-killed carcasses retailed in Loughborough were purchased on the hoof and slaughtered by town butchers. The majority of these supplies were drawn from the local cattle auction. A few butchers traded with local dealers, a few purchased direct from the farmer. More occasionally purchases were made at neighbouring towns or shipped from large markets further afield. Sometimes a butcher killed cattle fattened by himself. At this time, Lough-borough, with a population of 27,000, was served by 42 retail meat shops – that is, one shop on average for 161 families (assuming an average of four persons per family).

Wholesalers were also especially influential in pre-war meat distribution. For example, in the 1920s, practically all of London's supplies of fresh, chilled and frozen meats passed through Smithfield (Putnam 1923). With rising imports, large cold stores were built, especially in the South of England, for storing and distributing meat. The network for delivering meat from pro-duction to retailing became increasingly specialized and complex as exem-plified by the difficulties encountered in trying to organize the early wartime control and distribution of meat to serve London (Hammond 1962).

In summary, and in generalized terms, pre-Second World War meat supply was organized and structured around imports made possible by large-scale exploitation of the refrigeration 'chain' based on cattle-rearing on large land areas in countries like Argentina and New Zealand. The distribution and retail chains were highly specialized with wholesalers, local auctions and butchers being the principal agents involved along the chain. Manufactured products were largely confined to utilizing the 'left-overs', once the cuts/joints of meat had been prepared, and were used to make sausages and meat pies, for example.

From the 1950s onwards the characteristics of the post-war meat system were becoming delineated. Although beef remained the dominant meat, the post-war meat system is characterized by the remarkable industrial-ization of poultry, and its corresponding expansion in consumption. Historically, poultry had been associated with small or part-time agricultural holdings, but industrial techniques and the rise of supermarket retailing, which developed a specialized, yet mass distribution outlet for chicken, has seen per capita chicken consumption increase more than sevenfold between the 1950s and 1980s. Allied to this, home-produced meat has seen the gradual squeezing out of imports of other meats and increasing specialization and concentration in livestock production. In total, the consumption of meat, by carcass weight, has increased substantially in

Table 10.1 Annual per capita consumption of various meats in the United Kingdom (kg carcass weight)

Years	Beef	Lamb	Bacon		Offal	Poultry	Total
			Pork	Ham			
1950–54	17.6	9.8	4.2	10.3	1.7	2.5	46.1
1955–59	22.7	10.6	8.1	10.9	2.1	3.8	58.2
1960–64	22.4	11.1	9.4	11.5	2.4	6.5	63.3
1965–69	20.9	10.5	11.0	11.4	2.4	8.8	65.0
1970–74	21.1	9.0	11.9	10.8	2.0	11.3	66.1
1975–79	22.1	7.4	11.3	8.9	2.2	12.4	64.3
1980–84	19.1	7.1	12.8	8.6	2.2	14.3	64.1
1985–88	18.9	6.6	13.2	8.1	1.8	17.2	65.8

Source: Harrington (1988)

recent decades, contrary to expectations that the 'healthy eating' revolution and the growth of vegetarianism might suggest.

Meat consumption in all its forms (that is, including poultry), when expressed in terms of carcass weight, stood at 4.11 million tonnes per year for the United Kingdom in 1989 (MLC 1990). This is an increase from an average of 2.9 million tonnes a year for 1970–5 and from 3.5 million tonnes in 1987 (Harrington 1988). A major part of this massive increase in tonnage is from poultry meat, but taking this out of the total figures, the consumption of beef, veal, lamb and pig meat increased by 24% between 1970–75 and 1987. Looking further back, total per capita consumption of meat in the United Kingdom has risen from 46.1 kg carcass weight per head of population in 1950–4 to 65.8 kg carcass weight in 1985–88. Table 10.1 breaks these figures down by different meats.

The growth in meat distribution through supermarkets has been at the direct expense of specialist butchers, but this is contingent on type of meat. In 1992, 57.2% (51% in 1989) of poultry by volume was sold through supermarkets in comparison to 15.4% (18% in 1989) through butchers. However, in 1989, butchers were still the main source of household purchases of beef and veal at 44.5% in comparison to 36.7% sold through supermarkets. By 1992, supermarkets had overtaken butchers with 44.7% of purchases compared to 38.7% through butchers. These figures and those for other meats are detailed in Table 10.2.

By 1993 provisional figures showed the United Kingdom to be self-sufficient in the home-fed production of beef and veal (average of 98% for 1982–84); self-sufficient for mutton and lamb (average of 70% for 1982–84); self-sufficient for supplies of pork (average of 102% for 1982–84); (home-cured production of bacon and ham stood at only 43% of UK total supply);

Table 10.2 Percentage of household purchases (by volume) of meat by retailer

	Beef and veal		Lamb*		Pork		Bacon and Ham		Poultry		All meat**	
	1989	1992	1989	1992	1989	1992	1989	1992	1989	1992	1989	1992
Butchers	44.5	38.7	45.8	43.3	38.9	35.5	19.9	17.4	18.0	15.4	31.7	27.8
Co-ops	3.7	3.2	4.3	2.5	3.6	3.0	6.4	4.9	6.2	4.8	5.0	3.9
Super-markets	36.7	44.7	34.8	36.9	40.1	47.3	50.1	57.0	51.0	57.2	43.7	50.1
Inde-pendents	2.0	1.7	2.1	2.3	1.9	1.9	8.1	6.3	2.1	3.0	2.9	2.9
Freezer centres	5.1	4.6	4.8	5.8	4.7	3.8	4.2	3.8	9.8	10.1	6.4	6.4
Other retailers	8.0	7.1	8.2	9.2	10.8	8.5	11.3	10.6	12.9	9.5	10.3	8.9

Notes: *Includes mutton. **Includes offal and other meat.

Source: MLC (1992)

and supplies of poultry meat at 91% of domestic supply (average of 98% for 1982–84) (MAFF 1994). These figures demonstrate the success of the post-war meat regime in virtually eliminating imports that were so dominant in the pre-war meat system.

There have also been important changes in the consumption patterns for meat and meat products between the two meat systems. The use and development of meat-based manufactured products has been a significant post-war development in the UK food chain, often to match the demands of new technologies – microwaves, for example. An example of these new meat products is that of 'ready meals'. This market has grown enormously since the 1970s with a large range of new products and packaging techniques (MLC 1992). The ready-meals market is dominated by frozen products, although the fastest-growing sector in recent years is chilled meals. The majority of ready-meals are based on meat and poultry. Out of 147 ready meal products launched in 1991, 32% contained beef, pork or lamb and a further 27% contained poultry. Even in manufactured products the new meat 'mix' of the post-war meat system is replicated.

Another important change in the way meat is consumed is the growth in consumption of meat in catering. Out of total meat consumption in 1989, it is estimated 24% was through catering, MLC (1990). The 1989 menu survey, conducted by Gallup for the *Caterer and Hotelkeeper*, questioned catering establishments on menu preferences. Overall the top three main-course lunch selections were, in order, fish (and chips), hamburgers and steak. Burgers and steaks came very close behind fish, each commanding 9% of the market (10% for fish). Roast beef, meat pies and sausages were also popular. The top two selections for main dinner courses were steak and fish (both most commonly eaten with chips), with pizza and hamburgers rating joint third, (figures reported in MLC (1990)).

In summary, the post-war meat system has seen meat consumption expanded mainly by a remarkable increase in poultry consumption using industrial techniques that minimize land use (the same 'industrialization' of pork also took place in the UK), by the growing dominance of super-markets as the source of meat purchases as against specialist butchers (although this is differentiated by types of meat), by increasing self-sufficiency in meat supply, and by substantive changes in the way in which meat is prepared and consumed with specially manufactured products and catering outlets becoming increasingly important.

This generalized overview of the pre- and post-war meat systems is not meant to be an exhaustive list of all the important features of the two systems. Crucial to the structuring of the meat systems is the role of government, not only in regulating the industry and developing health and safety standards, but in 'brokering' the different conflicts and interests manifest in the meat systems, for example between different groups of agricultural interests and those of the consumer. A fuller description would have to detail the role of the state. Also, not explored in depth is the 'organic' properties of meat and the way that these have become integrated into the changing food chain, from ready meals to fast-food catering. However, the brief description provided is sufficient to suggest that import-ant and far-reaching change has taken place in the production and con-sumption of meat and meat products over the past 100 years and in the way that the industry has been structured to incorporate these changes.

Where does this leave the meat system of today? While different animal species used for meat are enabled to consume different feeds more or less productively, one form in which the meat system is being integrated is through the common dependence upon sources of feed. Productivity in animal husbandry[8] can be increased either through the efficiency with which animals convert feed into potentially consumable flesh or in the range and content of the raw materials that they consume.[9] Although this is a considerable oversimplification, the meat system is increasingly one in which a widening range of potential feeds are more or less cost-effective as inputs across different species, as FAO (1989, p. 29) puts it:[10]

> As computerized least-cost ration formulation spreads in the feed industry and among livestock feeders, even small changes in relative prices, will cause significant shifts in demand among available feed ingredients. . . . Since grains may be incorporated to make up as much as 75 percent of the rations for pigs and poultry the use of grains in animal feeding has become mainly a question of relative prices.

Apart from computerized feeding and formation of feed composition, them-selves associated with nutritional research, the intensive feeding of animals requires cost-effective 'housing', specialized and timely veterinary services, and drugs to treat and prevent diseases and to enhance digestive performance.[11]

Particularly 'advantaged' by these developments have been pig and poultry, especially chicken, due to 'the high conversion efficiency of these species' (FAO 1989, p. 18). This follows from their organic distinction from cattle and sheep as 'monogastrics' rather than ruminants, with a corresponding decline in the significance of pasture relative to grain and oilseed as a source of feed.[12] Consider the outcome for the UK chicken industry. While the number of days taken to fatten a bird to 4 lb has declined from sixty to thirty-nine days between 1966 and 1991 and the amount of feed required has fallen from 9 lb to 7.75 lb, this implies that bird consumption per day has risen by 13% – an economy in time and cost to market (HoC 1992).[13]

It is not possible to undertake an overview of agricultural trends here but there is a tendency towards specialization (most obviously in chicken and pig 'farming'), even if with the survival of some mixed farms and others devoted to the use of arable land for pasture and/or crops, possibly in rotation and to provide feed for own or others' animal husbandry.[14] Thus, we would expect developments in agriculture, if taken in isolation, to represent a breaking down of the meat system into its separate components. However, integration across the commodity chains has been displaced vertically, as in provision of inputs, but also in their use as outputs in creating meat products.

Manufacturers are often parts of large diversified food companies straddling a range of meat and other products. They also tend to be vertically integrated from, for example, hatching chickens and growing poultry through to the marketing of their own branded products, with some large poultry producers owning their own feed mills.[15] The range of products is expanding rapidly, covering branded/unbranded, fresh/frozen, canned/vacuum-wrapped, cooked/uncooked, complete and ready meals, whole birds or parts, etc. Bernard Matthews is a prominent meat producer, having established itself through a highly effective advertising campaign, moving from turkey products, for which it created an all-year demand, to other meats even if it chooses not to supply own-label retailers. It is best known for its convenience roasts, manufactured by coextrusion (meat stripped off animals and reconstituted):[16] 'The machine used by Bernard Matthews produces 65 foot long rolls of meat weighing 375lbs. The "logs" are frozen then cut and packed or processed (eg battered and crumbed) further. The result is fixed weight poultry and red meat products.'

Thus, the literature on shifts in meat-eating habits has emphasized a multiplicity of factors, price and income, changing meal habits, the influence of healthy eating and animal rights and welfare, eating out, microwaves and freezers, women going out to work and their (partial) displacement from the kitchen, the taste for greater variety, and the rise of more single households, and changing shopping patterns. We hope to have shown how these factors are structured relative to one another and now to show how they have had a complex impact on the taste for meats.

MEAT NORMS

Before examining the food norms for meat, first consider overall levels of purchases of the meat products covered. Table 10.3 is important in showing how many of the meats on average are purchased by the different age groups.[17] Clearly, the number of meats being purchased has been falling for all age groups but more purchases are made by the middle-aged, where both income and household numbers (and numbers of children) tend to be higher.

Table 10.3 Overall frequency of purchase of meats by age group

Age	<25	25–34	35–44	45–54	55–64	65–74	>75
1979	27.2	28.5	30.4	31.1	27.7	24.8	19.3
1984	21.7	24.2	28.3	27.3	24.1	20.9	17.3
1986	21.5	24.0	26.8	26.7	23.7	21.3	17.8
1989	18.1	22.4	25.5	25.3	21.9	20.3	16.2

Significantly, overall purchases of meat do not necessarily rise with income. As can be seen from Table 10.4, all income groups have experienced a fall in overall purchases but the highest income group (A1) purchases fewer meats than the lowest income group among the employed (D).[18] Indeed, as shown by Figure 9.1 in the previous chapter, the quantities of meat consumed by households has, over the past two decades, become increasingly inversely correlated with household income, although this is presumably explained to some extent by differential reliance upon eating out, which is excluded from the NFS over the period considered here.

As has already been indicated, the NFS is a survey of (approximately 7,000) households' weekly expenditure on foods purchased for consumption within the home, from which the data employed here are taken. Greater details about the NFS are to be found in the annual reports[19] and, concerning our use of them, in Chapter 8. However, two points need to be highlighted here. The

Table 10.4 Overall frequency of purchase of meats by income

Income*	A1	A2	B	C	D	E1	E2
1979	25.9	27.1	29.1	30.9	29.5	22.7	23.8
1984	24.3	24.9	26.3	26.9	25.1	19.5	21.3
1986	22.3	22.0	25.5	26.7	24.6	18.8	21.7
1989	21.7	21.5	24.1	24.9	22.7	18.9	19.4

Note: *Of head of household.

first is that the food categories used, as designated by a specific meat product such as chicken, are potentially composite both in the NFS definition of a food code (which may combine a number of products) and in our combining together two or more of the NFS food codes. Second, of necessity, the specification of socioeconomic variables must be operationalized. At times, the NFS categories are employed, as in age or head of household as already reported above. At other times, we have formed our own variables out of the NFS categories, to make income groups of reasonable size when subsampling by other variables – see next section.

THE HETEROGENEITY OF MEAT

Now we empirically demonstrate the heterogeneity of meats through the divergent patterns with which they are purchased, and how these patterns have changed, even over as limited a period as a decade.[20] Table 10.5 reveals how the proportion of the population purchasing each meat, ranked by the figures for 1989, has changed between 1979 and 1989. Some have increased, some have decreased, and some have remained stable in 'popularity'. Carcass meats other than poultry and pork have suffered, together with liver, but most processed meat products, other than sausages and cooked bacon, have more or less sustained or increased their frequency of purchase.

Now it might be argued that these changes merely reflect shifts in levels of income and relative prices for the variety of characteristics to be found across meats. However, as argued in Chapter 7, attempts to explain shifts in food demand through price and income elasticities, especially for meats, have proved remarkably unsuccessful and do, in any case, leave a large residual that is apportioned to underlying shifts in demand.

It might also be thought that the above table is charting the shifting impact of the bulk purchase syndrome – that some meats have become more amenable, others less, to consumption from the store of larger but less frequent purchases.[21] However, with some exceptions, the changes in the quantities purchased on a weekly basis follow the frequencies of purchase quite closely. The exceptions, defined here by a 10% or more deviation between average quantities purchased across the population and the proportion of the population purchasing, are of interest in their own right. All of the 'deviants' involve an increase in the quantities purchased by those purchasing (suggesting a bias towards the increasing role of bulk purchase). Thus, there are no meats for which the average size of purchase of those purchasing has significantly fallen.[22]

Consider, for example, ready meals. While the proportion purchasing has almost doubled from relatively low levels, the average consumption in ounces per person per week has increased by even more, so that the average weekly purchase has increased by 23.2%. Given that ready meals

Table 10.5 Absolute frequencies of purchase

	1979	1984	1986	1989
Beef	63.7	51.95	52.80	48.68
Uncooked bacon	66.14	56.58	53.81	47.93
Cooked bacon	39.93	37.08	36.95	38.13
Sausages	53.87	44.72	38.57	34.82
Chicken	32.09	32.91	34.55	33.60
Pork	33.34	31.59	31.91	27.22
Lamb	34.51	27.38	23.92	23.63
Meat pies	22.44	20.91	21.45	20.57
Corned meat	21.52	21.19	21.48	19.34
Cooked meat	20.50	22.04	21.51	18.28
Canned meat	23.38	18.58	18.50	17.22
Other frozen*	18.08	12.35	16.32	17.14
Deli/pâté	18.06	18.88	18.49	16.56
Cold pies	18.15	16.59	15.79	14.05
Liver/offals	22.43	16.11	14.40	11.03
Frozen burgers*	–	13.49	13.17	11.03
Ready meals	5.40	8.59	8.23	10.54
Cooked poultry	5.39	5.89	8.54	9.62
Turkey	2.47	6.47	5.68	5.46

Note: *No separate category for frozen burgers in 1979.

are supposed to represent the epitome of convenience, it is unlikely that increasing size of weekly purchase only signifies the bulk purchase syndrome, although ready meals are not necessarily fresh meals and may be taken from store. An alternative hypothesis, to the purchase of more such meals in the weekly shop, is their extension from single to other households with more members.

Three products, with the increase in changes in quantity purchased by those purchasing shown in brackets below, have experienced falls in overall levels of consumption. In other words, for the fewer purchasing, substantially more is being purchased – for sausages by (19.0%), canned meat (14.8%) and frozen burgers (12.2%, calculated from 1984 to 1989). As previously observed, this paradox of falling average quantity purchased with rising size of purchase by those purchasing, might be explained by a trend towards bulk purchasing – plausible for the freezer-bound burgers and the larder-bound canned meat. But the alternative, of a core group of consumers who go against the trend by consuming more rather than less, is more likely for sausages – with implications for health, overlooked if only examining average consumption for the population as a whole, given the fat content of sausages.[23]

There are three other deviants for each of which the quantity purchased by those purchasing has risen by so much that it significantly outweighs the fall in the number purchasing so that average quantity purchased over the population has increased. The products are cooked bacon (15.2%), corned meat (24.8%) and deli/pâté (14.4%). Unlike those products last discussed, the increasing quantities being purchased by those purchasing are in line with, if significantly greater than, the increase in average quantity purchased across the population. Interestingly, deli/pâté is a composite of two food codes – those associated with delicatessen and more traditional pastes and spreads. Both have witnessed an increase in the quantity purchased by those purchasing, the first by 13.6% and the second by 16.0%, but the average quantities purchased by the population have increased by 24% and decreased by 20%, respectively. Both of these products might be thought to be consumed relatively quickly; the first, however, has experienced a growth in popularity both in proportion purchasing and average quantity purchased across the population, whereas the second has suffered a fall in numbers purchasing and average purchased across the population even if those purchasing are buying larger quantities.

While meats are differentiated by their different and varied fortunes in spread and depth of popularity, they are also differentiated by the patterns of purchases according to the socioeconomic characteristics of households. As shown in Chapter 11, purchases of some, but by no means all, meats are particularly affected by social class (defined by occupational type) even correcting for income which, by itself, has a more limited impact on meat choice. Specifically, it is found that there is a heavy skew to higher classes for deli/pâté[24], cold pies and ready meals, and towards the lower classes for sausages, meat pies, corned, cooked and canned meat and burgers.[25]

Here, we focus upon age (of 'housewife'), a socioeconomic variable which cuts across both class and income (although the latter tends to rise and then fall with age). Table 8.1 (p. 172) contains the dramatrices by age, aggregated over the four sample years. In interpreting these figures, it is important to recall that they are aggregated over four years so that the average shifts in rankings per annum need to be scaled down by four. On this basis, it can be concluded that meat choice is heavily skewed to the old (or, more often, against the young) for lamb, cooked meat and liver/offals. On the other hand, there are strong skews to the young for canned meat, deli/pâté, frozen burgers, other frozen products and ready meals.

Because the pattern of overall meat purchases by age are of an inverted-V shape, where the dramatrices are skewed away from the young, the absolute proportion of the younger households' purchasing tends to be very low. This is so, for example, for liver and for lamb, with Table 10.6 illustrating the point for selected age groups.

On the other hand, if the skew is towards the young, then their absolute frequencies of purchase can even outweigh those of their greater

Table 10.6 Absolute frequency of purchase by age

Age	<25	35–44	55–64
Lamb			
1979	26.69	31.35	39.05
1984	14.11	27.92	29.67
1986	13.47	24.81	30.01
1989	10.52	21.14	27.62
Liver			
1979	18.18	23.18	25.10
1984	10.53	15.58	19.42
1986	10.00	13.67	16.08
1989	2.27	9.93	14.24

Table 10.7 Absolute frequency of purchase by age

Age	<25	25–34	35–44	45–54	55–64	65–74	>75
Frozen burgers							
1984	20.84	19.47	19.23	12.66	7.89	5.69	2.10
1986	19.59	18.23	17.09	13.57	8.54	6.11	4.38
1989	17.94	16.16	15.12	10.26	5.83	5.11	3.36
Frozen convenience foods							
1979*	32.69	22.59	23.43	19.28	12.14	8.54	6.63
1984	14.95	14.72	16.18	13.23	9.44	8.94	3.24
1989	22.68	22.38	21.40	17.38	13.38	10.64	7.18

Note: *Includes frozen burgers.

meat-eating elders (or, more exactly, middle-agers), as shown for frozen burgers and other frozen food in Table 10.7.

These results are modified once account is taken of other socioeconomic variables. Especially for liver, for example, but also for lamb, the age effect is reproduced for single or couple households without children but not for those with children. This is because the bias against these meats where children are present in the household is so great that the age effect tends to be totally dominated. On the other hand, for couple households without children, there is a skew for sausages away from the young; for ready meals, the skew to the young is much stronger for single households.

Interestingly, when account is taken of income, most of the age effects are reproduced but they tend to be stronger for the lower than for the higher income groups. In other words, age tends to have a more important impact upon meat purchases the more important is income as a constraint upon the household. Much the same is true of the impact of the presence of children. But the effect seems to be different according to the sort of child(ren) present. For lamb, for example, the negative effect of children is particularly pronounced for the presence of pre-school children, slightly mitigated by siblings at school. There are similar effects for liver (see Tables 9.2 and 9.3).[26]

The same, but opposite, effect applies in the case of frozen convenience food, illustrated in Table 9.3, for canned meat and also burgers (where the child effect tends to persist in the higher income groups) and, in much milder form, for sausages. In short, from these and other results, it appears that the presence of children has an effect both according to their numbers and their types, and the extent of the effect is greater the lower the income. But it must again be emphasized that this applies, in different ways, to some, but not all, meats.

The preceding discussion has established the heterogeneity of meats in two different ways. The first shows that meats are differentially purchased in terms of the quantities involved, the spread of popularity across households, and the ways in which these characteristics have changed over time. The second feature distinguishing meats is the variability of their attraction to consumers according to the latter's socioeconomic characteristics. We have demonstrated the complex and mixed effects of age, income, class, household composition and presence or absence of children.

CONCLUDING REMARKS

This still leaves open, however, the question of the relationship between these heterogeneous patterns of purchase and the meat system to which they are attached (or should it be meat systems?). At the proximate level of food choice itself, the variation across meats and socioeconomic factors would appear to suggest that there is little integral connection involved between meat systems. However, no account has yet been taken of the nature of the meat products themselves and their common attachment to socioeconomic determinants. To rectify this is to some extent speculative, though still open to empirical investigation both in principle and in practice even if beyond the scope of this contribution.

Consider, for example, the trend towards healthier eating and vegetarianism which is (too?) readily associated with the young as more open to adopting new eating practices, products, moralities and lifestyles. Certainly, as demonstrated above, this is reflected in their greater aversion to the traditional carcass meats, but is contradicted by a greater attachment to frozen burgers, ready meals and deli/pâté which, in addition, are characterized by their convenience. Indeed, it can be seen how a variety of influences other than the direct determinants of food choice itself are at

work. The supermarket delivers a very wide range of innovative manufactured meat products that allow for convenience in shopping, storage and
use, are not readily associated with health and animal welfare concerns,
and which can use as ingredients those parts of the animal (liver/offal) that
would otherwise go to waste or command limited demand.[27]

More generally, we suspect that the pressures to reduce (fatty) meat
consumption for health reasons are being contradicted by the use of meat
(products) as a continuing form of consumer gratification. This is evidenced
by the greater purchasing of meat by those on lower (but not the lowest)
incomes and of lower occupational status for whom, presumably, other
convenient and affordable forms of satisfaction are less readily available.[28] The
meat system seems to have adjusted in a number of ways: it has provided a
wider range of convenient products to serve all tastes and motives (including
its own profitability and the forms in which it is generated) whether for
consumption in the home or for eating out for which separate outlets serve
those of different status and income. Moreover, the impact of low income
seems to be particularly significant for the presence of children where the
possibly greater commitment to provide meat for the household leads to a
disproportionately greater dependence on those meat products that are both
cheap and designated as relatively unhealthy.

In short, while there is heterogeneity and segmentation in the markets
for meat, this depends to a great extent on the complex interaction of
economic and social processes that are common across all meats. While the
jury is still out, and the evidence yet to be fully collected and presented,
this leads us to work with the notion of a single meat system with separate
components. It is perhaps more important to recognize the shifting contours of the meat system, as they strengthen and weaken at different points
along the vertically organized SOP, than it is to come down with an
either/or verdict on its integral unity or separability. What is essential is to
connect the changing choices and meanings of meats to the SOPs that make
those choices and meanings a reality.

NOTES

1 As would appear to be the logic of analysis based on the 'world steer', for
example, in Sanderson (1986).
2 It has parallels with the more general 'diet paradox'; see Fine (1993b).
3 In any discussion of vegetarianism, it is always important to test any hypothesis
against its prevalence among a high proportion of the world's population
outside the West.
4 See Fiddes (1991), for example, who sees it as the consequence of the declining
importance of demonstrating control over nature. For Falk (1991), contrary to
Fiddes, aversion to meat (and other foods) is a consequence of being unable to
subject them to control and certainty. For Adams (1990), it is a complement to
the exercise of male power over women. See also Twigg (1983) for an
undifferentiated discussion of the meaning of meat.

5 See Adams (1990) for whom the obfuscation over the meaning of vegetarianism weakens its meaning and impact as part of a more general process concealing the significance of eating meat (or the flesh of any creature).

6 See Richardson *et al.* (1993 and 1994).

7 Not only with changing meal patterns but with the growth of convenience roasts, most notable in Bernard Matthews' turkey roll.

8 This is most simply expressed, though complicated by quality considerations, as the reduction in the cost of feed per effective weight of output which can itself be increased by MRM (mechanically recoverable meat), addition of water or other ingredients to add weight, bulk and colour, whether in joints, cuts or meat products.

9 Pulp waste from a variety of crops has increasingly been employed as animal feed. And, as a source of disease and food scares, the use of animal waste has arisen.

10 See also Eurostat (1990) and Woodhams (1988).

11 Large companies predominate across both agro-chemicals (herbicides, pesticides and fungicides) and fertilizers (nitrogen, phosphates and potash), less so for the latter where economies of scale are apparently less important (Key Note 1993a).

12 This has reduced the comparative advantage associated with the availability of pasture with the result that there has been a decline in the international trade in meat with the rise of poultry and pork. These trends are less pronounced in the developing world. Note that the substitutionism in this instance, from pasture to feed, and from ruminants to monogastrics, involves the intervention of industry but occurs within agriculture and not at its expense.

13 Over the same period, the weight of turkeys at twenty weeks has increased from 23.7 lb to 37.6 lb (males) and from 16.4 lb to 25.7 lb (females) and the weight of ducklings at seven weeks has grown from 6.5 lb to 7.2 lb. In 1956, chickens took eighty-four days to achieve a weight of 4 lb. These changes have not come about without attendant problems due to the accelerating intensity of production; while the mortality rate of chickens fell to 3% in 1975, it then rose again to 6% because of leg and metabolic disorders associated with the high growth rates and energy diets of the birds (Mattessons Wall's Limited, n.d.).

14 It is difficult from available figures to make an easy and sensible representation of the empirical trend towards specialization. But see the MAFF-produced annual, *Farm Incomes in the UK.*

15 For what follows, see Mattessons Wall's Limited (n.d.). Both breeding/hatching and egg-laying tend to belong to separate enterprises.

16 Mattesson Wall's Limited (n.d.). Buxted, another major meat manufacturer, retails both own and own-label products, the latter for Marks & Spencer and Sainsbury.

17 A listing of the meat products involved is found in Table 8.1.

18 The income groups are taken from the NFS, falling in level from A1 to D, with E1 and E2 being high- and low-level income for the unemployed. For more details, see Chapter 8.

19 See also Slater (1991) and Frank *et al.* (1984).

20 Note that Ritson (1988 and 1991b) identifies major shifts in underlying tastes in the 1980s.

21 The general presumption – with improved domestic technology (freezers), the increasingly important weekly shop, and with enhanced packaging and preservatives – is that frequency of purchase should decrease even if quantities purchased remain the same. For those products not purchased on a weekly basis, however it might be expected that frequency of purchase would increase

(given, for example, the capacity to extend freshness and its availability in 'convenience' stores).

22 The average size of purchase by those purchasing has only fallen for beef (4.5%), meat pies (5.7%) and cooked poultry (6.6%).

23 See Chapter 9.

24 All the more remarkable because this category is made up of both status spreads, such as pâté, and traditionally working-class spreads such as meat pastes. From quantity data, the former predominates.

25 These findings tend to be confirmed and even strengthened when correcting for other socioeconomic variables.

26 Tables 10.2 and 9.3 are only for households with adult couples, together with no, pre-school, school or both sorts of children.

27 The capacity of the food system to shift the form in which its products enter consumption is similarly demonstrated for sugar and dairy foods, see Heasman (1993) and Chapters 5 and 12. Note also the use of meat for the pet food industry.

28 See Chapter 11.

11

FOOD AND CLASS

This chapter is concerned with the class content of food. It is considerably aided by a recent article, Tomlinson and Warde (1993), which has reclaimed the high ground, against a post-modernist tide, for the significance of class distinctions. They have done so by assaulting their erstwhile opponents' favoured terrain – the area of consumption and of food in particular. By examining categories of food expenditure between 1968 and 1988, using data drawn from the UK Family Expenditure Survey (FES), they discover that class (as determined by occupation) remains a major correlate of consumption patterns. Employing discriminant analysis on food expenditure, they are able to identify the class of over 50% of all households by broad socioeconomic group. Within middle-class, single households even stronger conclusions are drawn: 'By 1988 one could identify the occupation class category of two middle class individuals out of every three by reading their grocery bills for a week' (p. 8).

The purpose of this paper is to develop the analysis of Tomlinson and Warde further, and it should be considered as a complement, rather than as an alternative, to their work. For, most obviously, there are a number of differences between the empirical studies involved. First, use is made of a different data set, the NFS, and over a different (and shorter) period, from 1979 to 1989. Second, attention is placed upon which of a select group of foods are purchased or not rather than upon broad categories of food expenditure.[1] Consequently, both of our analyses share in common the neglect of the average quantities of foods purchased, a focus that has persisted in many food studies because of the preoccupation with meeting the (average) nutritional requirements of a healthy diet. Incidentally, in this light, it should be observed that Tomlinson and Warde's conclusions are almost certainly understated. For a persistent finding of the NFS is that expenditure elasticities for food exceed quantity elasticities – the more you spend, the less quantity you buy in proportion. This has the implication that the wealthier purchase higher-quality foods which is liable to be a further aspect of distinction quite apart from the composition of expenditure. In other words, the better-off are liable to distinguish themselves not only by their spending patterns but also by buying better quality within those broad expenditure patterns.

A third difference is in the statistical methods employed. Tomlinson and Warde rely upon discriminant analysis which identifies which foods and classes tend to be correlated with one another (in levels of expenditure). This chapter uses the novel empirical techniques previously outlined to identify food norms, fully described in Chapter 8, searching for common or distinct patterns in the foods purchased or not by households distinguished by a range of socioeconomic variables.

A fourth difference, then, is the extent to which account is taken of other potential socioeconomic determinants of food choice. Tomlinson and Warde clearly correct for class but also establish its significance over and above income, with which it is generally correlated, by comparing two subsamples of two of the classes – one manual and the other professional, each member of which, for both classes, is required to earn a per capita disposable income of between £125 and £175 per week. They find the professionals go for wine and 'healthy' products, while the manual working class is inclined towards beer, cooked meats and sugar. Further, they take a marginal, if implicit, step towards acknowledging the importance of household composition, both by focusing on per capita income (correcting for numbers in the household) and by undertaking a specific analysis of single adult households (within the middle-class category).

However, as has been continuously repeated by the NFS in its annual reports, household composition appears to be a much more important determinant of food choice than either income or class, even after correcting for household numbers. It is hardly surprising, for example, that single households should have different food purchases than those with one or more adults and a number of children of a variety of ages. They will purchase less *and* differently. More attention is paid here to household composition, in particular to the presence or absence of children. In addition, our work has found age (of head of household) to be an important determinant of food choice, although we do not report on its interaction with class.[2]

It would appear, however, that the introduction of a range of correctives for other socioeconomic variables – age, children, income, household composition, gender, etc. – would have the effect of weakening the conclusions that Tomlinson and Warde seek to draw concerning the role that class plays as 'a principal causal mechanism and a central analytic tool' (p. 3). For class becomes one determinant among many; and tell me what foods you purchase and I will tell you your sex, your age, whether you have children or not and how many people are in your household.[3] A final difference with Tomlinson and Warde, then, concerns how such empirical results are to be interpreted, although it is suspected that the option offered here is both consistent with Tomlinson and Warde's stance and acceptable to them.

For their approach, no doubt inspired by the goal of contesting consumption as increasingly classless in its content, seeks to forge an immediate connection between individual class membership and the corresponding individual patterns of consumption. Significantly, as the title of their piece indicates – 'Social Class and Change in Eating *Habits*' (emphasis added) – there is nothing specific about food in what they do. For food, like clothing in the earlier days of sumptuary laws, is interpreted as both a symbol of class membership and as evidence of its continuing causal significance. But the latter not only has to be established, so also do the mechanisms by which it is determining. As Tomlinson and Warde observe in attempting to move beyond the use of (deficient) nutrition as an index of class difference (persistent though it is): 'Any interest in class division and class reproduction as a social process – concern for the symbolic, ceremonial and sociable aspects of food – is obscured if food is considered merely the precondition to health' (p. 3). By the same token, the identification of food patterns by class does not in itself reveal class reproduction as a social process even if extended in content from health to symbolic, ceremonial and sociable aspects of food.[4]

This point can be illustrated by a number of different hypothetical extremes. Suppose, for the sake of argument, that Fordist methods of food production and mass consumption had become predominant to the exclusion of all other forms of production and products – a tendency previously emphasized by a branch of the food systems literature.[5] Then, class differences would be reflected primarily through access to income with the wealthier consuming more of the same. The class system associated with Fordism would be reproduced through limited class distinctions in food consumption, other than by quantity. And, as there are strict limits to the capacity of the stomach if not the appetite, food distinctions would be eroded with growing incomes. In other words, the class nature of a Fordist regime would increasingly be reflected in the *absence* of distinctions by food consumption.

On the other hand, quantitative differences in income might lead to qualitative differences in consumption habits, as in eating out, with the poorer classes relying upon fast food as opposed to a fancy restaurant. Yet again, fast food might become the habitual form of convenient eating out for the wealthy while serving more as a special occasion for the worse-off. This would mean that the higher class might consume more of what is associated with the food patterns of the lower class.[6]

The purpose of these hypothetical examples, of greater or lesser empirical significance in practice, is to suggest that patterns of consumption are not the immediate reflection of class differences. Indeed, patterns of consumption may serve to obscure the underlying class relations upon which they are based as is so evident in so many other aspects of a modern, property-owning democracy.[7] Further, consumption in general, and of food in particular, will reflect and reproduce class relations in complex and a variety of ways. Indeed, it is essential to recognize that different foods will be articulated with class and other social relations and activities in different ways from one another.

In this light, two rather different conclusions follow. One is that the persistence of empirically identifiable class differences in consumption are all the more remarkable given that they are liable to have been both heavily modified and veiled by their interaction with other socioeconomic variables. The other is that the presence and identification of such class effects still leaves open to be discovered the mechanisms by which they are reproduced. Such is the implication, for example, of Mennell's (1987) discussion of the inferiority of English relative to French cuisine. For he suggests that distinction by food was less necessary for an English aristocracy, confident of its hierarchical position. He also refers to the difference in ethics (English protestantism) and relations between town and country. Hence, just as class distinctions by foods are differently constructed from one country to another, they are liable to be distinguished by foods within a country.

In short, both interpretatively and causally, Tomlinson and Warde seek a uniform and immediate identification between class and consumption. Yet, this is neither essential nor necessarily appropriate in forging a link between class and food. Significantly, Tomlinson and Warde's approach is not specific to food – it could, as previously observed, apply equally to clothes, homes or mode of transport for it simultaneously seeks an association between class membership and items of consumption. While this analysis pursues the same goal, even if with different methods and data sets, it does so against an analytical background specific to food which recognizes that class (and other social) patterns of consumption are bound to vary across foods according to the systems of provision to which they are attached.

We begin with an empirical estimation of food norms by class using our own methods. This is followed by a brief discussion of the implications of such exercises for the notion and validity of class as an analytical category.

FOOD NORMS BY CLASS

Table 11.1 indicates the percentage of the population purchasing each of the selected foods in the four years chosen for analysis. The foods are in order of 'popularity' for 1989. Quite clearly, some of the foods have witnessed substantial growth in spread of purchase, some have experienced substantial decline, while a few have changed very little.

Fortunately, by chance rather than by design, the frequencies of purchase of all the foods taken together is extremely even both across the

Table 11.1 Absolute frequencies of purchase

	1979	1984	1986	1989
Whole milk	97.79	87.55	78.06	69.92
Potatoes	71.64	66.85	67.12	64.90
Biscuits	70.81	64.12	64.97	61.79
White bread	`78.25	71.55	62.76	59.54
Eggs	77.20	68.93	64.44	53.09
Brown bread	39.00	44.57	53.08	47.38
Cereal	39.89	42.65	43.46	42.36
Skimmed milk*	4.00	13.69	26.38	39.54
Sugar	58.80	48.33	44.26	36.07
Margarine	45.65	46.36	44.78	35.77
Crisps	28.56	32.81	34.23	34.95
Chicken	32.09	32.91	34.55	33.60
Yoghurt	19.71	27.29	30.62	31.36
Juice	15.47	25.31	28.61	29.14
Butter	60.96	43.85	36.50	27.35
Spreads*	9.76	8.09	17.12	22.36
Ice cream	15.61	17.34	17.56	19.29
Chips	5.92	11.74	14.26	16.16
Burgers*	18.08	13.49	13.17	11.03
Ready meals	5.40	8.59	8.23	10.54

Note: *These foods have a shifting composition over time; see Chapter 8.

different social classes and across these for the years – at about 40%
(exactly the proportion of these foods, for example, purchased by social
class A in 1989, as shown in Table 11.2).

In addition, again fortuitously, the *differences* in frequencies of purchase
between one food and the next in popularity (whether above or below) is

Table 11.2 Percentage of purchases across all foods by social class

			Class		
	A	B	C	D	E
1989	40.0	38.8	39.9	39.7	41.9
1986	41.2	41.1	42.6	42.1	44.0
1984	41.5	41.5	42.2	41.6	41.2
1979	41.3	40.7	42.3	41.7	42.5

relatively small (with the exception of whole milk, especially in 1979 when, as the most 'popular' food, it enjoyed a gap of 20% over its nearest rival, white bread). As a consequence of these chance numerical properties, shifts in relative frequency for subsamples are liable to serve as a sensitive index of differences in absolute frequencies as well of underlying food norms as previously outlined in earlier chapters. Thus, for example, a shift upwards in the absolute frequency of a food for a particular social class, relative to other classes or the population as a whole, is likely to be picked up by the dramatrix (and must correspond to a downward shift in the absolute frequencies, and possibly the dramatrix, for one or more other foods).

Table 11.3 is made up by summing over the dramatrices for the four years. This has the advantage of drawing upon the results for each of the years but at the expense of eliminating any opportunity of revealing the presence of shifts in rankings even within as short a period as a decade. Accordingly, this is commented upon below where appropriate.

Table 11.3 Aggregate dramatrix for social class

	Class				
	A	B	C	D	E
Milk	0	0	0	0	−1
Potatoes	−3	−4	−6	−4	−6
Biscuits	6	6	4	0	1
White bread	−17	−6	3	5	6
Eggs	−2	−1	−1	−1	−1
Brown bread	11	7	−7	−9	−14
Cereal	2	4	5	5	4
Skimmed milk	13	9	−1	−3	−5
Sugar	−22	−16	−6	1	4
Margarine	−13	−10	−5	−1	3
Crisps	1	2	13	9	8
Chicken	−5	−8	−1	0	2
Yoghurt	17	9	2	−1	−2
Juice	21	14	0	0	−9
Butter	−2	−3	−3	−4	−5
Spreads	−3	−1	1	2	3
Ice cream	0	0	0	−4	−1
Chips	1	1	−1	0	7
Burgers*	−7	−4	3	4	7
Ready meals	4	1	2	1	3

Note: *Combined with other frozen convenient food in 1979.

In interpreting Table 11.3, it is important to bear in mind that it is aggregated over four years.[8] Consequently, it needs to be divided by four in order to give an average of the difference in rankings of the foods. Further, even where the entries by this criterion are not apparently significant, as for burgers for example, the difference (14) between the upward shift for the lowest class (+7) and the downward shift for the highest class (–7) is striking. Moreover, the entries for the other classes are monotonic, decreasing with higher class, suggesting that there is a systematic (but negative) relation or component of the food norm for burgers by social class.

Quite clearly, there are stronger rankings or skews towards higher classes for brown bread, skimmed milks, yoghurt and fruit juices, and towards lower classes for white bread, sugar, margarine and burgers (with exceptionally high ranking of chips for the lowest class in 1989). Of these, the skews have developed over the decade for white bread, skimmed milk, margarine, yoghurt, fruit juice and sugar (primarily between 1979 and 1984). For the other foods with skews, there is no consistent pattern for these emerging during the decade. This is clear evidence both of the persistence and of the rapid creation of difference in food norms between classes. On the other hand, there are foods for which there is no consistent (monotonic) pattern of purchase behaviour with class. Chicken is a good example, with its being purchased weekly by approximately one-third of the members of each of a number of household subsets of varying socioeconomic characteristics. For some foods, such as crisps, the pattern across class is in the form of an inverted-V. Although a well-defined pattern, possibly reflecting a skew towards distinction from the middle classes (whether by higher or lower classes), this is almost certainly not the result of class-specific behaviour, but the influence of other socioeconomic variables with which class is weakly associated. (Inverted)-V patterns are quite common, for example, with age which is itself associated with both income and the presence of children (in inverted-V form).

Table 11.4 confirms these results for the skews in class rankings by presenting the absolute frequencies for selected foods for the two extreme classes over the four years. In general, each class follows the overall trends (presented in Table 11.1), with the higher classes further advanced in changing eating habits towards brown bread, yoghurt and juice; and away from white bread, sugar and margarine. It also appears that the slight skew in the dramatrices towards higher classes for biscuits is an anomaly. It arises out of the particularly high frequency with which the lower classes purchase white bread (which, relative to absolute frequencies, depresses their rankings of biscuits).

But are these patterns of food purchases by social class confirmed, or do others emerge that are concealed in the aggregate, once account is taken of other socioeconomic factors? Quite clearly, class is highly correlated with income and may simply be functioning as a proxy for it. Remarkably,

Table 11.4 Absolute frequencies for select classes and foods

| | Biscuits | | White bread | | Brown bread | | Sugar | |
	A	E	A	E	A	E	A	E
1989	66.18	72.26	41.91	75.91	53.47	0.15	25.14	48.91
1986	65.31	75.19	44.90	80.45	69.73	43.61	33.33	54.14
1984	69.88	70.00	56.33	87.86	58.73	31.43	36.45	61.43
1979	71.85	77.84	63.05	92.78	55.43	23.20	50.15	74.23

| | Margarine | | Yoghurt | | Juice | | Burgers | |
	A	E	A	E	A	E	A	E
1989	30.64	48.18	53.47	27.74	49.13	21.17	9.54	22.63
1986	38.78	60.15	53.40	30.08	55.78	27.07	7.82	15.79
1984	39.46	54.29	42.47	17.14	45.18	13.57	9.34	22.14
1979	48.68	56.19	31.09	18.04	29.91	8.25	12.02	20.62 *

Note: *Burgers includes other frozen convenient foods in 1979.

however, if the effect of income is examined by itself, with the survey partitioned into six income percentiles, the resulting dramatrices aggregated over the four years, as before, reveal more limited shifts in rankings, and more mild monotonic patterns where these do emerge. This is illustrated in Table 11.6 (corresponding to Table 11.3 for class) which is preceded by Table 11.5 showing how purchases over all foods varies with income (corresponding to Table 11.2). It follows, even though there are not enormous differences in rankings, that those with higher incomes are still liable to purchase more of each good (although this eases off and even reverses for the highest incomes after 1984). Thus, for some foods, lower income is associated with higher frequency of purchase of certain foods, most obviously for white bread for example.

Table 11.5 Percentage of purchases across all foods by income percentile

| | Percentile* | | | | | | |
	1	2	3	4	5	6	7
1989	28.7	34.6	36.5	40.0	42.1	41.5	(37.5)
1986	29.7	36.2	38.7	41.6	43.4	43.0	(39.8)
1984	29.3	35.2	38.1	41.4	43.8	44.4	(39.0)
1979	30.7	36.5	40.3	43.4	42.4	43.6	(40.2)

Note: *1–6, lowest to highest percentile; 7, representing those households for which there are no data on family income

Table 11.6 Aggregate dramatrix for income percentiles

	Percentile					
	1	*2*	*3*	*4*	*5*	*6*
Milk	0	0	0	0	−1	−2
Potatoes	2	1	0	−2	−6	−3
Biscuits	−3	−3	−2	2	7	7
White bread	2	1	3	1	2	−6
Eggs	−1	0	−1	0	1	1
Brown bread	1	1	−3	−5	−7	4
Cereal	−5	−3	2	3	7	4
Skimmed milk	−3	−3	−5	−3	2	6
Sugar	2	4	2	−5	−6	−13
Margarine	−5	−3	0	−1	−8	−13
Crisps	−5	−2	1	10	12	7
Chicken	2	2	0	−3	−3	−3
Yoghurt	−2	−2	−1	2	5	4
Juice	−5	−7	0	0	4	14
Butter	9	2	−2	−4	−8	−3
Spreads	11	6	−2	1	2	−1
Ice cream	−5	1	−2	0	0	−1
Chips	2	−1	1	0	0	0
Burgers	2	1	5	4	−1	−3*
Ready meals	−1	−1	2	1	1	2

Note: *Combined with other frozen convenient food in 1979.

Such patterns over income groups are of less concern here than how income affects the impact of class. The strength of the class effects previously identified were further examined by subdividing the survey in two different ways. The first was by focusing upon class differences within three separate types of households: single adults, and couples with and without children. For white bread, brown bread, skimmed milk, margarine (more mildly – possibly reflecting the decline in spread on bread but also the association of margarine with health), yoghurt and fruit juice, the skews for class were all reproduced for each of these household types. For biscuits, the skew to higher classes was strongest for couples with children; for sugar, the skew did not apply to single-adult households (possibly because of infrequent bulk purchase syndrome); crisps did reveal a weak skew to lower-class households other than single; burgers had no lower-class skew for single households; and ready meals had a skew to higher classes for single households, a V-pattern for couples without children, and a skew to lower classes for couples with children.

The effect of class independent of income was investigated by dividing the households into five income groups prior to partitioning these by class.[9] Once again, even having corrected for income in this way, the class effects remained for white bread, brown bread, skimmed milk, sugar, margarine (more mildly), yoghurt, fruit juice and burgers. Otherwise, there are relatively few class effects within income groups. This suggests that of the two factors, class takes the leading role over income.

In short, the association of patterns of food purchases with social class is well established for a variety of foods even when account is taken of household composition and income. Indeed, for the foods considered here, class has a stronger effect than income. However, income does itself emerge as being more important than previously apparent, once other socioeconomic influences, especially the presence of children and age, are taken into account.

So far, then, the results reported here conform in type and content to those of Tomlinson and Warde, although it is worth emphasising that some, not all, foods are a mark of class distinction. The presence or absence of some items in the weekly shopping trolley is an index of class; but others, such as eggs, whole milk, potatoes, chicken and cereals, do not have class stamped upon them. But how do these food norms relate to their dependence upon food systems?

First, the industrialization of agriculture, and the manufacturing and processing of food products, has been associated with cheaper foods and higher incomes for most consumers, even if this is also associated with an extension of product variety. As foods in quantities and qualities have become available to all (or most) within the developed world, it is hardly surprising that class differentiation by foods should be uneven across them. For, if cheapness and being amenable to mass production, distribution and consumption is the basis upon which class distinctions are to be found, then there is no reason that these should be even across all foods and drinks in their weight (even if they do apply in each case). Further, if we posit a tendency towards cultural homogeneity (and, hence, tastes for foods), such processes are liable to vary in rhythm and incidence.

Second, then, as the emphasis has shifted away from getting enough food, even if potential physiological requirements have long been exceeded for most people and most nutrients, so food has been able to serve a shifting variety of roles, with different incidence of these across social classes. In particular, food is able to gratify the individual in a number of ways, and the extent to which it does so is liable to be influenced by the alternative forms of (non-food) gratification that are sought and available. It seems that the class patterns in food consumption that have been identified suggest a higher commitment to health in the higher classes. It might popularly be presumed that this is due to greater acceptance of, and action upon, health messages. Such a view is oversimplified. For surveys have frequently shown that there is often considerable knowledge of what is a healthy diet, although it is laced with a healthy scepticism about the shifting opinions of experts. Further, the incidence of smoking and alcohol consumption indicates that their most important determinants cannot be inequality in knowledge of their impact upon health – although the analogy is far from perfect, given the different social and physiological meanings of food and potentially addictive goods. Although this is only a loosely formulated hypothesis, and one for which it is difficult to (design a) test, an alternative view is that higher classes are more capable, and not just through income alone, of seeking gratification other than through food (at least as purchased for consumption in the home).[10] The most obvious direct connection between food and class (as occupational type) in this context would be in work satisfaction – that you eat more to compensate for lack of job satisfaction – but less direct mechanisms might also be in place.[11] Of course, this opens up a large number of subsidiary hypotheses about factors whose incidence might not only be questionable but which would be open to being complex and uneven by occupation, gender effects, etc., and from one to food and another. Thus, are lower occupations less gratifying (e.g. less stressful or stimulating) than higher? If so, what types of difference in gratification are involved, how are they experienced, and how do they give rise to attempted compensating gratification through food consumption as opposed to other activity?

These remarks are supported by the empirical results for eighteen meat products, examined in a similar exercise to that reported above. With some exceptions, especially for new and/or convenience products, the proportions of the population purchasing each meat have been declining (see Table 10.5). And, while the proportion of meats being bought by each class has declined, more meats are being purchased by the lower than by the higher classes. This indicates that meat-eating has, if anything, become reversed as a symbol of status, as illustrated in Table 11.7 showing by social class the proportions of all eighteen meats purchased. This might simply reflect stronger response to health messages about meat by higher classes. But, then, as will be seen, once we examine differences across meat products, it becomes difficult to explain why some lower-quality meats, especially offal, have proved particularly less appetizing to the lower classes over time.

This relative aversion to meat with higher class is even confirmed by the quantities of meats purchased per person per week, broken down by income rather than class. As Figure 9.1 indicates, over the 1980s, the ranking of income groups by quantities of meat purchased has been substantially reversed, with meat consumption increasing as income falls from A to E2.[12] These interpretations of indices of overall meat consumption are, by our own arguments, both crude and overgeneralized. They do,

Table 11.7 Percentage of purchases across all meats by social class

	Class				
	A	B	C	D	E
1989	21.1	21.2	25.1	25.0	27.9
1986	20.3	22.2	27.2	27.8	29.0
1984	22.1	23.5	27.4	28.1	29.1
1979	23.7	25.4	30.8	31.4	33.4

however, serve to illustrate the main point that the translation of class into (meat) eating habits is both complex, and contradictory, and the socio-economic and cultural mechanisms must be unravelled on a disaggregated (even meat-by-meat) basis.

This cannot be done here in detail. But consider the aggregate dramatrix for meat products (Table 11.8). There are clearly class distinctions in the rankings of some meats; a heavy skew to higher classes for deli/pâté[13], cold pies and ready meals, and towards the lower classes for sausages, meat pies, corned, cooked and canned meat (not all monotonic) and burgers. Unfortunately, both because of the difference across classes in overall meat purchases and the more uneven gaps between the absolute frequencies with which the meats are purchased, the dramatrix does not give as sensitive an index of changes in absolute frequency of purchase of meats across the social classes. This will be taken into account in the discussion that follows.

The food norms for meat products reveal just how complex is the relationship between class and consumption. For a product such as deli/pâté, with a lingering status appeal, the dramatrices are so strongly skewed towards higher classes that their absolute frequency of purchase exceeds that of lower classes despite the latter's greater proclivity for meat. Indeed, this is the only meat product for which the class skew is strongly reproduced within different types of households and for different income groups. For sausages, the positive skew towards the meat-eating lower classes means that their absolute frequencies of purchase considerably exceed those of the higher classes (although the skew is not reproduced for single households and any income group other than C) – see Table 11.9. All classes have experienced an absolute decline in purchasing, but the class skew has remained very strong.

On the other hand, for chicken, as previously noted, there tend to be even proportions across all classes, with a third of each purchasing weekly; the same applies to beef, at a level of 50%.[14] With higher classes purchasing less meat overall, this tends to lead to a slight skew towards them in the

Table 11.8 Aggregate dramatrix

			Class		
	A	B	C	D	E
Beef	1	1	0	−1	1
Uncooked bacon	−1	−1	0	1	−1
Cooked bacon	−1	0	1	−1	0
Sausages	−8	−4	−1	0	2
Chicken	7	4	2	−1	1
Pork	1	0	1	−1	1
Lamb	−4	−3	−11	−6	−4
Meat pies	−11	−5	1	7	−5
Corned meat	−12	−8	5	2	−3
Cooked meat	−6	−6	2	−3	5
Canned meat	3	−4	6	16	18
Frozen	3	1	6	6	0
Deli/pâté	24	21	4	−5	−7
Cold pies	8	6	−2	−2	−3
Liver/offals	−1	−1	−9	−8	−4
Burgers	−8	−2	1	6	7
Ready meals	11	5	3	1	1
Cooked poultry	2	1	0	1	3
Turkey	3	0	0	0	−1

Table 11.9 Percentage purchasing sausages by social class

			Class		
	A	B	C	D	E
1989	19.44	22.45	29.87	33.13	35.00
1986	20.83	25.90	35.12	40.91	51.52
1984	26.19	31.13	40.04	41.41	46.67
1979	41.18	40.33	50.08	47.59	57.14

dramatrices. Paradoxically, the same applies to liver/offal, for which lower-class aversion appears to have caught up with the higher classes in the 1980s (and overcome any inducement through cheapness). However, the most important (negative) factor associated with liver purchase is the presence of children (and, to a lesser extent, the age of head of 'household', with a relative aversion by the young). For lamb, age is an important factor. Yet, another pattern is revealed for ready meals. Despite a skew to the higher classes, which it shares with deli/pâté, its importance is increasing over time. Interestingly, the greatest increase in absolute frequencies has been for the unskilled classes, especially where children are present, whereas the greatest increase in ranking has been for the professional classes. Although class has some effect for ready meals, age has been a more influential variable. There would appear to be a complex interaction of tradition, innovation, convenience and status at work.

It is worth emphasising again, as for the earlier set of products, that there are many meat products for which there do not appear to be strong class patterns alongside the complexity of those patterns that do exist. In the case of meat products, this arises in part out of the gratification that has always been provided by eating meat even as alternative forms of gratification have become available, although many other factors such as age and presence or absence of children are important over and above class and income. Nor should it come as a surprise that such class distinctions by meat as can be identified are far from striking and even perverse in quantities consumed – any more than that an increase in owner-occupation should lead us to hesitate before declaring the death-knell of class politics. In generating food distinctions between classes, there is many a slip twixt cup and lip, and the class relations that generate food systems are not directly translated into corresponding patterns of consumption.

CONCLUDING REMARKS

Although the starting point of this chapter has been to develop further the analysis of the relationship between patterns of food purchases and social class, only limited progress has been made in establishing the causal mechanisms involved in creating the empirical associations that have been identified. Within our framework of analysis, however, this is not surprising for it is hypothesized that the ways in which distinctions are drawn in consumption, and especially for food which commands a decreasing proportion of income, are liable to vary from one product to another. Before drawing broader implications for the significance of class, it is worth drawing attention to a separate issue raised by Tomlinson and Warde. They find that the unemployed and those dependent upon welfare provision are moving towards distinctive patterns of food purchases, reflecting a polarization that they suspect might continue without a change in welfare policy.

Evidence from the overall frequencies of purchases of the foods considered here strongly support the idea of a marginal group of consumers – although the data have to be treated with caution for reasons elaborated below, and the connection to welfare dependency has not been examined directly. For, as previously observed (Table 11.2), although overall levels of

Table 11.10 Percentage of purchases across all foods for marginal groups

		Income	Expenditure
	Single adults	*Lowest percentile*	*Lowest percentile*
1989	25.5	28.7	18.0
1986	27.7	29.7	20.9
1984	26.9	29.3	20.1
1979	28.9	30.7	24.5

purchase of foods are relatively even across social classes at about 40%, the same is not true for other partitions of the population. What stands out is the sharp difference in overall purchases by those in the 'marginal' groups; the difference between the overall purchase of foods by those in the lowest percentile of household income and those in the second percentile is far greater than for between any other two percentiles; the same is true for those in the lowest percentile of food expenditure, and for single households. These levels are also declining and, for Table 11.10, should be compared with an overall average of 40%.

Now, lower levels of purchases for single households (fewer mouths to feed, more liable to eat out), for those on low income (less money available) and those making little expenditure (eating out or bulk purchases next week) are not necessarily causes for concern. However, the differences from the averages, and by comparison with the gaps elsewhere in the partitions, are so great as to suggest that there are a variety of socioeconomic conditions that lead to divergence from more standardized patterns of food purchases – and the same applies to single parents (primarily mothers) for reasons other than overall levels of purchase, although this has not been investigated in detail. This is not surprising given the increasingly standardized form apparently taken by food purchasing – the one big weekly shop. Those excluded from such norms, whether by virtue of income, access, level of expenditure or size of household, are liable to be marginalized from such standards and, one suspects in certain cases, to be marginally provided for whether in nutrition or gratification. Both for reasons of policy as well as for analysis, given the deception created by the average consumer, there is a need to focus upon the hard to feed as well as the hard to heat, to house and to employ.

Unfortunately, this lies beyond the scope of the present work. But it does allow the issue of class to be posed more sharply. As has been seen, patterns of food consumption do at times appear to reflect class position even if not always. This would appear to be evidence against a class explanation for consumption, at least in the absence of other, apparently equally important, factors. On the other hand, the presence of a strata of 'hard to feed', even amidst a world of plenty, suggests that class is of importance, at least at the margins where those who are on low income, unemployed, etc., can be perceived to arise out of the functioning of a *class system* that creates such conditions.

How is the evidence to be interpreted, and does it offer support for or against class analysis? Initially observe, however, that the evidence is constructed around *individual* households in two different ways. Class is identified with occupation of head of household, and consumption is identified with household purchases of food. This, and other statistical exercises, tend to be simply concerned with the presence or absence of correlations between these two sets of household characteristics.

This can be put in another way. There are many different ways of stratifying the population according to individual or household characteristics apart from occupational status and food consumption. Each of these necessarily depends upon inequalities although these need not necessarily reflect privilege, advantage or hierarchy (as in education, wealth and power), since the differences may be in ideological stance, gender, race or political preference, etc. But there is a presumption that class generates strong correlations between itself and the various forms of stratification, with class generally defined occupationally – whether directly (for head of households) or indirectly in the case of non-waged members of the household (do non-working wives take on the class membership of their husbands?). This individualistic notion of the effect or proof of class is strong even if the putative correlations are based upon social determinants. Analytical schemes concerning the processes of stratification through structures, consciousness and action, while relational in origin, are still often tied to outcomes at the level of (groups of) individuals.[15] The result is inevitably to overthrow class analysis on the grounds of counterexamples, such as the right-wing voting or attitudes of members of the working class (for which fascism is the more devastating counterpart). More sophisticated accounts that hold on to class analysis need to complement it with the incorporation of other factors such as gender, race, etc., and, even on this expanded terrain, reject any determinism attached to more complex stratification. If we cannot tell how people are going to vote from their class, gender and race, we can hardly expect to tell how they are going to eat.

This begs the question of how class is to be defined at the level of the individual, with occupational categories generally serving in default of more careful consideration. No doubt, the origins of this definition arise out of a generalization from the boss–worker polarity in which a finer division by the nature of the employer–employee divide is intended to breathe extra life into the correlations with income, health and other household characteristics. This sort of procedure has posed particularly acute problems for Marxist class analysis. For a number of separate criteria have emerged for the definition of the working class – as work is productive or unproductive (of surplus value, an issue which is itself controversial),[16] manual or non-manual, undertaking a capitalist function (supervisor, for example) or function for capitalism (police officer) or not, etc. These characteristics can also be attached to further derived criteria such as membership of a trade union or ideological stance towards the social order (unlikely to be oppositional if concerned with upholding the law).[17]

Such multiplicity of criteria, and the potential disjuncture between them in terms of class membership, prompted Ohlin Wright (1985) to suggest that individuals might occupy contradictory class locations – satisfying working-class membership, say, in some respects but not in others (a waged policeman or supervisor). As is apparent, ultimately leading Ohlin Wright to accept that his theory rests upon a Weberian rather than a Marxist methodology, the theory of class stratification is pitched at the level of the individual's characteristics. While the criteria concerned might be derived from Marxist concerns, though not unique to them, they are arbitrary to a certain extent both in content and scope. Further, the notion that class locations might be contradictory owes nothing to dialectics nor to the complexity of social structures, processes and relations – however these are understood philosophically and causally. Rather, the contradictory class locations are purely properties of individuals, who do not or, possibly, cannot satisfy all of the appropriate correlates of a single class position. By the same token, it is hardly surprising that there should be contradictory locations, as it were, in food consumption.

This suggests that, if the idea of class is to be a property of individuals, it must be complemented by a range of other, potentially 'contradictory', factors. Consequently, class is no longer privileged and must take its place as one factor among the others – why not contradictory gender, race or other locations, such as sexual orientation? But there is an alternative, since class can be relocated at the level of social relations. This is the way in which we understand class, reinforced by our study of food, despite apparent contradictory 'dietary locations'.

For class is, in the first instance, a simple and abstract relationship around production – best described by the duality between capital and labour. This cannot be projected directly onto individuals, although there are undoubtedly archetypal entrepreneurs and waged workers. From the capital–labour relation, systemic tendencies, structures and relations can be derived, their strength and role in part contingent upon historical and social developments, as for landed property and landowners for example.[18] More specifically, food systems can be understood as the particular way in which underlying class relations give rise to consumption, including patterns across the population.

In this light, it is inappropriate to test the conceptual validity of class by examining correlations at the individual level between patterns of consumption (or other practices and ideologies) and proxies for class relationships. Of course, teasingly, there may be and may appear to be such direct corre-lations. The working class cannot own private aeroplanes nor luxury mansions, and there will be more flexible and indirect constraints and influences on patterns of consumption which will tend to generate class characteristics at the individual level. Even so, it is essential not to identify patterns of production with those of consumption directly but to construct a relationship between the two analytically, by incorporating the inter-mediate steps between the social and the individual along the food system.

The same applies to class analysis in contexts other than consumption. Just as consumption, fish and chips and cloth claps, cannot be read off from occupational stratification, so the same applies to politicization, for example. The conflict between capital and labour creates the potential for social democratic and socialist parties to represent the interests of labour. Membership of such parties, and the content of their policies and practices, cannot be read off from their origins in the class relationships of pro-duction. In this respect, although the analogy should not be pushed beyond its methodological implications, the food and political systems are com-parable. Accordingly, the central question is whether the capital–labour relation is considered to be uniquely crucial to contemporary society and, if so, how it is structured and reproduced (or not) at more complex levels, whether in eating, voting or revolutionary consciousness.

NOTES

1 Of course, implicit in the work of Tomlinson and Warde is the definition, through discriminant analysis, of food norms by expenditure. This diverges from the NFS approach by the quality of food (and differences in prices paid for foods of the same quality).
2 The same applies to gender effects on food choice, although these are in part intra-household and difficult to discern from inter-household data. The best that can be done is probably to compare households in which one or other of the sexes is absent altogether. But see the discussion of single parents in the concluding remarks.
3 Paraphrasing the quip made by the French eighteenth-century gourmet Brillat-Savarin, 'tell me what you eat: I will tell you what you are' – often abbreviated to 'you are what you eat'.
4 This has been recognized elsewhere (Warde 1992, p. 15–16):

> There is a systemic connection between the driver of a combine harvester and the consumer of a bowl of cornflakes. But given an advanced division of labour, we cannot show anything but a contingent link between an individual's occupation and his/her taste in cereals.

See also Warde's (1990) introduction to the special issue of *Sociology* devoted to consumption.
5 For food systems literature, see Chapter 3.
6 Of course, the incidence of eating out is affected by a range of factors other than income and class, such as age, presence of children, whether in paid employment or not and household composition.

7 Thus, the presence of Tory-voting, share-holding manual workers does not in itself undermine the legitimacy of class analysis.

8 The presence of negative entries across the whole spectrum of class may appear anomalous – how can all classes rank a food lower than the overall norm? However, certain categories of the population have been excluded from the table, such as those on pensions, the unemployed and the armed forces. This might shift all the rankings shown by an absolute amount (relative to the rest of the excluded population) but does not affect their rankings relative to each other.

9 These were taken from the NFS income categories as follows (rather than our own categories formed by use of six percentiles): A1 and A2 were combined to form a single category, B, C, D and E2. For details of the levels of income involved for the various years, see Chapter 8.

10 See Mintz (1993).

11 Such considerations might suggest one reason that there is a correlation between income inequality and health over and above those due to low absolute levels of income – as highlighted in the work of Quick and Wilkinson (1991). Class as well as income inequalities might lead to unhealthy forms of gratification as a result of relative deprivation – as in obesity, smoking and alcoholism.

12 See also Nelson (1993, p. 116) who finds that 'there have also been recent reversals in some long-standing income-group rankings – sugar (1959), fish (1970), separated fats (1973) and eggs (1975)'.

13 All the more remarkable because this category is made up of both status spreads, such as pâté, and traditionally working-class spreads such as meat pastes. From quantity data, the former predominates.

14 Although such uniformity of purchasing behaviour is not reproduced for all socioeconomic partitions of the population.

15 See Crompton (1993) for a thorough review of the issues surrounding class and stratification.

16 See Fine and Harris (1979) for a review.

17 For a recent review, see Carter (1995).

18 Classes other than capital and labour can be derived logically from the capital–labour relation – those receiving (high) income in the form of wages, but not exploited in view of their function or professional or other qualification and those who are self-employed.

12

THE DAIRY SYSTEM

The UK dairy system has lurched from one dramatic upheaval to another over the past decade. The result is that the existing system has now reached the point of collapse and a 'brave new world' is dawning over the industry. This has been dramatically hastened with the UK government's 'deregulation' of the milk industry with effect from November 1994. Contributing to this fundamental breakdown in the existing system has been the spectacular growth in the liquid market for skimmed milks which now account for more than half of all household milk purchases; the slapping on of farmgate milk quotas by the EC in 1984 with immediate effect; supermarkets and dairy companies seeking to integrate farmers closer to what they see as market 'realities'; and government's varying stances and finally its apparently decisive role in shaping the dairy business.

Within our analytical framework, these events are explained as the transition from an SOP, centred for sixty years on the organic role of whole-fat liquid milk, to a new SOP being structured on an organic plurality of milks and milk products. We will identify the dairy system that previously prevailed from the 1930s onwards, distinguish it from the currently evolving dairy system, and trace out some of the features characterizing the transition between the two.

We begin, however, by outlining the elements that the two dairy systems have had in common. Each is a chain of provision combining various economic activities through vertical integration. Inputs may be manufactured, as in cattle feedstuffs, or be dependent upon own-grown feed for which availability of land is essential. Dairy herds may be of varying size and quality in terms of the quantity and content of the milk that they yield. Milk itself has to be processed, even if to be delivered in liquid form, and it has to be distributed, sold and consumed. Associated with each of these activities, there are also changing technologies and work practices, and the availability of finance whether through credit or internally generated profitability.

In terms of the organic content of the dairy system, attention should be drawn to the perishability and 'bulk' of milk. This is reflected in the duality between final products – between liquid milk (and fresh cream) that must be consumed relatively quickly and manufactured products, such as butter and cheese (and powdered and UHT milk as well as non-dairy products containing milk derivatives) that can last more or less indefinitely. The broad division between the two sorts of final products is attached to the SOP as a whole, through the capacity that is created in processing dairy milk and in the balance of inputs within dairy farming. In addition, the institutional structure governing the system is significant in terms of the ownership and control of the vertically organized chain of provision. In this, there is the question of how competition is arranged within and across the various agencies along the SOP, particularly given the perishability of milk and the potential volatility in its supply and demand. Inevitably, the role of the state has been important in governing the competitive process.

The difficulty lies less in outlining these descriptive characteristics of the dairy system than in confronting them with the appropriate analytical framework. Our starting point is the increasing intensity of production, usually associated with capital accumulation. In the United Kingdom, for example, milk producer numbers fell by 40% between 1966 and 1976 (71,197 in March 1976) and the decline continued with a 34% drop over the next ten years (46,740 in March 1987). Average herd size over this twenty year period increased from 25 cows to 67. Between 1976/77 and 1986/87, milk output rose from 13,647 to 15,364 million litres. However, the total number of dairy cows actually fell, from 3,228,000 to 3,135,000. The increase in production, therefore, was achieved by raising average yield per cow from 4,275 to 5,015 litres over the ten-year period (Roberts 1988).

Whatever the marketing conditions for liquid milk, the individual dairy farmer is able to produce surplus profitability by processing more feed, whether this be dependent upon more land, more cows, higher yields, more machinery, or more manufactured feed as opposed to pasture. What happens to that surplus profitability depends upon the functioning of the system as a whole. It can be extremely short-lived if leading to over-production and collapse in the price of milk unless, as is common for many agricultural products, state intervention is designed to protect farm incomes. Here, then, there are two extremes – one in which the surplus profitability associated with increasing intensity of production is appro-priated by the economy as a whole and eroded in the form of lower prices, the other in which it is retained by the producer.

But matters are more complicated than this because the argument as such is not specific either to dairy farming or agriculture more generally. These are distinguished by their dependence upon land, not so much in the natural sense (although this is important) as in the necessity of access to land. For it is equally possible that the surplus profitability is appropriated by a landowner in the form of rent. To a greater or lesser extent, this would moderate the incentive to increase intensity of production for its associated profitability would be shared with a landlord. Nor is this obstacle necessarily overcome by a system of owner-occupation – for the potential rents derived from expanding output become consolidated in the value of land, as a sharp constraint when a farmer seeks to obtain access to neighbouring property. In short, there is a complex relation between ownership of land, the incentive and capacity to increase output, and the latter's price (potentially enabling surplus profitability to accrue as interest paid for loans to finance land purchase). Clearly, this will be affected by the potential to exploit existing quantities of land more intensively which in turn depends upon the availability and efficacy of high-yield cows and manufactured feed.[1]

Now, consider the dairy system as it evolved from before the Second World War. It came into effect in England and Wales in 1933 with the establishment and operation of the Milk Marketing Board (MMB).[2] The scheme was developed and promoted by the National Farmers' Union, was endorsed by a poll of producers and was given, according to the terms of the 1931 Agricultural Marketing Act, the requisite ministerial and parliamentary approval. The Board was vested with powers over producers and had the ability to control prices. Cox *et al.* (1990, p. 83)[3] describe the Milk Marketing Board as:

> Arguably, the single most important development in agricultural policy during the inter-war years. . . . The MMB . . . was a major political innovation which revived the corporatist possibilities for agriculture and which has stood the test of time better than any other such arrangement affecting British agriculture.

The setting up of the MMB was also a victory for the milk producers over distributors. The previous decade had seen increasingly bitter disputes between the two as farmers, to overcome their market weakness, sought to improve their lot *vis-à-vis* distributors. The unevenness in the relationship between farmers and distributors (wholesalers) stemmed from milk's central organic nature, namely its perishability, its bulk and its seasonality. In the mid-1800s two-thirds of total milk production went into cheese and butter manufacture, but by the 1930s this had dropped to a quarter as a result of dairy imports from the Commonwealth, facilitated by refrigeration. On the other hand, liquid milk consumption had doubled between 1883 and 1923 and, by the 1920s, raw milk production for the liquid market dominated the dairy sector. This made producers, with a highly perishable product, heavily reliant on distributors who used this vulnerability to try to control prices in their favour. In addition, distributors in some regions were becoming increasingly concentrated in contrast to the large number of producers.

However, allied to the producers' economic concerns was the growing importance of liquid whole milk as a 'healthy eating' product. This organic property of milk, that it is rich in vitamins and minerals, had placed its production in the arena of public health with schemes like the free school milk programme, started in 1927. Consolidating these health issues with producer interests, the MMB put into practice a market structure geared to supporting the dairy industry by maximizing returns to producers through the production of liquid whole milk. The MMBs secured surplus profitability to farmers by serving as a barrier to vertical integration with implications for the pricing of perishable and non-perishable dairy products. The past decade has seen a nibbling around the edges of this structure and the beginnings of vertical integration more directly with retailers and product manufacturers. This has challenged and undermined the existing SOP for milk and milk products in a number of significant ways. Before these are examined in more detail, a brief description is given of the essential workings of the dairy system that is currently being undermined.

HOW THE DAIRY SYSTEM HAS OPERATED

A central feature of this dairy system has been that farmers have not had direct supply contracts with dairy companies. Rather the MMB, on behalf of producers, exercised, in effect, monopoly power over the sale of their product. Swinbank (1987) describes this as involving a three-stage process. Farmers, who have been compelled to register with the MMB to produce milk for sale except in clearly defined circumstances, have made raw milk available to the MMB which in turn was the sole seller of raw milk to the dairy companies. These manufactured milk products and prepared liquid milk for sale to consumers and caterers. The price that the dairy companies paid for raw milk was determined in the Joint Committee,[4] composed of the Dairy Trade Federation (DTF), representing buyers, and the MMB. The price of raw milk was, therefore, differentiated by end use (for example, butter or cheese – see Table 12.1), but farmers received a 'pooled' price, after deduction of Board expenses, regardless of the actual usage of the milk from their farm.

The practical functioning of the milk marketing scheme was dependent on this complex pricing policy operated through the MMB, but also reflecting government policies on milk pricing. For the purposes of this discussion the general principles only are outlined as they relate to the SOP.[5] A key component, then, has been price differentiation for milk dependent on its final use. In particular, the price for liquid milk has been highest, and the MMB served the farmers' interests by pressing for maximum sales within this submarket. Table 12.1 illustrates the different prices obtained for the (same) milk depending on its use.

However, the pricing and supply system for raw milk was not as simple as implied by the figures in Table 12.1, since the prices represent an

Table 12.1 Average return for wholesale producers of milk in England and Wales (pence per litre)

Product	1990/91	1991/92
Liquid market	23.914	24.759
Cream	18.556	18.790
Chocolate crumb	19.027	19.117
Condensed milk*	18.900	18.850
Whole-milk powder	18.071	18.494
Cheese	16.557	17.706
Butter	16.513	17.482
Other products	19.085	19.410
All wholesale milk	20.460	21.436

Note: *Includes evaporated milk.

Source: Federation of United Kingdom Milk Marketing Boards

'average' for each use; the figure for 'cheese' hides different prices for different cheeses, for example. The MMB also operated an allocation system which involved 'calling' milk from low-value usages to higher-value outlets whenever those higher-value markets could absorb a larger supply. So, for example, if a manufacturer of chocolate crumb needed a certain supply of milk at the same time as a butter manufacturer, the milk would be diverted or called for the chocolate crumb use, and the butter manufacturer forced to wait until a suitable supply next became available.

In this way, the liquid market always had priority over supply, followed in descending order by other higher-value products. If supplies were short, then the Board would direct milk away from the lowest-value usage and, in particular, from the factory using such milk that lay closest to the one (making higher-value products) that was facing a shortage. Negotiating the raw milk price was also a complex procedure and differed from product to product. For some products agreed formulae were laid down, reducing the scope for negotiation. For example, there was the CATFI system (Common Approach to Financial Information) for determining processing and distribution costs for butter, but this did not necessarily make conditions surrounding butter manufacturing readily transparent, as Swinbank (1986, p. 45) warns: 'It should be noted . . . that the British butter market is not easy to understand, and that a major study would be required to encompass the complexities.' National pricing was further complicated by the provisions within the CAP for the dairy sector, with a target price for milk, intervention buying for products such as butter, and export refunds (subsidies).

With the MMB serving as a buyer of last resort for all milk producers, the milk marketing scheme also served to limit comparative advantage between milk producers as reflected, for example, in regional differences, nearness of producers to manufacturing sites, more efficient producers, etc. This policy was reinforced by government interventions to set a national retail price for milk (up until 1985). Thus, the milk marketing scheme (MMS) has proved immensely successful in securing incomes and a regular cash flow for farmers, especially small and medium-sized producers.[6]

The priority of the liquid market over other uses of milk was sustained, before the United Kingdom's entry into the EEC in 1973, by a policy that permitted the fairly free importation of manufactured milk products, from Commonwealth countries in particular. The price at which they could be landed effectively determined the price at which the MMB could sell raw milk for manufacture. The extent of the price differentiation could be large. For example, in 1970 and 1971, the Board obtained more than twice the return for sales of raw milk for the liquid market in comparison to the average return for manufacturing – 23.61 as compared to 9.20 pence per gallon (Swinbank 1986).

From the time of the United Kingdom's accession to the EEC in 1973, the prices paid for milk destined for manufacture improved and the differential between them and the liquid price narrowed. Traditionally the liquid milk market in the United Kingdom has been much greater than other EU countries. In 1988, for example, 44% of UK milk was used for liquid consumption compared to an EU average (excluding Spain and Portugal) of 20% (NCC 1990). The emphasis on liquid sales and the resulting supply and pricing system has also been blamed for holding back innovation in the dairy industry. For example, in July 1985 makers of blue Stilton were paying nearly 28% more for their milk than were Cheddar cheese manufacturers (Swinbank 1986). The NCC (1990, p. 10) points out:

Britain has the ability to produce a wide variety of cheeses for instance, but the existence of the milk marketing scheme acts against this. A monopoly which exists to solely promote liquid milk production acts against innovation – it directs supplies of milk from manufacturing.

However, the tensions of maintaining this structure, geared to producing high returns to producers for liquid whole milk, in the face of a changing and increasingly industrial set of food complexes has been a contributory factor to the demise of the existing dairy system. Swinbank (1987) notes that buyers are seeking not so much to process raw milk in its entirety into milk products (with low-value byproducts such as whey). Rather, the aim has been to use the constituents of raw milk and their manufacture into less traditional products, including imitation milk products in combination with vegetable fats and proteins. The limited industrialization of the dairy industry, therefore, is not simply because agriculture has confronted capitalism with a natural production process (Goodman et al. 1987, p. 1), but due to the management of these processes in favour of agricultural rather than industrial interests (although the development of such hybrid milk products can be interpreted as a form of substitutionism).

THE DAIRY REGIME IN THE 1980S

Although not discussed in detail, it is clear from the brief description above that to protect producer incomes, the checks and balances within the dairy system evolved in both complexity and rigidity within the MMS. It also displays the strength of the dairy system; for example, the MMS in England and Wales remained essentially intact even with the United Kingdom joining the EU. This was achieved through the negotiation of a lengthy transition period and the introduction of special legislation. In practice this meant, after an initial five-year transition, that special legislation (council Regulation 1422/78) was introduced by the EC to allow the UK MMBs to continue. There was a further redrafting in 1981 to reflect the requirements imposed by EEC law (Colman 1992). However, at EU level, the technological treadmill of the milk production process – the ability to generate ever-expanding output intensively, and the guarantee of farmer profitability for this – saw the dairy industry create massive surpluses. Support for milk and milk products grew to become the single largest item in the EC agricultural budget, peaking in the late 1970s at around 46% of the total (Milk Marketing Board 1989). The EC Commission confronted the agricultural budget difficulties and dairy product surpluses head-on with the imposition of milk quotas in April 1984.

Before discussing the implications of the EU-wide imposition of milk quotas on the dairy industry in England and Wales, trends and the changes in industry structure within the then dairy regime will be outlined. The dairy industry is the largest single sector of the UK food and drinks industry. In 1989, milk from UK farms was valued at over £2 billion and the retail value of products made from it netted £4.5 billion per annum; dairy products accounted for 16% of UK consumer expenditure on food (Harding 1989).

The MMB (England and Wales) was Europe's fourth largest food producer and second largest dairy producer (behind Nestlé). In 1989, the MMB had a turnover of just under £2.25 billion and collected 11.5 billion litres of milk from more than 32,000 producers. Five companies – Express Dairies, Unigate, CWS, Northern Foods and Dairy Crest – bought two-thirds of total milk produced. The MMB was the sole shareholder of Dairy Crest Ltd, and the latter bought around one-quarter of all milk produced (the relationship between MMB and Dairy Crest is discussed in more detail in the following pages).

At the other side of the farm gate, dairying has seen improvements in productivity driven by increasing economies of scale and new technology. Through the MMB's strict quality and compositional criteria, achieved through price incentives, raw-milk[7] production appears to exhibit the

Table 12.2 Dairy industry: number of producers and processors in England and Wales

	Wholesale milk producers[a]	Organizations[b] receiving ex-farm milk	Establishments[c] receiving ex-farm milk
1970	79,011	312	581
1975	58,532	192	398
1980	42,725	151	341
1985	36,119	150	300
1990	31,283	178	328
1991	30,289	188	337
1992	29,233	197	332

Note:

[a] Wholesale milk producers is the term used by the MMB to denote those registered producers who have entered into a contractual agreement whereby they may sell their milk (in its raw bulk condition) to the MMB.

[b] In many cases a number of 'establishments' may be under the same ownership: such a group of establishments is referred to as an 'organization'.

[c] A specific individual milk-processing plant (be it creamery or dairy) is referred to by the term 'establishment'.

Source: Federation of United Kingdom Milk Marketing Boards 1992.

classic symptoms of Fordist agriculture – standardized, mass-produced output subject to a technological treadmill. In the case of dairying, this includes the use of feed concentrates to increase yields, milking equipment and type of parlour, veterinary support, etc. Producer numbers in dairying fell by 43% from 1973 to 1983, the number of dairy cows declining by 5% over the same period. However, there was an increase in average number of dairy cows per herd, up from 40 in 1973 to 71 in 1991. There were fewer small producers and more large producers, with the number of producers with more than 100 cows increasing over 50% between 1973 and 1983 (Milk Marketing Board 1989). Table 12.2 details the reduction in the number of wholesale milk producers together with the number of organizations and establishments active in the dairy industry.

The number of dairy cows in England and Wales fell by nearly 13% between 1980 and 1990 (2,672,000 cows compared to 2,324,000), but yield per cow rose between 1979/80 and 1989/90 by 7.5% from 4,715 to 5,070 litres per annum. The number of cows in herds of sixty or more increased to 74% of total cows (2,251,800) in 1991 from 67% of total cows (2,633,800) in 1981 (all figures adapted from Federation of United Kingdom Milk Marketing Boards 1992).

THE IMPLICATIONS OF MILK QUOTAS FOR THE DAIRY REGIME

The unusual and dramatic impact of milk quotas resulted from their immediate implementation. National guaranteed quantities (quotas) were to be calculated based on deliveries in the 1981 calendar year, plus 1%. The United Kingdom had its quotas assessed on producers' 1983 wholesale deliveries, less 9% and opted for the 'Formula B' or 'dairy-based' levy scheme.[8] The quota scheme was to run for five years. In 1988 the system was extended for a further three years and, in 1992, for a ninth year up to 31 March 1993. From 1 April 1993 the current regulations were repealed and replaced by new ones. Table 12.3 shows that between 1983/84 and 1991/92 sales off farms through the MMB in England and Wales fell by 17% (40% for butter and nearly 50% for skimmed-milk powder).

There are differing views on the impact of quotas on the dairy industry in England and Wales. Williams (1993, p. 2)[9] describes quotas for British dairy farmers as: 'A particular disappointment, not only because they have prevented expansion of milk supply in a net importing country, but also because they had to be imposed on a marketing system that had special difficulty in adapting to them.'

However, Hubbard (1992), for example, argues that farmers adapted quickly to the sudden imposition of quotas, responding initially by reducing both cow numbers and the level of feeding. In this sense cows have become like machines – their number can be and their throughput can be

Table 12.3 Milk sales off farms through the MMB in England and Wales

Year (April to March)	Million litres
1969/70	10,022
1974/75	11,115
1979/80	12,775
1981/82	12,694
1982/83	13,654
1983/84	13,610
1984/85	12,604
1985/86	12,688
1986/87	12,750
1987/88	11,912
1988/89	11,578
1989/90	11,632
1990/91	11,549
1991/92	11,239

Source: Federation of United Kingdom Milk Marketing Boards.

reduced (the latter implying a shift away from manufactured feed and greater reliance upon pasture when reducing yield).

Further, the impact of quotas has to be considered in the context of longer-term trends within the dairy industry (see earlier section on these between 1973 and 1983). The quota system has not seen a dramatic change in the industry's structure. The rate of industrial change has slowed down partly due to quotas, but the general economies of scale have continued to accrue, with growing concentration of production in larger units. Further, the profitability of dairy farming has increased (in comparison with other sectors of farming) as a direct result of quotas. The Milk Marketing Board (1989, p. 1), in examining the first five years of milk quotas, stated that average returns from milk had been pushed up and producer prices had also risen significantly both in nominal and real terms: 'As a means of restricting output and increasing prices, quotas have clearly been extremely effective.' With a cap on production and higher prices for raw milk, producers took steps to pass the cost of quotas up the food chain. As described below, input suppliers and labour have borne the brunt of these costs and, unlike farmers, have had no redress.

Thus, producers cut costs by altering feed practices and reducing the use of purchased compounds (with which they found they had been 'over-feeding' when there was no limit on milk supplies during the 1970s!). By 1989, over 1,000 producers had stopped using them altogether, and others had changed the way they were used. The result, in the five years from 1984, was a saving in purchased feed of approximately 40% (Milk Marketing Board 1989). This, in turn affected the feed industry; nationally, the number employed in the compound feed sector declined from 16,000 to 12,500 between 1983 and 1987 (Cox *et al.* 1990).

Farmers also reduced their own labour requirements. Between 1983/84 and 1989 the number of hired workers employed on dairy farms fell 27% (while dairy farm numbers fell 17%). The vast majority of these had been full-time workers, where nearly 13,000 job losses occurred. Just over half of all hired job losses in the entire agricultural sector in England and Wales over this period took place on dairy farms, yet these farms comprised less than one-fifth of all agricultural holdings (Milk Marketing Board 1989). As Cox *et al.* (1990, p. 101) put it: 'To a considerable extent then, the crisis and costs [of milk quotas] were diverted from the farmers to other sectors of the rural economy or class groupings in agriculture and the food system more generally.'

In addition, milk quotas unexpectedly also produced a new and lucrative source of income – the quota allocation itself. It is argued below that the most significant impact of quotas in the context of change within the current dairy regime has been the trade that has developed in the sale and leasing of quotas between producers.[10] The reason for this is that the value of quotas has fundamentally altered the relationship in dairying between land, landlords and tenants as well as undermined the concept of the

Table 12.4 Milk quota leasing and transfer in England and Wales

Year	1986/87	1987/88	1988/89	1989/90	1990/91	1991/92[a]
1. Total transactions	3,252	5,665	7,328	9,917	13,076	16,912
2. Quantity of milk involved (million litres)	195.0	254.7	341.5	468.1	602.1	690.0
3. % of milk quota	1.6%	2.2%	3.0%	4.1%	5.2%	6.1%
4. Producers leasing *out* quota	1,475	2,397[b]	2,685[b]	3,511[b]	4,696[b]	6,451[b]
5. Producers leasing *in* quota	3,010	4,878[b]	6,080[b]	7,802[b]	9,318[b]	10,905[b]

Notes:
[a]As administered by the MMB.
[b]Includes a small number of producers who leased both in and out.

Source: Federation of United Kingdom Milk Marketing Boards, *UK Dairy Facts and Figures* (various years)

pooled scheme for milk that has restricted comparative advantage between producer and regions.

In the five-year period reviewed by the Milk Marketing Board (1989), the MMB calculated that well over a third of all wholesale producers either bought, sold or leased quota and that the money changing hands represented a significant proportion of dairy farmers' incomes. In particular, it was estimated that over the first five years of quota sales, £250 to £350 million had been paid from the industry to outgoers (that is, of people leaving the industry). Table 12.4 shows the rapid growth in the trade in the leasing of quotas with total transactions increasing more than fivefold between 1986/87 and 1991/92.

Generally, higher prices for milk, lower input prices, improvements in technology and reduction in the level of global quota will raise the leasing price (Hubbard 1992). Hubbard points out that reductions in input prices are the main contributory factor in raising leasing prices in real terms and, with animal feed accounting for around two-thirds of total variable costs in the dairy enterprise, lower feed prices have been of particular significance.

More important, Hubbard shows that quotas have replaced land as the fixed input in dairy farming to become the ultimate repository of economic rent. He calculates that the total values of assets of all dairy farms in England and Wales in 1990 were estimated at £13 billion, with land and buildings, inclusive of quotas, accounting for £8.8 billion. Subtracting from this figure the estimated value for quotas (£4.4 billion) gave a value for land

and buildings, exclusive of quota of £4.4 billion. In comparison, total asset value of dairy farms in 1983 (prior to quotas) was £15 billion (in 1990 prices), with land and buildings accounting for £9.5 billion. In real terms, total asset values in the industry fell by 13% over this period with the value attached to quotas being more than offset by the 54% fall in value of land and buildings (£5.1 billion in 1990 prices). Hubbard (1992, p. 45) argues: 'It seems reasonable to conclude that the dramatic decline in real value of land and buildings in the milk sector has occurred as a direct consequence of quotas.' At the same time the purchase price of quotas has risen to around 40 pence per litre (representing twice the wholesale milk price) while, since 1986, the leasing price increased from 3 to 7 pence per litre (Hubbard 1992).

THE IMPACT OF MULTIPLE RETAILERS AND LOW-FAT MILKS ON THE DAIRY SYSTEM

The activity of the major retailers in the 1980s has effectively destroyed the consensus that previously existed for the marketing of liquid milk. Until then the cornerstone of the dairy regime for distribution of liquid milk was the doorstep delivery. The competitive pricing of milk and the development of alternatives to whole milk (skimmed, semi-skimmed, etc.) have substantially undermined doorstep deliveries. Deliveries by the milkman have declined from 84% of retail liquid milk sales in 1983 to 65% in 1991, with most of the decline occurring since 1987/88 (Key Note 1993b).

Before 1980, it was uncommon to find milk on sale at less than the maximum retail price for doorstep delivery, and shop sales were often more expensive than those on the retail round (Swinbank 1986). Sainsbury was the first major retailer to start competing on price when, in June 1980, it began selling pasteurized milk in its stores at 16 pence a pint, 0.5 pence cheaper than the price on the round. The retailers also looked to display a range of milk products (unheard of until the 1980s). Swinbank (1986, p. 42) also quotes the comments of Sainsbury's chairman, Sir John Sainsbury, when, in February 1981, he is reported as saying that the price for shop sale of milk was fixed in a cartel-like arrangement to force shops to sell at a higher price than the doorstep price. Further, Sir John is reported to have said that the DTF policy also seemed to have the effect of inhibiting the development of the sale of different kinds of milk – skimmed and semi-skimmed for slimmers, vitamin-added and flavoured milk for children. In addition, until 1984 the dairy trade refused to discount milk bought in bulk by supermarkets in order to protect doorstep deliveries (NCC 1990).

As outlined earlier, the dairy system had been set up around the 'organic' principle of whole milk. Over the past decade the quality of whole milk in the diet has been challenged on the basis of its fat content. Whereas the 'goodness' of whole milk could previously be used as a positive endorsement by milk producers, ultimately the butterfat (around 4% of whole milk consists of fat) component has been used to contribute to its decline. The healthy eating debate involving dairy products centres on the 'fat' wars, that is dietary advice warning against consuming too much saturated fat (eg butterfat) while at the same time increasing consumption of polyunsaturated fats (improving the P:S ratio), advice that has also been skilfully used by a number of margarine manufacturers to their advantage.

For household purchases of liquid milk, trends in healthy eating have contributed, in the space of a few years, to whole-milk consumption being reduced to less than half of total milk consumption with low-fat milks (skimmed and semi-skimmed) for the first time exceeding full-fat milk consumption in the second quarter of 1992 (MAFF 1992). For the total liquid milk market, whole milk consumption has declined from 82% in volume terms in 1985, to 59% in 1990 and 54% in 1991, Key Note (1993b).

However, as described below, the production of low-fat milks, while apparently fitting in with current dietary trends, has been used in attempts to maximize profits for some dairy interests *outside* the MMB's milk marketing scheme. In this way low-fat milk production exposed a weakness within the structure of the dairy system as administered by the MMB, posing a serious threat to the MMB's survival and proving an object of legal action. It also serves as an example of how the organic properties of food within a specific SOP can prove crucial to the functioning and operation of the structure of that system: in this case, how an apparently unimportant loophole in the MMS, that is the processing of whole milk to skimmed milk, has been increasingly exploited and the existing structures, based on maximizing profits through the retail sale of liquid whole milk, have been unable to accommodate this within the existing scheme and demand for a plurality of liquid milk markets.

The crux of the problem, for the MMB, and the weakness of the MMS has proved to be the concept of the pooled price paid to all milk producers, irrespective of the end use of their milk, and the question of what is understood as the processing of milk. Colman (1992) describes in detail the background behind these two issues. In particular, he documents the disputes that have arisen between the MMB and producer-retailers (PR) and producer-processors (PP)[11] who have sought to retain the returns from the final point of sale of their products outside the discipline of the pooled price.

Colman (1992) cites three examples of where this has occurred – first, regarding on-farm processing of milk into butter, cheese and cream. This had not presented the MMB with a problem since the MMB's selling price of milk for these purposes is less than the pool price paid to producers for milk, and quantities have been small. Hence the MMB would not be concerned if such on-farm processors were not party to the MMS because by opting out (or being exempted) they would be foregoing any share of returns from selling their milk to higher-valued uses through the pooling

249

system. However, such processors have taken full advantage of the MMS by selling their milk to the MMB at the pool price and buying back at the appropriate (lower) price for their own (manufacturing) use.

Second, and more seriously, is the problem relating to low-fat milk and the on-farm treatment of low-fat milks. At first, because the total milk passing through the PP and PR sector was small, the MMB chose to overlook when some milk in the sector was turned into, and sold as, low-fat milk and did not impose its levy on milk for low-fat liquid sale, treating it as a processed product. Since, however, low-fat milks command the same wholesale and retail prices as whole milk, this loophole enabled PRs and PPs to avoid the levy on direct sales into the liquid market and thereby secure an advantage over other milk producers. As Colman (1992, p. 132) explains:

> And since the 'market' for low-fat milk has grown rapidly at the expense of that for whole milk, it is not surprising that the PR–PP sector has taken advantage by increasing the proportion of its total throughput which is non-levy-bearing low-fat milks. Given the advantage through not paying levy has been around 4 pence per litre (ppl) against an average pool price of 19 ppl, there is a powerful incentive to move into producer-retailing and processing and to capture an increasing proportion of the liquid milk market for low-fat milks.

Third, Colman shows how categories of exemption from the MMB's powers have also been exploited, in particular the option of withholding for export. He uses the example of Strathroy Milk Marketing Limited, set up in 1989 in the Northern Ireland MMB area. By mid-1991, this company had arrangements with over 300 producers to withhold over 100 million litres of milk for export. Between January 1989 and March 1991, 88.6 million litres of milk were exported to the Republic of Ireland under the withholding provision for export. In addition, the company supplied skimmed and semi-skimmed milk to Tesco in England while exporting the separated cream to the Republic of Ireland. The legality of this had been challenged by the Northern Ireland MMB. What each of these examples illustrates is the vulnerability of the dairy system to breaches in the structural separation that had been provided for farmers through the role of the MMB.

MANUFACTURING AND THE DAIRY REGIME

The major organic property of raw milk, its perishability, locked into the producer-driven regime, had set the manufacture of milk products into a moribund structure. As mentioned above, the priority of the dairy regime had been liquid milk with manufacturing taking second place. This is also compounded by the organic factor of the seasonality of milk production. For example, in Britain, twice as much milk is available for manufacture in

May as in August (Grant 1991). Up until 1973 this relationship was further affected by fairly open imports of manufactured dairy products. Table 12.5 gives an estimation of the production of milk products in the United Kingdom. While this gives a broad-brush picture of production, the aggregate figures conceal the complexity of the market and more recent change. For example, no figures are given for yoghurt production nor is there an indication of branded products. Production has been further complicated by the ability to sell products into intervention and, in recent years, EC action to reduce product surpluses with the quota system.

The manufacture of dairy products in England and Wales is dominated by a relatively small number of companies (see earlier). The market concentration has been made more problematical by MMB's ownership of Dairy Crest. The MMB originally became involved in dairy processing through the construction of plants in areas where there were no facilities for using milk for manufacture. Its presence in the industry was increased in 1979 when it purchased sixteen of Unigate's plants, pushing up the MMB's share of milk going to manufacture from 27% to 50%. Hence the MMB became not only the monopoly supplier of milk to the dairy companies, but also owned the largest dairy company itself. Concern about this led to the government's decision to set up an investigation into Dairy Crest by the firm of management consultants Touche Ross. The Touche Ross report of 1985 made it clear that Dairy Crest did not act like a normal commercial company, but was concerned to maximize returns on milk for the farmers who ultimately control the MMB (Grant 1991). An important part of the emerging structure of the new dairy system is the place and role of Dairy Crest, with it being hived off as an independent commercial dairy company.

The dominance within the SOP for liquid whole milk sold through doorstep deliveries had seen less priority attached to manufactured dairy products. The result is that in the United Kingdom these have been dominated by commodity-style products. For example, 62% by volume, of all cheese made is 'Cheddar'. Despite sharp falls in retail butter sales, the differentiated pricing scheme of the MMS has meant that sometimes UK brands of butter have disappeared temporarily from retail outlets (Hollingham and Howarth 1989). The UK retail market for dairy products, in particular innovative products, has been met by imports and a mass of foreign manufacturers have entered the UK dairy market (Key Note 1993b). To illustrate the importance of these other sources of supply for manufactured dairy products, Table 12.6 gives figures for total volume of UK imports of milk and milk products between 1986 and 1991.

The growing concentration of the whole dairy industry, the activities of Dairy Crest, quotas effectively capping milk supplies and hence increasing the power of the MMB over who gets supplied with milk, and the innovative and competitive nature of the dairy market fuelled by retailers

Table 12.5 Estimated production of milk products in the United Kingdom (thousand tonnes)

Product	1978	1979	1980	1981	1982	1983	1984	1985	1986	1987	1988	1989	1990	1991
Total cheese[a]	215.9	234.0	237.1	243.4	243.8	245.1	246.3	255.7	257.7	263.9	288.9	279.9	313.2	288.6
Cream	117.1	123.9	126.4	124.0	125.2	124.8	122.6	125.2	128.7	129.1	143.7	146.9	152.0	151.2
Condensed milk	185.9	174.4	142.7	147.2	154.8	131.8	123.6	120.0	113.2	121.0	127.1	n.a.	n.a.	n.a.
Milk powder	326.8	287.1	301.8	318.6	365.9	390.7	357.7	372.3	408.7	344.4	288.8	n.a.	n.a.	n.a.
Butter	163.3	160.5	168.4	171.6	215.5	240.8	205.5	201.9	221.7	176.5	141.7	131.0	136.8	109.8

Note: [a] Excludes cheeses made from skimmed and low-fat milk.

Source: Federation of United Kingdom Milk Marketing Boards 1992

Table 12.6 Total UK imports of milk and milk products (tonnes)

	1986	1987	1988	1989	1990	1991
Butter	140,627	118,765	121,750	111,746	107,533	98,808
Butteroil	3,707	4,899	4,950	4,832	5,464	4,932
Cheese: Cheddar	99,380	80,167	104,328	77,851	90,505	75,551
– processed	20,489	20,742	23,863	25,139	29,465	29,109
– blue vein	5,962	5,737	5,936	5,403	5,623	5,688
– other	46,831	53,487	64,286	70,381	76,361	81,856
Total cheese	172,662	160,133	148,413	178,773	201,955	192,204
Condensed milk:						
– sweetened	594	920	1,205	1,869	1,491	1,753
– unsweetened[a]	8,485	8,878	8,629	8,133	9,574	8,736
Chocolate crumb	23,812	25,404	35,741	43,259	52,884	49,869
Milk powder:						
– whole[b]	2,231	2,470	1,924	2,951	2,468	3,108
– skimmed	8,989	7,858	8,936	15,552	6,537	7,699
Whey powder	10,266	14,264	19,220	19,415	21,175	19,130
Cream: fresh	3,187	3,821	2,842	2,663	2,420	3,137
– sterilized	1,367	1,086	139	154	18	–
Yoghurts[c]	33,624	33,504	41,852	54,985	71,382	85,736
Liquid milk[d] (litres)						
– packaged	3,851,556	5,865,957	10,541,950	16,923,760	20,262,545	35,845,962
– bulk	25,833,025	30,129,955	32,627,641	15,135,549	13,870,460	23,426,732

Notes:
[a] Includes skimmed condensed.
[b] Includes semi-skimmed milk powder.
[c] Natural and prepared.
[d] Whole, semi-skimmed and skimmed milk.

Source: Customs and Excise (adapted from Federation of United Kingdom Milk Marketing Boards)

and importers, have all helped to contribute to increasing acrimony between the MMB and DTF in the Joint Committee over handling the problems of low returns for manufacture, especially in the light of the large share of total raw milk production going to manufacture. Williams (1993) describes a fundamental shift in the role of the Joint Committee from a consultative body to that of a decision-making body in 1981 as a result of changes in Community Regulations. Swinbank (1986) says that the uneasy relationship between the MMB and DTF in Joint Committee seemed to have worked reasonably well until the relatively recent past. He gives four reasons why this relationship altered. First, the market changed with more milk going to manufacturing; second, changes in industry structure, in particular the expansion of Dairy Crest's activities; third, the ending of the government's price-fixing powers over liquid-milk and the entry of retail stores into the liquid milk market and consumer concerns over butter fat; and, fourth, stringent EC policy towards the dairy sector, especially quotas.

In short, the changing position of manufacturing in the dairy industry was giving rise to larger and more powerful alliances, including many milk producers, looking to redefine the structure of the current dairy regime in a way more favourable to their interests. This centres around greater vertical integration, with dairying becoming more unified into industrial food supply and the upstream activities of retailers. This new structure is being shaped by the desire to concentrate on some of the less exploited, until relatively recently, organic properties of milk and use these to help fashion a different, more flexible, type of dairy regime.

THE NEW DAIRY SOP

In this chapter, state policy has not been examined in detail, although it is a key enabling factor in the way that the dairy regime works. Government policy, for example, has given statutory force to the MMB as well as defining and setting the limits of its power. There have also been telling interventions in the system, from giving the dairy trade more say in Joint Committee and fixing the retail price of milk to negotiating reform of the CAP. Government has now taken action to end the previous dairy system to which it originally gave regulatory authority six decades ago. The Queen's speech of 6 May 1992, presaged The Agricultural Deregulation and Marketing Bill which will provide for the abolition of the MMSs and deal with consequential matters such as the treatment of the assets of the MMBs. At the time of writing, the Agriculture Bill which will abolish the MMB had completed its House of Commons stages and is due to come into effect from April 1994 (*Milk Producer*, July, 1993).

The dairy system has been driven by the capacity to produce ever larger quantities of raw milk at ever decreasing unit costs. The forces that have collectively undermined the structure of the previous dairy system have followed from the resulting conflicts of interest throughout the dairy SOP. Producer restructuring has centred around the erosion, but cushioning, of small-scale producers, and this has led to the creation and strengthening of entrenched interests. Manufacturing interests faced with capped raw-milk supplies under quotas and increasingly innovative competitors can no longer rely on unlimited commodity-style production. The multiple retailers have played a pivotal role by taking on the central pillar of the current dairy regime – the market for liquid milk. They have attacked this on two fronts: first, through price cutting (in comparison to doorstep deliveries), and second, in developing a range of liquid milks other than whole milk alone. They have also found shelf space for innovative dairy products such as yoghurts, fromage frais and speciality cheeses.

Finally, dietary and marketing trends have led to the creation of a new healthy eating definition of dairy products, in particular low-fat versus full-fat dairy products. The essential organic cornerstone of the current dairy regime, butterfat, has been successfully challenged; first, by changing consumer eating habits, and second, by strong competition from other fats and oils. The new dairy regime is creating a SOP through vertical (dis)integration, with producer interests segmenting in response to the needs of other parts of the dairy system. This will see the pooled concept disappear, helped by the movement of milk quotas between producers to those best able to integrate into the new system. In addition producers will become more closely tied to decisions and activities further up the SOP – it has been suggested that by the mid-1990s farmer control of milk supplies beyond the farm gate will diminish from about 85% at the end of the 1980s to 30% (*Farmers' Weekly*, 22 December 1989, p. 40).

The mode of the emerging structure and institutions of the new system are not yet clear. It is too early to assess critically the operation and structures of the new milk system. However, it is already clear that the transition is far from smooth and is proving a source of acrimony at a personal as well as at a commercial level.[12] The MMB in England and Wales has responded to its imminent abolition by launching Milk Marque in January 1993 – a new cooperative for England and Wales dairy farmers which will start trading when the MMB ends in 1994. Milk Marque is inviting all dairy farmers in England and Wales to join it and sign a contract to sell all their milk to them. Milk Marque in its campaign to persuade dairy farmers to join is emphasising the continuation of stability which, it argues, was always a strong feature of the MMS. In competition to Milk Marque, the big dairy companies, such as Northern Foods and Nestlé, are also making their case for dairy farmers to supply them exclusively. The new system represents increasing vertical integration within the industry with the intention of cutting out the middleman represented by the old MMB and the new Milk Marque. However, the reality has proved to be the replacement of a regulated monopoly, the MMB, with a private one in the form of Milk Marque.

However, the new system of provision for milk will mean, in theory, that for the first time in sixty years dairy farmers will be able to choose to whom to sell their milk. However, it should be noted that the four biggest dairy companies will buy two-thirds of liquid milk, and 70% of all dairy products are sold through just six supermarkets (*Milk Producer*, January 1993, p. 6). The prospect seems to be one of displacing the publicly owned MMBs by a few privately owned but integrated dairy corporations. This will not simply be the switch from public to private, with some corresponding change in vertical and horizontal industrial structure. It will also lead to a shift in how surplus profitability is generated and appropriated along the dairy chain. The immediate effect has been a sharp rise in liquid-milk prices and uncertainty and reorganization within the industry.

Northern Foods, for example, one of Britain's biggest dairy companies, has been hard hit by the milk shake-up. In March 1995, it reported that it was shedding 2,200 jobs in a restructuring of the company's operations. It warned that its 1994/95 pre-tax profits would fall by 25%. Chairman Chris

Hashins was reported as blaming these outcomes both on the supermarket price war, which has seen many retailers selling milk at below cost, and on the deregulation of the milk market in England and Wales which had resulted in higher milk wholesaling costs (*Financial Times*, 24 March 1995, p. 23). More telling as far as the structure of the new dairy regime is concerned, the company said that it expected doorstep deliveries of milk to fall to 30% of sales by 1997, down from 60% of the overall market in 1990 and 45% in 1995.

Developments within the dairy system have presented the customer with new products (whether in the various forms of milk or other dairy products) as well as new ways of obtaining them with the particularly sharp rise in the sale of dairy products (especially milk) through supermarkets. In addition, health concerns have prompted the consumption of less butterfat. In this light, how have consumers responded? We have applied our methods to the NFS data for select dairy products.

DAIRY NORMS

Table 12.7 indicates the proportions of the whole sample of households (which we have termed absolute frequencies) that have purchased the dairy products selected for analysis. Whole milk, cheese, margarine, butter and cream have all experienced falls in absolute frequency of purchase, and yoghurt, (semi-)skimmed milk, and low- and reduced-fat spreads have had increases. On the face of it, this indicates a favourable shift towards healthy eating with the substitution of the second set of products for the first. Such impressions are confirmed by quantity analysis from NFS annual reports; with minor exceptions, trends in quantities purchased per person closely correlated with trends in frequency of purchase per household.

The extent and rhythm of these changes in absolute frequencies has differed from product to product, with cream falling between 1979 and 1984 and then holding its level, whereas butter and margarine have experienced continuous decline, the former dramatically. However, it is to be expected that these changes will also differ across households.[13] This was investigated by a wide variety and large number of socioeconomic variables – listed in Chapter 8 – for each of the years.

Now, one of the problems with these variables, irrespective of the statistical methods employed, is the high degree of correlation between them. Social class, (family or head of household) income, food expenditure, presence of children, household size, working wife, etc., all tend to be positively correlated with one another. On the other hand, the young and the old are both more liable to be of smaller household size and of lower income. A factor analysis for 1989 of social class (numerically indexed), age, family income, food expenditure and household composition (indexed by size, counting children as half) explained 80% of the

Table 12.7 Absolute frequency of purchase of products

	1989	1986	1984	1979
Whole milk	69.92	78.06	87.55	97.79
Cheese	63.92	68.11	66.87	71.38
Margarine	35.77	44.78	46.36	45.65
Yoghurt	31.36	30.62	27.29	19.71
Semi-skimmed milk	28.10	15.11	13.60^1	4.00^2
Butter	27.35	36.50	43.85	60.96
Skimmed milk	15.41	13.53	–	–
Cream	14.26	14.26	14.82	19.14
Low-fat spreads	12.72	11.24	8.09^3	9.76^4
Reduced-fat spreads	10.33	6.24	–	–

Notes:
[1] Skimmed milk not subdivided.
[2] Other milk, excluding UHT, powdered, etc.
[3] No separate category of reduced fat.
[4] Other fats.

variance across the households by two principal factors alone, one heavily loaded on class, age and income of head of household, the other on food expenditure and household composition.

In terms of absolute frequencies, that is the number of households purchasing an item and not how often they do so, the variable that gave the most regular set of results is overall food expenditure. The sample population was divided into six percentiles and, with all but a few exceptions, the absolute frequency of purchase increases monotonically with food expenditure. Some of the figures for 1989 are indicated in Table 12.8, for which the frequencies are shown for the top and the last-but-one percentile.

It is also apparent from Table 12.8 that the relative frequencies of the two displayed percentiles are different from one another – the fifth ranks milk above cheese but it is the other way around for the first and both diverge from the rankings for the population as a whole – by inspection with the figures for 1989 from Table 12.7.

Such relative frequencies or rankings allow consumption norms to be investigated. As observed, while the higher percentiles purchase more of everything, they may or may not do so with the same priority of preference from one product to the next. Table 12.9 indicates the relative frequencies of the six percentiles in ascending order; a positive (negative) figure represents a movement up (down) in the percentile's ranking of the food concerned relative to the population ranking as a whole, with the same ranking if a zero is shown. By looking at the columns of the array, these figures can be interpreted as showing the most common order in which the

Table 12.8 Absolute frequency of purchase by fifth and first percentile of food expenditure

	5th percentile	*1st percentile*
Whole milk	68.1	73.4
Cheese	52.4	86.4
Margarine	27.5	49.5
Yoghurt	20.6	53.8
Semi-skimmed milk	24.4	36.8
Butter	22.2	41.6
Skimmed milk	13.9	22.3
Cream	8.2	28.7
Low-fat spreads	9.1	19.3
Reduced-fat spreads	7.8	12.6

Note: Overall, average proportions of the products purchased by each percentile are, in ascending order of overall food expenditure: 16.6, 25.4, 29.6, 34.2, 37.1 and 42.4.[4]

products would be acquired within the percentile groups relative to the population as a whole.

Table 12.9 shows extremely regular movements in rankings across the percentiles. For all but butter and margarine, the dramatrix entries are monotonic with food expenditure. Looking across the rows, whole, skimmed and semi-skimmed milk, and low- and reduced-fat spreads all decrease in ranking, and cheese, yoghurt and cream all increase in ranking. The movements are far more pronounced for yoghurt, semi-skimmed milk

Table 12.9 Dramatrix for food expenditure percentiles, 1989

	Decreasing percentiles					
	1	*2*	*3*	*4*	*5*	*6*
Whole milk	0	0	0	−1	−1	−1
Cheese	0	0	0	1	1	1
Margarine	−1	0	0	0	0	−1
Yoghurt	−3	−2	0	0	0	1
Semi-skimmed milk	2	1	0	−1	−1	−1
Butter	1	1	0	1	1	1
Skimmed milk	1	0	0	0	−1	−1
Cream	−2	−1	−1	0	1	1
Low-fat spreads	1	1	1	0	0	0
Reduced-fat spreads	1	0	0	0	0	0

and cream. For butter and margarine, there is the mildest of movements, in the form of a V-shape, inverted for margarine.

Now what is striking about these results is the extent to which they contradict the absolute movements in frequencies over time (see Table 12.7). For yoghurt and whole milk, this is not so, but the relative rankings of all of the other foods is in the opposite direction – if including butter and milk which decline sharply in absolute frequency.

Why is this of significance? It implies that as more is spent, those who spend more do take on the 'new' products (since absolute frequencies are higher) but they are also relatively more likely to retain the 'old' products which is why their relative frequencies are higher. High spenders adopt the new patterns of consumption but shed the old products slower than they adopt the new.

This is open to the interpretation that the health message does get across but is undermined for those households that spend more than others on food for whatever reason. We are mindful, however, that we are only dealing with purchase or not, and not with quantities purchased. It could be argued that a bigger spend is more liable to be spread across the products for variety (in which case the health message is not working) or because of the greater range of tastes to be satisfied within a week. Two households, for example, may have exactly the same per capita consumption patterns, but the larger of the two finds it possible to buy all foods on a weekly basis. These matters warrant further investigation but lie outside the scope of our research, since quantity analysis as such is precluded. However, it should not be presumed that, because a household is of larger size, it consumes a wider variety of foods in order to accommodate potentially different tastes. The opposite might occur since foods may have to be found that satisfy all common, and not each set of, tastes – a highest common factor rather than least common denominator type of argument. Clearly, however, the outcome for intra-household divergence of preferences is dependent on the degree of independence of choice at mealtimes which is generally perceived to have risen.

The results for the dramatrix for food expenditure for 1989 were not so sharply delineated in the corresponding dramatrices for the earlier years. Indeed, the patterns are very much weaker for 1979, if not non-existent, and only gradually emerge through the other years. In addition, both for 1989 and for the earlier years, absolute and relative frequencies were investigated for a number of subsamples of the population, themselves broken down by further socioeconomic variables. Thus, for example, each household type was studied as if it were the whole population.

The reason for doing this was to examine whether food expenditure was showing the most sharp results because of its correlation with other variables and to isolate the independent impact of these.[15] In general, the results for the dramatrices for these other variables were weaker than for food expenditure, and more so the earlier the year. This suggests that food expenditure is an important determinant, and that the other variables act indirectly through it (so that family size, for example, leads to changed consumption patterns more because more is spent than because of difference in family size as such).[16]

There were, however, some exceptions to these generalities. Before mentioning these, it is worth outlining how they were investigated in terms of the relationship between absolute and relative frequencies. Consider the latter first. Suppose that for the whole (sub)sample, the frequency of purchase of two foods is quite close – as in semi-skimmed milk and butter for the whole survey for 1989, for example. Then, in breaking the sample down by some socioeconomic variable, it is more likely that there will be a shift in their relative ranking as revealed in the dramatrix. Less likely is a non-zero entry implying a shift between two foods whose overall absolute frequencies are far apart. Consequently, the foods can be partitioned, differently for each year, according to their susceptibility to shift in ranking – the partitions for 1989 are whole milk and cheese; margarine, yoghurt, semi-skimmed milk and butter; and skimmed milk, cream, low-fat and reduced-fat spreads.

The relationship between absolute and relative frequencies is such that significant or monotonic movements in the dramatrices may be associated with small changes in the absolute frequencies; and, large or monotonic movements in absolute frequencies may not show up in the dramatrices because of the lack of movement between partitions. This is illustrated for cream and yoghurt, for example, in Table 12.10 for couple households broken down by age of housewife.

For 1986, both cream and yoghurt are monotonic in the dramatrix but this is not so for absolute frequencies although, significantly, the breach for the latter for 45–54-year-olds is associated with a high level of overall purchases – the average number of dairy purchases in ascending age cohort are 28.9, 30.0, 30.7, 33.1, 31.6, 31.4, 28.1 and 28.6. On the other hand, there is little to show for the dramatrix in 1984 either for cream, whose absolute frequencies are irregular as before, or for yoghurt even though it has perfect monotonicity as in 1986.

It is results such as these that confirm how important food expenditure is as the most significant variable explaining the sorts of variation examined. But some other results do emerge. Older people, especially senior citizens, and, to a lesser extent, the unemployed tend to have higher ranking of margarine, butter and low- and reduced-fat spreads; the latter is a taste shared by the young. Movements for semi-skimmed milk are more pronounced than for skimmed milk. Margarine and butter tend to be ranked lower by those of higher social class and income, with semi-skimmed milk ranked higher. The presence of children tends to weaken or erode altogether the relationships otherwise found to be present.

Table 12.10 Results by age of housewife

Age	<25	25–34	35–44	45–54	55–64	65–74	>75
1984							
Absolute frequencies							
Cream	15.48	16.86	14.69	19.80	15.66	15.40	10.53
Yoghurt	31.55	30.98	28.67	21.48	21.55	15.19	10.53
Dramatrix							
Cream	0	−1	−1	0	0	1	1
Yoghurt	0	0	0	0	0	−1	0
1986							
Absolute frequencies							
Cream	8.82	14.13	17.20	16.86	17.27	17.56	13.02
Yoghurt	34.12	31.16	28.66	32.84	20.39	15.50	11.83
Dramatrix							
Cream	−4	−2	−1	−1	0	1	1
Yoghurt	−1	−1	0	0	0	0	1

How are these results to be interpreted? First, the consumption of products such as margarine and butter have persisted as traditional with the older households. A different age factor is with reduced- and low-fat spreads, possibly associated by young households with some degree of cheapness and health. Presumably, the importance of the age factor in these respects explains the relatively even dramatrix by food expenditure for butter and margarine for 1989 (see Table 12.9). Cream, however, seems to combine the characteristics both of tradition and expense, although its use may have been encouraged or upheld, after an initial fall for health reasons, by the growing taste for dairy desserts following upon the rising popularity of the taint of health associated with yoghurt. Finally, those of higher class and income have tended to adopt semi-skimmed milk and to have dropped margarine and butter more readily – although this does not extend to other indices of healthy choice not already indicated as associated with food expenditure.

CONCLUDING REMARKS

By way of conclusion, let us assess where our analysis might be considered distinctive and illustrative of our previously developed approach. First, our methodology is to examine food consumption from the perspective of SOPs which are distinct and particularly organically dependent. While incorporating many of the insights from the food systems literature, we do not believe that these can be applied in too generalized a fashion. The rhythms of the UK dairy system, for example, do not correspond either in time or across its various components to the stylized rise and fall of Fordist agriculture. And the industrialization of agriculture – as understood in terms of substitutionism and appropriationism in the analysis of Goodman *et al.* (1987) – has witnessed the persistence and expanding role of organic ingredients even if in uneven and diverse ways. Vegetable oils have substituted for butter fat but, with the rise of skimmed milk, butterfat has been diverted to new products, such as fancy desserts, or has entered the manufacturing system more extensively as in the production of cheeses.

Second, we have defined consumption norms in terms of purchase or not rather than by average quantity purchased, while allowing such norms to vary by household characteristics. These norms have been identified by novel statistical techniques from NFS data. For dairy products, food expenditure, however it may itself be determined, is found to have become of decisive importance although other factors, such as age, class and income, have also been of importance over and above expenditure. Their significance varies from one product to the next – for reasons presumably reflecting price as well as capacity and willingness to respond to changing advice on what is a healthy diet.

Finally, our results give some insight, in the case of dairy products, into the apparent paradox that connects the meteoric rise in healthy foods with continuing persistence of (dairy) fat in the diet. From the perspective of choice, those spending more are more likely to purchase healthy products but often continue to rank traditional products more highly in their purchasing behaviour than those who spend less. Over a lifetime, as household circumstances change, patterns of consumption also change. More expenditure is associated with household size (including children), income and age (up to a point). At various times over the life-cycle, there will, then, be susceptibility to raising the ranking of less healthy dairy products. Thus, the health message may well be getting across but it needs to be accompanied by the lesson of less as well as different. This is hardly palatable to the commercial interests within the dairy system even if its restructuring can be credited with making such a variety of healthy products available. The imperatives to produce continue to drive consumption even if the mechanisms and incidence of how and by whom has been open to change.

NOTES

1 See Chapter 3 for these arguments in a more general context.
2 Five Milk Marketing Boards have been established in the United Kingdom. The largest covered England and Wales and was created in 1933, three boards for

Scotland were established in 1933 and 1934 and that for Northern Ireland in 1955. Only the England and Wales MMB is discussed here.

3 This section draws heavily on the factual information in Cox *et al.* (1990).

4 The Joint Committee, between the MMB and the Milk Distributive Council (after 1973 the Dairy Trade Federation), formed in 1955, was a move by government to strengthen the position of the dairy trade in relation to producers (Cox *et al.* 1990). The role of the Joint Committee has been to negotiate the price of milk for manufacture and, since 1985, for the liquid market as well. In 1979, the Joint Committee and its negotiating role were placed on a statutory footing which was in part a response to concern within the EC at the monopolistic powers of the MMB.

5 For detailed descriptions of the intricacies of milk pricing policies and the role of government policy since the Second World War, see Hollingham and Howarth (1989).

6 The government 'fixed' the retail price for liquid milk from 1954 to 1985 when the powers to do so became the responsibility of the Joint Committee.

7 There are four legal categories of milk. First, 'raw milk', that is milk not subject to any processing whatsoever; second, 'whole milk', that is milk standardized to a minimum 3.5% fat content; third, 'semi-skimmed', that is milk standardized to a fat content of between 1.5% and 1.8%; and, fourth, 'skimmed', that is milk standardized to a fat content of not more than 0.03%.

8 Cardwell (1992) describes the legislative arrangements for implementing the EC milk quota scheme. In short, each member state was entitled to produce milk and milk products up to a guaranteed total quantity amounting to milk deliveries during the 1981 calendar year plus 1%. Should production exceed that total, a 'superlevy' would become payable (in addition to the existing Co-responsibility Levy which continued in force). For the purpose of implementing the superlevy, each member state had a choice between two formulae. Under Formula A reference quantities were allocated to individual producers and the superlevy was payable by them on any excess production. Under Formula B, reference quantities were allocated to purchasers, as in the UK case through the MMBs. The superlevy became payable on deliveries to those purchasers in excess of the reference quantities allocated. The purchasers then passed on the superlevy to individual producers in accordance with their contribution to the excess. At the start of the scheme the rate of superlevy was 75% of the milk target price under Formula A and 100% under Formula B. In practice, under Formula B the MMB with its 'pooled' milk purchases, for the purposes of the superlevy, could 'transfer' production between producers who were under their quota with those who were over quota and derive an aggregate total.

9 In the paper by Williams (1993) there is a note saying that the author was, until his retirement, Director of Economics of the Milk Marketing Board for England and Wales.

10 A milk quota is 'leased' for use within the existing marketing year or purchased for use over the lifetime of the (quota) scheme.

11 Producer-retailers pasteurize, bottle or pack and retail their own milk; producer-processors sell their own bottled or packed milk to a retailer (that is, in their own right rather than through the MMB).

12 See *Sunday Times*, Business Section, 28 August 1994, p. 3.

13 Another important factor in determining the changes in the absolute frequencies over time is the changing composition of the (survey) population. Chesher (1991), for example, points to the reduction in household size by 7% between 1979 and 1989, with 26% fewer children and young adults aged

between 9 and 17 years, with some compensating increase in the number of middle-aged (+2%) and older males (+11%). Also there has been an increase in the proportion of those in sedentary occupations, usually associated with lower food consumption. These changes in household composition will affect the calculation of our norms – and it might have been a worthwhile exercise to have estimated them for a standardized composition – but the impact of socioeconomic variables within years will not be affected.

14 Note that the food expenditure variable is for all, and not just dairy, foods.

15 For each year, a hundred or so analyses were compiled for various combinations of variables and inspected for absolute and relative frequencies, the latter through the dramatrices.

16 This is in contrast to the application of similar methods to the ownership of consumer durables; see Fine *et al.* (1993) for example. More significant results were obtained by partitioning the sample.

Part V

WHITHER FOOD STUDIES?

13

SUMMING UP AND FUTURE DIRECTIONS

Throughout this book, we have been concerned both to employ and to justify four central themes. First, the consumption of food is determined by a complex chain of activities. Second, the impact of any one determinant is dependent upon its interaction with the others; it cannot be examined appropriately in isolation from the other factors making up the food system. Third, it is necessary to distinguish between different food systems since these will be structured and develop differently from one another, even where they have certain elements in common. Fourth, food systems are themselves distinguished from other SOPs by virtue of their organic content.

These insights have also allowed us to offer some critical insights into the present state of food studies. It tends to constitute a body of knowledge and analysis drawn from a disparate set of disciplines. These are poorly integrated, if at all, and they generally focus upon particular aspects of food systems at the expense of how they function as a whole. Even if there is some recognition of the need for a truly interdisciplinary approach, progress has remained limited.

This is in part because the different disciplines, from which food studies is drawn, continue to have a dynamic of their own, quite independent of the continuing problems of studying food. Consequently, these developments can be applied to food, and they will then reinforce, rather than break with, disciplinary autarchy. It follows that the window of opportunity that has been opened up for an interdisciplinary food studies will not necessarily be grasped, and old patterns will be reproduced even if in new ways. Further, the theoretical content of food studies will continue to overlook the specificity of food, what we have termed its organic content, in anything other than name.

What follows will illustrate these themes both in terms of material that has not yet been covered in the book and in anticipation of issues to be covered in the subsequent volume.

THE FOOD INDUSTRY AS INDUSTRIAL ECONOMICS

Industrial economics has, apart from models of perfect competition and oligopoly, been heavily influenced by the structure–conduct–performance (SCP) paradigm. Oversimplifying, as the terminology suggests, this takes the size distribution, or industrial structure, of a sector to be given. From this, it is argued that particular pricing or other strategies will be adopted by corporations, with definite outcomes in terms of profitability. More recently, a new industrial economics has emerged, in which game theory is prominent. In particular, corporations take into account the impact of their strategies on those of their rivals, and modify their behaviour accordingly. In addition, there is a further innovation in that the structure of the industry is not taken as given but is itself a consequence of the choice of firms either to enter or to exit from the industry.

A leading representative of this new approach is Sutton (1991). His book has been extremely influential, and Schmalensee (1992, p. 125) advises that, 'every serious student of industrial economics should read John Sutton's *Sunk Costs and Market Structure: Price Competition, Advertising, and the Evolution of Concentration*'. What is significant for our purposes is that the examples chosen by Sutton to illustrate his theory are all taken from the food industries. Consequently, they have been prominent in food studies as a guide in how the food industry should be analysed.

Essentially, Sutton divides the (food) industries into two types.[1] For the first, the product is homogeneous and the key parameters in the industry are the fixed overhead costs for an individual firm and the overall size of the market. The greater the overhead costs and the smaller the market, the lower the number of firms that can be accommodated by the industry. In the long run, firms can enter the industry and will have the incentive to do so as long as the industry allows more than normal profits. The lower the ratio of fixed costs to market size, the fewer will be the number of firms that are able to make a profit. For the more firms there are, the more demanding for the industry is the total of fixed costs to be covered. In short, there are liable to be fewer firms, the higher the fixed costs and the lower the market size. Putting this the other way around, as the ratio of market size to fixed costs increases, so the potential number of firms in the long run increases indefinitely. If it were otherwise, those firms in the industry would make ever-larger profits as market size increases, and this would create an incentive for other firms to enter.

Exactly how many firms there are, and what prices will be charged, however, depends upon the way in which competition is fought within the industry by the existing firms. For example, suppose that competition is very intense within the sector, so that whenever there is an increase in output and drop in price from any source (whether from an existing producer or new entrant), the response is to engage in a price war. Because of the threat of such retaliation, and the consequent disastrous falls in profits, new entrants are liable to be discouraged. It follows that, other things being equal, the more competitive is an industry internally in the sense described, the lower is the number of firms to be found in the industry. Paradoxically, this contradicts traditional economic thinking in which competition is generally associated with larger number of firms.[2]

The outcome is potentially different for industries of the second type, characterized by a further source of competition. So far, the level of overheads has been taken as given. But the competitive advantage of each firm may be enhanced by increasing its expenditure on fixed capital. This could be to improve the quality of the product, even artificially through advertising to create product differentiation and brand loyalty, or through research and development to reduce production costs. Exactly the same considerations apply as before as far as the number of firms in the industry is concerned. Only now it is tempered by increasing fixed costs as market size increases. Suppose, for example, that demand is highly responsive to advertising. Then, as market size increases, there might be such an incentive to attempt to capture the higher levels of demand that advertising, now an endogenous component of fixed costs, might rise more than in proportion. In other words, there is no guarantee that the number of firms within the industry will increase indefinitely with market size. Rather, it is advertising expenditure or the like that increases, discouraging new entrants. The result is a potential upper bound to the number of firms in the industry irrespective of the overall level of demand.

Here, the details of the arguments just presented are not so important as the method involved. Although breaking with the SCP paradigm, it does share certain aspects in common. First, the conditions of supply (costs) and demand (market) are given even if they can vary over time and can be manipulated by the degree of competition through advertising expenditure and price setting. Second, the analysis is organized around the notion of (long-run) equilibrium even if this might only be specified by the presence of upper and lower bounds on the number of firms according to the nature and intensity of competition. Third, the whole thrust of the analysis is to provide a general theory, applicable to all (food) industries in principle, with a focus upon horizontal competition within a well-defined sector (to determine the number of firms, the level of overheads and output price).

From our perspective, these are considerable weaknesses. Of concern is the methodology surrounding equilibrium, contrasting as it does with our own approach based on tendencies, structures and contingent outcomes. Much that is taken as given in Sutton's analysis needs to be explained. In addition, Sutton does not, and does not intend to, provide a theory specific to food. He just chooses such industries by way of illustration, expecting any other industry to follow suit. By default, then, the preoccupation with horizontal forms of competition necessarily precludes what we take to be crucial components of any study of food industries. This is that they should be located analytically within the food system of which they are a part, and that they should be distinguished from one another.

For Sutton, this can only be done according to whether they do allow for variable fixed costs or not.[3] Thus, sugar is specified as a food industry of the first type. In Chapter 5, however, we have shown how important are a whole range of vertically integrated factors that cannot be reduced to the parameters of his model, not least the competing sources of raw sugar and competition between refiners on this basis, as well as the shifting patterns of use of refined sugar both within the food industry and within the home. An example of the second type of industry, in which advertising makes up an important part of fixed costs, is chocolate confectionery. No doubt, the Sutton model does capture a part of what is going on in such industries. But, equally, it will tend to overlook other factors, such as the dynamic between own-label and branded products. The imperative to spend heavily on advertising branded baked beans, or other products, follows from the need for them to cross the threshold of demand that places them on superstore shelves where, paradoxically, they compete with the store's own-label products.

THE COSTS OF THE EU

The EU's CAP has long presented apparent anomalies, such as higher prices within the EU than those that prevail upon world markets, and the accumulation of surplus output in the form of mountains, lakes and the like. Economists have attempted to estimate what the cost of the CAP has been to consumers. In general, there is contempt for what is taken to be the archetypal prejudices of consumers who are presumed to take these symptoms of economic inefficiency as indicative of massive waste at their expense. The pursuit of the interests of a small minority of farmers in foreign EU lands are perceived to have been imposed by an equally distant bureaucracy. In the words of Ritson (1991a, p. 119): 'The consumer voice has typically been poorly articulated, and its arguments have been inconsistent and incoherent.' It is not our intention here to rescue the consumer (all of us, after all) from these harsh accusations, although we doubt whether the inconsistency and incoherence involved is any less than in any other area of public opinion. What 'consumers' recognize, however imperfectly and accurately, is that the EU's CAP forms a part of the food system over which they have relatively limited control. It is hardly surprising that the overt exercise of power within that system by the CAP, again however correctly understood, should be endowed with an exaggerated responsibility for the extent of the deficiencies in food provision. What, however, is the more consistent and coherent way in which to investigate the impact of CAP?

According to conventional economic analysis, CAP is to be seen as bringing about a shift in or along supply curves. Although the mechanisms of support by which this is done are varied and complex, this means that EU prices will be higher than those on the world market for two different reasons. First, non-EU supply is excluded to a greater or lesser extent by quotas and tariffs. Second, if EU prices support a higher output than consumers are prepared to purchase, then the EU will export and depress world prices (unless output is stored). Consequently, calculations by economists of the impact of the CAP on consumer welfare do *not* proceed on the basis of the difference between world and EU prices. This is perceived to be a substantial overestimate of the cost to consumers. For it is reasonably argued that in the absence of the CAP, EU prices would indeed be lower but not by as much as the difference with world prices with the CAP in place. For, in the absence of the CAP, EU supply would be lower, and this would bid up world prices (especially if EU dumping ceased or if its demand for imports from the rest of the world increased). Consequently, economists have tended to argue that the costs of CAP to the consumer are quite limited. It is even argued that healthier diets have been encouraged by the higher prices prevailing for nominally unhealthy foods such as butter, sugar and meat.

This, however, is to take a very limited view of the role and scope of the CAP. As is realized in these analyses and calculations, even if often only implicitly, they do involve a counterfactual. What would happen if CAP were withdrawn? An answer, as observed, is usually offered in terms of a shift in supply. But we all know that the repercussions would be considerably more dramatic. Quite apart from the disruptive effects of political action liable to be taken by farmers, an alternative form of state policy towards agriculture would have to be put in place. Otherwise, for example, markets would become highly unstable. This means that we cannot simply construct a non-CAP schedule of supply on the basis of the CAP schedule. Abolition of CAP would require more fundamental changes in economic and political conditions.

This does not go unrecognized. In Ritson's (1991a) account, alternative policy measures are hypothesized. But, by the same token, we would emphasize a broader scope of analysis and take the counterfactual – what would happen if other policies were in place – in other directions if not eschewing this approach altogether. For it is necessary to see the CAP as both a cause and an effect of the structure and development of the EU food system. Accordingly, it fits within a set of economic and political processes that cannot be varied independently of one another. Thus, in different ways from one product to another, EU agriculture is structured in relation to the other components of the food system. It is necessary to understand how farming relates to the food industry as well as to changing forms of processing, retailing and consumer habits. As has been seen in this volume for dairy products and

271

sugar, the evolution and impact of the CAP cannot be simply read off from shifting supply curves, however accurately measured.[4]

This is one path that might continue to be taken by economists in the future, partly as a result of improved modelling and estimating techniques and partly as a result of the stimulus to this sort of exercise that has been inspired by the wish to assess the impact on agriculture of the Uruguay Round of GATT. In the second volume, we assess these arguments concerning the cost of the CAP in much greater detail, suggesting that the scope of factors incorporated and how they interact with one another has been unduly limited. Hence, it is hardly surprising that the consumer should be berated by economists for exaggerating the impact of the CAP on their diet; for consumers do have a correct, if ill-formed, understanding of the extent to which food is filtered through CAP as part of the functioning of the EU food systems as a whole. The phenomena of food mountains and lakes, as well as the large differences between EU and world prices, are correctly taken to be symbolic of the functioning of this food system, even if the quantification involved is misleading.[5]

FOOD AND HEALTH

An understanding of the role of the CAP as part of the EU food system is essential if the policy-making process is to be satisfactorily analysed. This applies not only to the policy towards agriculture but towards other areas of the food system as well. In particular, again following a logic of supply and demand, it is readily concluded that, from the point of view of healthy eating, the impact of the EU has been relatively limited because it has only changed prices to a limited extent and quantities consumed even less (and, as previously observed, even in healthier directions).

Again, there is a counterfactual involved here, and it is one that leaves very little room for eating patterns to be otherwise. Essentially, it takes preferences for food as given and unaffected by EU policy. This is all the more remarkable as no account is given of how food preferences are formed. Of course, there is a presumption that the CAP as such should have only a limited influence over the formation of consumer tastes, as opposed to their satisfaction. But, much the same might be said about each aspect of the food system taken in isolation. It is the working of the system as a whole that needs to be assessed, both in its serving and creating food needs.

This is well illustrated, quite apart from the persistence of sugar, cream and fat in the UK nation's diet, by the Norwegian experience. Thus, given our emphasis upon the role of the food system as a whole in determining what we eat, it is hardly surprising that we should argue that food policy must potentially address each component of the food system and not just the immediate determinants of food choice by the consumer. In this way, it would prove possible to uncover how policy interventions might be neutralized or even reinforced by the operation of the food system. Norwegian experience of food policy provides a salutary lesson. It has often been recognized as uniquely seeking to coordinate interventions to promote healthy eating with agricultural policy. While rightly praised for attempting to merge the two policy areas that are usually separately formulated and implemented, as well as being inconsistent with one another, initial optimism about the impact of such policy coordination has given way to disillusion. This can be shown to be the result of insufficient commitment to exercise control over the imperatives of the food system and the economic and political interests to which they are attached, primarily farming interests in Norway.

An even more dismal record is found for UK food policy. It has failed even to address the goal of coordination between food and agricultural policy. Consequently, the range of policies that influence the nation's diet has been and continues to be mutually incompatible and is more attuned to the commercial imperatives residing within the food system, whether in response to farmers, industrialists or retailers. In short, it is essential to see food policy as part of the food system, not as an externally generated intervention to shift us towards healthier diets even if this is the ideology with which it is imbued. Anyone with the slightest acquaintance with the debates and conflicts over food labelling and advertising will be well aware of the extent to which the dissemination of healthy eating information is severely constrained. These insights concerning the relationship between the food system and health policy will be taken up in the second volume, with Norway and the United Kingdom as comparative case studies.

FOOD AND INFORMATION

To a large extent, healthy policy around food has been designed to inform consumers of what they should eat in the hope that this will enable them to meet their preferences for a healthy diet if they have them, and to move their preferences in that direction otherwise. These informational campaigns are based upon (shifting and contested) scientific knowledge that is designed to trickle down to consumers through leaflets, etc.

The weight of such propaganda is very limited relative to the resources devoted to 'information' by commercial interests through advertising and packaging (and, indeed, account must be taken of their presence in determining the scientific knowledge itself in the funding of research and in their nominees serving as members of learned and advisory bodies). More commercially disinterested lobbyists in the field of healthy eating tend to be labelled as food fads or even terrorists, although the veracity and importance of what they seek to communicate is gargantuan relative to the mass of advertising which constitutes the most common formal means of communicating food information.

As already indicated, this is at best a partial exercise if no account is taken of how such information interacts with the food system as a whole. If, for example, agricultural policy is designed, possibly implicitly or indirectly, to provide for a certain level of output – of sugar, say – and if this output is neither exported nor stockpiled, then it must be consumed. So food policy in conjunction with the food system is presented with the task of getting that food into stomachs. The only question is how and whose. Consequently, health policy around food information campaigns merely forms one factor in redistributing the nation's diet among consumers. It is the food that has to trickle down rather than the information which, not surprisingly, is more readily absorbed by the better educated and informed and with the time, money and other means by which to lead a healthy life. In the case of sugar, while the message has got through, with considerable reduction in its direct consumption of sugar from the bowl, it has increasingly been used instead as an industrial ingredient – particularly in carbonated drinks but also in a wide range of processed foods.

As a further example, consider milk. Superstores have encroached upon sales from doorstep deliveries and have provided a range of healthier products in the form of skimmed and semi-skimmed milks which have grown in popularity quite dramatically and have just exceeded 50% of sales. This is a sure indication of the ability of the health message to get through to the front lines. But something has to be done with the cream! Apart from its use as an ingredient for other manufactured foods, it is to be found in the even more varied range of products to be found in the adjacent dairy cabinets. The popularity of their contents, such as desserts and fancy cheeses, has also grown exponentially. There appears to be a zero-sum game – however much we improve our diet, it tends to be at the expense of somebody else's.

Consequently, healthy diet campaigns are liable to be limited or even counterproductive in their effects, with the incidence of their impact upon dietary change possibly increasing the dispersion of eating behaviour. Those with poor diets might worsen their food intake; the 'improvement' might only affect those who do not need it. Of course, the above argument has been made on the basis of entirely unrealistic assumptions; that output is fixed and must be consumed. But it does serve to indicate one among many ways in which healthy eating campaigns might trickle down to the consumers. There is an analogy with tax evasion and avoidance. If government has to raise the same amount of revenue through taxation, these activities merely result in expenditure (corresponding to the food systems' alternative methods or persuasion and processing) to shift the incidence of the tax burden. The same applies to the food we consume.

The previous argument is limited not only because of the extremely special assumptions about the supply of food but also because of its equally limited understanding about how healthy eating campaigns trickle down, to a greater or lesser extent, to different sections of the population. While this is the model of food knowledge underlying and rationalizing such campaigns, it is seriously inadequate. It is necessary to examine what might be termed the food information system. Most of the discussion of how we obtain food beliefs, with the notable exception of anthropology, has primarily been oriented around what is perceived to be the practical, policy goal of shifting consumers' beliefs and, consequently, their purchasing behaviour and diet. This is an erroneous analytical starting point on two closely-related but distinct scores.

First, the notion of knowledge, information or beliefs that is employed is seriously inadequate both in its scope and the failure to recognize how ideas about food are generated, employed and frequently subject to inconsistency and fluidity. The creation of food beliefs needs to be related to a food information system that includes health messages and other sources of knowledge such as advertising, but which is fundamentally dependent upon the functioning of the food system itself as a source of practical knowledge – not least in how we cook, shop and eat.

Second, not surprisingly, the impact of healthy eating advice has to be understood in the context of the functioning of the food system as a whole, and not merely at the proximate determinants of food choice alone. Indeed, in parallel with our suggestion for the formation of a food studies discipline, it is possible to organize the food information literature according to how it recognizes, or contributes to the understanding of, food systems, the food information system and the interaction between the two. Thus, the formation of our food beliefs is informed by what we eat, how it is provided and how information is constructed, delivered and received around all of these activities. This cannot be reduced to the simple shifting of food choice according to campaigns, more or less effective, designed to induce us to favour one food or diet as opposed to another.[6]

WHAT IS DIET?

These issues are also taken up in detail in the second volume, along with a more general consideration of the notion of diet.[7] One of the enduring features of food studies is the idea that diet represents a coherent and integral object of study. This is so, for example, of the British diet. By this is often meant the average per capita consumption of food. Quite clearly, this shifts over time and, at any one time, is different by region, class, age, income, etc. Accordingly, it makes no more sense to talk about the British diet than it does to talk about the British weather. It is a more or less convenient descriptive category which, like all averages, can conceal more than it reveals to the extent that there is dispersion around the mean.

Yet, much of the food studies literature is organized around the centrality of diet. In economics, it is attached to Engel's Law and the hypothesis that we are liable to spend a well-defined but declining proportion of our income on food as income increases. For dietitians, it is defined physiologically by the level and composition of nutrients that are required for a healthy human, by analogy with other animals, and depending upon physique and levels of activity, etc.

We adopt a different approach. For diet is the *outcome* of a complex set of processes that are not necessarily coherent, consistent and connected to one another. It is both mistaken and even misleading to approach diet as a primary causal factor, whether resulting from nutritional or utility-optimizing targets. Food consumption simply does not work in this way. As has been argued repeatedly, how food gets into our stomach is differentiated by one SOP to another. Even at the proximate level of food choice alone, the influences involved are highly disparate. Perhaps the appropriate analogy here is less with the weather than with clothing. While there are notions of national or customary dress, these have paled into insignificance against the variety of clothing that is now available. Further, while individuals do have a 'wardrobe', it too is highly variable and shifting, with individuals adopting different forms of dress for different occasions and in deference to changing forms of self-representation or lifestyle. This leads us to draw back from talking about the nation's or even an individual's overall 'dress' except as an extremely loose descriptive device. Exactly the same ought to be applied to diet. We are often engaged in a separate set of activities and influences, and these are connected to different socio-economic processes when we move from the consumption of one food to another. In short, in modern parlance, diet needs to be deconstructed, in meaning as well as in the complex and differentiated material practices by which it is constructed.

CONCLUDING REMARKS

We hope that this commentary whets the appetite for our second volume in which we apply the analysis developed here to the problems of diet, and food information and policy. Our recurring theme is that food consumption has to be addressed in terms of the differentiated food systems to which it is attached. Moreover, while much of the literature within food studies does not follow this imperative and focuses narrowly upon one or other aspect of food systems, it still constitutes a sound basis on which to construct an alternative. For, in its constituent disciplines, the literature provides a wide coverage of the different components of the food system. At times, the narrowness and nature of the analysis renders it of limited interest and use, as in much of the mechanical demand analyses within economics. But, especially if setting aside generalizations based on 'horizontal' factors, the vast majority of the literature can be usefully (re-)employed by integrating it together, around the joint themes of specific food systems and their organic content. We hope that this will provide the future direction for food studies, although the dangers of intra-disciplinary retrenchment should not be underestimated.

NOTES

1 In this account, we follow the representation of Sutton given by Schmalensee (1992) even though it is an oversimplification and possibly open to doubt. For a fuller critique, including a more formal technical presentation, see Fine (1994d).
2 This perverse result is in part because of the assumption of fixed overheads which implies the presence of economies of scale. These are generally precluded by the theory of perfect competition or, at least, average costs are generally presumed to rise for individual firms after a certain level of production. Note that the economy in the case considered here will be more productively efficient, the fewer the number of firms, since fixed costs are replicated less often.
3 And, of course, according to the degree of internal competition and the underlying conditions of supply and demand.
4 Interestingly, the attempts to measure the impact of '1992', the elimination of many of the impediments to a common market within the EU, was based to a large extent on the restructuring of industry that would result from larger markets. However, the presence of such scale economies is generally absent from calculations of the costs of the CAP.
5 Significantly, Ritson (1991a) suggests that it is more appropriate to treat consumers as consumers of food alone rather than as having a broader range of interests, such as the environment and the level of taxation. And, in a remarkable parallel with the discipline of food studies itself, each of these and other topics are treated separately from one another in the chapters of the volume that he edits with Harvey (1991).
6 For a striking illustration of this approach, see Fine (1995a).
7 See Fine (1993b).

REFERENCES

Abbott, G. C. (1990) *Sugar*, London: Routledge.

Adams. C. (1990) *The Sexual Politics of Meat: A Feminist–Vegetarian Critical Theory*, London: Polity Press.

Afarinkia, M. (1989) *Land Reform in Iran*, University of London, unpublished PhD thesis.

Albert, B. and A. Graves (1988) *The World Sugar Economy in War and Depression*, London: Routledge.

Allen, P. (ed.) (1993) *Food for the Future: Conditions and Contradictions of Sustainability*, New York: John Wiley.

Anderson, K. (1994) 'Multilateral Trade Negotiations, European Integration, and Farm Policy Reform', *Economic Policy*, no. 18, April, pp. 13–52.

Anderson, K. and R. Tyers (1991) *Global Effects of Liberalising Trade in Farm Products*, London: Harvester Wheatsheaf.

Arce, A. and T. Marsden (1993) 'The Social Construction of International Food: A New Research Agenda', *Economic Geography*, vol. 69, no. 3, July, pp. 293–311.

Atkins, P. (1988) 'Redefining Agricultural Geography as the Geography of Food', *Area*, vol. 20, no. 3, pp. 281–3.

Avery, W. (ed.) (1991) *World Agriculture and the GATT*, London: Lynne Rienner.

Aykroyd, W.R. (1967) *Sweet Malefactor: Sugar, Slavery and Human Society*, London: Heinemann.

Baker, P. *et al.* (1990) 'The Simulation of Indirect Tax Reforms: The IFS Simulation Program for Indirect Taxation (SPIT)', Institute of Fiscal Studies, Working Paper No. W90/11.

Ball, M. (1980) 'On Marx's Theory of Agricultural Rent: A Reply to Ben Fine', *Economy and Society*, vol. 9, no. 3, pp. 304–26, reproduced in Fine (1986).

Banks, J. *et al.* (1993) 'Quadratic Engel Curves and Welfare Measurement', Institute of Fiscal Studies, mimeo, March.

Beardsworth, A. and T. Keil (1993) 'Hungry for Knowledge? The Sociology of Food and Eating', *Sociology Review*, November, pp. 11–15.

Beck, U. (1991) *The Risk Society*, London: Sage.

Becker, G. (1981) *A Treatise on the Family*, Cambridge: Harvard University Press.

Belk, R. (ed.) (1992a) *Highways and Buyways*, Provo: Association for Consumer Research.

Belk, R. (1992b) 'Collecting for a Consumer Culture', in Belk (1992a).

Berlan, J. (1992) 'The Historical Roots of the Present Agricultural Crisis', in Friedland *et al.* (1992).

Bernstein, H. (1979) 'African Peasantries: A Theoretical Framework', *Journal of Peasant Studies*, vol. 6, no. 4, July, pp. 421–3.

Bernstein, H. (1982) 'Notes on Capital and Peasantry', in Harriss (1982), reproduced from *Review of African Political Economy*, 1979, no. 10, pp. 60–73.

Bernstein, H. *et al.* (eds) (1990) *The Food Question: Profit vs People?*, London: Earthscan.

Bernstein, H. and B. Campbell (eds) (1985) *Contradictions of Accumulation in Africa: Studies in Economy and State*, London: Sage.

Bhaduri, A. (1977) 'On the Formation of Usurious Interest Rates in Backward Agriculture', *Cambridge Journal of Economics*, vol. 1, no. 4, December, pp. 341–52.

Bijker, W. *et al.* (eds) (1992) *The Social Construction of Technological Systems*, Cambridge: MIT Press.

Birch, G. and K. Parker (eds) (1982) *Nutritive Sweeteners*, London: Applied Science Publishers.

Bird, J. *et al.* (eds) (1993) *Mapping the Futures: Local Cultures, Global Change*, London: Routledge.

Blundell, R. (1988) 'Consumer Behaviour: Theory and Empirical Evidence – A Survey', *Economic Journal*, vol. 98, March, pp. 16–65.

Bonnano. A. *et al.* (eds) (1994) *From Columbus to ConAgra: The Globalization of Agriculture and Food*, Lawrence: University of Kansas Press.

Borrell, B. and R. Duncan (1990) 'A Survey of the Costs of World Sugar Policies', The World Bank, WPS 522, Policy, Research and External Affairs Working Paper (International Economics Department).

Bowler, I. (ed.) (1992a) *The Geography of Agriculture in Developed Market Economies*, Longman: Harlow.

Bowler, I. (1992b) 'The Industrialisation of Agriculture', in Bowler (1992a).

Bowler, I. and B. Ilbery (1987) 'Redefining Agricultural Geography', *Area*, vol. 19, no. 4, December, pp. 327–32.

Brewer, R. and R. Porter (eds) (1993) *Consumption and the World of Goods*, London: Routledge.

Brown, A. and A. Deaton (1972) 'Surveys in Applied Economics: Models of Consumer Behaviour', *Economic Journal*, vol. 82, December, pp. 1145–236.

Brown, J. (1958) 'Seasonality and Elasticity of the Demand for Food in Great Britain since Derationing', *Journal of Agricultural Economics*, vol. 13, pp. 228–49.

Burawoy, M. and Skocpol, T. (eds) (1982) *Marxist Inquiries: Studies of Labor, Class and States*, Chicago and London: The University of Chicago.

Burnett, J. (1989) *Plenty and Want*, 3rd edn, London: Routledge.

Busch, L. (1990) 'Agricultural Commodities: The Complex Path from Production to Consumption', paper presented at the Annual Meeting of the Association for the Study of Food and Society.

Busch, L. *et al.* (1989) 'Science, Technology, and the Restructuring of Agriculture', *Sociologia Ruralis*, vol. XXIX, no. 2, pp. 118–30.

Busch, L. and W. Lacy (eds) (1986) *The Agricultural Scientific Enterprise: A System in Transition*, Boulder: Westview Press.

Busch *et al.* (1991) *Plants, Power and Profit: Ethical, Social and Economic Consequences of the New Biotechnologies*, Oxford: Basil Blackwell.

Buttel, F. and D. Goodman (1989) 'Class, State, Technology and International Food Regimes: An Introduction to Recent Trends in the Sociology and Political Economy of Agriculture', *Sociologia Ruralis*, vol. XXIX, no. 2, pp. 86–92.

Cannadine, D. (1983) 'The Context, Performance and Meaning of Ritual: The British Monarchy and the "Invention of Tradition"', in Hobsbawm and Ranger (1983).

Cardwell, M. (1992) 'General Principles of Community Law and Milk Quotas', *Common Market Law Review*, vol. 29, no. 4, pp. 723–47.

Carter, B. (1995) 'A Growing Divide: Marxist Class Analysis and the Labour Process', *Capital and Class*, no. 55, spring, pp. 33–72.

CEFS (1990) *Annual Statistics*, Brussels: Comité Européen Fabricants de Sucre.

Central Statistical Office (various years) *Annual Abstract of Statistics*, London: HMSO.

Chalmin, P. (1990) *The Making of a Sugar Giant: Tate & Lyle 1859–1989*, Chur, Switzerland: Harwood Academic Publishers.

Charles, N. and M. Kerr (1986a) 'Food for Feminist Thought', *Sociological Review*, vol. 34, no. 3, August, pp. 537–72.

Charles, N. and M. Kerr (1986b) 'Eating Properly, the Family and State Benefit', *Sociology*, vol. 20, no. 3, August, pp. 412–29.

Charles, N. and M. Kerr (1988) *Women, Food and Families*, Manchester: Manchester University Press.

Charsley, S. (1992) *Wedding Cakes and Cultural History*, London: Routledge.

Chesher, A. (1991) 'Household Composition and Household Food Purchases', in Slater (1991).

Chesher, A. and H. Rees (1987) 'Income Elasticities of Demands for Foods in Great Britain', *Journal of Agricultural Economics*, vol. 38, pp. 435–48.

Colman, D. (1992) 'The Breakdown of the Milk Marketing Schemes', *Oxford Agrarian Studies*, vol. 20, no. 2, pp. 129–38.

Commission of the European Union (1992) *European Figures*, Luxemburg.

Consumers in the European Community Group (1983) *The Sweet Smell of Excess: The EEC Sugar Scandal*, London: CECG.

Cook, I. (1994) 'New Fruits and Vanity: The Role of Symbolic Production in the Global Food Economy', in Bonnano *et al.* (1994).

Cowan, R. (1992) 'The Consumption Junction: A Proposal for the Research Studies in the Sociology of Technology', in Bijker *et al.* (1992).

Cox, D. (1970) *Analysis of Binary Data*, London: Methuen.

Cox, G. *et al.* (1990) 'The Political Management of the Dairy Sector in England and Wales', in Marsden and Little (1990).

Crawford, W. and Broadley, H. (1936) *The People's Food*, London: William Heinemann.

Crompton, R. (1993) *Class and Stratification: An Introduction to Current Debates*, London: Polity Press.

Cronon, W. (1990) *Nature's Metropolis: Chicago and the Great West*, New York: Norton.

Currie, E. (1987) 'How NutraSweet Has Opened Up New Opportunities by Marketing a Food Ingredient to the Consumer', KAE Product Development Conference, 24 March.

Curry, J. (1993) 'The Flexibility Fetish', *Capital and Class*, no. 50, summer, pp. 99–126.

Dahlberg, K. (1993) 'Regenerative Food Systems: Broadening the Scope and Agenda of Sustainability', in Allen (1993).

Deaton, A. (1985) 'Panel Data from the Time-Series of Cross-Sections', *Journal of Econometrics*, vol. 30, no. 1, pp. 109–26.

Deaton, A. and J. Muellbauer (1980) *Economics and Consumer Behaviour*, Cambridge: Cambridge University Press.

Deerr, N. (1949) *The History of Sugar*, vol. 1, London: Chapman and Hall.

Deerr, N. (1950) *The History of Sugar*, vol. 2, London: Chapman and Hall.

Department of Health (1989) 'Report of the Panel on Dietary Sugars. Committee on Medical Aspects of Food Policy. Dietary Sugars and Human Disease', *Report on Health and Social Subjects*, no. 37, London: HMSO.

Department of Health (1991) 'Dietary Reference Values for Food Energy and Nutrients for the United Kingdom: Report of the Panel on Dietary Reference Values of the Committee on Medical Aspects of Food Policy', *Report on Health and Social Subjects*, no. 41, London: HMSO

Desor, J. *et al.* (1977) 'Preference for Sweet in Humans: Infants, Children and Adults', in Weiffenbach (1977).

Dobbing, J. (ed.) (1987) *Sweetness*, Berlin: Springer-Verlag.

Dyson, T. (1994a) 'Population Growth and Food Production: Recent Global and Regional Trends', *Population and Development Review*, vol. 20, no. 2, June, pp. 397–411.

Dyson, T. (1994b) 'World Population Growth and Food Supplies', *International Social Science Journal*, no. 141, September, pp. 361–85.

Eurostat (1990) *Animal Feed: Supply and Demand of Feedingstuffs in the European Community*, Luxembourg: EC.

Falk, P. (1991) '*Homo Culinarius*: Towards an Historical Anthropology of Taste', *Social Science Information*, vol. 30, no. 4, pp. 757–90.

FAO (1989) *Aspects of the World Feed–Livestock Economy: Structural Change, Prospects, and Issues*, Rome: Food and Agricultural Organisation.

Federation of United Kingdom Milk Marketing Boards (1992) *UK Dairy Facts and Figures*, Thames Ditton.

Fiddes, N. (1991) *Meat: A Natural Symbol*, London: Routledge.

Fine, B. (1979) 'On Marx's Theory of Agricultural Rent', *Economy and Society*, vol. 8, no. 3, pp. 241–78, reproduced in Fine (1986).

Fine, B. (1980) 'On Marx's Theory of Agricultural Rent: A Rejoinder', *Economy and Society*, vol. 9, no. 3, August, pp. 327–31, reproduced in Fine (1986).

Fine, B. (1983) 'The Order of Acquisition of Consumer Durables: A Social Choice Theoretic Approach', *Journal of Economic Behaviour and Organisation*, vol. 4, pp. 239–48.

Fine, B. (ed.) (1986) *The Value Dimension: Marx versus Ricardo and Sraffa*, London: Routledge & Kegan Paul.

Fine, B. (1987) 'Labour Market Theory: A Critical Assessment', Birkbeck Discussion Paper, No. 87/12, reproduced in shortened form as a *Thames Paper in Political Economy*, 1990.

Fine, B. (1989) *Marx's 'Capital'*, 3rd edn, London: Macmillan.

Fine, B. (1990) *The Coal Question: Political Economy and Industrial Change from the Nineteenth Century to the Present Day*, London: Routledge.

Fine, B. (1992) *Women's Employment and the Capitalist Family*, London: Routledge.

Fine, B. (1993a) 'Modernity, Urbanism, and Modern Consumption: A Comment', *Environment and Planning D, Society and Space*, vol. 11, pp. 599–601.

Fine, B. (1993b) 'Resolving the Diet Paradox', *Social Science Information*, vol. 32, no. 4, December, pp. 669–87.

Fine, B. (1994a) 'Towards a Political Economy of Food', *Review of International Political Economy*, vol. 1, no. 3, pp. 519–45.

Fine, B. (1994b) 'Towards a Political Economy of Food: A Response to My Critics', *Review of International Political Economy*, vol. 1, no. 3, pp. 579–86.

Fine, B. (1994c) 'Diamonds, Coal and Oil: Towards a Comparative Theory of Mining', *Review of Political Economy*, vol. 6, no. 3, July, pp. 279–302.

Fine, B. (1994d) 'Competition and Market Structure Reconsidered', mimeo.

Fine, B. (1995a) 'Towards a Political Economy of Anorexia', *Appetite*, no. 24, pp. 231–42.

Fine, B. (1995b) 'Towards a Political Economy of Consumption', in Miller (1995).

Fine, B. (1995c) 'Entitlement Failure?', mimeo.

Fine, B. (1995d) 'Playing the Consumption Game', mimeo.

Fine, B. (1995e) 'Reconsidering 'Household Labor, Wage Labor, and the Transformation of the Family'', *Review of Radical Political Economics*, forthcoming.

Fine, B. and L. Harris (1979) *Rereading 'Capital'*, London: Macmillan.

Fine, B. and Leopold, E. (1993) *The World of Consumption*, London: Routledge.

Fine, B. and J. Wright (1991) 'Digesting the Food and Information Systems', Birkbeck Discussion Paper, no. 7/91, December.

Fine, B., N. Foster, J. Simister and J. Wright (1992a) 'Consumption Norms, Diffusion and the Video/Microwave Syndrome', SOAS Working Papers in Economics, no. 19, May.

Fine, B., N. Foster, J. Simister and J. Wright (1992b) 'Access to Phones and Democracy in Personal Communication: Myth or Reality?', SOAS Working Papers in Economics, no. 20, May.

Fine, B., N. Foster, J. Simister and J. Wright (1992c) 'Who Owns and Who Wants to Own a Car? An Empirical Analysis', SOAS Working Papers in Economics, no. 21, May.

Fine, B., N. Foster, J. Simister and J. Wright (1992d) 'Consumption Norms: A Definition and an Empirical Investigation of How They Have Changed, 1975–1990', SOAS Working Papers in Economics, no. 22, May.

Fine, B., N. Foster, J. Simister and J. Wright (1992e) 'Consumption Norms for Durables: Evidence from the General Household Survey', SOAS Working Papers in Economics, no. 23, May.

Fine, B. *et al.* (1993) 'Consumption Norms, Trickle-Down and the Video/Microwave Syndrome', *International Review of Applied Economics*, vol. 7, no. 2, June, pp. 123–43.

Fischler, C. (1980) 'Food Habits, Social Change and the Nature/Culture Dilemma', *Social Science Information*, vol. 19, no. 6, pp. 937–53.

Fischler, C. (1988) 'Food, Self and Identity', *Social Science Information*, vol. 27, no. 2, pp. 275–92.

Fischler, C. (1989) 'Cuisines and Food Selection', in Thomson (1989).

Flux, A. (1930) 'Our Food Supply Before and After the War', *Journal of the Royal Statistical Society*, vol. 93, pp. 538–56.

Frank, J. *et al.* (1984) 'Britain's National Food Survey: Whose Purpose Does It Serve?', *Food Policy*, February, pp. 53–67.

Friedland, W. (1984) 'Commodity Systems Analysis: An Approach to the Sociology of Agriculture', *Research in Rural Sociology and Development*, no. 1, pp. 221–35.

Friedland, W. *et al.* (eds) (1992) *Towards a New Political Economy of Agriculture*, Boulder: Westview Press.

Friedmann, H. (1978) 'World Market, State, and Family Farm: Social Bases of Household Production in the Era of Wage Labor', *Comparative Studies in Society and History*, vol. 20, pp. 545–86.

Friedmann, H. (1982) 'The Political Economy of Food: The Rise and Fall of the Postwar International Food Order', *American Journal of Sociology*, vol. 88, supplement, pp. S248–86, reproduced in Burawoy and Skocpol (1982).

Friedmann, H. (1987) 'The Family Farm and the International Food Regimes', in Shanin (1987).

Friedmann, H. (1990) 'The Origins of Third World Food Dependence', in Bernstein *et al.* (1990).

Friedmann, H. (1993) 'The Political Economy of Food: A Global Crisis', *New Left Review*, no. 197, January/February, pp. 29–57.

Friedmann, H. (1994a) 'Premature Rigour: Can Ben Fine Have His Contingency and Eat It, Too?', *Review of International Political Economy*, vol. 1, no. 3, autumn, pp. 553–61.

Friedmann, H. (1994b) 'Distance and Durability: Shaky Foundations of the World Food Economy', in McMichael (1994b).

Friedmann, H. and McMichael, P. (1989) 'Agriculture and the State System', *Sociologia Ruralis*, vol. 19, no. 2, pp. 93–117.

Frijters, J. (1987) 'Sensory Sweetness Perception, its Pleasantness, and Attitudes to Sweet Foods', in Dobbing (1987).

Gardner, B. (1992) 'Changing Economic Perspectives on the Farm Problem', *Journal of Economic Literature*, vol. XXX, March, pp. 62–101.

Geissler, C. and D. Oddy (eds) (1993) *Food, Diet and Economic Change Past and Present*, Leicester: Leicester University Press.

Gibbon, P. and M. Neocosmos (1985) 'Some Problems in the Political Economy of "African Socialism"', in Bernstein and Campbell (1985).

Giddens, A. (1991) *Modernity and Self-Identity: Self and Society in the Late Modern Age*, Cambridge: Polity Press.

Giddens, A. (1992) *The Transformation of Intimacy: Love, Sexuality and Eroticism in Modern Societies*, Cambridge: Polity Press.

Glennie, P. and N. Thrift (1992) 'Modernity, Urbanism, and Modern Consumption', *Environment and Planning D: Society and Space*, vol. 10, no. 4, pp. 423–43.

Glennie, P. and N. Thrift (1993) 'Modern Consumption: Theorising Commodities and Consumers', *Environment and Planning D: Society and Space*, vol. 11, pp. 603–6.

Glinsmann, W. *et al.* (1986) 'Evaluation of Health Aspects of Sugars Contained in Carbohydrate Sweeteners: Report of Sugars Task Force', *Journal of Nutrition*, vol. 116, Supplement, pp. S1–S216.

Goodman, D. (1992) 'Some Recent Tendencies in the Industrial Reorganization of the Agri-Food System', in Friedland *et al.* (1992).

Goodman, D. and Redclift (1981) *From Peasant to Proletariat: Capitalist Development and Agrarian Transitions*, Oxford: Basil Blackwell.

Goodman, D. and M. Redclift (eds) (1989) *The International Farm Crisis*, London: Macmillan.

Goodman, D. and Redclift, M. (1991a) *Refashioning Nature: Food, Ecology and Culture*, London and New York: Routledge.

Goodman, D. and M. Redclift (eds) (1991b) *Environment and Development in Latin America*, Manchester: Manchester University Press.

Goodman, D. and M. Redclift (1994) 'Constructing a Political Economy of Food', *Review of International Political Economy*, vol. 1, no. 3, autumn, pp. 547–52.

Goodman, D. and M. Watts (1994) 'Reconfiguring the Rural or Fording the Divide? Capitalist Restructuring and the Global Agro-Food System', *Journal of Peasant Studies*, vol. 22, no. 1, October, pp. 1–49.

Goodman, D. and J. Wilkinson (1990) 'Patterns of Research and Innovation in the Modern Agro-Food System', in Lowe *et al.* (1990).

Goodman, D. and J. Wilkinson (1994) 'Agro-Food Futures: Towards a Polyvalent Agro-Food System', mimeo.

Goodman, D. *et al.* (1987) *From Farming to Biotechnology: A Theory of Agro-Industrial Development*, Oxford: Basil Blackwell.

Grant, W. (1991) *The Dairy Industry: An International Comparison*, Aldershot: Dartmouth.

Greaves, J. and D. Hollingsworth (1964) 'Changes in the Pattern of Carbohydrate Consumption in Britain', *Proceedings of the Nutrition Society*, vol. 23, pp. 136–43.

Greaves, J. and D. Hollingsworth (1966) 'Trends in Food Consumption in the United Kingdom', *World Review of Nutrition and Dietetics*, vol. 6, pp. 34–89.

Grenby, T. (ed.) (1987) *Developments in Sweeteners*, 3rd edn, London: Elsevier Applied Science.

Grigg, D. (1993a) 'The European Diet: Regional Variations in Food Consumption in the 1980s', *Geoforum*, vol. 24, no. 3, August, pp. 277–89.

Grigg, D. (1993b) 'International Variations in Food Consumption in the 1980s', *Geography*, vol. 78, no. 3, July, pp. 251–66.

Grigg, D. (1993c) 'The Role of Livestock Products in World Food Consumption', *Scottish Geographical Magazine*, vol. 109, no. 2, September, pp. 66–74.

Grigg, D. (1993d) *The World Food Problem*, 2nd edn, Oxford: Blackwell.

Grigg, D. (1994) 'Income, Industrialisation and Food Consumption', *Tijdschrift voor Economische en Sociale Geografie*, vol. 85, no. 1, pp. 3–14.

Halsbury, *Halsbury's Laws of England* (1986), 4th edn, vol. 52, London: Butterworths.

Hammond, R. (1946) 'British Food Supplies, 1914–1939', *The Economic History Review*, vol. XVI, no. 1, pp. 1–14.

Hammond, R. (1962) *Food: Studies in Administration and Control*, vol. 3, London: HMSO.

Harding, F. (1989) 'Dairy Products', in Spedding (1989).

Harrington, G. (1988) 'Meat and Meat Products: Changes in Demand and Supply', *Proceedings of the Nutrition Society*, vol. 47, pp. 315–21.

Harris, S. (1984) 'The UK Sugar Economy', 30th Congress of the International Confederation of European Beet Growers (CIBE), Kensington Town Hall, London.

Harris, S. (1985) *Review of the EC Sugar Market: Report for the World Bank*, Washington DC: World Bank.

Harris, S. *et al.* (1983) *The Food and Farm Policies of the European Community*, Chichester: John Wiley.

Harriss, J. (ed.) (1982) *Rural Development: Theories of Peasant Economy and Agrarian Economy*, London: Hutchinson.

Hausman, J. *et al.* (1984) 'Econometric Models for Count Data with an Application to the Patents–R&D Relationship', *Econometrica*, vol. 52, no. 4, July, pp. 909–38.

Heasman, M. (1987) *One Lump or Two? Current Challenges Facing Sugar in the UK*, Food Policy Research Unit, University of Bradford Briefing Paper.

Heasman, M. (1988) *Influence of Changing Patterns of Sucrose Consumption on Industrial Users*, unpublished doctoral thesis, University of Bradford.

Heasman, M. (1989) 'Sugar and the Modern Food System', *British Food Journal*, vol. 91, no. 3, pp. 9–16.

Heasman, M. (1990a) 'Nutrition and Technology: The Development of the Market for "Lite" Products', *British Food Journal*, vol. 92, no. 2, pp. 5–13.

Heasman, M. (1990b) 'What the Papers Said: A Review of Regional Newspaper Reports on Sugar, Diet and Health between September 1987 and October 1990', mimeo.

Heasman, M (1991) 'Lite Products: An Attitudinal Survey of British Food and Drink Manufacturers', *British Food Journal*, vol. 93, no. 7, pp. 12–16.

Heasman, M. (1993) 'The Persistence of Sugar in the British Food Supply, 1900 to the Present Day', SOAS Department of Economics Working Paper, no. 35, October.

Heasman, M. (1994) 'The Political Economy of Sugar: A Systems of Provision Approach', mimeo.

Heasman, M. and A. Schmitt (1994) 'The Impact of Sweeteners on European Union Sugar Supply: A Systems of Provision Approach', mimeo.

Heckman, J. (1979) 'Sample Selection Bias as a Specification Error', *Econometrica*, vol. 47, pp. 153–61.

Henderson, J. (1989) *The Globalisation of High Technology Production: Society, Space, and Semiconductors in the Restructuring of the Modern World*, London: Routledge.

Hills, J. (1994) 'A Global Industrial Policy. US Hegemony and GATT. The Liberalization of Telecommunications', *Review of International Political Economy*, vol. 1, no. 2, summer, pp. 257–79.

Hirschoff, P. and N. Kotler (eds) (1989) *Completing the Food Chain: Strategies for Combating Hunger and Malnutrition*, Washington: Smithsonian Institution Press.

Hobhouse, H. (1985) *Seeds of Change*, London: Sidgwick & Jackson.

Hobsbawm, E. and T. Ranger (eds) (1983) *The Invention of Tradition*, Cambridge: Cambridge University Press.

HoC (1992) *The Trade Gap in Food and Drink*, House of Commons Agricultural Committee Second Report, 112–I&II, Session 1991/92, London: HMSO.

Hoggart, K. (ed) (1992) *Agricultural Change, Environment and Economy*, London: Mansell Publishing.

Holderness, B. (1985) *British Agriculture Since 1945*, Manchester: Manchester University Press.

Hollingham, M. and R. Howarth (1989) *British Milk Marketing and the Common Agricultural Policy: The Origins of Confusion and Crisis*, Aldershot: Avebury.

Hollingsworth, D. (1985) 'Rationing and Economic Constraints on Food Consumption in Britain Since the Second World War', in Oddy and Miller (1985).

Hooks, B. (1992) *Black Looks: Race and Representation*, London: Turnaround.

Hubbard, L. (1992) 'Milk Quotas and Farm Asset Values', *National Westminster Bank Quarterly Review*, August, pp. 38–48.

Hussain, A. and K. Tribe (1980a) *Marxism and the Agrarian Question*, vol. 1: *German Social Democracy and the Peasantry, 1890–1907*, London: Macmillan.

Hussain, A. and K. Tribe (1980b) *Marxism and the Agrarian Question*, vol. 2: *Russian Marxism and the Peasantry, 1861–1930*, London: Macmillan.

Ironmonger, D. (1972) *New Commodities and Consumer Behaviour*, Cambridge: Cambridge University Press.

ISA (1987) *The Influence of Changing Lifestyles on Food and Drink Consumption in Europe*, London: International Sweeteners Association.

Jackson, P. (1993) 'Towards a Cultural Politics of Consumption' in Bird *et al.* (1993).

James, P. *et al.* (1980) 'Is Food Intake under Physiological Control in Man?', in Turner, M. (ed.) (1980) *Nutrition and Lifestyles*, London: Applied Science Publishers.

Jones, A. and S. Makings (1931) *Some Aspects of Meat Distribution and Consumption: A Study Based On Conditions In Loughborough – 1930*, Loughborough: Midland Agricultural College.

Keat, R. *et al.* (eds) (1992) *The Authority of the Consumer*, London: Routledge.

Keen, M. (1987) 'Zero Expenditures and the Estimation of Engel Curves', *Journal of Applied Econometrics*, vol. 41, pp. 277–86.

Kenney, M. *et al.* (1989) 'Midwestern Agriculture in US Fordism: From the New Deal to Economic Restructuring', *Sociologia Ruralis*, vol. 19, no. 2, pp. 131–48.

Kerr, M. and N. Charles (1986) 'Servers and Providers: The Distribution of Food within the Family', *Sociological Review*, vol. 34, pp. 115–57.

Key Note (1993a) *Agrochemicals and Fertilizers*, Key Note: Hampton.

Key Note (1993b) *Milk and Dairy Products*, Key Note: Hampton.

Kim, C. and J. Curry (1993) 'Fordism, Flexible Specialization and Agri-Industrial Restructuring: The Case of the US Broiler Industry', *Sociologia Ruralis*, vol. XXXIII, no. 1, pp. 61–80.

Kloppenburg, J. (1988) *First the Seed: The Political Economy of Plant Biotechnology, 1492–2000*, Cambridge: Cambridge University Press.

Kotz, D. (1994) 'Household Labor, Wage Labor, and the Transformation of the Family', *Review of Radical Political Economics*, vol. 26, no. 2, June, pp. 24–56.

Kotz, D. (1995) 'Reply: Analyzing the Transformation of the Family', *Review of Radical Political Economics*, vol. 27, no. 2, June, pp. 116–23.

Krugman, P. and A. Smith (eds) (1994) *Empirical Studies of Strategic Trade Policy*, Chicago: Chicago University Press.

Lancaster, K. (1966) 'A New Approach to Consumer Theory', *Journal of Political Economy*, vol. 74, pp 132–57.

Landell Mills (1989) *Sweetener Analysis*, Oxford: Landell Mills.

Le Heron, R. (1993) *Globalized Agriculture: Political Choice*, Oxford: Pergamon Press.

Lee, V. A. (1981) 'The Nutritional Significance of Sucrose Consumption: 1970–1980', *Critical Reviews in Food Science and Nutrition*, January, pp. 1–47.

Lloyd, E. (1936) 'Food Supplies and Consumption at Different Income Levels', *Journal of the Proceedings of the Agricultural Economics Society*, vol. 4, no. 2, pp. 89–120.

Long, N. and J. van der Ploeg (1988) 'New Challenges in the Sociology of Rural Development: A Rejoinder to Peter Vandergeest', *Sociologia Ruralis*, vol. XXVIII, no. 1, pp. 30–41.

Long, N. *et al.* (1986) *The Commoditization Debate: Labour Process, Strategy and Social Network*, Wageningen: Wageningen Agricultural University.

Lowe, P. *et al.* (eds) (1990) *Technological Change and the Rural Environment*, London: David Fulton Publishers.

Lund, P. and B. Derry (1985) 'Household Food Consumption: The Influence of Household Characteristics', *Journal of Agricultural Economics*, vol. 36, pp. 41–58.

Lyle, P. (1950) 'The Sources and Nature of Statistical Information in Special Fields of Statistics: The Sugar Industry', *Journal of the Royal Statistical Society*, Series A, CXIII (Part IV), pp. 531–43.

Lyson, T. and C. Geisler (1992) 'Toward a Second Agricultural Divide: The Restructuring of American Agriculture', *Sociologia Ruralis*, vol. XXXII, no. 2/3, pp. 246–63.

MacKay, D. (1987) 'The Food Manufacturers' View of Sugar Substitutes', in Grenby (1987).

MAFF (various years) *Household Food Consumption and Expenditure*, annual report of the National Food Survey, London: HMSO.

MAFF (1968) *A Century of Agricultural Statistics: Great Britain 1866–1966*, London: HMSO.

MAFF (1994) *Agriculture in the United Kingdom 1993*, London: HMSO.

Mahler, V. (1986) 'Controlling International Commodity Prices and Supplies: The Evolution of United States Sugar Policy', in Tullis and Hollist (1986).

Mann, S. and J. Dickinson (1978) 'Obstacles to the Development of Capitalist Agriculture', *Journal of Peasant Studies*, vol. 5, no. 4, July, pp. 466–88.

Marsden, T. (1992) 'Exploring a Rural Sociology for the Fordist Transition: Incorporating Social Relations into Economic Restructuring', *Sociologia Ruralis*, vol. XXXII, no. 2/3, pp. 209–30.

Marsden, T. and R. Munton (1991) 'Global Food Strategies and Environmental Change: Some Preliminary Considerations', *Fresh Fruit and Vegetables Globalization Network*, Working Paper No. 7, University of California, Santa Cruz.

Marsden, T. *et al.* (1986) 'The Restructuring Process and Economic Centrality in Capitalist Agriculture', *Journal of Rural Sociology*, vol. 2, no. 4, pp. 271–40.

Marsden, T. and J. Little (eds) (1990) *Political, Social and Economic Perspectives on the International Food System*, Aldershot: Avebury.

Marsden, T. *et al.* (eds) (1990) *Rural Restructuring: Global Processes and Their Responses*, London: David Fulton.

Marsden, T. *et al.* (eds) (1992) *Labour and Locality: Uneven Development and the Rural Labour Process*, London: David Fulton.

Mattessons Wall's Limited (n.d) *Poultry Working Group Report.*

Mayhew, M. (1988) 'The 1930s Nutrition Controversy', *Journal of Contemporary History*, vol. 23, pp. 445–64.

McKenzie, J. (1986) 'An Integrated Approach – With Special Reference to the Study of Changing Food Habits in the United Kingdom', in Ritson *et al.* (1986).

McMichael, P. (1992) 'Tensions between National and International Control of the World Food Order: Contours of a New Food Regime', *Sociological Perspectives*, vol. 35, no. 2, pp. 343–65.

McMichael, P. (1993a) 'World Food System Restructuring under a GATT Regime', *Political Geography*, vol. 12, no. 3, May, pp. 198–214.

McMichael, P. (1993b) 'Agro-Food Restructuring in the Pacific Rim: A Comparative International Perspective on Japan, South Korea, the United States, Australia, and Thailand', in Palat (1993).

McMichael, P. (1994a) 'Global Restructuring: Some Lines of Inquiry', in McMichael (1994b).

McMichael, P. (ed.) (1994b) *The Global Restructuring of Agro-Food Systems*, Ithaca: Cornell University Press.

McMichael, P. and F. Buttel (1990) 'New Directions in the Political Economy of Agriculture', *Sociological Perspectives*, vol. 33, no. 1, pp. 89–109.

McMichael, P. and D. Myhre (1991) 'Global Regulation vs. the Nation-State: Agro-Food Systems and the New Politics of Capital', *Capital and Class*, no. 43, spring, pp. 83–105.

Meghir, C. and J. Robin (1992) 'Frequency of Purchase and the Estimation of Demand Systems', *Journal of Econometrics*, vol. 53, pp. 53–85.

Mennell, S. (1987) 'On the Civilizing of Appetite', *Theory, Culture and Society*, vol. 4, no. 3, pp. 373–403.

Mennell, S. *et al.* (1992) *The Sociology of Food: Eating, Diet and Culture*, London: Sage, reproduction of the special issue of *Current Sociology*, vol. 40, no. 2.

Messer, E. (1984) 'Anthropological Perspectives on Diet', *Annual Review of Anthropology*, vol. 13, pp. 205–49.

Milk Marketing Board (1989) *Five Years of Milk Quotas: A Progress Report*, Thames Ditton.

Miller, D. (ed.) (1995) *Acknowledging Consumption*, London: Routledge, forthcoming.

Mintz, S. (1985) *Sweetness and Power. The Place of Sugar in Modern History*, Harmondsworth: Penguin.

Mintz, S. (1993) 'The Changing Roles of Food in the Study of Consumption', in Brewer and Porter (1993).

MLC (various years) *Meat Demand Trends*, Milton Keynes: Meat and Livestock Commission.

Monopolies and Mergers Commission (1981) *S. and W. Berisford and British Sugar Corporation Ltd: A Report on the Proposed Merger*, HC241 1980/81, London: HMSO.

Monopolies and Mergers Commission (1987) *Tate and Lyle plc and Ferruzzi Finanziaria SpA and S. and W. Berisford plc: A Report on the Existing and Proposed Merger*, CM89, London: HMSO.

Monopolies and Mergers Commission (1991) *Tate and Lyle plc and British Sugar plc: A Report on the Proposed Merger*, CM1435, London: HMSO.

Moran, W. (1992) 'Globalisation and Agricultural International Trade', *Environment and Planning A*, vol. 24, pp. 771–74.

Morris, M. (1979) *The State and the Development of Capitalist Social Relations in the South African Countryside: A Process of Class Struggle*, PhD thesis, University of Sussex.

Moskowitz, H. (1971) 'The Sweetness and Pleasantness of Sugars', *American Journal of Psychology*, vol. 84, no. 3, pp. 387–405.

Munton, R. (1992) 'The Uneven Development of Capitalist Agriculture: The Repositioning of Agriculture within the Food System', in Hoggart (1992).

Murcott, A. (1983a) 'Cooking and the Cooked: A Note on the Domestic Preparation of Meals', in Murcott (1983b).

Murcott, A. (ed.) (1983b) *The Sociology of Food and Eating*, Aldershot: Gower.

Murcott, A. (1989) 'Sociological and Social Anthropological Approaches to Food and Eating', *World Review of Nutrition and Dietetics*, no. 55, edited by G. Bourne, Basel: Karger, pp. 1–40.

Murdoch, J. (1994) 'Some Comments on "Nature" and "Society" in the Political Economy of Food by Way of Reply to Fine', *Review of International Political Economy*, vol. 1, no. 3, autumn, pp. 571–7.

NACNE (1983) *A Discussion Paper on Proposals for Nutritional Guidelines for Health Education in Britain*, The Health Education Council, London: National Advisory Committee on Nutrition Education.

NCC (1990) *Milk Marketing in England and Wales*, National Consumer Council, London: HMSO.

NCC (ed.) (1992) *Your Food: Whose Choice?*, National Consumer Council, London: HMSO.

Nelson, M. (1993) 'Social-Class Trends in British Diet, 1860–1980', in Geissler and Oddy (1993).

Nicol, W. (1982) 'Sucrose: The Optimum Sweetener', in Birch and Parker (eds) (1982).

Oddy, D. and D. Miller (eds) (1976) *The Making of the Modern British Diet*, London: Croom Helm.

Oddy, D. and D. Miller (eds) (1985) *Diet and Health in Modern Britain*, London: Croom Helm.

Ohlin Wright, E. (1985) *Classes*, London: Verso.

Orr, John Boyd (1937) *Food, Health and Income*, 2nd edn, London: Macmillan.

Palat, R. (ed.) (1993) *Pacific-Asia and the Future of the World-System*, Westport, Connecticut: Greenwood Press.

Pancoast, H. and W. Junk, (1980) *Handbook of Sugars*, 2nd edn, Westport, Connecticut: AVI Publishing.

Pearce, I. (1964) *A Contribution to Demand Analysis*, Oxford: Oxford University Press.

Pelto, G. and P. Pelto (1985) 'Diet and Delocalisation: Dietary Changes since 1750', in Rotberg and Rabb (1985).

Perelman, M. (1979) 'Obstacles to the Development of Capitalist Agriculture: A Comment on Mann and Dickinson', *Journal of Peasant Studies*, vol. 7, no. 1, October, pp. 119–21.

Perren, R. (1978) *The Meat Trade in Britain 1840–1914*, London: Routledge & Kegan Paul.

Pesaran, M. and R. Smith (1992) 'Estimating Long-Run Relationships from Dynamic Heterogeneous Panels', paper presented at the Fourth Conference on Panel Data, Budapest, June.

Pudney, S. (1989) *Modelling Individual Choice: The Econometrics of Corners, Kinks and Holes*, Oxford: Blackwell.

Putnam, G. (1923) *Supplying Britain's Meat*, London: George G. Harrap.

Quick, A. and R. Wilkinson (1991) *Income and Health*, London: Socialist Health Association.

Rayner, A. *et al.* (1993) 'Agriculture in the Uruguay Round: An Assessment', *Economic Journal*, vol. 103, November, pp. 1513–27.

Raynolds, L. *et al.* (1993) 'The "New" Internationalization of Agriculture: A Reformulation', *World Development*, vol. 21, no. 7, pp. 1101–21.

Reinhardt, N. and P. Barlett (1989) 'The Persistence of Family Farms in United States Agriculture', *Sociologia Ruralis*, vol. XXIX, no. 3/4, pp. 201–25.

Richardson, N. *et al.* (1993) 'Current Attitudes and Future Influences on Meat Consumption in the UK', *Appetite*, vol. 21, no. 1, pp. 41–51.

Richardson, N. *et al.* (1994) 'Meat Consumption, Definition of Meat and Trust in Information Sources in the UK Population and Members of the Vegetarian Society', *Ecology of Food and Nutrition*, forthcoming.

Ritson, C. (1988) 'Special Study of Meat and Meat Products', in NFS annual report, London: HMSO.

Ritson, C. (1991a) 'The CAP and the Consumer', in Ritson and Harvey (1991).

Ritson, C. (1991b) 'The Consumption Revolution', in Slater (1991).

Ritson, C., L. Gofton and J. McKenzie (eds) (1986) *The Food Consumer*, Chichester: John Wiley.

Ritson, C. and D. Harvey (eds) (1991) *The Common Agricultural Policy and the World Economy: Essays in Honour of John Ashton*, Wallingford: CAB International.

Roberts, D. (1988) 'Changes in the Demand and Supply for Milk and Dairy Products', *Proceedings of the Nutrition Society*, vol. 47, pp. 323–9.

Rolls, B. and M. Hetherington (1989) 'The Role of Variety in Eating and Body Weight Regulation', in Shepherd (1989b).

Ross, E. (1980a) 'Patterns of Diet and Forces of Production: An Economic and Ecological History of the Ascendancy of Beef in the United States Diet', in Ross (ed.) (1980b).

Ross, E. (ed.) (1980b) *Beyond the Myths of Culture: Essays in Cultural Materialism*, New York: Academic Press.

Rotberg, R. and T. Rabb (eds) (1985) *Hunger and History: The Impact of Changing Food and Production Patterns on Society*, Cambridge: Cambridge University Press.

Rozin, P. (1989) 'The Role of Learning in the Acquisition of Food Preferences by Humans', in Shepherd (1989b).

Ruivenkamp, G. (1987) 'Social Impacts of Biotechnology on Agriculture and Food Processing', *Development*, vol. 4, pp. 58–9.

Sahlins, M. (1988) 'Cosmologies of Capitalisms', *Proceedings of the British Academy*, vol. 74, pp. 1–51.

Sanderson, S. (1986) 'The Emergence of the 'World Steer': Internationalisation and Foreign Domination in Latin American Cattle Production', in Tullis and Hollist (1986).

Sayers, S. (1994) 'Moral Values and Progress', *New Left Review*, no. 204, March/April, pp. 67–85.

SCF (1987) *The Report of the Scientific Committee on Food on Sweetness*, Cs\EDUL/S6- FINAL, Brussels: EC.

Schmalensee, R. (1992) 'Sunk Costs and Market Structure: A Review Article', *Journal of Industrial Economics*, vol. XL, June, pp. 125–34.

Schmitt, A. (1995) draft doctoral thesis, School of Public Health, Université Catholique de Louvain, Bruxelles.

Schiwech, H. (1985) 'Gaps in Knowledge and Misconceptions about Sugar and Nutrition', *Proceedings of the World Sugar Research Organisation Scientific Conference*, pp. 85–107.

Scott, D. (ed.) (1988) *Anorexia Nervosa and Bulimia Nervosa: Practical Approaches*, London: Croom Helm.

Scranton, P. (1983) *Proprietary Capitalism: The Philadelphia Textile Manufacturers, 1880–1885*, Cambridge: Cambridge University Press.

Scranton, P. (1989) *Figured Tapestry: Production, Markets, and Power in Philadelphia Textiles, 1885–1941*, Cambridge: Cambridge University Press.

Sen, A. (1967) 'Isolation, Assurance and the Social Rate of Discount', *Quarterly Journal of Economics*, vol. 81, no. 1, February, pp. 112–24, reproduced in Sen (1984).

Sen, A. (1981) *Poverty and Famines*, Oxford: Clarendon Press.

Sen, A. (1984) *Resources, Values and Development*, Oxford: Blackwell.

Shanin, T. (ed.) (1987) *Peasants and Peasant Societies: Selected Readings*, 2nd edn, Oxford: Blackwell.

Shepherd, R. (1989a) 'Factors Influencing Preferences and Choices', in Shepherd (1989b).

Shepherd, R. (ed.) (1989b) *Handbook of the Psychophysiology of Human Eating*, London: John Wiley.

Shepherd, R. and C. Farleigh (1989) 'Sensory Assessment of Foods and the Role of Sensory Attributes in Determining Food Choice', in Shepherd (1989b).

Slater, J. (ed.) (1991) *Fifty Years of the National Food Survey, 1940–1990*, London: HMSO.

Smil, V. (1994) 'How Many People Can the Earth Feed?', *Population and Development Review*, vol. 20, no. 2, June, pp. 255–92.

Smith, I. (1978) 'The Development of Natural Sweeteners as Alternatives to Cane and Beet Sugar', *Journal of Agricultural Economics*, vol. 29, pp. 155–62.

Sobal, J. *et al.* (1993) 'Teaching the Sociology of Food, Eating, and Nutrition', *Teaching Sociology*, vol. 21, no. 1, January, pp. 50–9.

Southgate, J. (1984) *The Commonwealth Sugar Agreement 1951–1974*, London: C. Czarnikow.

Spedding, C. (ed.) (1989) *The Human Food Chain*, London: Elsevier Applied Science.

Stevens, C. and C. Webb (1983) 'The Political Economy of Sugar: A Window on the CAP', in Wallace *et al.* (1983).

Stone, J. *et al.* (1954) *The Measurement of Consumers' Expenditure and Behaviour in the United Kingdom, 1920–1938*, Cambridge: Cambridge University Press.

Sutton, J. (1991) *Sunk Costs and Market Structure: Price Competition, Advertising, and the Evolution of Concentration*, Cambridge: MIT Press.

Swinbank, A. (1986) 'The Political Economy of Milk Pricing in England and Wales', *Food Marketing*, vol. 2, no. 1, pp. 34–54.

Swinbank, A. (1987) 'The Political Economy of Food: The Case of the Dairy Industry', *Food Marketing*, vol. 3, no. 1, pp. 21–39.

Symes, D. (1992) 'Agriculture, the State and Rural Society in Europe: Trends and Issues', *Sociologia Ruralis*, vol. XXXII, no. 2/3, pp. 193–208.

Tarrant, J. (1992) 'Agriculture and the State', in Bowler (1992a).

Thomson, D. (ed.) (1989) *Food Acceptability*, London: Elsevier.

Tomlinson, M. and A. Warde (1993) 'Social Class and Change in Eating Habits', *British Food Journal*, vol. 95, no. 1, pp. 3–10.

Tracy, M. (1989) *Government and Agriculture in Western Europe 1880–1988*, 3rd edn, New York: Harvester Wheatsheaf.

Tullis, F. and W. Hollist (eds) (1986) *Food, the State, and International Political Economy: Dilemmas of Developing Countries*, Lincoln: University of Nebraska Press.

Turner, B. (1982) 'The Government of the Body: Medical Regimens and the Rationalization of Diet', *British Journal of Sociology*, vol. 33, no. 2, June, pp. 254–69.

Twigg, J. (1983) 'Vegetarianism and the Meaning of Meat', in Murcott (1983b).

Tyers, R. and K. Anderson (1992) *Disarray in World Food Markets: A Quantitative Assessment*, Cambridge: Cambridge University Press.

Urry, J. (1993a) *The Tourist Gaze: Leisure and Travel in Contemporary Society*, London: Sage.

Urry, J. (1993b) 'Time, Leisure, and Social Identity', mimeo.

van der Ploeg, J. (1990) *Labor, Markets, and Agricultural Production*, Boulder: Westview Press.

Vandergeest, P. (1988) 'Commercialization and Commoditization: A Dialogue Between Perspectives', *Sociologia Ruralis*, vol. XXVIII, no. 1, pp. 7–29.

Wallace, H. *et al.* (eds) (1977) *Policy-Making in the European Communities*, London: John Wiley.

Wallace, H. *et al.* (eds) (1983) *Policy-Making in the European Community*, 2nd edn, London: John Wiley.

Warde, A. (1990) 'The Sociology of Consumption', *Sociology*, vol. 24, no. 1, pp. 1–4.

Warde, A. (1992) 'Notes on the Relationship between Production and Consumption', in Keat *et al.* (1992).

Watkins, K. (1991) 'Agriculture and Food Security in the GATT Uruguay Round', *Review of African Political Economy*, no. 50, March, pp. 38–50.

Watts, M. (1994) 'What Difference Does Difference Make?', *Review of International Political Economy*, vol. 1, no. 3, autumn, pp. 563–70.

Webb, C. (1977) 'Mr Cube versus Monsieur Beet: The Politics of Sugar in the European Communities', in Wallace *et al.* (1977).

Weiffenbach, J. (ed.) (1977) *Taste and Development*, Washington DC: Government Printing Office.

Wernick, A. (1991) *Promotional Culture: Advertising, Ideology, and Symbolic Expression*, London: Sage.

Whetham, E. (1976) *Beef Cattle and Sheep 1910–1940*, Cambridge: University of Cambridge, Department of Land Economy.

WHO (1987) *Environmental Health Criteria*, Geneva: World Health Organization.

Williams, R. (1993) 'The Future of Milk Marketing', *Journal of Agricultural Economics* vol. 44, no. 1, pp. 1–13.

Willis, S. (1991) *A Primer for Daily Life*, London: Routledge.

Winson, A. (1992) *The Intimate Commodity: Food and the Development of the Agro-Industrial Complex in Canada*, Toronto: Garamond Press.

Woodhams, R. (1988) *Feedgrains to 1993: the Challenge of New Markets*, EIU Special Report, no. 1156, London: Economist Intelligence Unit.

Wursch, P. and N. Daget (1987) 'Sweetness in Product Development', in Dobbing (1987).

Young, B. (1987) 'Sugar, Children and Television Advertising', Research Report No. 15, Health Education Authority.

Young, J. (1990) *The Market for Low and Light Foods: Symposium on Low and Light Foods and Drinks – Meeting Consumer Demand*, Reading: Leatherhead Food RA, 26 April, 1990.

INDEX

Notes: 1. Most references are to the United Kingdom unless otherwise specified;
2. Most references are to food, which is therefore largely omitted as a qualifier

Abbott, G.C. 84
absolute frequency of purchase 171,
    257–8, 260–1, 263
acceptable daily intake (ADI) 137, 145
access: to finance 32; to food, unequal
    13–14, 16, 25, 26, 56; to land 44–5,
    47
acesulfame K (E950) 133, 136–41, 145
Achard, F. 127
ACP (African, Caribbean and Pacific
    countries): sugar 79, 89, 94–7, 106,
    108, 122, 124, 128, 133–4, 140;
    theory of food systems 56, 57
Adams, C. 215, 216
addiction 148; *see also* alcohol;
    smoking
additives 49; *see also* artificial
    sweeteners
advertising: artificial sweeteners 141;
    differentiating food systems 63, 70;
    econometrics 147; meat 208; sugar
    105, 111, 118–19
Advisory Committee *see* National
    Advisory Committee
Afarinkia, M. 56
Africa 56, 57; sugar 79, 94, 97, 106, 128
age of householders: class 230–1;
    dairy 256–7, 261, 262, 264;
    econometrics 153, 154; meat 202,
    204, 209, 212–14; norms 171–2, 180,
    181, 256–7, 261, 262
Agricultural Deregulation and
    Marketing Bill (1992) 254
Agricultural Marketing Act (1931) 239

agriculture 273, 274; artificial
    sweeteners 134–5; capitalist
    economy 41–4, 56;
    commoditization 42–5; dairy 190,
    197, 237–46 *passim*, 249, 251, 255,
    263; economics of food 17–20;
    'farm problem' 17, 19; geography
    22; meat 207–8; protectionism 17,
    18, 27; rotation 48, 98, 99; subsidies
    17–18; substitutionism 48–51, 53,
    57–8, 216; sugar 78, 87, 97–9, 108,
    120; technology 46, 48, 49, 87–8,
    99, 216, 237, 243–4; theory of food
    systems 32, 61–4; uniqueness of
    food's dependence on 36; unstable
    38; *see also* industry and food; land
aid, food 91
alcohol: artificial sweeteners 140; as
    car fuel 90; class 219, 228;
    econometrics 161, 164; low income
    and children 185, 186; sugar 90,
    102, 104, 114; *see also* brewing; wine
almost ideal demand system (AID)
    156, 162
amino acids 101
Anderson, K. 17–18, 27
animals *see* livestock
anorexia 72
anthropology 24–5
antibiotics 126
appropriationism/appropriation 262;
    agriculture 48–51, 53, 57–8; of
    subsidies by rich 47, 98; sugar
    87–8, 121

292

INDEX

computers 148–9
confectionery 80, 82, 101–3, 104, 113–14, 126; artificial sweeteners 140; low income and children 185
Congo (Brazzaville) 128
Consumers in European Community 126
consumption: artificial sweeteners 139; differentiating food systems 60, 62, 63, 64, 66–7, 69–70, 73; failure to develop satisfactory 'junctions' 70; meat 205–6; theory of food systems 32, 35–6, 37, 55; variability of 67; *see also* commodity; consumption and sugar supply; econometrics
consumption and sugar supply: EU 135–6, 144; learning before Second World War 99–103; NACNE recommendation 117; peak (1950s–70s) 104–7; statistics 95, 100, 102, 114, 122–3, 135–6, 143; in UK 78, 95, 99–102, 104–5, 113–14, 117, 122–3, 143; world 89, 95
contingency 33, 34, 120
convenience foods 40, 174; sugar 115, 120, 121; *see also* canned products; frozen foods; ready meals; snack foods
Cook, I. 72
cooked meat 208, 211, 212, 219, 229–30; norms 172–3, 178
cooking equipment *see* technology, household
Cooperative Wholesale Society 243
'core' eaters 164
corn syrup 74, 88–9, 132
corned meat 211, 212, 229–30; class 229–30; norms 172, 178
corner solution 148, 161–2
costs 268; agriculture 17; artificial sweeteners 133, 136, 142; EU 270–2; sugar 135; *see also* prices
Cowan, R. 70
Cox, D. 162, 239, 246
Crawford, W. 100–1
cream 238, 241, 249, 252–3; norms 175, 176, 256–61; problem of 274
credit and agriculture 45
Crompton, R. 236
Cronon, W. 72
Cuba 79, 96
'Cube, Mr' 105
cubes, sugar 96

Currie, E. 142
Curry, J. 55, 58, 59
cyclamate (E952) 136, 137–8, 139, 145

Daget, N. 84
Dahlberg, K. 56
Dairy Crest 243, 251, 253
dairy system 12, 237–64; agriculture 190, 197, 237–46 *passim*, 249, 251, 255, 263; class 197–8, 222–4, 226, 227, 256–7, 260; differentiating food systems 72; econometrics 158; healthy diet 239–40, 248–9, 254, 256, 259, 262; income 256–7, 260, 262; industry 250–4; new SOP 254–6; norms 175–7, 179–82, 256–61, 262; operation of 240–3; quotas 245–8; regime in 1980s 243–4; retailing 248–50, 253, 254, 255–6, 263, 274; sugar 98, 120, 126, 136–8, 140; theory of food systems 37, 59
Dairy Trade Federation (DTF) 240, 248, 253, 263
Deaton, A. 156, 162, 163, 164
Deerr, N. 127
Delessert, B. 127
deli/pâté: class 229, 230–1; meat system 211, 212, 217, 229–31; norms 172–3, 178
demand and demand analysis 276; almost ideal 156, 162; econometrics 148, 150, 155–6, 159–60, 162, 165; food studies 16–17, 20; low income and children 186; NFS 150–8; pent-up desire for sweets 104; supply 15, 21, 32; *see also* preferences
Denmark: sugar 135–6, 139
dependency on food aid 91
Derry, B. 165
descriptive framework 31–2
Desor, J. 126
desserts *see* puddings
deviance: from healthy diet 16, 21; hunger as 14
diabetes mellitus 117, 130
Dickinson, J. 47, 57
diet: balanced *see* healthy diet; defined 275–6; paradox 59; *see also* food
dietetic and slimming foods 90, 133, 185; *see also* 'lite' products
differentiating food systems 9–10,

295